Never Seen the Moon

Never Seen

the Moon

The Trials of Edith Maxwell

SHARON HATFIELD

UNIVERSITY OF ILLINOIS PRESS

URBANA AND CHICAGO

To Jack Wright

© 2005 by the Board of Trustees
of the University of Illinois
All rights reserved
Manufactured in the United States of America
C 5 4 3 2 1

⊗ This book is printed on acid-free paper.

Library of Congress Cataloging-in-Publication Data
Hatfield, Sharon, 1956–
Never seen the moon : the trials of Edith Maxwell /
Sharon Hatfield.
p.   cm.
Includes bibliographical references and index.
ISBN 0-252-03003-6 (cloth : alk. paper)
1. Maxwell, Edith, 1914–1979—Trials, litigation, etc.
2. Trials (Homicide)—Virginia—Wise.
3. Women—Virginia—Social conditions.
I. Title.
KF224.M35H38   2005
345.73'02523'09755743—dc22   2004025265

CONTENTS

Illustrations follow pages 30 and 90.

PREFACE

In every locality there are two or three "big stories" that have served as defining moments in the collective life of a community. In some instances, monuments or roadside markers have been erected to connect people with those far-distant events, but more often the stories live on only in the moldering dreams of retired journalists or in unspoken chapters of family lore. In 1990 I had the good fortune to learn of such an event that happened in Wise County, Virginia, a coal-mining community in the Appalachian mountains where I had worked as a reporter some years earlier. The tale I heard from Evelyn Slemp, a dedicated collector of local history, was that of schoolteacher Edith Maxwell, found guilty of killing her father in 1935. Maxwell had been famous once, then mostly forgotten—and though she had served a prison sentence, questions about her culpability lingered a half century after her celebrated trials. Older residents who could still recall her case kept coming back to one memorable detail: Maxwell's insistence that she had struck her father in self-defense with no more substantial a weapon than a high-heel shoe.

The story immediately piqued my interest, even as I wondered if it could possibly have any lasting significance. It was not until I visited a university library that I began to realize how one family's catastrophe had affected many people beyond the stony ramparts of Wise County. Searching through microfilm, I was amazed to discover that Maxwell had been a celebrity of national and international proportions from 1935 to 1937. I found that hundreds of articles about her had appeared in the Hearst newspapers and the *Washington Post*, while publications such as *Time, News Week*, the *New Yorker*, and detective magazines also took notice. Influential writers and commentators such as James Thurber, Walter Winchell, and Ernie Pyle had weighed in on the case. The Central Press Association distributed a picture of "curfew slayer" Edith Maxwell as the first photograph in a series depicting "outstanding news happenings of *world* interest during the year 1935 [emphasis added]."

Over the next several years I would learn that a cowboy singer had penned a song in her honor, Warner Brothers made a movie, wealthy bluebloods of eastern society staged fundraisers, and thousands of ordinary citizens wrote letters and signed petitions on her behalf. In the end, even First Lady Eleanor Roosevelt became involved in efforts to free her.

I became intrigued by the question of why Edith Maxwell's case had captured the imagination of millions of depression-era readers when the thirteen other homicides reported in Wise County in 1935 had not. What lessons did her story have to teach them—and us? How was it possible that someone so famous had become so obscure over the decades? And how could I, an Appalachian woman, tell Edith's story in a way that would honor the culture we both shared without papering over some unpleasant truths?

Driven by these questions, I began an odyssey that would eventually take me to California, Florida, Richmond, Virginia, and Washington, D.C., in search of answers. Today, after more than twelve years of research, I can honestly say that I do not have a complete understanding of what occurred in the Maxwell home on the night of July 20–21, 1935. Despite two trials that generated voluminous pages of sworn testimony, the mystery of what happened to Trigg Maxwell endures. Edith, her mother Ann, and her little sister Mary Katherine probably never revealed the full truth of what had occurred within the walls of the family's four-room dwelling. The prosecution, lacking eyewitnesses, had to rely almost entirely on circumstantial evidence and failed to produce a definitive murder weapon. In later years, Edith made private statements that seemed to contradict what she had said publicly at her first trial. I'm not sure all the answers will, or indeed can, ever emerge.

Yet I have learned enough of Edith's remarkable story to know that hers was not just the horrible human dilemma of a young woman accused of patricide. Rather, her case played out against a background of larger social concerns that swept America during the 1930s. Many of those same issues—feminism, domestic violence, prejudice against people who were "different," and the precipitous slide of news toward entertainment—remain with us today, and that is why the Edith Maxwell story can be regarded as a harbinger for debates that would still divide American society some seven decades later.

Writing in the *New Yorker,* James Thurber described the Edith Maxwell saga as "one of the most interesting trials since the Scopes case," referring to the famous "monkey trial" that had riveted national attention on Dayton, Tennessee, in 1925. Although Thurber chose to comment from afar, about sixty other journalists actually traveled to remote Wise County in 1935 and 1936 to cover the case of the celebrated schoolteacher.

Among those who made the trek into the Appalachian mountains were some of the best and worst of the national press corps. Scripps-Howard newspaper columnist Ernie Pyle, who would later become famous for his World War II dispatches, was working as a roving correspondent when the Maxwell case surfaced. He spent several days in Wise County, where he met Maxwell, interviewed her friends and neighbors, and subsequently filed several insightful stories about her family and the people of Wise County.

In contrast to Pyle's astute portraits of mountain people stood the stories written by the Hearst press and correspondents for the United Press wire service—articles that idealized Maxwell even as they reinforced stereotypes about her native Appalachian culture. For example, Arthur Mefford, a writer for Hearst's *Daily Mirror* tabloid, depicted Edith as the epitome of culture and refinement while describing her neighbors as "slatternly women and gangly men [who] rise each day to take up the dull business of living."

Relying on stereotypes gleaned from decades-old romantic novels and magazine sketches, and more recently from silent films, the writers of these sensational articles engaged in wholesale condemnation of mountain society, which, they said, treated women as slaves held under a 9 P.M. curfew. From that skewed perspective Edith was thought to have been punished for her "book-larnin'" and "store-boughtened" clothes rather than for any crime she may have committed. One writer reportedly declared that Edith had never seen the moon until she went off to college because she was not allowed up stay up after dark. Such irresponsible statements led newspaper editor Virginius Dabney to complain in *The New Republic* that "few cases have ever been buried under a thicker coating of journalistic horse-feathers, baloney and banana oil than this Maxwell case."

Though replete with cartoonish images, the reports of the yellow press did garner a large national following for Maxwell, even as they ridiculed and infuriated residents of southwest Virginia. Some newspapers crossed the line from journalism to activism, helping to raise money for Edith's appeal. The reputable *Washington Post* started a defense fund to "free Edith Maxwell," and its less reputable rival, the *Washington Herald*, soon followed. Her cause was also taken up by notable press figures of the 1930s such as Walter Winchell and Evalyn Walsh McLean.

Shortly after Edith's first conviction in November 1935, her brother Earl sold the exclusive rights to her story to the Hearst newspapers, which wasted no time in packaging Edith's supposedly first-person accounts into racy exclusives. Her lawyers defended this business transaction as a source of money for Edith's defense. From then on Edith's fortunes and those of the Hearst empire were intertwined in a mutual quest for "justice" and "profit," an arrangement that brings into question whether the media crusade ultimately helped or harmed Edith's outcome in the legal system even as it catapulted her to national celebrity. By making Edith a staple item of media consumption, her handlers had unleashed a willful genie—widespread publicity on an almost unimaginable scale.

Blind justice is the ideal of American jurisprudence. The power of the mass media to affect the outcome of a legal case—the so-called court of public opinion—has, however, had an undeniable impact on our judicial system. In some instances journalistic muckraking has rendered a great public service by helping free the innocent, as idealistic reporters of the 1930s believed they were doing by advocating for Edith Maxwell. But the opposite can also be true in situations where the victim's or defendant's celebrity seems to overwhelm the justice system and render the facts of the case irrelevant. Both these contradictory impulses were at work in the Maxwell case. Sadly, some of the followers who flocked to her side were more galvanized by the bizarre nature of a tragic situation than by a desire to separate fact from fiction.

It is also important to ask how Edith Maxwell's journey to the brittle heights of celebrity affected her personally. Was she, as prosecutor Fred Greear suggested, a calculating murderess who "openly boasted" that the press would free her? Or was she, as Norton, Virginia, newspaper editor Pres Atkins believed, ultimately a victim of her own fame? Although Edith's notoriety and youthful good looks often worked in her favor, evidence also suggests that constant adoration by the press and public fanned in her the flames of misguided ambition. By 1941 many observers were convinced that media celebrity had become a glittering juggernaut for Edith Maxwell.

———

Was the death of Trigg Maxwell, Edith's father, "just another sordid murder," as the prosecutor claimed, or was it an empowering female reaction to years of physical and verbal abuse by the male victim? Many eastern liberals, such as members of the National Woman's Party (NWP), chose the latter interpretation and were quick to attach wide sociological implications to the Maxwell family tragedy. Not only were party activists personally moved by Edith's plight but they also saw her possible vindication as a chance to expand women's rights—and, at the same time, to advance the party's political agenda.

Of particular concern was the fact that Edith had been tried by an all-male jury. The NWP had for many years worked to attain jury service equality on a state-by-state basis, but by the mid-1930s only twenty-one states allowed women to sit on juries. NWP attorneys entered the Maxwell case and were successful in raising this constitutional issue at the circuit court and state appellate levels. One of them, state senator Gail Laughlin of Maine, participated briefly in the second trial, mesmerizing the court-room audience with her mannish looks and Yankee demeanor—and by being the first woman to argue before the Wise County bar. Yet Laughlin's evident distaste for hillbilly culture made her, in some observers' eyes, a liability to the defendant.

Edith Maxwell's eventual disavowal of the NWP, probably encouraged and orchestrated by Earl Maxwell, illustrates that the grand ideology of social change cannot exist in a vacuum. It must operate along a broad con-tinuum of human needs and wishes. Separated from party activists by age, culture, and social class, Edith Maxwell could never be the feminist icon they had sought to create. Beyond that, her desire to be free was sometimes at cross-purposes with martyrdom. Not so surprisingly, she lost a possible opportunity to have the federal courts rule on the fairness of the all-male jury, just as they had declared the inequality of an all-white jury pool in the famous Scottsboro case involving black defendants in 1932. She walked away from a chance to make *real* history—to make a lasting impact rather than just a media splash. But once again, the Maxwell case had proven to be a "tar baby" that sullied the motives, however well-intentioned, of the many groups and individuals vying to free Edith Maxwell.

Although it is not so uncommon for an unsolved mystery to gather unto itself the stuff of legend, the taboo aspect of Edith Maxwell's crime made it especially appealing to readers in the depression. By committing an act of female-on-male violence, Edith Maxwell had turned up the volume on a subject that was barely a whisper in the 1930s. Not until the 1970s and 1980s would the right of a woman to defend herself against an abusive male family member become the topic of widespread public discussion. The often-related issue of children who kill their parents also has received a thorough public airing, with considerable evidence showing that many of these children—but not all—suffered from parental abuse. The debate has eventually come full circle with extreme cases like that of the Menendez brothers, in which the "abuse excuse" was not considered a justification for murder. In retrospect, the Edith Maxwell case may be regarded as a bellwether to this intensely emotional contemporary issue.

⸺

The challenge to journalists to transcend—or at least be aware of—their cultural biases was probably a subject seldom discussed in ethnocentric city newsrooms of the 1930s. For much of the twentieth century the press routinely used racist and sexist language that was reflective of American society as a whole, language that was dismissive of anyone "other" or "different." To become the mainstream heroine demanded by the times, Edith Maxwell was set apart from her community and, in effect, asked to renounce her native Appalachian culture—with devastating results for her and her family and neighbors.

Although celebration of diversity has more recently become a goal of our society, prejudice against traditional Appalachian culture remains strong in the United States. Present-day jokes about outhouses and incest can be traced back to the local-color writers of the late nineteenth century who created stereotypes that were recycled by yellow journalists of the 1930s and magnified by feature films and television. *Never Seen the Moon* can thus be read as a cautionary tale about the dangers of demonizing minority cultures by imposing mainstream values.

Some of the older residents of Wise County who still remember the Maxwell media frenzy often share a common lament, "Why did the press have to print a picture of a cow walking down Main Street?" This is a telling response because that particular image likely is real—not staged as were some of the other published photos. Cows *did* occasionally wander down the main throughfare of the town of Wise in 1935. Yet, residents might argue, the detail is true, but the selection of details all adds up to a false picture. A journalist first has the obligation to get the facts straight, then to order them in a coherent whole. And as their own words reveal, several of the writers covering the Maxwell case failed to be either accurate or culturally aware. The legacy of their failure, and of others' before and after, is not merely the wounded pride of a few townspeople but a lingering deep scar in the Appalachian psyche.

It is important to remember, however, that kernels of truth can lie buried in the most outrageous stereotypes. Wise County women in the 1930s were not slaves, were not legally restricted by curfews, and often had a great deal of autonomy in their own homes, but their role in public life was limited. As in many other locales in the 1930s, virtually all legal and political discourse—whether by police officers, judges, attorneys, or politicians—was conducted by men. Accepted standards of behavior for men and women were also different. One thing is virtually certain: Had Edith

Maxwell been a twenty-one-year-old man, out late on Saturday night, this story would never have happened. Perhaps the meddlesome "outsiders," though often arrogant and condescending, were in a better position to question why things should continue as they always had been.

Who, then, can best tell the stories of Appalachia—or of any place, people, or way of living? I was drawn to this question often during the writing of this book. Writers, broadcasters, and filmmakers not rooted in Appalachia have told the region's story for generations, but the one they were telling was certainly *not* a myth of progress. For every local writer determined to skate over the darker chapters of Appalachian history, there have been legions of outside voices ready to denounce mountain people as primitive and other. Even notable historians such as Arnold Toynbee, who in 1935 called Appalachians "the American counterparts of the latter-day white barbarians of the Old World," fell victim to this unfortunate worldview.

These pages establish that the coverage of the Edith Maxwell case by outsiders often was biased, simplistic, and unfair—an indictment of Appalachian culture rather than an examination of the cycle of family violence from which Edith could not escape. There is no one simple answer to the question of why Edith Maxwell was given an extremely harsh sentence in light of the available evidence. I would like to think that my Appalachian heritage, and the years I spent in Wise County, give me special insights. That does not mean that only those born and reared in Appalachia are qualified to examine its history. Indeed, there is the temptation for insiders to try to overcompensate for past injustices. A writer's background will inevitably shape her vision of the world, but there is still the obligation to tell the truth as honestly as one is able to construct it.

Although I am no longer a resident of Wise County, Virginia, I am still very much a part of the wider Appalachian community. I feel a strong sense of responsibility to both of these "publics." I also acknowledge the intense suffering that both the Maxwell and Dotson families endured during those trying times nearly seventy years past. Yet Edith's story long ago transcended being a family saga or even a remarkable piece of Wise County history. Hers is an American story, one in which our notions of women's equality and power, of the vast freedoms and terrible responsibilities given to the mass media, as well as the integrity of our legal system, were severely put to the test.

ACKNOWLEDGMENTS

This book would never have been attempted without the late Evelyn Dale Slemp's alerting me to the Maxwell case. Like a wise woman of old, she issued the call to initiation that started me on a journey for which I am profoundly grateful.

Several mentors have helped me personally and professionally over the years. At the start of my career, Greg Edwards, a dedicated journalist who was then managing editor of the *Coalfield Progress* newspaper, taught me what it meant to be a reporter. Much later, Dru Riley Evarts, Patricia Westfall, and Judith Yaross Lee of Ohio University provided expert guidance in the early stages of this project. I also wish to acknowledge my mentors at Goucher College—Diana Hume George, Lisa Knopp, Kevin Kerrane, and Leslie Rubinkowski—who not only offered sound writing advice but also set a stellar example of the writing life.

Appalachian scholars have also influenced this work. As I first began to formulate research strategies, I found inspiration in Altina Waller's throughly researched and groundbreaking book *Feud.* Editor Jerry W. Williamson, a noted authority on Appalachian films, dazzled me with his breadth of knowledge and eventually published a portion of my research about *Mountain Justice* in the *Appalachian Journal.*

During the course of my quest, many librarians and archivists assisted me in countless ways. Among these are Minor Weisiger, Vincent Brooks, and Jennifer Davis McDaid of the Library of Virginia; Stuart Ng of the University of Southern California; and Robin Benke of the John Cook Wyllie Library of the University of Virginia's College at Wise. Film archivist Stephen Gong of the University of California at Berkeley provided expert advice that led to my locating the film *Mountain Justice.* David Parker of the Motion Picture, Broadcasting and Recorded Sound Division of the Library of Congress was instrumental in making the film available to me for study, as was Turner Entertainment.

The hunt for archival photos was nearly as exciting as the search for the film and historical documents. I acknowledge the excellent assistance of Tom Gilbert of AP/Wide World Photos; Jenay Tate, editor and publisher of the *Coalfield Progress;* Joanne Slough of the *Richmond Times-Dispatch;*

and Jennifer Spencer of the Sewall-Belmont House in Washington, D.C. Graphic designer Peggy Sattler lent her expertise in scanning images.

The Wise County Historical Society and the Historical Society of The Pound were immensely helpful to me, both through the books they have published and the conversations I have had with their members. I owe a special debt of gratitude to Brenda Dotson Salyers of the Historical Society of The Pound, whose dedication to preserving the heritage of her community is unmatched. I deeply appreciate the assistance of these organizations, while noting that any mistakes or misinterpretations are my own. In addition, Wise County Circuit Court Clerk Gary Rakes and his staff provided cheerful and expert guidance on locating documents at the courthouse.

Several current or former Wise County residents graciously shared their reminiscences with me, including Kenneth Asbury, Frances C. Roberson, James C. Roberson, Glenn Dotson, Burgess Cantrell, Chances Kelly Varson, Virgil Craft, Agnes Ellison, Guy Roberts, and Norman Crouse. I am especially grateful to Jim Robinson, Edith Maxwell's nephew, for a lengthy and informative interview. Vivian Barker Wright opened her home in Wise to me as I was tracking down the story. Further, I am most grateful to Edith Maxwell's son, Randall O. Abshier, who provided information about the later years of her life.

The Ohio Arts Council gave crucial support by awarding me a creative writing fellowship for nonfiction in the early 1990s, enabling me to travel to distant locations seeking archival documents. I was also fortunate to work with the Historical Society of The Pound to secure funding from the Virginia Foundation for the Humanities and Public Policy, which resulted in a public forum on the Maxwell case being held in Pound during Heritage Days in 1994.

I have also been lucky to live in a community of writers who have carried on a dialogue with me through many phases of this work. I thank the Illiterati Writers' Group of Athens, Ohio, for their camaraderie and insights. I am also grateful to Marta Mills, Mark Shelton, Peggy McCarthy, Greg Edwards, and Lee Smith for reading early drafts of this book.

Judith McCulloh, assistant director of the University of Illinois Press, has contributed her expert editorial eye as well as a long-standing belief in this project. Press staff members Mary Giles and Seth Killian also provided valuable assistance. Others who have helped me in ways large and small include Kyle Citrynell, Bob Fox, Pam Durban, Tom French, Patsy Sims, Blaine Dunlap, Gurney Norman, Nyoka Hawkins, Gillian Berchowitz, Danny Miller, Anoa Monsho, Mary Jo Cartlegehayes, Stephen Kimber,

Lynn Adams, Tim Smith, Sandra Williams, Carol Sue Gilbert, Sam Gilbert, Mary Makin, Alan O'Leary, Don Baker, Judy Jennings, Evelyn Mills, Beth Roberts, John Roberts, Edward L. Henson, Gary Slemp, Debbie Mace, Bonnie Riley, Betty Dementi, Curtiss Ellison, Alan Stein, Kathy Stein, Jo Carson, Bob Kerber, Jean Spires, Elizabeth Storey, Geoff Buckley, Sandy Plunkett, Frank Hunter, Mildred Davis, and Burns Gilliam.

My own family has shaped this work through their unwavering support: my parents, Jean Davis Hatfield and William G. Hatfield; brothers John Hines and Ben Hines; my aunt, Ferne Davis Lambdin; and cousin, Garry Ely. I especially thank my parents for providing a home where the "life of the mind" seemed every bit as real, and often more compelling, than our everyday lives.

And, finally, this project would never have been possible without the love and encouragement of my husband, Jack Wright. Over the years, Jack has played the roles of editor, critic, traveling companion, and fellow sleuth—and this book is the better for it.

Never Seen the Moon

1   *"No Fire Here"*

The small, boisterous cafes and roadhouses were just beginning to close as Saturday night reeled toward Sunday morning in the tiny Appalachian border town of Pound, Virginia. On July 20–21, 1935, two years after the lifting of Prohibition, the Pound community was flexing. At joints like the Joyland, the Rendezvous, and the Little Ritz, a mostly male clientele of coal miners and farmers were enjoying their own brand of cafe society. Here the rhythms of fiddles, rather than violins, provided the soundtrack to the depression years, and from bottles of beer and white lightning flowed giddy distraction that no champagne could match. But Saturday night could not last forever. Within a few hours the rowdy jigs would give way to the unadorned beauty of Old Regular Baptist hymns. In darkened farmhouses and above-street apartments, Pound's less exuberant citizens had already tucked themselves into bed.

In his imposing three-story "rooming house" on Main Street, Chant Branham Kelly had retired shortly after midnight, but as the hour approached 1 A.M., sleep had not yet come. At forty-one, Kelly had already made a name for himself as the brilliant developer who, in the space of thirteen years, had transformed Pound from a crossroads hamlet to a bustling village. As he flipped idly through a magazine in his second-floor bedroom, a car suddenly pulled up to the Maxwell residence, which sat just three feet from Kelly's building. Kelly had known blacksmith Trigg Maxwell and his wife Ann for more than ten years. By the sound of things, the Maxwells' attractive twenty-one-year-old daughter, Edith, must be returning from a date. Even though the hour was late and Edith was a schoolteacher, the Kelly household was accustomed to such comings and goings. Edith was a gal who seemed to ignore the usual female restrictions.

The car pulled away almost immediately. Within minutes, Kelly heard angry female voices muffled in the thick night air. He could not understand what was being said, but he was concerned enough to jump out of bed and pull on a bathrobe. As Kelly searched for a belt to secure his "kimona," as he called it, concern accelerated to alarm. The female cadences had fallen silent, giving way to a voice he was sure belonged to Trigg Maxwell.

"Oh, Lordy," the voice cried over and over.[1] Each time, Trigg would finish up the sentence with something too low and indistinct for Kelly to understand. Kelly listened for perhaps five minutes, then decided to act. He did, after all, own the village drugstore. Maybe Trigg was ill and needed help.

All was quiet by the time Kelly reached the street, but he decided to walk over to the Maxwells' anyway. The modest one-story structure sat in a row of buildings sandwiched between the road and the Pound River, its forty-foot front bordering the unpaved main street and its rear supported by stilts extending thirty feet down to the surface of the water. A false two-story facade, painted white, gave the appearance of a storefront and attested to the fact that the home had been converted from a garage some years earlier. With a mind toward economy, Trigg had partitioned his building into two apartments, one for the family and the other rented out to the post office.

Kelly crossed in front of the house to the side farthest from his own building. In the semidarkness he noticed that the door to the Maxwells' enclosed side porch was open about a quarter of the way. Both the porch and the door were covered by latticework, which afforded a measure of privacy from passersby on the street. Nonetheless Kelly could make out a figure on the porch, which he recognized as that of the Maxwells' youngest daughter, eleven-year-old Mary Katherine.

"It's Chant," the girl said to someone inside.

Edith immediately came to the door but did not open it any wider. Like a Greek oracle she spoke from the shadows behind the latticework, her tall, slender silhouette adding authority to her words. "There's no fire here, Chant. You had better go on home."

Kelly silently brushed off Edith's remark as a joke. He walked a little closer and said he wanted to help Trigg if he were hurt. Edith again told him to go home. Instead, Kelly backed up a few steps and tried to peer in a front window where he thought the groaning might have been coming from earlier. He could see no one but heard shuffling sounds, as if someone were walking through the house.

"Edith, what's wrong?" he persisted, once more taking a few steps in her direction.

"Oh, it's just another old drunk Trigg," she responded with a trace of annoyance. "This is none of your affair, so please go on."

Kelly reluctantly returned to the second-story living quarters he shared with his invalid wife Lucille, her two sisters, and a nurse. He was giving Edith the benefit of the doubt about her "no-fire-here" joke. Surely she wasn't referring to the horrific fire that had swept his home just a year or so before, forcing his wife to jump from a high window and break her back—a fall that had left her permanently paralyzed. Instead, he reasoned, she was probably just bantering the way people did when they saw somebody speeding down they road: they'd holler, "Wonder where the fire is?" all in good humor.

Unfortunately, Kelly was becoming more convinced by the minute that some calamity *had* happened at the Maxwell home. Even now, he could still hear shuffling noises next door as if people were hurrying about inside. Suddenly the Maxwells' radio began playing loudly, obliterating the other sounds. Faced with Edith's assurances, what could he do? Kelly finally went back to bed but was too distracted to continue reading. Other members of his household had also been disturbed by the racket but were now settling back to sleep. Kelly lay there, studying the situation, wishing he could do the same. After eight or ten minutes the Maxwells' radio abruptly fell silent.

———

"Chant, wake up, daddy is dying. Chant, hurry, come over here."

Kelly instantly recognized the wailing voice below the window as that of little Mary Katherine Maxwell. It was now about 2:30 A.M. More than an hour had passed since Kelly had been turned away from the Maxwell home, and it now appeared that his worst misgivings had come true. Something terrible had happened to Trigg.

Kelly bolted down the stairs for the second time that Sunday morning. He paused long enough to awaken his sister-in-law, Martha Strange, and Lovell Sowards, a boarder who ran a nearby cafe. He did not wait for them to dress but quickly followed Mary Katherine next door.

A frame structure without indoor plumbing, squeezed onto a postage-stamp-sized lot, the Maxwell home was subdivided into four rooms that connected without hallways. The front door led directly into the living room, where Edith slept on a studio couch. To the right was her mother's bedroom, shared with little Mary Katherine. On the back side, facing the river, Trigg's room was on the left and the kitchen on the right. Running down the right side of the house was the long, narrow porch where Kelly had earlier been turned away by Edith.

Mary Katherine now frantically beckoned Kelly in. He found the porch still dark, but golden light from the other rooms bathed Trigg Maxwell's inert form as it lay in the doorway separating porch and kitchen. Kelly's neighbor had been a tall, vigorous man accustomed to years of demanding physical labor; now he was stretched out on his back, unconscious and barely breathing. Trigg's head and torso rested on the porch while his legs extended about eighteen inches into the kitchen. He was dressed in long underwear, socks, and sock supporters. Ann Maxwell, still in her nightgown, was standing at her husband's feet. Edith had her arms around her mother.

Kelly immediately began to administer resuscitation exercises by raising and lowering Trigg's arms. Trigg responded by breathing a bit more strongly. Encouraged, Kelly kept up the exercises for several minutes but was wondering if help would soon arrive. Edith had gone next door to summon Dr. E. L. Sikes, the village physician.

Within moments, a half-dressed Dr. Sikes walked in and knelt to take Trigg's pulse. Kelly stopped moving Trigg's arms and examined his head for any signs of injury. He immediately noticed that Trigg's head was wet. A circular area underneath his head also was damp, but the substance was only water, not blood. It was not until Kelly looked a second time that he noticed a small cut on the top of Trigg's head. He pointed out the wound to Dr. Sikes, but by this time Trigg's breath was once again flagging alarmingly.

"Do something for him. Can't you do something?" Ann Maxwell kept pleading.

"He needs heat," Dr. Sikes said.

Lovell Sowards, Kelly's boarder, had come over to help. The doctor instructed Sowards to retrieve the family's electric iron, which had already been plugged into a socket in the front room. Sikes evidently was hoping that the application of heat might help Trigg ward off shock. Sowards went to check on the iron twice, but each time it stubbornly remained cold. Time was slipping away.

"There's nothing more I can do," Dr. Sikes announced. "I'm going home to dress."

The physician returned to his combination home and office next door, leaving Kelly to continue his frantic efforts. Kelly resumed the respiration exercises, but this time Trigg's breathing improved only briefly. Though he was rapidly becoming exhausted, Kelly kept up the exercises until Trigg ceased breathing entirely. From the time he heard Mary Katherine's call, his neighbor's life had ebbed away in less than fifteen minutes.

A log three feet in diameter and two feet tall—hewn from the trunk of a great sycamore—sat on the porch just inches from Trigg Maxwell's head, bearing silent witness to the events of Saturday night. The massive wooden stump, stripped of its bark and mounted on three 2 x 4 legs, served as the Maxwells' meat block, where they routinely carved pork and beef with a knife, saw, and little hand hatchet. Trigg's body lay by the block. Had he lived two more days he would have turned fifty-three.

Even in the face of tragedy there was much work to be done. One of the first tasks was to notify Trigg Maxwell's relatives and friends. Mary Katherine and one of Kelly's boarders went to the nearby home of Trigg and Ann's married daughter, Gladys Robinson, who was the postmaster in the other half of the Maxwell building. Gladys and her husband Clay awakened their children and hurried to the scene. Mary Katherine returned as well. Clay stayed at the Maxwells only briefly before leaving to summon Vernon "Bunk" Maxwell, Trigg's brother, and send telegrams to far-flung Maxwell relatives. Trigg and Ann's fifteen-year-old daughter Anna Ruth, who was staying overnight with relatives in Wise, was not expected home for several more hours. Lovell Sowards and some of the other men began sawing boards on which to lay out the body.

As neighbors entered the house, Edith, Ann, and Mary Katherine—all talking at once—excitedly told everyone that Trigg had fallen and hit his head on the meat block. Some would recollect that the women said Trigg was drunk; others wouldn't remember it that way. Edith told Mabel Maxwell Mullins, Trigg's niece, that Trigg had been "acting queer, talking about picking blackberries" and that she had hidden his clothes to keep him from getting out. Mullins would later testify to an extraordinary exchange that allegedly took place that night between Edith and her older sister Gladys: "Don't say, Edith, that Poppy was drunk," Gladys said.

"Gladys, don't think that I would tell a lie and the old man dead," Edith responded.

⎯⎯

The first active-duty police officer did not appear on the scene until approximately 5 a.m., some three hours after Trigg's death—and then almost by accident. Trooper Warren Edison Orr, who had joined the state police only the previous month, had been patrolling the Pound area that Saturday night with another "speed cop," as the troopers then were known. Shortly before dawn, Orr's partner dropped him off at his own car, which had been parked near the Maxwell residence practically all night. Orr hadn't been at the car three minutes when Mary Katherine beckoned him to her house.

As Orr approached he saw Edith and Ann standing in the macadam road that served as Pound's main street. He urged the distraught women to get out of the street for their own safety. Orr went inside, glanced at Trigg's body lying on a cot, and privately inquired of Dr. Sikes what had happened. After a brief conversation with the doctor, Orr went on his way, apparently satisfied that no foul play was involved.

Inside the Maxwell home, however, some of Trigg Maxwell's relatives were growing skeptical of Edith and Ann's account of the evening's events. Chant Kelly had already let it be known to some of those present that a "racket" had preceded Trigg's death. Additional doubts may have been raised by Dr. Sikes's observation that Trigg had suffered "a lick to the head." By dawn the decision had been made to have an autopsy performed. Ann opposed the procedure, preferring to send the body to a funeral home in Wise for conventional preparation, but she apparently was overruled by her in-laws. It was a most unusual step, a defining moment for family members who believed Ann and Edith and for those who doubted.

A hearse bearing Trigg Maxwell's body soon was en route to the Fred H. King Funeral Home in Norton, Wise County's largest town, some twenty miles from Pound. King, a veteran of more than seven thousand embalmings, had obligingly come over to the Maxwell home and picked up the body himself. Returning to the funeral home before 6 A.M., he surveyed the body with a practiced eye. Trigg Maxwell's visible injuries consisted of a cut and two bruises on the head, a small cut on the hand, bruises on his forearm, and a blackened left eye. King carefully sewed together the slightly ragged cut on the forehead and immediately began the embalming process.

It was King's understanding that the dead man's relatives—son-in-law Clay Robinson, brother-in-law Lee Skeen, and brother Vernon Maxwell—had made arrangements for a private autopsy later that Sunday. For reasons unexplained, however, King proceeded to embalm *prior to* the autopsy. The undertaker finished his work in about two hours, then decided to have breakfast and await the arrival of the doctors.

—

Wise County Sheriff J. Preston Adams was having a very busy weekend. Just hours after Trigg Maxwell had died at Pound, Orbin Baldwin was felled by two shots from a .32–caliber pistol as he stood shaving at his home on Bear Branch near Norton. The man had died instantly, and his wife, Ida, had admitted shooting him. The mother of six was being held at the jail in Wise, the county seat. As this most untranquil Sunday wore on, Adams was on his way to Pound to confront two more murder suspects.

Adams followed the winding road down the mountain from Wise, arriving at the Maxwell home around 11 A.M. In his hands was a warrant for Edith and Ann's arrest on suspicion of murder, sworn out by Trigg Maxwell's relatives. Mother and daughter received the sheriff in the tidy front room that had moonlighted as Edith's bedroom.

At twenty-one, Edith was a head taller than her somewhat frail, forty-eight-year-old mother. With her fashionably permed brown hair parted down the middle and a figure kept pencil-slim through years of walking and playing basketball, Edith appeared striking even in this vulnerable moment. Her almond-shaped, gray eyes studied the sheriff in disbelief as he informed her of her arrest.

"It's a sight to be accused of something like this," Edith told him. "I'm a teacher. I keep them [the parents] up."

As Adams and his deputy sheriff led them to a car, Edith found herself consoling her mother. "Don't worry, there's nothing to it," she told Ann.

Even before the suspects had been taken to the county jail at Wise, police had begun a thorough canvass of the premises. Fred Greear, the young commonwealth attorney who liked to investigate his cases personally, had driven across the county from his home in Saint Paul as soon as he heard the news. By early afternoon he had arrived to make sure the deputies missed nothing.

To the casual observer, everything was in its place, giving no clue that the head of the house had lately been struck down. But a closer examination yielded clues that hinted of a violent struggle. Even with the July heat, certain spots on the uncarpeted floors of the Maxwell kitchen seemed oddly damp, raising suspicions that they had recently been mopped. In Trigg's bedroom, however, some dried spots of blood apparently had been overlooked. In the kitchen, nestled in the fire chamber of the cook stove, were the burned remains of what could have been a man's shirt. On the porch, a wet sheet with an attached safety pin, a pillow, and a pillowcase had been stuffed into a banana crate. These soggy bedclothes—stained with what appeared to be blood—were on the bottom, other dry articles having been placed on top of them. A thorough inspection of the meat block turned up no blood, no hair, or any evidence it had been wiped off.

Despite these promising leads, Greear and the deputies were mystified as to what type of weapon could have inflicted the cut on Trigg Maxwell's head. There seemed to be no end to the array of harmless-looking household instruments that could have been used. As deputies sifted through the possibilities inside, other officers surveyed the muddy waters of the

Pound River flowing eastward a scant three feet behind the Maxwell home. In the past, quick-thinking bootleggers along Main Street had been known to throw a whiskey bottle out a back door or window and into the river as police closed in. Why not someone with more deadly evidence to hide? Recent heavy rains, however, had made an effective search impossible. Sand and mud reached a depth of six feet at this part of the river, ensuring that it would never have to yield its secret—if indeed there was a weapon embedded in the murky bottom.

—

As Fred Greear drove toward the jail in Wise, some thirteen miles from Pound, he was carrying on the seat beside him a trophy from the fledgling murder investigation. The just-completed search of the Maxwell kitchen had finally turned up an electric iron with what looked like dried blood around the edges. True, the iron was not a forensic certainty—but at least it was something to go on.

Greear pulled his car to the curb in front of the jail and surveyed the familiar faces of court-watchers who were staring at him from the street corner and from doorsteps along Main Street. Observing the comings and goings of people at the jail and courthouse was a favorite pastime in this county seat. Taking pains not to disappoint his audience, Greear sprang from the car and dramatically held up the iron for all to view.

As the prosecutor entered the jail with his prize he was probably anticipating a battle of wits with the Maxwell women. He might have regarded the case as an opportunity to add yet another notch to his string of legal victories. But Greear could scarcely have realized as he stepped through the jail door that he was entering the pages of history. He could not have imagined that the slender young woman who waited nervously in her cell was destined to become a symbol of empowerment for women across the country, nor could he have anticipated that his beloved Wise County itself would be put on trial. It was a case that would test the very fabric of the community yet ultimately would be resolved at the highest levels of power.

2   The Purloined Peas

Wise County, Virginia, the birthplace of Edith Maxwell, was in 1935 an isolated mountain district in the heart of what sociologists would eventually refer to as "hard-core" Appalachia.[1] It would not be until thirty years later that Congress formally drew the map of Appalachia, defining this mountain region east of the Mississippi as a two-hundred-thousand-square-mile area that includes all of West Virginia and portions of twelve other states.[2] But Appalachia had long existed in the national consciousness as the land of moonshine, coon dogs, and feuding mountaineers.

In Virginia, too, it had long been recognized that the mountain counties west of Roanoke had a distinct culture that had somehow transmuted on its journey from the Greek-columned country houses of Old Virginia to the rough-hewn log cabins perched on steep hillside farms. In the river valleys of the Roanoke, the New River, the Holston, the Clinch, and the Powell, life had a resonance not shared by denizens of the state capital at Richmond, nearly four hundred miles to the east. It was true that this part of the state had a fierce allegiance to Virginia traditions; mountain school children were just as proud as their flatlander cousins to lay claim to Washington and Jefferson. Further, this part of the state had clung to Virginia and the Confederacy while neighboring counties with prevailing Unionist sentiments had split off to form West Virginia in 1863.

In matters of geography, economics, and lifestyle, though, it was obvious that the Virginia mountaineers had more in common with their highland neighbors in Kentucky, North Carolina, West Virginia, and Tennessee than with residents of Piedmont and Tidewater Virginia. People back then, as today, liked to point out that a resident of Lee County, in the extreme southwest, was geographically closer to eight or nine other state capitals than to Richmond. But that distance almost always seemed to translate into a troublesome law of gravity: with increased distance from the political center came diminishing political clout. By 1935 it was not surprising that a University of Pennsylvania professor would proclaim Appalachia a "blighted" area, lagging behind the rest of the nation in education, income, and public services.[3] In southwest Virginia, so constant was the refrain that "the state stops at Roanoke" that a scheme was once proposed to unite the mountain region of Virginia with those of Kentucky and Tennessee in a new state, Katenva. But the plan came to naught, and southwest Virginia would remain a largely ignored—although exotic and mysterious—satellite of Richmond. From frontier times onward, mountain people became accustomed to solving problems their own way, without outside help, or interference.

———

A writer in the 1930s once remarked somewhat naively that the history of southwest Virginia began when the first white men laid eyes on it. But the Cherokees of Tennessee and North Carolina saw it differently. According to their tradition, the Great Spirit had created the region as a seasonal hunter's paradise for many different tribes that followed the ancient buffalo traces, entering the territory from homelands to the north, west, and south. It was given to none of them to live there but for all to enjoy the streams, waterfalls, and dense forests of hickory, oak, poplar, and rhododendron in which panther, elk, bear, and deer abounded.

By 1750—143 years after the English landed at Jamestown—European scouts and adventurers had begun to foray into the Virginia backcountry. Tradition has it that the first of these scouts to set foot in what would later become Wise County was Christopher Gist, the head of a surveying party returning east after exploring the lower Ohio Valley. Gist's travels through Wise County in 1751 would earn him the distinction of having a river (Gist's River, later bastardized as "Guest River") named after him as well as a high school in Pound, which was to be Edith Maxwell's alma mater.

Another interloper in this vast wilderness was said to be Jonathan Swift, an English adventurer who supposedly had worked a rich vein of silver somewhere in southwest Virginia or eastern Kentucky—possibly near Pound. On a visit to the mine around 1753, Swift and a partner coined some of the metal into French crowns and carried two horseloads of the money back to their homes in North Carolina. Swift soon returned to resume mining, but to his dismay he could not locate the seam of silver ore. After days of fruitless searching, Swift gave out (or sold) maps purporting to show its location. Some dismissed the entire story as a hoax designed to conceal a counterfeiting operation, but true believers would continue to pour into the mountains for the next hundred years in search of the fabled wealth.

Most who risked their lives on the Virginia frontier in the latter half of the eighteenth century were looking for something more elemental than silver: land they could farm. Settlers of mostly English, German, and Scots-Irish extraction gradually pushed the frontier westward one river valley at a time, meeting violent resistance from Native Americans defending their hunting grounds. From base camps on the Clinch River, the legendary North Carolinian Daniel Boone would eventually spearhead further migration down Powell Valley, through the Cumberland Gap, and into the Kentucky Bluegrass. But present-day Wise County, lying north of the Clinch, was off the beaten track and remained largely uninhabited until after the Revolutionary War.

As the area that would become Wise County grew safer for white settlers in the 1790s, they began trickling in from the older river fortresses to the south and west, settling along mountain streambeds where bottomlands were hospitable to farming. The names these pioneers chose for their communities reflected their abiding kinship with the landscape. Creek, Fork, Branch, and Run bespoke the fanning out of settlement along the Powell, Guest, and Pound Rivers; Spur, Ridge, Mountain, and Rock suggested the limitations these travelers encountered. Still other place names whispered of the Native Americans who had lately tramped through these woods. The community of Cranes Nest was the legacy of the Indian chieftain Crane, whose lieutenants had scratched his graceful waterfowl emblem on the soft bark of trees to mark his campground.

By the mid-1800s, residents in this locale still were part of Lee, Scott, and Russell counties, but visiting a courthouse to transact business meant a hard day's ride and staying overnight. In response to a citizens' petition, Wise County was carved from the three original ones in 1856. It was named for the incumbent governor, Henry Alexander Wise, described by a later historian as "an inveterate chewer and swearer" and "one of the last great individualists in Virginia."[4] In keeping with the unfettered character of its namesake, the new county was estimated to be 97 percent wilderness.

The state legislature decreed that a county seat should be established on the Daniel Ramey farm at Big Glades, a 708–acre tract sitting atop a broad plateau in the center of the county. A team of commissioners selected one acre of the Ramey farm for the public square and called the new town Gladeville, later known as Wise Court House and finally as Wise. About five hundred men voted in the first general election in 1856.

Although Wise County's pioneer women had no say in worldly affairs such as politics—and as Protestants, no heavenly role model that was remotely female—they often held sovereignty over matters of life and death. Giving birth and assisting others in labor, nurturing the sick, spinning and weaving, and planting and harvesting were all activities that attested to women's generative power. Their resourcefulness often meant the difference between death and survival.

The story is told of the early settler Betty Ramsey, who with her husband White (or Whitley) carved a beachhead in the virgin forest near Norton. Back then, farmers had to save their own seeds from year to year for replanting, for, as the Ramseys might have said, seeds in frontier communities were "scarce as hen's teeth." One spring morning Aunt Betty arose early and planted her garden with peas before going to the fields to assist her husband. When the couple returned home in the evening, they discovered that their chickens had invaded the garden and pecked all the peas out of the freshly turned soil. Determined to save her future harvest, Aunt Betty marched out to the henhouse in the early dusk, armed with a butcher knife and needle and thread. By the light of a flaming pine torch she examined the craw of each bird in the roost. Finally she came upon one rooster whose throat was bulging with the purloined peas. Deftly she made an incision, reclaimed the precious seeds, and sewed the bird's wound as precisely as if it had been a seam in a patchwork quilt.

This pattern of life—farming and small-scale timbering—continued through the early decades of Wise County, though it was sometimes disrupted during the tempestuous Civil War years. The forbidding mountains that surrounded the county stood as sentinels to its isolation, limiting commerce and contact with other areas but perhaps contributing to a sense of shelter and community within. In the latter part of the nineteenth century, however, eastern land speculators and capitalists had come to regard Wise County not as a Shangri-La but as a marketplace where quick fortunes could be made by extracting the abundant coal deposits that had lain undisturbed for millions of years.[5]

Like rich men trying to enter heaven through the eye of a needle, the railroad companies began to thread their tracks through the encircling mountain rims by either following river beds or blasting tunnels. At the natural landmark known as Bee Rock, honeybees had lived and stored nectar for untold generations until they were dislodged by repeated dynamite blasts set off by a construction crew building a railroad tunnel.[6] By 1891 the Louisville and Nashville and the Norfolk and Western lines had reached Norton, cementing that community's destiny as the business hub of Wise County.

On the heels of railroads came speculators who enticed landowners to sell their coal-rich holdings for as little as 50 cents an acre. Farmers who had previously raised their own vegetables and livestock now turned to mining and found themselves, as one writer put it, "dependent hirelings of corporations."[7] Still others became prosperous members of the merchant class that sprung up to support the burgeoning industry. In the space of 100 years, the white settlers had gained dominion over the Indians, only to be supplanted themselves by a new monarch—King Coal.

———

Standard-gauge railroads took longer to reach the Pound River section of northern Wise County, preserving its isolation well into the twentieth century. Circled by nearly impenetrable mountains, Pound was almost a world within a world. During the first decades of settlement it was wild country, ideally suited for bushwhacking an enemy, discreetly carrying on a prosperous moonshining business, or even bewitching a truculent neighbor. These activities naturally became the stuff of legend.

In a place where tall tales abounded, nobody was even sure how Pound (or "The Pound," as residents call it) got its name. Tucked away in a narrow valley, the village sprang up on a bend in the river, which flows northward to the Big Sandy and finally to the Ohio. Some people think the name echoes down from pre-pioneer times, when Native Americans supposedly stole horses from settlements farther east and impounded them on the rich bottomland in the bend of the Pound River, stringing grape vines over the landward side to form an enclosure.

Others speculate that the name originated from the mill that William Roberson, an early pioneer and ancestor of Edith Maxwell, built on that spot. He moved to Pound in 1836 and built a horse-driven mortar and pestle to pound grain into meal.[8] Recent scholarship, however, suggests that the name Pound was already firmly established before the mill was built; the river and town may bear the name of an English immigrant family named Pound or Pounds.

One of the most famous stories associated with Pound would gain it national notoriety in the 1890s, when the mystical preacher and physician M. B. "Doc" Taylor allegedly ambushed and killed several members of the rival Mullins family near Pound Gap. Seen by some as a Robin Hood figure who helped care for the poor, old Doc had several friendly hiding places in the rough country around Pound and eastern Kentucky. But the law regarded Taylor as a homicidal madman. He was ultimately captured, tried, and sentenced to death. Brought to the scaffold in Wise with great fanfare, Doc had dressed in snowy white and publicly vowed to rise again on the third day. Despite his failure to appear, he was later immortalized by the novelist John Fox Jr. as the villain "Red Fox" of *The Trail of the Lonesome Pine.*

If Pound Gap had sometimes proved to be a deadly crossing, the settlement below it had seen its share of bloodshed as well. Above all, Pound was a border area, and armed clashes between Kentuckians and Pound residents were commonplace around the turn of the century. Some of the violence was organized, but at other times a chance encounter with a stranger—or even a spat with a beloved companion—could lead to violent death, especially at the numerous barrooms that had sprung up in the shadow of Pine Mountain. The times were so rough that at one section of Pound, called Donkey, the bodies of the Kentucky dead were often laid out for their relatives to retrieve from Virginia territory.

By the 1930s the homicides were much less frequent, yet people who kept count of such things would tell you there had been more than fifty killings within a ten-mile radius of the village since the earliest settler days. On a July night in 1935, the name of Trigg Maxwell would come to be added to that list. But the circumstances of Trigg's death—suspicions he had been done in by his womenfolk, at home, secretly, and in the dead of night—did not fit the customary scenario. The Maxwells' fellow citizens would have to think about this case in a different way.

Was Trigg's death, as is often the case, a mirror image of his own aggression—his own violence impulsively turned back on itself? Or was this a carefully premeditated plan to solve a long-standing grievance? Could the death have been unintentional? These were questions for Wise County justice to decide.

3   *"A Two-Hour Grilling"*

The *Knoxville News-Sentinel* reported on Monday, July 22, that Trigg Maxwell was beaten to death with an electric iron. "Mr. Maxwell's head bore deep wounds and the tell-tale iron was found near the body," the story said. Although the conjecture about the iron was presented as fact by the newspaper, Wise County authorities still were not sure exactly how Trigg Maxwell had died.

Commonwealth attorney Fred Greear was in his office at the Wise County Courthouse that Monday, carefully sifting through the results of an autopsy performed on Trigg Maxwell's body the day before. Two Norton physicians had ruled that the fatal wound had been a sharp blow to the head that pierced the covering of the scalp. Although the doctors found no skull fracture, they said the blow had been sufficiently severe to cause blood clots to form at the base of the brain. But could this blow have been incurred through a fall, as the Maxwell women maintained?

Greear had been immediately skeptical of the "meat block" story of Trigg Maxwell's death, partly because obvious efforts had been made to clean up the scene of the "accident." Now, reading the autopsy report, he learned that Trigg had sustained at least three blows to the head and had bruises on his arms—curious details that only heightened the prosecutor's suspicions. Greear felt confident he could convince the Wise County grand jury, which was already in session with other cases, to issue indictments against both Edith and Ann. His expectations of a light docket for the upcoming court term had suddenly vanished.

By the summer of 1935, Fred Bonham Greear had been a lawyer for twelve years. He was regarded by colleagues as an intellectual and man of ideas. Often arriving at the office before 8—and staying until midnight if necessary—the University of Virginia Law School graduate already had tried more cases at age thirty-six than some attorneys do in a lifetime. Upon filling the commonwealth attorney slot in 1932, he had jumped into the job with a vengeance, not only prosecuting a record number of felony cases but also acting as a financial advisor to the Wise County board of supervisors. He even went so far as to become a manager of the county poor farm, turning it from a money drain into a profitable operation.

Even with all these duties Greear was never too tired to attend to the vagaries of local politics. In the 1931 election cycle he had been the easy choice of the Democratic Party and handily defeated his Republican opponent. Now, in July 1935, another election was just a few months away.

When a Wise County Democratic candidate thought of votes, his reveries must have invariably turned to Pound. The area had for many years been a bastion of the Democratic Party; the clannishness for which Pound families were famed also translated into large voting blocks come election time. It was said that the heads of one or two influential families could walk into a local gathering and command two hundred votes in the blink of an eye. Large Democratic pluralities in Pound precincts ensured that the area would be well represented at the county Democratic convention. Not surprisingly, quite a few Pound politicians were elected to county government.

Fred Greear, who had been a Democratic player since 1923, inevitably had brushed shoulders with Pound Democrats—including the Maxwell family—during the course of his political campaigns. Greear sometimes stayed overnight at the home of Trigg's brother, Fred, when he was in Pound hunting votes. Another brother, Vernon "Bunk" Maxwell, was a tireless worker for the party, and Trigg's brother-in-law Lee Skeen was a former Wise County sheriff.[1] Trigg himself had been a delegate to the Democratic Convention a few months before his death, although Greear would later say that he did not know Trigg personally.

Within a few months all these relationships would lead to charges that the Maxwell case had become a "political football," and Greear's own motives would be called into question. The prosecutor, however, would always maintain that it was, to him, "simply another murder case," a family dispute that had turned violent. A talented orator with the drive to excel, Greear had earned a stellar reputation in southwest Virginia as a trial attorney. Now, with the Maxwell case looming, his career was about to play out—quite unexpectedly—on a much larger stage.

———

As Greear had anticipated, the county grand jury quickly returned indictments on Monday, charging both Edith and Ann with murder. By appealing directly to the grand jury, Greear was able to sidestep the procedure called a preliminary hearing, where the commonwealth would have been required to show that it had sufficient evidence to try the Maxwell women. Now Greear had the indictments, but they lacked the specificity he needed to fully develop the state's theory of the case at trial.

Edith Maxwell had been confined to the Wise County Jail since midday on Sunday, in the custody of the jailer, Jim Dotson, who happened to be her mother's half-brother. Ann herself had posted a $3,000 bond that Sunday and returned home, where she had taken to her bed in emotional distress. Some reports said bond was denied to Edith, whereas others said it was set at an unattainable $6,000, suggesting that she was considered more culpable, or capable of flight, than Ann. At any rate, Edith was feeling vulnerable and lonely despite a visit from a college girlfriend.

Greear began pressing Edith for a more believable explanation than the "meat block account" she had maintained since her arrest. On Tuesday, the prosecutor and Sheriff J. Preston Adams sat down with her for a formal interview. Displaying a cool presence of mind for a woman barely past her teens, Edith asked to have her uncle, Gernade Dotson, a well-known attorney, present during questioning. Greear shrugged off the request, saying it wasn't necessary, and began asking Edith about the type of weapon that had been used. "What did you kill your father with?" Greear would say over and over.

Edith finally broke under the relentless questioning, apparently telling a story quite different from the one her lawyers would eventually present in court. On July 24, Greear announced to the press that Edith had admitted striking her father with the deceased's own shoe as he threatened to whip her for staying out late. If the following report in the *News-Sentinel* is an accurate reflection of what Edith told the prosecutor, her statement was potentially very damaging:

> The confession, coming after a two-hour grilling, told of a scuffle that started while the father was in bed last Sunday morning and allegedly occurred because the girl had stayed out late on the night previous.
> "He scolded me for coming in late, between 12 and 1 o'clock Sunday morning, and said he was going to whip me," Attorney Greear quoted the girl as saying. "He made a couple of passes at me with his hand, as I was sitting in a chair near the bed. I saw the shoe, picked it up and struck him."[2]

Less than forty-eight hours after her arrest, Greear had exacted Edith's admission that she had hit her father. It was a key point, one he would otherwise have a hard time proving. The three words in a prosecutor's mantra—means, motive, opportunity—were gradually coming into focus. A father and his grown-up daughter living under the same roof certainly had the opportunity to engage in a family dispute behind closed doors, and now, Edith was telling him she had used a shoe as a weapon. But could a man's flat-heeled shoe, rather than an iron, really inflict that kind of damage? Was the motive simply a disagreement over Edith's staying out late, or were other matters involved? It was far from being an open-and-shut case.

———

After several days of incarceration, Edith had a visit from her mother. Ann threw her arms around her daughter and began to cry.

"Honey, if you hadn't told this, you wouldn't have been in here now," Ann told Edith.

"Mummy, they told me you had told it."

"No, your mummy never has told nothing."[3]

Fred Greear was in the enviable position of having two suspects charged with the same crime. Although the newspapers would sometimes say that Ann Maxwell was indicted "as an accessory" to murder, Edith and Ann were jointly indicted on the same charge. With Edith in jail and Ann at home, psychological games were inevitable.

The available evidence suggests that Greear may have wasted no time in telling Edith that her mother—and even little Mary Katherine—had been talking to him.[4] It is not known whether they gave him incriminating information, but the uncertainty of it all was bound to rattle even the most self-possessed suspect. Having dual defendants could eventually work in Greear's favor. But where two street hoodlums might readily squeal and blame each other, Ann and her daughter shared a strong emotional bond—one not easily broken by even the most determined inquisitor.

Throughout the ordeal ahead Edith would steadfastly refuse to implicate her mother for even the slightest wrongdoing. Solidarity with Ann had long been her credo when trouble came. Still, in going beyond the meat block story and admitting to a fight with Trigg, Edith had given the little bulldog prosecutor a bone to worry, a thread that could unravel the fabric of their lives.

4 *Becoming "Miss Edith"*

In the upcoming murder trial of Edith Maxwell, her father's people and her mother's would soon find themselves arrayed on opposite sides of the courtroom, just as if they were guests seated at a church wedding. The chain of events that ultimately would lead to this unhappy juxtaposition in 1935 had indeed been set in motion by a wedding some three decades earlier. Perhaps some of those same relatives had been present when H. Trigg Maxwell married Wilby Anna "Ann" Dotson in the summer of 1904. It is uncertain how the eighteen-year-old bride and twenty-two-year-old groom first met, but they apparently had lived around Pound all their lives and may have known each other as children.

It could safely be said that both young people were from good fami-

lies, old pioneer stock. All Ann had to do was count back three generations, to her great-grandfather Simon Dotson, who had settled in the area
around 1820 and sired a clan of southwest Virginia Dotsons—including
the county's first sheriff. Daniel, Simon's son and Ann's grandfather, married the miller's daughter at Pound and made a homeplace about two
miles southeast of the village in a remote area called Bold Camp, which
was originally named "Bowl Camp" by hunters in earlier times.

Daniel's son, Marcus De Lafayette Dotson, was born in 1850 at Pound.
"Fate," as he was nicknamed, became a prosperous farmer and also operated a gristmill and sawmill near Bold Camp. Fate was twice widowed and
married a third time before his death in 1923, siring at least seventeen
children. His first wife was Letha Hylton of Pike County, Kentucky, with
whom he had one son and four daughters, including Ann Dotson Maxwell,
born in 1885. The son, William Washington Gernade Dotson, seventeen
years Ann's senior, was said to have been so hungry for an education that
after farm chores were done he "studied at night by the light of pine knots
and hickory chips, and later, from the light of a brass roundwick kerosene
handlamp."[1] Gernade became a lawyer, and by the time of Ann's marriage
in 1904 he was serving as Wise County's commonwealth attorney.

Trigg Maxwell, too, could boast of long-standing ties to Wise County,
especially on the side of his mother Martha's people, the Gilliams. In 1842
his maternal great-grandparents, John and Mattie Gilliam, had followed a
typical migration pattern into the area, moving northward from Copper
Creek in Scott County, Virginia. Family tradition says that John traded a
pony and a hog rifle for more than seven hundred acres on Glady Creek,
about two miles from the present-day town of Wise. When Wise County was
formed in 1856, John Gilliam was elected commissioner of the Gladeville
District and was also named the county's first overseer of the poor. His son
Ira (pronounced Ah-ree), a minister, was elected county commissioner of
revenue and eventually served as sheriff.

Despite this promising beginning, the Gilliam family suffered a series
of reversals during the Civil War. Two of John's sons signed on with the
Confederacy at Wise Courthouse but deserted after learning that their
father had moved the rest of the family north to Kentucky and was fighting for the Union. John himself survived captivity as a prisoner of war,
narrowly escaped hanging for treason by the Confederates, and lived to
the age of eighty-four. His sons William and Lilburn, and his wife, Mattie,
succumbed to smallpox, however, and another son died of pneumonia
during the conflict.

The effects of these wartime upheavals on William's young daughter

Martha have not been recorded, but by all accounts she became a devoutly religious adult, a figure of piety in the Methodist church. In November 1875, at fifteen, she married Elbert W. Maxwell.[2]

The Maxwells, like the Dotsons and the Gilliams, were longtime residents of southwest Virginia, but their entry into Wise County must have followed a more meandering path. A journalist wrote in 1936 that "the first Maxwell, so far as they [the family] can learn, went into the Cumberlands on the heels of Daniel Boone."[3] According to historian Luther Addington, the Maxwells came to Pound from North Carolina, which is also the locale from which Boone migrated. The Maxwell family's early years in Virginia, however, remain something of a mystery.[4] Trigg's father, Elbert, was born in what is now southern West Virginia and apparently moved to Wise County as a youth. It is not known how he met Martha Gilliam, but one can infer that the match bore the approval of her family; her uncle, Ira Gilliam, performed the wedding ceremony in 1875.

Twenty-four-year-old Elbert and his teenage bride set up housekeeping just outside of Pound proper, on the road leading to mountainous Bold Camp. Eventually a narrow-gauge railroad was built to haul timber from Pound to a sawmill near Wise. According to family tradition, once Elbert got a job with the railroad he "never walked again," preferring to ride on horseback. He also managed to integrate himself within the local Democratic power structure, serving a term as Wise County treasurer from 1895 to 1899.[5]

Elbert and Martha became the parents of ten children, eight of whom reached adulthood. The sons were Trigg, Vernon, Fred, Edgar, and Napoleon; the daughters were Clora, Venie, and Lockie. Elbert was a landowner who had achieved enough prosperity to afford extras for his children; he and Martha took pride in ordering baby Lockie's clothes from Macy's Department Store in New York.

Although tabloids would later speak of a long-standing feud between the Maxwells and the Dotsons, nothing in the existing record supports the idea of a Montague-and-Capulet-style union. In fact, Trigg's parents, along with Ann's father and stepmother, sold the young couple a sixteen-acre tract on Bold Camp for $200 in November 1904, just a few months after their marriage. Whatever problems would arise between the families later, Edith Maxwell's parents-to-be were starting out together on the solid footing of their own mountain farm.

Nonetheless, the young couple had to confront a world far different from that of their parents' generation. Life in Wise County had changed dramatically during Ann and Trigg's childhood and adolescence. By the time of their marriage, hunting and subsistence farming—traditional ways of life for decades—were giving way to rapid industrialization. With outside corporations purchasing vast tracts of timber and coal land for pennies an acre, what a young man could hope to become was now shaped by decisions made in New York, Philadelphia, and England. Money—and perhaps social status—was gaining newfound importance.

What a young woman could become, however, was still largely determined by her choice of a husband. A teenager like Ann probably had hoped to marry well, possibly to find someone of the same social standing as her brother Gernade, the well-connected attorney over in Wise. But to Ann's disappointment, Trigg would follow a much more typical path for a young Appalachian man of apparently limited education. On his marriage license application, Trigg listed his occupation simply as "farmer." In turn, Ann's in-laws would come to regard her as someone who thought more highly of herself than she had reason to.

During their early years together, Trigg and Ann Maxwell apparently lived on Bold Camp as previous generations had, sheltering their growing family in an unpainted frame house set on a steep hillside. At the time of Edith's birth there on April 24, 1914, the couple already had two daughters, Gladys and Alma, and a son, Earl.

When Edith was six years old, Trigg decided to abandon farming and move the family five miles away to Jenkins, Kentucky, where he got a job in the coal mines. His brother Vernon, having returned from World War I with Clay Robinson, a buddy from West Tennessee, likewise worked in the Jenkins mines, and Lockie Maxwell, Trigg's thrifty and independent sister, had landed a position in Jenkins as the postmistress.

Located across Pound Gap at the foot of Pine Mountain, Jenkins was a made-to-order town, constructed in 1911 solely as a launching pad for Consolidation Coal Company's venture into the pristine Elkhorn coalfields of eastern Kentucky. Trigg Maxwell's family arrived around 1920.[6] They found a bustling model coal town of about a thousand dwellings, complete with stores, churches, schools, hotels, and a hospital, water system, power plant, and YMCA. Supplementing the indigenous Scots-Irish labor force were Italians, Poles, Albanians, Hungarians, Slavs, and African Americans who had come to taste the risks and rewards of the coal boom.

In exchange for free housing, electricity, water, and an average wage of 35 cents per hour, a "Consol" miner was expected to work in dangerous and stressful conditions. Even though the company provided safety demonstrations for its Jenkins miners, the threat of serious injury or death from roof falls or mechanical accidents was a day-to-day reality. A life insurance agent once remarked that he never bothered to try to sell policies to coal miners because the frequent payouts would render this group a poor investment. Fortunately, the coal company did provide burial insurance.

When Trigg Maxwell, nearing forty, took the job at Consol, the Maxwells probably had the most hard currency they had ever seen up to that point in their marriage. At least a portion of Trigg's wage, however, was paid in scrip—money printed by Consol and redeemable only in the company's stores. It is uncertain whether the Maxwells were in a position to get ahead or, more likely, just provide for the immediate needs of the family. But by moving just a few miles from their mountain farm they had entered a different world.

In her ghostwritten autobiography, Edith said relocating to Jenkins from Pound "was like going to a large city for the first time." She recalled Jenkins as "a particularly well-kept little town, with nice clean streets, and row upon row of neat well-kept and nicely painted homes." It was here that Edith first entered school, fell in love with moving picture shows, and enjoyed tomboyish pleasures such as hiking, fishing, and shooting marbles.[7]

Above all, the picture that emerges from Edith's childhood is that of a close relationship with her mother. Although Ann did occasionally spank Edith, she managed to convey what we would today call unconditional love, spreading a soft blanket of emotional protection that would perhaps allow her daughter to truthfully say years later, "My childhood in Jenkins was a very happy one. It is just crammed full of fond memories."[8]

Some of the happiest of those recollections revolved around Ann's abilities as a storyteller. Sitting at her mother's knee in the evening, Edith loved to hear tall tales such as the one about Tatertoe Johnny, the prototypical mountain preacher who consumed vast quantities of food at every home he visited. "Old Tatertoes"—so called because of the enormous big toes he had on each foot—became in Ann's telling, "the man who ate the thirty-nine biscuits" at one meal. Anytime one of her children would pile up food on the plate, Ann was certain to elicit smiles by quickly pronouncing the hungry youngster "Old Tatertoes."[9]

Nonetheless, there were a few holes in this sheltering coverlet that even Ann could not mend. Ann's relationship with Trigg had been undermined by frequent quarrels since their days on Bold Camp, and as their son, Earl grew older, he, too, began to clash with his father. In her autobiography Edith recalls a devastating incident that allegedly occurred when she was about seven. In a scenario eerily similar to Edith's future battle with her father, Trigg got drunk one night and attempted to whip his teenage son. Earl resisted and knocked his father to the floor, but apparently neither one of them was seriously injured. The next morning Trigg arose and gave Earl a thrashing. Ann and Edith watched in mournful silence as the boy packed his bags and left. He would not return, even for a visit, for several years.[10]

—

During the Maxwells' sojourn in Kentucky, Pound—like most of the rest of the country—was enjoying the heady success of the Roaring Twenties. The time had come, said *Crawford's Weekly* in Norton on December 17, 1927, when the populace "doesn't take the Heavenly Hereafter quite as seriously as it did ten years ago. Men and women who were praying for a home above, and neglecting their daily affairs, are now busy trying to get good homes . . . for their families. Problems of the Here and Now concern them—education for their children, happiness for their families, comparative comfort and reasonable security. . . . Ten years ago all Norton preachers used to despise the very word, science. The auto was wicked. Now they own them."

By 1927 Trigg had decided to move the family back to Pound to share the new prosperity the community was enjoying. The ongoing transformation of the old wagon road through Pound Gap into a modern, hard-surfaced highway was stimulating the construction of new homes and store buildings. Pound's first high school had also been built while the Maxwells lived in Jenkins, surely an attractive prospect for a family that now included not only thirteen-year-old Edith but also little sisters Anna Ruth and Mary Katherine.

Perhaps having grown accustomed to small-town life, Trigg and Ann chose to live in Pound rather than return to their property on Bold Camp, which was rented off and on by tenant farmers. Trigg owned a piece of land in the middle of town, which he planned to develop as both rental property and living quarters for the family. After Edith finished the seventh grade at Jenkins, the Maxwells moved into their new home in Pound. The move to Jenkins had taken an entire day by wagon; the return trip took only an hour by truck. The shortened travel time also meant that Trigg could commute to his job in the mines. Although he did not own a car, he apparently had no trouble finding rides with other Consol miners.

The Pound Gap road project left some local residents almost delirious at the prospects of improved transportation between Virginia and Kentucky. Not only Pound merchants but also those further south in Wise and Norton stood to prosper from the Kentucky trade. About three thousand people ascended the mountain to Pound Gap to attend the opening ceremony for the new road on November 19, 1927. Chill winds clawed at the backs of the audience but scarcely cooled the rhetoric wafting down from the speakers' platform. Dignitaries from both sides of the state line enticed the crowd with visions of industrial development. "The occasion lacked not that crowning glory which must have been evident when the golden spike was driven at the completion of the first transcontinental railroad in the Far West," reported *Crawford's Weekly*.

For all the grandiosity, it was a lighthearted affair. The mayor of Norton, Virginia, poked gentle fun at the emissaries from Kentucky, saying he was "agreeably surprised to see that my new friends are not wearing coonskin caps, homespun clothes and yarn socks." Others wished openly that Prohibition could go away for just one day. Young ladies from Norton and Jenkins ceremoniously cut the ribbon, and a privileged few then continued the celebration at a nearby hotel.

The mood soured ten days later, however, when a mob stormed the Letcher County jail at Whitesburg, Kentucky, some twenty miles from Pound Gap, and with virtually no opposition seized Leonard Woods, a black prisoner accused of murdering a white man from Virginia who had worked as a mine foreman in Kentucky.

The tale had begun a few days earlier, when Woods allegedly gunned down young Herschel Deaton near Jenkins after Deaton refused to give Woods and two female companions a ride in his coupe. Wise Countians turned out in large numbers for Deaton's funeral, which was conducted in his hometown of Coeburn, Virginia, by members of the Knights Templar and the Blue Lodge. Sentiments festered but for a few hours. Barbershops in Virginia hummed with the news that there would be a "neck-tie party" in Kentucky that night. Who wished to join the mob?

Thirty-six cars with Virginia license plates crossed the mountain to the Fleming coal camp, where they waited for a mob composed mostly of Kentuckians to saw through the bars of Wood's cell in Whitesburg. The Kentuckians returned with their prisoner to Fleming, where the two contingents joined and drove to the place on the Kentucky side where Deaton had been shot. As the mob prepared to lynch its prize, officers from Jenkins—fearing a backlash from the black coal miners in the camps—begged them to do it somewhere else.

The mob complied and headed back up Pine Mountain to Pound Gap, arriving about 3 A.M. Just over on the Virginia side stood the reviewing stand that had served as a monument to cooperation between the sister states. The crowd hung Woods from a wooden beam on top of the stand and—reportedly firing from Kentucky soil—riddled his body with such a hail of bullets that the rope was shot in two. Then somebody got the idea to burn the corpse. A woman, said to be one of many females in the crowd, obligingly retrieved gasoline from her car. The crowd watched in satisfaction as Woods's clothing was set afire. Eventually they melted away into the night, but not before souvenir hunters had picked bullets from the blistered body.

Newspapers throughout Virginia were predictably outraged. Bruce Crawford, the crusading editor of *Crawford's Weekly,* condemned the act in the strongest terms, writing on December 10, "To justify that lynching is . . . to revert to a primitive state that gives the lie to all our claims to Christian enlightenment and human progress." Neither prosecutors in Virginia or Kentucky, however, seemed willing to track down those responsible. The perpetrators were never punished, but the episode did result in the Virginia legislature passing an antilynching law early in 1928. Leonard Woods would become the last recorded lynching victim in the Old Dominion, his death an atavistic reminder of a more barbarous time.

———

By the end of 1928, local historian James Taylor Adams declared that the "crimson history" of the Pound community was now "bleached in modern progress." According to Adams, "Education has banished the lust to kill; the passion for the blood of an enemy; the disrespect for law and order that was once the heritage of every boy and girl born on the Pound."[11] Had he been giving a walking tour, Adams might have pointed with pride to the largest building in town—the brick and stone Christopher Gist High School that sat across the river from the Maxwell home.

Before its completion in 1924, high-school-age students had to seek classes in Jenkins, Wise, and Clintwood or perhaps, more commonly, end their formal education. With the opening of the new school, complete with four classrooms and two basketball courts, students in the immediate Pound area could study English, arithmetic, history, science, and foreign languages without having to board away from home.

Those who lived on the "town" side of the river had their choice of walking to a footbridge about a half-mile below the school or crossing directly in front of the building by whatever means possible. According to a former pupil, "Wading the river or walking on ice or even swimming became the normal method of travel for most students who lived on the 'other side'"—a somewhat dangerous practice that anxious school administrators never could entirely curb.[12]

Edith, still a bit of a tomboy, probably would have scorned the footbridge. All through high school she excelled at basketball, making the Pound girls' team as an eighth-grader and eventually playing on the all-county team. Her only academic disappointment was failing mathematics her first year—a mistake she determined never to repeat. By her senior year, Edith recalled, she was an ambitious student who tried to excel at everything—a voracious reader who exhausted the small school library and an amateur actress who "always strove to sweep the audience right off their seats" at school plays. Mathematics still remained difficult, yet Edith remained confident she would pass all her subjects.[13]

"Graduation went off like a charm," Edith said of a night in June 1932 when she and eleven classmates gathered at Chistopher Gist for the traditional accolades. "My mother and sisters were very proud of me. Maybe my father was, too. I don't know. Because, being a very quiet man, he didn't say much about it that I know of."[14]

In the middle of that summer, Edith told her parents about the dream she had cherished since childhood—of becoming a nurse. Trigg and Ann were aghast. Such work was just not suitable for a young woman, they argued. If Edith intended to pursue a profession, teaching was the logical and genteel choice. She reluctantly gave in. She was accepted at the Radford, Virginia, State Teachers College, about 150 miles northeast of Pound, to begin her studies in the fall of 1932. "My parents decided for me," she would say of her career.[15]

Raising the $700 needed for tuition and expenses seemed nearly impossible at first. Edith wrote to Radford, seeking financial aid, and obtained a loan of $350 to cover tuition. She spent the rest of the summer worrying about where the remainder of the money would come from. Finally, Trigg appealed to his sister Lockie, the postmistress at Jenkins, who without hesitation agreed to lend her the other $350.[16] Everything had fallen into place.

When fall came, one of the town boys drove Edith to Norton to catch the train to Radford. Although still disappointed that she was not bound for nursing school, Edith was filled with resolve. "Life keeps right on moving along no matter what happens to our dreams," she would say in her autobiography. "So I picked up the pieces of mine."[17]

Professors at Radford State Teachers College would eventually tell reporters that Edith Maxwell exhibited "no signs of wildness" in the strict atmosphere of the all-female school she attended from 1932 to 1934.[18] With the guidance of Dr. John Preston McConnell, an ardent temperance crusader and church leader of national stature, students were expected to become moral as well as intellectual paragons for their future charges.

It was a silk-stocking setting, ideal for such a mission. Charmingly situated on forty-five acres overlooking the New River, the college had inherited the building and oak-shaded grounds of a former boom hotel. Since its opening in 1913, enrollment had grown to several hundred, and brick buildings had been added. A journalist in the 1930s wrote approvingly that "Radford is large enough to give to country girls seeking to fit themselves for teaching all the urban atmosphere they need, and small enough to retain the sympathetic rural touch needed for the intimate, exacting art of teaching in the great rural areas."[19]

Edith Maxwell, a country girl arriving in a town of nearly six thousand inhabitants, found herself "painfully shy" for the first time in her life. Even though other women from rural backgrounds were studying there, Edith soon noticed that her occasional references to feeding the chickens or slopping the hogs back home were sometimes met with ridicule from other students. And she continually felt ashamed of her wardrobe, which she deemed to be shabby.

She took comfort in rooming, at least part of the time, with her cousin, Ruth Baker, whose mother, Venie Baker, was a sister to Trigg. After her cousin's departure, Edith developed a close friendship with another Wise County girl, Katherine Green, who was to remain her confidante and supporter throughout the difficult years ahead.

Gradually, Edith's self-consciousness disappeared, and she began to enjoy campus and town life, particularly trips to the drugstore soda fountain and the movies. She also continued to develop the athletic talent she had demonstrated in high school, receiving her "monogram" for both basketball and soccer at Radford. Of her studies, she said later, "The work was interesting, even though I hadn't particularly wanted to be a teacher."[20]

Faculty member Joe Young West, who taught Edith both years, recalled that he "found no occasion to question her integrity." In a letter to the governor in 1938, West said, "I found her to be a well-mannered dependable young woman. Her scholastic ability was slightly above the average, and her interest in her work made her a pleasant person to work with. She was a hard worker and rather unassuming. Never did she have to be corrected in class for any sort of misconduct or for inattention."[21]

As her time at Radford drew to a close in the spring of 1934, Edith reluctantly turned to thoughts of home. According to her autobiography, she would have preferred roaming in what she perceived to be greener pastures, but instead she came back to Pound out of a sense of obligation. Trigg and Ann, although only about fifty, were considered to be getting on in years, and there were the two younger girls, Anna Ruth and Mary Katherine, to feed, clothe, and educate.

Strapped by the depression, Edith's parents reasonably could have expected her to make a financial return on her education. Now that she had obtained her teacher's certificate, it was only logical, in their eyes, that she return to Pound. In her autobiography, Edith tells of her decision: "It was just taken for granted, it seemed, that I was to stay home and do my share. I was impressed with the fact that it was my duty. My parents had always been good to me. And I would have done anything for my mother."[22]

But Earl Maxwell, perhaps aided by hindsight, would later say that he had begged his sister not to go back home.

———

With coal fires to be built and water to be carried, the life of a country schoolmarm was far from glamorous. Edith Maxwell, however, could count herself fortunate to have a job. Hard times had hit Wise County. By early 1935, more than 2,100 families—about 20 percent of the population— found themselves on relief. In the depths of that winter, more than fifty jobless men and boys had become so desperate for food that they illegally shot a flock of three hundred migrating robins, which resulted in the hunters' arrest. The one-room Mullins School, located north of Pound between Edwards Gap and Red Onion Mountain, was a proverbial golden goose for the Maxwell family. Here, in a white-painted building with a small bell tower, "Miss Edith" spent the 1934–35 school year teaching a class of forty-two youngsters in grades one through seven. Her monthly salary—variously reported to be $65 and $73.50—compared favorably with her father's $18 a week wage at the coal mines and far surpassed the average monthly public relief benefit of $11.23 per family. Edith could even afford to take a three-mile taxi ride from her parents' home to the school, splitting the fare with another woman who taught nearby.

In her autobiography, however, Edith later said that the Mullins School was not a choice assignment despite its relatively short distance from her home. Nevertheless, she fondly recalled her days at what she called the "tarpaper shack" on the banks of Meade Creek, where in addition to teaching the three R's she would frequently hold pie suppers to raise money for school supplies. "I enjoyed it more than I ever dreamed that I would be able to."[23]

An acquaintance of Edith's recalled in 1994 that she was a "good teacher," one so popular that patrons of the school sometimes gave her live frying chickens as tokens of appreciation. A former pupil, however, remembers Edith more for her frequent absences than for her teaching, recalling that Ann Maxwell would come to the school as Edith's substitute. Another former pupil recalled that Edith moved her desk from the center of the room to the window, where she could watch the road. When visitors would drive up and honk their horns she would unexpectedly declare recess, cross the foot log across Meade Creek, and hold lengthy private conversations. Another observer noted that Edith tended to dismiss her class early and arrive back home just as the school in town was letting out.

These bits of information suggest that Edith may have been a reluctant teacher, trying to cut the corners of a prescribed life.[24] Perhaps she regretted not having become a nurse, or perhaps she simply would have preferred to be somewhere else. As the ghostwriter put it, Edith's worst fear about remaining in Pound was that "like the Indians' horses, my dreams and hopes would be impounded within the encircling river—not overnight, but forever."[25]

Although Edith may have felt these strictures about her life in a private moment, she was certainly no drudge. The intoxication of having a paycheck was strong. She paid her parents $6 a week for room and board, made payments on her school loan, fixed up the house with linoleum rugs, and spent the rest on herself. For the first time in her life she had extra money to buy clothes and books. She even went so far as to purchase the floor-model radio that would play ever so briefly during the final hour of her father's life.

"To be a school teacher in my part of the country," noted Edith, "a girl has to have an absolutely clean bill of health to begin with, or she doesn't qualify for the job. . . . you can understand, I believe, just how difficult it would be for her to sow any wild oats, or even mild ones for that matter, without its becoming the talk of the whole countryside."[26]

Twenty-one-year-old Edith, however, did not seem overly worried in the summer of 1935 that school board members might be peeking around every corner. Her family still did not own a car, but she had no compunct-about hitching rides or hailing taxis. In the language of the tabloids, Edith was "always goin' places where she could mingle with persons of her own intelligence."[27] In truth, it was not so much intellectual repartee she sought but a new kind of fun—fun of a higher order than one might find at, say, a square dance or pie supper that her mother or grandmother might have enjoyed.

A few other young women of Edith's acquaintance—quite well brought up and respectable—had also been influenced by the flapper age. They could be counted on to share a cigarette or maybe even doctor a cup of coffee with something stronger. A favorite weekend pastime was to take down the beds at somebody's house, roll up the scatter rugs, and dance the night away. The women typically did not have dates for these get-to-gethers, but a large group of men and women would innocently enjoy each other's company. They were, as one resident described them, "the bright young set."

Even within this venturesome group Edith seemed to be the one most often testing—and sometimes breaking—the bounds of accepted behavior. As she noted, there was no legal curfew to keep Wise County women home after dark, but in some quarters "car riding" was still suspect. Going around on Saturday night without a chaperone, as Edith sometimes did, was sure to cause talk.

"The evidence does not disclose that she was guilty of any more reprehensible conduct than keeping late hours with young men," a Virginia Supreme Court justice would later observe.[28] And Edith, too, could easily have argued that had she been a twenty-one-year-old male, no one would have bothered to question her comings and goings. Such a lifestyle, however, was hardly typical for a respectable mountain schoolteacher in the summer of 1935.

As Edith's lawyers would later present it, her future as a teacher had been secure. Having completed her first year of teaching in May, she had been rehired and was hoping to be assigned a "better" school the following fall—perhaps one larger or closer to town. All had been well with Miss Edith's prospects until her shocking arrest on a murder charge.

Some around Pound, however, were telling prosecutor Fred Greear that Trigg Maxwell had been worried about his daughter's reputation, fearing that Edith's behavior might endanger her job and thus the family's livelihood. Whether his beliefs were well-founded or not, the outcome was the same. According to the *Coalfield Progress*, Trigg and Edith had argued over her late hours and "alleged attentions to a certain man" on that fatal Saturday.

Earl Maxwell puts a sheltering arm around his sister, Edith, in this photo, probably taken during the mid-1920s. Edith looked up to her worldly older brother, who took her on trips to Detroit and Cincinnati and bought her an evening gown. Earl would later lead the battle to win Edith's acquittal, although his fundraising tactics sparked controversy even among her supporters. (Photo from *Actual Detective Stories*)

Trigg Maxwell, a hard-working and popular coal miner, held traditional views about women's behavior—and objected to his twenty-one-year-old daughter Edith's going out at night. (Photo from *Actual Detective Stories*)

The Maxwell home on Main Street in Pound (on left) had been converted from a garage and contained the post office as well as the family's living quarters. It was here that Trigg Maxwell died in the early morning of July 21, 1935. (Photo from *Actual Detective Stories*)

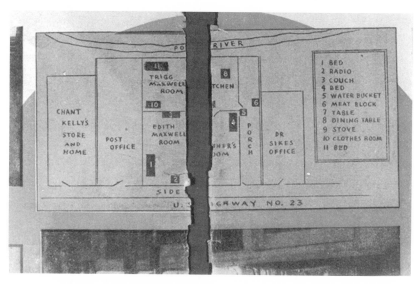

In the Maxwell home, Trigg's bedroom was at the left, rear corner and Ann's was on the right front. At the first trial, the defense contended that Edith struck Trigg with a shoe while struggling in Ann's room; the prosecution argued that the injuries to Trigg had been inflicted in *his* bedroom with a more lethal weapon. Note the enclosed porch off the kitchen where neighbors found Trigg lying unconscious beside a meat block. (Photo from *Actual Detective Stories*)

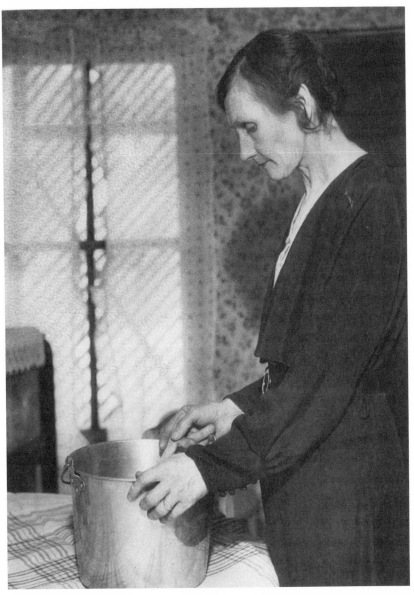

Edith's mother, Ann Dotson Maxwell, prepares a meal in the kitchen of her home at Pound in November 1935. The food was intended for Edith, who was jailed at Wise awaiting an appeal of her first conviction. (AP/Wide World Photos)

Edith taught at the one-room Mullins School near Pound before her arrest.
Local residents bristled at its subsequent description in the *Washington Post* as "a
tarpaper shack." (© *Richmond Times-Dispatch;* used with permission)

The building with a car parked in front is Shorty's, named for proprietor
Shorty Gilliam. This was the cafe in Wise, Virginia, where Edith spent part of
the evening of July 20, 1935, shortly before Trigg Maxwell's death. It was also
the spot where she, Judge Ezra Carter, and news reporters heard a radio broadcast of King Edward's abdication speech during a break in Edith's 1936 trial.
Gilliam's brother sometimes operated the restaurant under the name "B. F.'s
Café." (Photo courtesy of Jack Wright)

Edith's brother and sisters pose in New York City before a February 1936 rally to raise money for her defense. Left to right, Mary Katherine, twelve; Earl, thirty-one; and Anna Ruth, sixteen. (AP/Wide World Photos)

Judge Henry Alexander Wise Skeen presided at Edith's 1935 trial but recused himself from the retrial after learning that he was her distant cousin. (Photo courtesy of the *Coalfield Progress*)

5   *"A Man of Easy-Going Disposition"*

One of the largest crowds ever seen at Pound gathered at the Methodist church on Tuesday afternoon, July 23, for Trigg Maxwell's funeral. The whitewashed one-room structure, adorned with a bell tower, sat on a high bluff overlooking Main Street. It had long been a spiritual beacon for Trigg's mother, Martha, and her sisters, "shouting Methodists" who had been faithful workers in the church. Today, a crush of people—including many prominent citizens from Wise and Dickenson counties—had ascended the wooden stairs leading up from the street to pay last respects to her son. Rain inauspiciously pelted the mourners as they tried to squeeze inside the building.

Trigg and Ann's daughter Alma, who lived in Detroit, and Trigg's brother Napoleon, who had moved to Washington state, had already sent word they would not be able to make the long journey back to Pound. The family was expecting Earl Maxwell, the only son, to arrive from New York City in time for the funeral, but as the minutes ticked by it became obvious he had been delayed.

The downpour showed no signs of letting up as the afternoon dragged on. Amid some private grumbling from those who wanted to proceed, the decision was made to wait for Earl and for better weather. The family rescheduled the service for Wednesday at the home of Edith's sister and brother-in-law, Gladys and Clay Robinson, who lived just down the hill from the church.

While funeral preparations were being made that Tuesday, Edith had been undergoing a withering interrogation by prosecutor Fred Greear in his office at Wise. Her admission that she had struck her father was still fresh ink on the page when Edith, in the custody of Sheriff J. Preston Adams, set out for Pound in the afternoon to view the body at the Robinson home.[1] In her own mind, the trip back to familiar surroundings almost seemed to be a reward for talking, but her satisfaction was to be short-lived.

Edith had been at Gladys's only a few minutes when her mother and one of her sisters became hysterical. Whether the outburst was related to Edith's confession is unknown, but one can only imagine her mother's reaction if this were the moment when Ann learned that Edith had told authorities about the fight at the Maxwell home on Saturday night. Sheriff Adams apparently cut short the visit and returned his young prisoner to jail. The *Bristol Herald Courier*, a southwest Virginia daily, reported that Edith "left without shedding a tear."

By Tuesday evening, handsome, thirty-year-old Earl Maxwell was stepping off the train in Norton after his arduous journey from New York City. His return to Wise County marked his succession as head of the family and chief protector of his beleaguered mother. Over the next two and a half years Earl would play the crucial role of legal strategist, press agent, devoted advisor—and, some would say, Svengali—to his sister Edith.

Earl had left the Maxwell home in Jenkins some fourteen years before his father's death and made his way to Chicago, where he held a number of jobs, including one as a butcher for a meatpacking company. He quickly curbed his mountain accent and learned to talk "proper," calling Trigg "Dad" instead of "Poppy" as his sisters did. Earl also picked up the habit of not chatting with people on the street unless he actually knew them. During a lengthy visit to Pound in the late 1920s these "citified" ways had earned Earl the reputation of being stuck-up, although Edith said he wasn't. A tall, well-built man who had a head for business, Earl had since moved on to New York City and was working as a wholesale candy salesman when he received a telegram summoning him to the funeral.

His first stop after leaving Norton was to visit Edith at the Wise County Jail. Although born nearly a decade apart, the two apparently had formed a special bond when Edith was young. In her autobiography she recalls her distress at seeing her teenaged brother leave home after fighting with their father. Over the years Edith remained emotionally close to her only brother and loved to read his letters. During her time in high school and college he had taken her on trips to Detroit and Cincinnati and bought Edith her first evening gown. Earl had urged his sister to leave Wise County after she finished at Radford, but she refused to do so for the sake of their mother—a decision she perhaps now regretted. In the days to come she would always follow his advice to the letter.

———

Like a newsreel rewound and replayed for an insatiable audience, throngs of mourners again flocked to the center of Pound on Wednesday for Trigg

Maxwell's funeral. Although Earl Maxwell could now attend, postponement of the service from the previous day had only fueled the grief of some of his father's relatives and friends. Word of Edith's confession—plus a newspaper headline proclaiming "Dry-Eyed Girl Views Body of Father She Beat to Death"—had further stoked the fires of resentment. To those who sided with Edith, her desire to attend the funeral was no doubt understandable, yet to those who had already judged her a murderess it was something of an outrage to see her again arriving in Sheriff Adams's car.

Adams drove up to the entrance of the Maxwell family home on Main Street, cut the motor, and got out—yet his lone passenger made no move to step into the strangely silent crowd. Edith instead remained in the car and sent word that she wished to see her sister Gladys, at whose home the services were to be held. As she waited for her message to be delivered, hostility seemed to blanket the air. "She ought to be lynched," muttered one of Trigg's sisters. Then some union miners, presumably Trigg's co-workers at Jenkins, approached the car and urged the sheriff to "take the girl out of here."

Sheriff Adams envisioned events suddenly spinning out of control. He drew himself up and spoke sharply to those nearest the car. With his hand resting lightly on his still-holstered pistol, he barked a warning and ducked behind the steering wheel. Adams abruptly made a wide arc in the middle of the street and wheeled the car back up the winding road to Wise with sirens wailing. Only eight years before, a mob had seen fit to summarily execute a black murder suspect up on the mountain above Pound. Although a woman had not been lynched in Virginia in recent memory he was not about to take a chance on making history. For the time-being his prisoner was better off in jail.

———

The front porch of Gladys and Clay Robinson's home had been transformed into an outdoor sanctuary for the Wednesday afternoon service. There, reported the *Coalfield Progress*, the Maxwell coffin was displayed "amid a great profusion of flowers." Two of Trigg's fellow miners from the United Mine Workers local stood before it holding American flags, and a choir intoned the familiar hymns "Nearer My God to Thee" and "Rock of Ages." Some mourners fainted in the sweltering air.

Ann, now under indictment for her husband's murder, attended the funeral. Three ministers conducted the service, two of them delivering short sermons whose content is now lost to history. Although it is not known if anyone gave a eulogy, a letter written afterward by one of Trigg's neighbors summed up the community's regard for the slain man: "He . . . [was] a man of easy-going disposition, well informed on the topics of the day and admiring the finer instincts of human nature, and especially the finer qualities of womanhood, which he sought to instill into his daughter."[2]

After the last prayer was uttered, Trigg Maxwell's nieces led the procession to the cemetery, casting flowers along the way.

6   *The Mountain Code*

Had it not been for an enterprising reporter loath to sit at his desk in Washington, D.C., the tale of the headstrong schoolteacher and her overbearing father might never have sounded beyond the hills of southwest Virginia. But to Fulton Lewis Jr., a writer employed by William Randolph Hearst, the Edith Maxwell case may have appeared as a rich lode waiting to be unearthed from the heart of Appalachia, a commodity potentially every bit as valuable as the sparkling gems of coal that were torn from the mountains daily and funneled to markets on the East Coast. As Wise County's Pres Atkins, publisher of the weekly *Coalfield Progress,* so deftly put it, the Maxwell case was "an answer to a metropolitan city editor's prayer."

Lewis, in fact, had been a city editor at the Hearst-owned *Washington Herald* before moving on the Washington offices of the Universal Service and the International News Service, two Hearst news-gathering agencies that distributed stories nationally and overseas. Lewis's syndicated column, "The Washington Sideshow," was carried in about fifty newspapers. Although only in his early thirties he was at the top of his game as a print journalist, often scooping the competition with his investigative reports on the inner workings of government. He seldom missed a chance to attack political opponents, especially the champions of Roosevelt's New Deal. Lewis would eventually make the switch from print to radio and become an award-winning commentator as well as an avid supporter of Sen. Joseph McCarthy. In July 1935, however, he was simply a newshound who had caught the scent of something that compelled him to venture far from his 275–acre Maryland farm.

How and why Lewis became interested in a story in remote southwest Virginia—more than four hundred difficult miles from the nation's capital—remains a mystery. People in Wise County speculate that someone connected with the Maxwell case—perhaps Earl Maxwell or even Fred Greear—brought the story to his attention. Or, Lewis simply may have read brief Associated Press reports and decided to cover the case himself.

To be sure, reporters in southwest Virginia had not been idle in the days following Trigg Maxwell's death. Regional daily newspapers had jumped on the story almost immediately, and the *Coalfield Progress* published two page-one items in its weekly edition. Except for mentioning the prominence of the Maxwells and the Dotsons, these news reports contained little out of the ordinary. In the eyes of regional editors, the Maxwell story had begun as a murder case, although one that perhaps deserved slightly more ink because the suspects were women from a well-connected family. The involvement of Fulton Lewis Jr. and the Hearst organization, however, soon would catapult the Maxwell story into the realm of symbol and myth.

Back in the 1890s, when Wise County was absorbing the shock waves of its first industrial revolution, American journalism was witnessing a cataclysmic upheaval of its own. Sensationalism in news reporting reached unprecedented heights with the emergence of so-called yellow journalism, the result of a cutthroat circulation battle between New York publishers Joseph Pulitzer and William Randolph Hearst.[1] In an effort to snare more readers, the rival capitalists trivialized the news through publicity stunts, sensational writing, and outright gimmickry; faked interviews, fraudulent pictures, and misleading headlines were tools of the trade. Even worse, their newspapers' hot-headed coverage of Spanish "atrocities" in Cuba whipped up public frenzy for starting the Spanish-American War.

Writer H. L. Mencken—himself a controversial figure—reminisced about journalists of the 1890s with his trademark irreverence:

> The old time city room . . . was full of pleasant fellows, but the majority of them were bad journalists. . . . To the fundamental problems of their craft they apparently gave no thought; or if they did, it was furtively and diffidently. Such grave questions were for editorial writers, managing editors, business managers, owners, and other such superior fauna. Thus there was little professional spirit in the city room, despite its exalted *esprit de corps*. The boys were not like fellow doctors or fellow lawyers; they were more like fellow Elks.[2]

Concerted public criticism succeeded in reining in the yellow papers by the start of World War I, but journalism was destined to go through oscillating cycles of excess and retrenchment. Mencken, writing in 1925, believed that the new journalism schools were turning out more professional graduates with "a lively sense of the essential dignity of journalism."[3] Others, however, were less sanguine, especially when it came to crime reporting. Critics wondered whether some of the more irresponsible press reports actually hindered the cause of justice.[4]

But the fedoraed, often armed, men who were soldiers in the tabloid war that raged the mid-1920s had little time for such lofty considerations. Circulation was the goal, and exaggerated tales of murder and mayhem were surefire ways of attaining it. Far from being detached observers, reporters for the yellow papers often compromised themselves by working directly with police to apprehend suspects in return for scoops. And if the wheels of justice seemed to move more slowly than the printing press, the newspapers could raise a public outcry that forced the police to make summary arrests and pressured the courts to convict on little evidence.

Sometimes a crusading editor became an arm of the prosecution run amok, endangering the defendant's right to a fair trial. In other cases, however, the yellow press had been able to generate considerable public sympathy for the defense—whether deserved or not. In the courtroom at any spectacular trial could be found a contingent of "sob sisters," women writers who often won favor for their subjects through the use of flowery language and greeting-card sentimentality.

Now, with Fulton Lewis Jr. steering a course for Wise County in July 1935, the sob sisters would soon find the perfect subject in Edith Maxwell. Within days of her arrest the winsome young woman would begin to take on a persona larger than life.

———

While citizens of Wise County, Virginia, were learning from their local newspapers about the arrest of a twenty-one-year-old teacher, people in the nation's capital were reading in theirs about a fairytale princess locked away in an evil fortress in a faraway land. About the only connection between the two accounts is that both were purported to be about Edith Maxwell.

Hearst's *Washington Herald*, which was especially interested in poignant stories about women, told readers on July 26: "Mob violence shall not touch one blond hair on the head of Edith Maxwell, the twenty-one-year-old belle of the Blue Ridge Mountains, who clubbed her father to death with a hob-nailed boot when he interfered with her one true love." That astonishing statement, like several that followed in the next few days, contained kernels of truth that were lavishly coated with error. Edith had dark hair, not blond; Wise County is located in the Cumberland Mountains, not the Blue Ridge; and there is no real evidence that Trigg and Edith argued over her "one true love." The *Herald* further reported that Edith, "whose beauty is the talk of Big Notch Gap" (a nonexistent place), had "crumpled beside the casket of her father" before the funeral and was being "held virtually incommunicado" at the county jail.

These titillating vignettes set the stage for a series of five Universal Service feature stories that exploded across the pages of the *Herald* from July 29 to August 2, 1935. The articles—four of which carried the byline of Fulton Lewis Jr.—carved out a giddy prototype for thousands of future stories. "The true battle on August 20, when Edith goes on trial before spectacled Judge H. A. W. Skeen, is between the 8 o'clock curfew of 'The Pound'—tawdry spattering of mountain shacks—and the right of modern youth to come and go as it pleases," Lewis wrote.

In his view, the mountaineers had no respect for "gov'ment law," only the "archaic family code of the mountains" that made a man an absolute despot in his own home. New highways were blamed (or credited) for bringing the "invading doctrines of the outside world" into conflict with the "curfew tradition of his [Trigg's] forefathers." According to Lewis, Trigg Maxwell "believed in the philosophy of the mountains, which resented every mode of new living brought to the Pound by the invasion of hard surface roads."

Edith was introduced to readers as a "vigorous, red-blooded American girl" who "believed a girl could remain away from home after dark, provided she behaved herself and kept true to the dictates of modern decency." The *Herald* ran a photograph of Edith, sitting on a bench with an unidentified "boyfriend," the words "love, honor, and oh baby" scrawled across the photograph by an unknown scribe. The effect was to make Edith seem modern—even daring. Lewis presented other mountain women, however, including Edith's mother, as "tired-eyed and old before their time." Of Ann Maxwell he condescendingly wrote, "Her slatternly clothes, her straggling hair are beyond even the magic of civilization to transform . . . but the germ is there. It has bred resentment against the law of the mountains and understanding for youth's mutiny against it."

According to Lewis, the killing had brought mountain society into a state of "bitter social insurrection," with Edith leading the "uprising against 'the code.'" "Pound Afire," screamed the *Herald*'s headlines. "Conservatives Call It Mean Business." Likewise, Raymond Meade, the young man who had given Edith a ride home on the night of Trigg's death, was ludicrously transformed into a revolutionary who had long fostered "a discontent of mountain existence."

Although Lewis seldom bothered to present anything resembling the prosecution's side, he had to account for the seeming paradox of "city-trained" Fred Greear, who was only in his mid-thirties. How could an enlightened University of Virginia Law School graduate like Greear—"properly a recruit to these militant ranks of youth"—possibly prosecute another college graduate such as Edith? Sadly, Lewis reported, the commonwealth attorney was only doing his job: "Young Fred Greear must take the side of the archaic dogmas of dying mountain traditions, however firmly he may be convinced of the righteousness of the youthful crusade."

Lewis's series not only defined the stock characters in the Maxwell melodrama but it also contained some startling information. Although an earlier Universal Service report in the *Herald* noted Edith's "strange confession" that she had killed her father with "a heavy shoe," Lewis put a surprising spin on the description of the alleged murder weapon. In his July 29 article the weapon was identified as a "high heeled shoe" and later in the series as a "French-heeled shoe" and a "frail, feminine shoe." During the struggle between Edith and Trigg, the newspaper said, Edith "seiz[ed] the nearest object—by strange irony a high heeled shoe she purchased in the days when she went to normal school in the outside world—[and] she beat him off in self defense."

The transformation of the father's work shoe into a lady's high-heel shoe provided a potent symbol of women's empowerment, but it served another function as well. Lewis predicted the defense would call "at least one outstanding surgeon" to testify that a lightweight slipper could not have caused Trigg's death. In a statement that would prove remarkably prescient, the reporter noted that "modern medical science will be called . . . in defense of Edith Maxwell."

From Lewis's big-city vantage point, being modern had gotten Edith into big trouble; now her only hope was to find a modern savior—someone, no doubt, from the "outside."

7 Buying Time

As the *New York Daily Mirror* put it, Earl Maxwell
was "an entirely modern young man" who "rose like a knight of old to
champion the cause of beauty in distress—his sister." He had intended
to stay in Wise County only for a few days after Trigg's funeral, but the
seriousness of Edith's predicament changed all that. His devotion to his
sister and their mother was absolute; now it would lead him on a most
unexpected and unwelcome quest. He would have to take a leave of absence from his job as a traveling salesman to clear their names. With a trial
date of August 20, 1935, looming large, his first task was to find them a
lawyer.

Of the thirty-five attorneys then practicing in Wise County, most had
established offices in the coal towns of Big Stone Gap and Norton or at
the county seat at Wise. Clintwood, in neighboring Dickenson County, was
home to fourteen more. But Earl told the *Washington Post* that he initially
had trouble finding a single lawyer willing to take the case. In his mind,
these multiple rejections added up to a single conclusion: They were all
leery of signing on with an unpopular defendant. But there was the matter
of money to be considered as well. The Maxwells had managed to keep
food in the cupboards, but they were a cash-poor family with little to offer
a prospective attorney except, perhaps, notoriety.

It would have been natural for Earl Maxwell to turn to William Washington Gernade Dotson—his mother's brother—for legal counsel. A re-
spected senior member of the Wise County bar and a former commonwealth attorney, "Uncle Nade" was still practicing law at age sixty-seven.
It appears that Dotson did offer advice to Edith and Ann from the very
beginning, and as the situation grew more desperate he eventually offered
to represent them at trial. Yet Earl was reluctant to place his uncle at the
helm of the defense. "We thought he wouldn't stand much show, being
a close relative and all," Earl told the *Post*.[1]

The family relationship might have been one reason, but it could
not have been the only one, because Earl went on to say that *he himself*
wanted to represent Edith in court but could not do so because he had

never been admitted to the bar. The fact that he, too, was a close relative did not seem to matter. Perhaps Earl simply hated to impose such a heavy burden on his elderly uncle—or maybe there were other, more arcane, considerations. At any rate, he continued to hunt for another lawyer.

Earl's search took him to Clintwood, where Dickenson County commonwealth attorney Alfred A. Skeen received him in his white-columned brick mansion opposite the courthouse. Hailing from a local pioneer family, Skeen had been a ten-year-old schoolboy in 1880 when Dickenson County, Virginia's "baby" county, was formed. By 1935 he had practiced law for four decades and had served as county judge. Although he was now the county prosecutor, the position was not considered full time, and he handled a private practice as well. Skeen listened to Earl's story and agreed to take the case. The two men then invited Gernade Dotson to assist with the defense. Earl finally had managed to line up competent representation, but the time to prepare for trial was growing short.

Historian Charles Johnson has described Gernade Dotson as "a man of influence and of very large relationship in Wise County, being related to many prominent families of both major political parties."[2] Since his first try for office in 1899 Dotson had parlayed those connections into a successful career in politics. His only defeat came in 1915, when he lost his third race for prosecutor to a Republican challenger. All in all, Dotson would spend sixteen years as commonwealth attorney between 1899 and 1931. According to Johnson, he was a vigorous prosecutor who had "sent five men to the hangman's noose, two white and three colored." Despite the Old Testament character of this grim work he was a devoted Sunday school teacher at the Methodist Episcopal church and a "big-hearted man" who opened his home in Wise to an endless stream of visitors.

In the 1920s—midway through his career—Dotson represented Wise and Dickenson counties in the Virginia House of Delegates for two terms, but eventually he returned to local politics. In his last bid for commonwealth attorney in 1927, Dotson surprisingly had played the role of political maverick. Although the Democratic Party had renominated the incumbent Vernoy Tate, Dotson—who thus far had been a model Democrat—decided to run as an independent. The Republican Party did not field a candidate. Dotson eked out the victory by only twenty-four votes, once more proving his popularity with the voters but no doubt alienating at least a segment of the Democratic Party leadership. At the end of his fourth term on January 1, 1932, he turned over the reins of power to a man who would eventually help write a most disturbing chapter in the Dotson family history—Fred Bonham Greear.

——

By 1935 commonwealth attorney Fred Greear's excellence as an orator was well known in southwest Virginia, yet the grieving relatives of Trigg Maxwell were taking no chances on Greear's being outgunned in the upcoming trial. Shortly after Trigg's death, his elderly mother, Martha Gilliam Maxwell, had traveled to Wise to line up additional prosecutors. The petite, bespectacled Martha Maxwell took money from her "budget"—the old-time name for wallet—and offered it to help obtain a conviction. Prominent Wise attorney Oscar M. Vicars and his young associate Lewis McCormick were recruited to assist Greear.

The lawyers were readying themselves to joust before seventy-six-year-old Henry Alexander Wise Skeen, judge of the Wise County Circuit Court and a cousin of defense attorney Alfred A. Skeen. The eldest son in a family of Scots extraction, Henry Skeen had grown up on a farm in the fertile Powell Valley section of the county. As a young man he had eagerly sought out teachers wherever and whenever he could find them. Skeen himself became a teacher in Kentucky but returned to Wise County after a few years and began reading law. He was admitted to the bar in 1887 and set up a law practice in Big Stone Gap, where he was soon elected mayor.

Skeen was appointed judge of the county court in December 1891, the same month he turned thirty-three. By 1899 he had ascended to the Seventh Judicial Circuit, a job that entailed traveling on horseback to courthouses in Lee, Wise, Scott, Dickenson, and Buchanan counties. Although physically frail, he contended with heavy dockets and spent about eleven months of each year hearing cases. Wise County eventually became its own judicial circuit—the Thirty-third—with Judge Skeen presiding. By 1935 the long horseback rides had been replaced by a twenty-mile automobile commute between his home in Big Stone Gap and the courthouse at Wise, still not an inconsiderable trip over narrow mountain roads.

As he prepared to hear motions on the Maxwell case that August, the aged judge probably had little inkling of the notoriety that would soon be heaped upon him. Within a few months he would become a target of lampooning journalists—some of whom would find him a living antique, a relic from a more patriarchal past. It would also be duly noted that the judge was distantly related to Trigg's brother-in-law, former sheriff B. Lee Skeen, who was siding with the prosecution. Others would point to his kinship with defense attorney Alfred A. Skeen. In a mountain county such connections were hard to avoid. Yet the Maxwell case would invite a level of scrutiny heretofore unknown in the old judge's career, an exacting and often cynical examination of "mountain justice."

—

Most big-city reporters preparing to cover the Maxwell trial in August 1935 would have been hard-pressed to locate Wise County on a map. Only a diligent search would have revealed its presence at 37 degrees north, 82 degrees west, a distant corner of Virginia tucked up hard against eastern Kentucky. Yet for nearly thirty years this mountain border region had existed in the mythic imagination as the "Land of the Lonesome Pine." It was *this* topography—sculpted in vivid detail by novelist John Fox Jr. in 1908—that was destined be reexplored by the yellow press as they covered the Edith Maxwell case.

Some reporters packing their bags that August probably included a copy of Fox's novel, *The Trail of the Lonesome Pine*, for handy reference. After all, they loved to flirt with the notion that life imitates art. It was not unusual to find news stories of the early twentieth century laced with references to popular fiction or the classics. It was equally common for prominent literary figures to write about important trials.

The novelist Theodore Dreiser, for example, was recruited to cover the sensational Hall-Mills murder trial in 1926 because of his depiction of a courtroom scene in his novel *An American Tragedy*.[3] In 1935, when a man named Newell Paige Sherman allegedly drowned his wife by tipping over a canoe, newspapers were quick to note the "horrible parallel" with the plot of Dreiser's novel. Sherman was instantly dubbed "the *American Tragedy* slayer."

In casting about for a fictional world that Edith Maxwell could inhabit, the more fanciful members of the press would find a ready-made universe already constructed by Fox in the pages of *The Trail of the Lonesome Pine*. Set in Wise County and neighboring Kentucky in the 1890s, the book provided a convenient mental reference point for reporters covering the Maxwell case because it was probably the most popular work about Appalachia that they (and their readers) had ever encountered. After its publication in 1908, *The Trail of the Lonesome Pine* was adapted into a stage play; silent films followed in 1916 and 1923. In 1936 Paramount would score a box-office success with its remake of the movie in Technicolor.[4] The tale's longevity was a testament to Fox's power as a storyteller as well as to the power of the mass media to keep recycling it for new audiences.

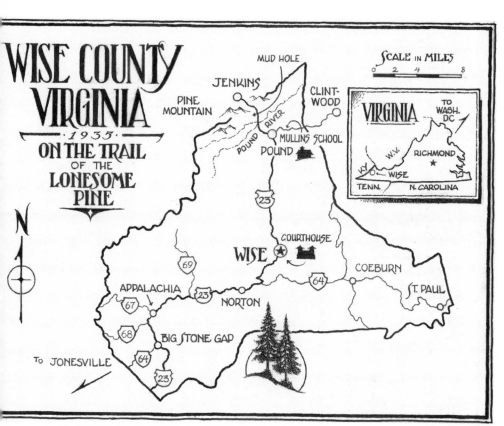

(Map courtesy of Sandy Plunkett)

The almost incessant references to Fox's literary creation would finally prompt one Wise County newspaper editor to quip that "most of the news stories on the Maxwell case have been written in hotel rooms with a bottle of 'corn' [liquor] in one hand and *The Trail of the Lonesome Pine* in the other."[5] It is easy to see why some reporters would look to Fox's fictional heroine, the beautiful June Tolliver, to find a literary "double" for the real-life Edith Maxwell. As Fox tells it, Tolliver is a mountain girl who travels from an isolated cabin to the Kentucky Bluegrass and finally to New York to get an education. Like Edith Maxwell, she returns home only to get caught up in family conflicts—in this case a virulent feud between the Tolliver and Falin clans. This fictional golden-haired heroine eventually becomes engaged to engineer Jack Hale, an "outsider" who has come to the mountains to seek profits in the burgeoning coal industry. First, though, he spends considerable amounts of his own money to send June to expensive schools, where she is taught to clean her fingernails and banish her mountain accent.

Most of her male relatives, whose lifestyle runs counter to the "flying wedge of civilization" thrust upon them by coal barons, are portrayed as murderous ruffians who oppose progress. Espousing a theory now discarded by scholars, one of Fox's more learned characters explains that the natives behave badly because they are "contemporary ancestors," an ill-bred, clannish people who resist modernizing influences—particularly the rule of law—and live just as the eighteenth-century pioneers did.

When Hale joins the local police force and hunts down Tolliver's kinsman "Bad Rufe," she has to choose between loyalty to her family or to Hale. Should she testify against her relative at a murder trial? Is the "real" June Tolliver more comfortable in traditional homespun garb or in the cloth suits worn by city women? Can she be modern without betraying her culture and kin? Throughout all her struggles, the "lonesome pine" serves not only as a majestic symbol of mountain wilderness but also as a source of spiritual renewal for the young heroine.[6]

Folklore surrounding *The Trail of the Lonesome Pine* had become a linchpin of tourist attraction in Wise County by 1935. The Colonial Hotel in Wise had picture postcards reflecting its location "on the trail of the lonesome pine," and Fox's home in Big Stone Gap had been carefully preserved. The publication of *The Trail of the Lonesome Pine* came at time when rural Americans were leaving family farms in droves and moving to cities, where they aspired no longer to be hillbillies or hayseeds but mainstream, "modern" people. When June Tolliver does just that, the young women of Wise County might have seen her journey as a fulfillment of their own hopes and dreams. But if some did identify with June, they also knew that Fox's portrayals of her feuding, fighting relatives and the half-mad preacher Red Fox were larger than life, not typical of their ancestors who had lived during the tempestuous 1890s. Local residents seemed to understand that the Fox book *was* fiction—and even if some parts were based on true stories, it had all happened a long time ago. They would be horrified to learn that these literary depictions from forty years earlier soon would be presented nationwide as sketches of actual living conditions.

In the eyes of the Hearst press it was inevitable that Edith Maxwell, with her evening gown and trips to Detroit and Cincinnati, would become "the lovely Trail of the Lonesome Pine Girl," or as Fulton Lewis had so outlandishly described her, "the Joan d'Arc of the Lonesome Pine." And as night follows day it was equally inevitable that Edith's fellow citizens would become the loutish foils of the current drama. Hearst tabloid writer Arthur Mefford, for one, would describe people "on the Trail of the Lonesome Pine" as "slatternly women and gangling men" who rise each day to "take up the dull business of living."[7] Only a favored few "enlightened" hillbillies were to be spared his contempt.

Reports like these soon would infuriate the citizens of Wise County, who liked to consider themselves as up-to-date as people in other places. Indeed, they felt that evidence of progress was all around them, if only reporters would take the time to see. The last links to the pioneer era were rapidly being obliterated, as the old log houses were torn down and replaced by structures of lumber and brick. Illiteracy had been cut to less than 10 percent. Elderly folks who had grown up using flaming pine-knot torches for illumination now enjoyed electric lights. The granny women and herb doctors who had nurtured the sick were gradually being replaced by physicians recruited by the coal companies and railroads. Nobody would be caught dead posing for a photo with a rifle slung across his chest or puffing on a corncob pipe.

Wise County residents were proud of the advances that had been made, yet they loved to dip into the well of collective memory, to talk of their colorful and fractious past as imagined in *The Trail of the Lonesome Pine*. Now, it seemed that the yellow press was about to seize one of the community's most powerful images and turn it into a doctored photograph, a badge of shame.

———

Although the case of Ann and Edith Maxwell was attracting far greater attention, the first murder trial set for the August term of Judge Skeen's court was that of Ida Baldwin. On August 19 she appeared in the second-story courtroom at the Wise County Courthouse to answer charges she had murdered her husband, Orbin, at their home near Norton on July 21. Fred Greear was assisted at the prosecutor's table by Gernade Dotson, who, ironically, would be opposing him later in the term as one of Edith Maxwell's defense counsel. Ida Baldwin's fate was to be decided by twelve men because state law did not allow women to serve as jurors.

Baldwin admitted shooting her husband but said she did so in self-defense. Testifying for more than an hour, the pregnant mother of six said he had threatened her life and that of her sixteen-year-old daughter on several occasions. And though initial reports said Orbin Baldwin was shot down "while shaving," Ida Baldwin testified that he had menaced her with a razor during a quarrel.

The court reduced the murder charge to manslaughter before giving the case to the jury late in the day. The men hearing the evidence apparently found sympathy with the defendant, declaring her not guilty after deliberating only forty-five minutes. At least in the Baldwin case it seemed that a group of mountain men had found female-on-male violence comprehensible, even justifiable. Would a different jury reach the same conclusion about the Maxwell women?

A curious crowd, said to be one of the largest in the county's history, eagerly wedged itself into Judge Skeen's court the next morning for the start of Edith and Ann's trial. Expectation blanketed the room as everyone waited for the old judge to gavel the proceedings to life. By 8:30 A.M. deputies had to be stationed at the courtroom doors to prevent more spectators from entering. Late arrivals continued to line the corridors outside.

Sprinkled among the farmers, miners, teachers, and housewives attending the trial were reporters from the Associated Press, United Press, and Universal Service. This handful of journalists had the power to put Wise County on the map, to reach millions of readers with whatever version of reality they chose to construct. Their presence did not go unnoticed by Judge Skeen. The freakish pretrial publicity surrounding the Maxwell case—much of it ballyhooing the "mountain code" and "the Land of the Lonesome Pine"—had begun to irritate the white-haired jurist. According to the *Coalfield Progress*, he advised correspondents in the courtroom "to refrain from highly colored and lurid details, under threat of citation for contempt of court."

At the defense table, the team of Alfred A. Skeen and Gernade Dotson had been bolstered by a last-minute recruit. Wise attorney Robert P. Bruce, a former state senator, had signed on about forty-eight hours before the scheduled start of the trial. Like Dotson, Bruce was a former Wise County commonwealth attorney who had made a name for himself as a crime fighter. During the 1890s, when rapid industrialization ignited a shocking flare-up of crime in the county, Bruce had diligently prosecuted some of the region's most violent men. Now in his seventies, the "silver-tongued orator" was still racking up courtroom victories, but more often they were for the defense. Just the day before he had helped gain an acquittal for Ida Baldwin.

Nonetheless, defense strategy had not had time to jell, and Skeen, Bruce, and Dotson knew it. When the Maxwell case was called, they immediately presented the judge with a written motion for a continuance. It said that Edith had been unable to raise defense funds because of being in jail and that Ann had been hampered by a "weakness" that had come over her after her husband's death. Arguing forcefully for a postponement, Skeen told the court that the question of fees had not been settled and that he had not had time to fully investigate the case. He threatened to withdraw if the trial began at once.

Skeen's gambit worked. The judge discussed the motion for about fifteen minutes with all six lawyers involved and then agreed to postpone the trial. He told the crestfallen audience that the case would be heard at the October term of circuit court to give the defense more time to raise money. He also granted a defense request to try Edith and Ann separately. This decision, although little remarked upon in the press, was a momentous victory for Ann, given that her alleged role in Trigg's death had never been publicly sketched out by the prosecution. Edith, however, had already admitted striking her father. Greear immediately chose to try Edith first.

The defense attorneys won these two key motions, yet they did not prevail on every legal point. As additional grounds for the continuance, they had asked Judge Skeen to rule that public sentiment was so squarely against the Maxwell women that they could not receive a fair trial until some time had passed. Judge Skeen rejected that argument but nonetheless agreed to postpone the proceedings.

Ann was again released under her previous bond, but, curiously, the defense lawyers made no attempt to have Edith freed from the county jail. She was returned to her cell after the brief hearing. Greear told reporters that the case would probably come to trial sometime in November.

Skeen, Bruce, and Dotson—with the invaluable assistance of Earl Maxwell—now had about ninety days to fashion a defense. They had managed to buy precious time, but the Maxwell case was not about to retire permanently to the back pages of the newspaper. If anything, the interlude was destined to give public sentiment more time to build. More energy would accrue to the hurricane gathering strength outside the borders of Wise County.

Country people who could decode nature's messages—adepts who reckoned by the number of fogs in August and the thickness of caterpillar fur—were predicting fine fall weather. But Edith, confined to the three-story, red-brick jail next to the courthouse, would have little opportunity to observe the change of seasons. The basement where she and the other women prisoners were kept was said to be a vermin-ridden dungeon where inmates slept three to a bed. Although such overheated prose was the predictable work of the tabloids, even local officials conceded the need for a complete renovation. Corroded water and sewer pipes, coupled with insufficient bathing facilities for the prisoners, made proper sanitation impossible, according to Sheriff Adams. The jail also lacked facilities for segregating youthful offenders from the adult population. By 1935 prisoners in federal custody were not permitted to be detained there, even briefly. A dramatic jail-break by eight prisoners in mid-July 1935 made the front page of the *Coalfield Progress* and prompted Wise County's board of supervisors to investigate conditions at the jail.

Such unflattering press reports might have pained the jailer, Jim Dotson, if he happened to read them, but they were nothing compared to the quandary of having one's own niece as a prisoner. Jailers are traditionally part of the law enforcement establishment and work closely with the sheriff and commonwealth's attorney. But Dotson also had to balance his official duties with concern for his half-sister's family. One visiting reporter said of the jailer: "Far from favoring his niece, he leans backward in the effort to avoid seeming to do so."[8]

Despite these family tensions Edith fared far better than the average prisoner. Earl brought her a bed soon after her arrest and continued to supply fresh linens each week. Special meals prepared by family members were a welcome change from the regular jail menu of gravy and biscuits for breakfast and "soup beans" for lunch and supper. She was eventually allowed to have an electric heater to blunt the autumn chill.

As the days dwindled toward her trial date, now officially set for November 18, 1935, Edith began receiving sympathetic letters from all over the country. She heard from preachers, her former teachers at Radford, and lawyers offering to help with her case. One of her attorneys bought her some postcards to answer the mounting piles of mail.

The fires of press coverage, banked low during early fall, were stoked by the immediacy of the long-awaited trial. Some journalists preparing to cover it were aware that editors expected them not only to report but also, and above all, to interpret the news. Fulton Lewis Jr. had set the standard back in the summer with his exaggerated tales of the "mountain code" that Edith supposedly had violated. Not to be outdone, many who followed him were also anxious to find larger meanings in the anguish of the Maxwell family saga. As the *Literary Digest* put it, they were "striving to establish the sociological significance" of the case.[9]

A correspondent for the United Press, most likely Harry Ferguson, apparently had already decided that the upcoming trial was not really about familial murder but about community morals:

> Wise, Va., Nov. 17—A curfew siren sent hoarse noises up the trail of the lonesome pine tonight, and the hill people boarded up their cabins because tomorrow everybody will be up early to start for "Gov'ment Court," where pretty Edith Maxwell goes on trial for killing her father with a frivolous, sharp-heeled shoe that he thought was a sin to wear.
>
> And sometime this week when the last witness has been heard and all the lawyers have spoken, twelve men will file into a stuffy room to decide whether it is a sin for a twenty-one-year-old girl to stay out with a boy until midnight.
>
> Trigg Maxwell thought it was. And that is why he waited behind the door of his house one night last July, planning to whip his black-haired daughter so that never again would she be away from her own fireside after 9 P.M.[10]

Luther F. Addington, Edith's former principal and one of her favorite teachers at Christopher Gist High School, was deeply troubled by these outlandish reports. As he later pointed out, not only were there many factual errors, such as a reference to the nonexistent 9 P.M. curfew for women, but the writing also showed vast ignorance of the geography and speech patterns of the county. Why, for one thing, did the scribes insist on putting the dialect of the Deep South in the mouths of Wise Countians when mountain accents were quite different?

On the evening before the trial Addington visited some of the out-of-town reporters—including the writer of the United Press story—in a hotel room and found his worst fears about the yellow press confirmed.

"Just what kind of clothes do they wear out in the hills?" one of them asked Addington.

"Haven't you been out to see?" he shot back.

Addington learned that the group of reporters had not gone out into Wise County's countryside at all; they had stayed on the main road, U.S. Route 23, and had filed pretrial stories from their hotel rooms in Wise. One admitted that they had stopped in Pound only briefly, "long enough to mail a post card back home to show that we had been there." Nonetheless, stories would continue to stream forth about hillbillies walking down mountain trails, wives dutifully following their husbands, on the way to "Gov'ment court"—a curious phrase that nobody in Wise County would ever have thought of uttering.

"Every section has its own peculiarities and misfortunes," Addington would later write. "But when a sensational trial is seized upon to use as a skeleton on which to hang the imaginings of the yellow pressmen the true citizen feels that an injustice has been wrought at the expense of his home section."[11]

This sense of violation had no doubt been felt by some of the "true citizens" of Dayton, Tennessee, who had experienced a similar media onslaught just ten years earlier. Their small Appalachian community had been put on the map by the Scopes "monkey trial," a great, gaudy piece of theater that had been stage-managed by H. L. Mencken and backed by a Greek chorus of about a hundred other journalists sent to cover the story in 1925. Now, some reporters were hoping that the Maxwell case would become a 1930s' revival of the famous show trial, which had pitted defense lawyer Clarence Darrow against prosecutor William Jennings Bryan.

Like Edith Maxwell, the defendant in the monkey trial was a teacher, but there most of the factual resemblance between the two cases ended. John Scopes was a high school biology teacher who volunteered to test a Tennessee antievolution law by teaching the theory to his students. Scopes was convicted of a misdemeanor—later overturned on a technicality—but was vindicated in the eyes of the public. Edith, however, had been caught up in the court system totally against her will.

Edith Maxwell and John Scopes, however, did have something in common, at least in the eyes of some observers. They were "modern," up-and-coming young people with the "proper" outlook. At the same time Scopes received favorable press attention, his opponents' beliefs and lifestyle were put on trial. Christian fundamentalists were certainly on the wrong side of history in opposing evolution, but their views were seldom respectfully presented by the press. Finding "sociological significance" may have been the ideal, but the glaring light of the media circus tended to eclipse serious reflection. Ridicule fell not only on prosecutor Bryan but also on the citizenry of Dayton, whom Mencken declared to be "local primates," "yokels," "morons," "anthropoids," "hillbillies," and "half-wits."[12]

Perhaps, in a way not intended, the press was right. The two cases *were* alike in that local people—Appalachian people—were seen as old-fashioned and out of step with the times. Little wonder, then, that Harry Ferguson of the United Press would presage the start of the Maxwell trial this way: "The self-imposed regulations under which these people live along the Trail of the Lonesome Pine also will be on trial, just as an abstract theory was on trial in the Scopes' case at Dayton, Tenn."[13]

Even before the opening gavel of Edith Maxwell's trial the case had assumed epic proportions far beyond the question of guilt or innocence. In the space of four months it had gone from a murder investigation to a referendum on the Appalachian way of life. How would the jury respond to such pressure?

𝟾 *Witness for the Prosecution*

On the morning of November 18, 1935, hundreds of citizens stood in line, eight or ten abreast, outside the clock-towered courthouse on Wise's main street. Set back from the road by a low rock wall and shallow front yard, the stone structure stood as a monument to local craftsmen who, with the help of a six-yoke team of oxen, finished it in 1897.

Although the courthouse was relatively new, its checkered marble floors scarcely worn by the tramp of years, history surrounded it like ether. The whipping post used in the early days of the county—its primary function being to punish men who abused their wives—had long since vanished. Likewise, the thirty-by-forty-five-foot, hewn-log building that had served as the original courthouse had been burned to the ground by raiding Federal troops during the Civil War.

The invisible past nonetheless enjoyed a vivid afterlife. Older people in the crowd could still recall the ghastly spectacle of the public gallows, later dismantled, upon which seven men had been hanged for murder before the advent of electrocution. Now the trial about to get under way in Judge Henry Alexander Wise Skeen's second-story courtroom promised to be a spectacle in its own right. Many in line that Monday morning probably sensed that something important was about to happen, but few could have foreseen that the day would usher in one of the largest media events in the annals of Appalachia.

Reporters from the three major wire services were on hand to cover the trial of the "Lonesome Pine girl." Messengers stood at the ready to ferry bulletins to the Western Union office at nearby Norton, which was expecting to wire ten thousand words daily to a world whose interest had been piqued by pretrial stories. Over the objections of Judge Skeen, news photographers had posted themselves at vantage points throughout the courtroom and upstairs gallery, where occasional camera flashes revealed their presence.

The high-ceilinged courtroom provided a grand, theatrical setting for the administration of justice. The judge's bench, flanked by tables for news reporters, anchored the south end of the room. Directly in front of Judge Skeen's perch was the jury box, where the jurors were to sit in two rows—five in front and seven in back—facing the audience. On the jury's left, the prosecutors manned a long table perpendicular to the jury box. Fred Greear sat in the middle, with Oscar M. Vicars on his right and Lewis McCormick on his left. The defense had a similar table on the jury's right, where Earl and Edith took their places beside Robert P. Bruce and Alfred A. Skeen. The jury box and lawyers' tables formed three sides of a square, with the witness stand occupying the fourth side facing the jury. The court reporter and court clerk worked at low desks near the front of the enclosed area.

A railing with ornate metal curlicues separated the audience from this main stage of action. The rest of the room was given over to two rows of nine pews each, which were packed with spectators long before court was to convene. More onlookers—many dressed in their Sunday best—took up standing room at the sides and back. According to the Associated Press, "Spectators for the most part listened with the absorbed interest of theater-goers at a stirring drama" as the trial unfolded.[1] Many brought lunch with them out of fear of losing their seats. Babies alternately dozed and wailed on their mothers' laps. A bailiff would have to chase curious schoolchildren out of the building throughout the day.

A pool of thirty men had been called as potential jurors. Along with the lawyers, Judge Skeen questioned them himself. Care was taken that none of the Maxwells' neighbors or kin would be impaneled—or anyone who lived within two miles of Pound. Three candidates were disqualified for being distant relatives of Edith; another was excused because he had caught a ride with prosecutor Greear while hitchhiking to court that morning.

It took only half an hour to seat the twelve-man jury in whose hands Edith's fate now rested. Glancing to their right to size up the defendant, they would have seen a tall, graceful woman stylishly dressed in a white shirtwaist, brown skirt, and suede shoes. Her expression may have been partially cloaked by the half-veil that tumbled to her nose from a brown hat. Edith, in turn, would have observed a group of well-meaning mountain men who had much more in common with Trigg than with her. Would old-fashioned chivalry prevail, or would they identify with the husband and father whose life had ended so abruptly? Only one thing was certain: A jury of her peers, the birthright of every citizen, was merely a hollow promise.

———

Back in the 1700s an English lord had remarked that "a man's home is his castle," a sentiment that became firmly embedded in the law. More recently, Edith Maxwell had shown that sometimes in America in the 1930s a woman's home was *her* castle, too. She had done this by coolly turning a worried Chant Kelly away from her door on the night of July 21, 1935, prolonging the agonizing moments in which her father's extremity could remain a private matter. Now it was commonwealth attorney Fred Greear's job to breach the ramparts of this protected space, to shine a light into the dark corners of concealment.

Had modern forensic science not been in its infancy, it likely could have told a tale worthy of an old mountain ballad, a refrain of blood spots crying up from the floor. Greear's investigators had uncovered considerable physical evidence suggesting that a violent struggle had occurred in the Maxwell home, yet the prosecutor had no experts to tell him what it all meant—and nothing to steer him away from faulty conclusions. If objects inside the house could not be counted on to tell the story definitively, he would have to rely on Chant Kelly, who just moments after the fatal struggle had teased the very perimeter of Edith's domain. And when the time came, Greear would present the damning words of a genuine eyewitness—Edith's own confession.

As soon as Greear and Alfred A. Skeen finished their opening arguments, the commonwealth called Kelly to testify. Throughout the trial, other witnesses would often refer to Kelly as "Chant Branham" because few had yet become accustomed to calling him by his newly acquired legal name. Chant had decided in early 1935, at age forty, to adopt the surname of his father, John W. Kelly. The elder Kelly, who was English, had come to the southwest Virginia–east Tennessee area in the hire of a British firm developing the area's vast mineral resources. Mary Branham, Chant's mother, was descended from one of the old pioneer families of Pound. Chant was born in Cumberland Gap, Tennessee, in 1894, but his parents separated when he was a baby. Mary returned to Pound and raised her son in the Mill Creek community on the old family farm, which he inherited at age nine upon the death of his grandfather.

There was much for the jury to admire in the man who took the witness stand that Monday morning. As a footloose teenager he had followed a young man's dream of adventure: roaming the West and Mexico, supporting himself with railroad and construction work. And as a soldier in the army he distinguished himself in the Vera Cruz, Mexico, expedition of 1914. He eventually returned to civilian life and attended colleges in West Virginia and Tennessee. By 1922 he was ready to go home.

Once back in Pound, Kelly married Lucille Strange and embarked on a varied career as owner of a pool room, drugstore, restaurant, and boardinghouse. For many years he served as both postmaster and barber, having learned the latter occupation while in the army. Townspeople also might have suspected that he harbored a technological genie in some dark, sulfurous bottle in his drugstore, for Kelly was a man who had the first telephone in Pound, and his wife and daughters enjoyed pumped-in water and electric lights from his very own Delco power plant.

Besides his entrepreneurial feats, Kelly was widely known for civic-mindedness. Shortly after Judge Skeen made the name change official on March 18, 1935, the *Coalfield Progress* had congratulated Kelly in a page-one story, calling him "one of Wise County's most loyal boosters" and praising his efforts to bring electricity and a water system to all residents of Pound. Prosecutor Greear would have the easy task of questioning a most popular and credible figure.

Kelly's story had changed little from the one he first told on the night of Trigg Maxwell's death. He had been reading in his second-floor bedroom about 1:10 A.M. on July 21 when he heard "feminine voices" engaged in "a racket" at the Maxwell home next door. Upon hearing Trigg's cries of "Oh, Lordy," he hurried to their doorstep, only to be turned away by Edith.

Soon a radio began playing loudly at the Maxwell house, muffling the sound of footsteps scurrying across the floor. Back on the second floor of his building, Kelly heard Edith's voice float up from the street. As later testimony would show, Edith had fled her house clothed only in a princess slip. Kelly heard her telling her little sister, Mary Katherine, to go get her clothes because she was going somewhere to spend the night. After five or ten minutes the radio was turned off. Nearly half an hour later he heard Mary Katherine hollering for him. "She told me to come, that her daddy was dying," Kelly recalled.

This time he descended by a set of stairs leading down to his drugstore. He left the lights on and the doors open in case he should need first-aid supplies. A few quick steps brought him once again to the Maxwell home, where Trigg was unconscious and struggling for air. Mary Katherine, Edith, and Ann all told Kelly that Trigg had fallen against a meat block that was sitting on the porch about three feet from his head. Despite Kelly's attempts to help Trigg breathe, he died about 2:30 A.M., some fifteen minutes after the neighbor's help was sought.

Later on the first day of the trial, Commonwealth Attorney Greear would call four other members of Kelly's household to testify about the loud disturbance that had riveted their attention early on the morning of July 21. Kelly's two sisters-in-law and two male boarders substantiated parts of his story, and one of the women, Verna Hubbard, added important—and incriminating—new information.

Hubbard testified that she "heard a fuss start just as soon as she [Edith] got in." Whereas Kelly had heard "feminine voices talking as though they were in a racket with someone," his wife's sister was more specific. Hubbard said she could hear Edith and Trigg's voices raised in argument but could not understand what was being said. She also could hear "scuffling" inside the house. A few minutes later, Hubbard glanced down from a second-floor window and saw Edith standing directly below in the narrow space between the Kelly and Maxwell buildings.

"Mary Katherine came out there after her," Hubbard told the court, "and while she was out there Carson Hubbard passed and asked her what was the matter and she didn't reply, and Mary Katherine came out and tried to get her to go back in the house and she didn't go right then.[2] She [Mary Katherine] come back out and said, 'Edith, come back in the house. Daddy's got blood all over hisself.' She said, 'Well, bring my dress and shoes.' I don't know whether she brought them or not. I could hear Trigg groaning like he was hurt, saying 'Oh, Lordy,' or something that I couldn't tell what, and he was groaning and going on."

The implications of Verna Hubbard's testimony would do much to bolster the commonwealth's case. The fight had occurred quickly, damage had been inflicted on Trigg Maxwell's head within moments, and there had been copious amounts of blood. According to the prosecution's theory, there was so much blood that it had taken the Maxwell women anywhere from thirty to forty-five minutes to set the house to rights before Chant Kelly and the other neighbors were allowed in. Although this testimony did not rule out the possibility that Trigg may have been the aggressor in the fight, the delay in seeking medical attention made Edith and her mother seem, at best, cold and uncaring.

Greear kept Kelly on the witness stand all Monday morning. After the star witness had completed his story of being turned away from the Maxwells' door, the prosecutor questioned him about what he had found when he finally got inside the house. During the resuscitation attempt, Kelly had noticed that Trigg's hair was wet, although there was no blood on him. "I had it in mind that he was hit, and hit in the head," he testified. Although it was hard to see on the darkened porch, Kelly finally located a small wound on Trigg's head just back from the hairline. When he examined the meat block later that night, he could find no evidence of blood or hair on it. On the kitchen floor, however, Kelly had found both blood stains and wet areas that appeared to have been recently mopped.

Kelly remained at the home until about 4 A.M. Sunday, helping other neighbors and relatives lay out the body, and apparently returned shortly after daylight. Greear asked him about any possible weapons found in or near the house. The witness testified he had spotted a coal axe with an eighteen-inch handle on the porch where Trigg died. Kelly searched the Maxwell home for a hatchet he said Trigg owned but could not find it.

By noon Kelly had completed his powerful story of the circumstances surrounding Trigg Maxwell's death. When court resumed after lunch Greear would be ready to steer Kelly's testimony toward the question of motive.

Hearst writer Edward B. Lockett was finding the trial of the Lonesome Pine girl every bit as colorful as he'd imagined. He considered the mountain audience to be "morose and sullenly talkative"—a perfect foil for Judge Skeen's lively and unpredictable courtroom behavior. Lockett noticed that Skeen seldom presided from the bench at all. Because of his deafness, the elderly judge would seat himself in a cane chair near the witness stand when someone was testifying, cocking a hand behind his bad ear. At other times, Lockett observed, the old man with a high starched collar would wander around the room. He sometimes engaged in "violent bickerings" with lawyers on both sides. All in all, Lockett thought, the outlandish scene was worthy of a Hollywood movie, with a judge straight out of central casting.[3]

What the Washington, D.C., correspondent may have failed to recognize, however, was that substance, more than style, was what counted in a murder trial. Eccentricities aside, seventy-six-year-old Henry Alexander Wise Skeen would consistently demonstrate that he had still the mental muscle to control his courtroom.

———

"Prior to this time [July 21] had you heard any argument between Edith Maxwell and her father?" Greear asked Kelly right after lunch. The question prompted a flurry of objections from defense attorney Alfred A. Skeen, who said the prosecution had to show actual threats of violence, not just a history of having arguments. After discussing the matter with the lawyers in chambers, Judge Skeen ruled that Kelly could testify about an argument at the Maxwell home the previous year.

"Mr. Maxwell and Edith was into a racket," Kelly said. "As I saw them he come up the stairway and went in the house or in the side porch, rather, with a shovel or pick or something of the kind, some tool in his hand and they was in the racket. They both went in the house and the racket continued and got violent and she run out of the house and he stayed in the house or in the porch, and she told him that she would burst his old brains out. I don't know whether she intended that for any future—." The court quickly cut off Kelly's speculation. "Just tell what she said," instructed Judge Skeen. "That is for the jury to say."

But the prosecution's star witness remained virtually unflappable under cross-examination by Alfred A. Skeen, who questioned him skeptically about the circular spots in the kitchen and another one Kelly had found on the porch near the dead man's right elbow. How did Kelly know the floor had been washed? Wasn't that a conclusion on his part? Kelly was forced to restate his answer, saying he had seen what appeared to be blood stains on a wet floor and that he had observed the stains again after the floor had dried. In the end, Skeen's tenacity made little difference; Kelly left the stand with his story intact.

Lovell Sowards, Kelly's boarder who had tried to help save Trigg's life, also testified about the odd wet spots on the Maxwells' floor. But Greear's major purpose in putting him on the stand apparently was to tell of an incident that had happened on the Saturday afternoon preceding Trigg's death. The story was intended to hammer away at the question of motive, but incidentally, it also managed to illustrate the stifling quality that can sometimes overwhelm small-town life. Sowards ran a restaurant in Pound. Edith stopped by to drink a Coca-cola. As she went out on the street she encountered filling station attendant Arch Vance. According to Sowards, the two stood "very affectionately," bodies touching. Trigg Maxwell was near the restaurant and apparently observed the scene. Father and daughter then walked down the street talking, but Sowards could not hear what was said.

Judge Skeen was disturbed by the turn Sowards's testimony had taken. Without waiting for the defense to object, he quickly declared the episode inadmissible. "All that goes out, Gentlemen of the Jury, as far as that man and woman are concerned. . . . It has no relation up to this time." Greear promised to lay the proper groundwork and recall Sowards later in the trial.[4] Another witness later testified that Edith had told Trigg during their walk down the street, "If you don't like it, what are you going to do about it?"

During cross-examination of Sowards, Alfred A. Skeen scored one of his first victories when he elicited the fact that Sowards had sold Trigg three beers in the hours leading up to his death. Trigg had purchased one around 5 P.M., another "about dark," and a third between 12:30 and 1 A.M. Of course, three beers spaced over seven or eight hours would not have had much effect on a tall, well-built man like Trigg Maxwell, and in any case Sowards insisted that he at all times appeared sober. Yet Skeen hinted—but could not prove—that Trigg may have been imbibing at other places that Saturday night as well.

The commonwealth's next witness, Ned Deaton, swore that Trigg had not been intoxicated. Deaton, who operated another restaurant less than two hundred yards from the Maxwell home, said he had talked to him for more than an hour that night, beginning at 11:30 or 12:00, and had noticed nothing unusual. A waitress at Deaton's also vouched for Trigg, testifying that he had looked sober when he came in the restaurant to buy an orange soda pop. Before the trial was over, a half-dozen people would swear that Trigg was not drunk. And, if he hadn't been, how could he have fallen so precipitously in the familiar confines of his own little house?

With his next batch of witnesses Greear would attempt to show that Edith Maxwell had nursed a homicidal rage against her father for years— and that the events of July 20–21 had been premeditated. Ruth Baker, Edith's first cousin, said Edith had mentioned killing her father "dozens of times" during the 1933–34 school year when the two roomed together at Radford State Teachers College. But Ruth admitted she had never tried to warn her Uncle Trigg and did not tell her mother—Trigg's sister—of the threats until after his death.

Alta Cantrell, a Pound teacher who had also attended Radford with Edith, remembered a college conversation in which Edith said she cared more for her mother than her father, "that she didn't care anything for him." Another witness, taxi driver Everett Holyfield, said Edith told him in 1934 that "she hated him [her father] so she couldn't keep from laughing if she seen him laid out dead."

Conrad Bolling, a teacher, recounted an incident from July 1934 in which he was driving Edith and four other young people around the county on a pleasure trip. Edith and another male passenger were seated in front. On the way to Mill Creek they passed Trigg Maxwell near a bridge. Bolling, explaining that he and Edith were "big friends," said he teasingly told her that her father would whip her when she got back home. In Bolling's recollection, Edith responded, "I would just like for him to try it. I would just kill him." Edith added that she would be glad if Trigg was dead. "I told her she should be ashamed of herself," Bolling testified, "and she said there wasn't any need of being ashamed, it was the truth."

For those who believed Bolling's account it was as if the future had hurled itself backward for a brief moment in 1934, revealing the impending tragedy with utter clarity. And from the defense's perspective, his story had stung like a sniper's bullet. The witness had not told his damaging recollection until the day of the trial, so Edith's lawyers were ill-prepared to counter it. Robert Bruce, who was sharing cross-examination duties with Alfred A. Skeen, could do little except obtain the names of the others who had been riding with Bolling and Edith. Before the afternoon was over, however, the defense would spring a surprise of its own.

Greear's next two witnesses were G. T. Foust and T. J. Tudor, the local physicians who had performed the autopsy on Trigg Maxwell at a Norton funeral parlor after the body had been embalmed. Their examination revealed that Trigg had suffered three blows to the head, two that bruised the scalp and another that cut through the scalp and into the periosteum, the membrane covering the skull. The lacerating wound commenced about one inch back of the hairline and extended lengthwise for three-quarters of an inch. The two other head blows had landed a little farther back—one to the right and one to the left of the cut—but did not break the skin. More bruises discolored the back of the left forearm and back of the left hand. A small cut was observed on the little finger of the right hand.

Dark, swollen areas around the victim's eyes and nose had led the doctors to expect a fracture at the base of the skull, but when they opened the cranium, none could be found. Instead, they saw large blood clots at the base of the brain. The doctors concluded that Trigg had died of brain injury from trauma to the front part of the head. The three-quarter-inch-long lacerating wound was deemed to be the fatal injury.

Special Prosecutor Vicars asked both men to give their opinions on what type of instrument could have inflicted that wound. In Dr. Foust's view, "It must have been somewhat sharp . . . because the cut was fairly clean." Dr. Tudor in turn testified that the mortal wound "in all probability was made with an instrument that had a sharp surface or at least a right-angle surface. Of course it might have been possible for some other kind of instrument with a tremendously hard blow to have cut, but if it had been, it would probably have fractured the skull."

So far the medical evidence had gone as the prosecution probably had anticipated. Both doctors' testimonies were consistent with the commonwealth's theory that Trigg Maxwell had been struck with a sharp-edged metallic object. That seemed to cast doubt on Edith's July 1935 statement to Fred Greear that she struck her father with a rubber-heeled man's shoe while fending off an attack. Greear prudently had seized Trigg's work shoes as evidence, confident he could show—if the need arose—that such an object could not have been the murder weapon. As Alfred A. Skeen methodically worked his way through a cross-examination of Dr. Tudor without inflicting any real damage, Greear's confidence level could only have increased. Apparently, no one on the prosecution team was ready for the jab that Skeen was about to administer. The defense attorney recalled Dr. Foust to the stand.

"Doctor, I hand you a shoe that will later be introduced in evidence, and I will ask you to examine the same and state whether or not in your opinion that shoe is capable when wielded with considerable force of making the wound or wounds which you found on the man's head?" In Skeen's hand was a brown, high-heeled woman's slipper. The wooden heel, covered with a thin layer of leather, was of a typical shape—circular at the back and sides, straight on the front. The straight edge of the heel measured about three-quarters of an inch, the same as the length of the laceration on the victim's head.

"If you hit hard enough this heel could make a laceration," responded Dr. Foust, who conceded that the shoe could have made the bruises as well. Dr. Tudor was also recalled, and, like Foust before him, he could not rule out the shoe as a possible source of Trigg Maxwell's injuries. "It is just a question of how much force could be put behind a shoe of this weight," Tudor said.

Greear scoffed at the very idea. As he later wrote in a detective magazine, "It was a light, sleazy thing of straps and patches with a light wooden heel, leather tipped, which showed no evidence of either blood or hair. It was scarcely as formidable as Cinderellas's slipper and it seemed incredible that the slipper could have inflicted the death wounds."[5] Skeen offered no explanation for the origin of the mysterious footwear, nor did the prosecution demand one. The high-heeled T-strap with its perforated leather trim was duly passed to the jurors for inspection. Greear, the meticulous preparer, had been caught short. "This came as a complete surprise to me," he wrote, "the first inkling I had that she would change her story and not mention the father's shoe."[6]

Recovering somewhat, Vicars took another turn at questioning the doctors, but he never succeeded in getting them to completely disavow the high-heeled slipper. Alfred A. Skeen had made sure that the upcoming testimony of his own witnesses would not be torpedoed by the commonwealth's medical experts.

—

Fred Greear had long been convinced that no shoe of any kind had killed Trigg Maxwell, yet his own search for a definitive murder weapon had proved elusive. The iron that county policeman Ed DeLong had seized from the Maxwell kitchen—the one that Greear had displayed so triumphantly in front of the jail back in July—was still a prime candidate. Now, with Delong on the stand, Greear was attempting to introduce it. Alfred A. Skeen had protested. "We object to the introduction of the iron in evidence unless they can show that the wound was inflicted by it," he said.

The Dickenson County lawyer was, of course, asking for a proof that the prosecution could not deliver. The forensic tests that are routinely performed in today's homicide cases were still decades off. There is nothing in the record to indicate, however, that even a rudimentary chemical analysis of the dark spots on the iron was ever performed. Were the discolorations blood, as the prosecution implied, or were they melted linoleum, as the defense would later suggest? In a *Liberty* magazine article written in 1935, Earl Maxwell had dared the prosecution to have the iron tested—but apparently neither prosecution nor defense ever did so. Citizens of that era had no reason to expect sophisticated testing, however;

the jurors would base their decision on instinct and common sense rather than scientific probabilities. Without hesitation, Judge Skeen accepted the iron as evidence.

Despite this victory, Greear's further questioning of DeLong suggested that even the prosecutor had less than total faith in the iron as the weapon. "Did you find any hatchet or hammer there?" he asked the policeman. Delong replied that he had not, but he also mentioned that he had noticed a short-handled "coal axe" on the Maxwells' porch, probably the same one Chant Kelly had observed. Yet DeLong testified that he did not seize the axe as evidence, and Greear did nothing further to connect it with the crime.

The commonwealth attorney also sought to introduce a pillowcase and sheet—both apparently blood-stained—that DeLong had found in a barrel on the Maxwells' porch during the police search. DeLong said both items were wet when he discovered them "down about a third of the way in the barrel" with other clothing on top. The implication was that the items had been on Trigg Maxwell's bed on the night he died and that someone had tried to conceal them.

Alfred A. Skeen was again ready with an objection. Unless the commonwealth could show that Edith put the bedclothes there, they would not be admissible. Greear countered that the items were found in the house where the homicide was committed and that the defendant had been present. Judge Skeen ruled for the defense, effectively ending DeLong's testimony.

Sheriff J. Preston Adams—the man who had adroitly steered Edith from harm's way on the day of her father's funeral—was the next prosecution witness. The commonwealth attorney was fond of pointing out that Edith had changed her original story, and with Adams on the stand, he was planning to bring the point home to the jury with devastating results. When Adams arrested Edith just hours after her father died, she immediately told him that her father had been drunk and fell against the meat block. Later, during her interrogation in Greear's office, she had admitted striking Trigg Maxwell with *his own shoe* shortly before his death. Now that the defense had brought in a lady's slipper, it appeared that Edith would be changing her story once again. These contradictions would become all the more obvious when the jury heard her previous explanations.

Sheriff Adams took his seat facing the jury. Like a hypnotist leading his subject down a well-worn path, Greear expertly guided Adams's testimony to a day in July 1935 when Edith was brought from the jail to Greear's office for interrogation. Suddenly a shadow fell across that path. Judge

Skeen began to pepper the sheriff with questions of his own. Did anybody make promises to Edith to induce a confession? Did she make it of her own free will? What exactly was said to her?

The sheriff, who probably had been expecting a routine introduction of the statement, found himself on the hot seat. "Shall I tell it in detail? I said, 'If you did this, don't make a mistake and deny it and then let it be proved on you.'"

"Wait, wait," responded Judge Skeen. "Gentlemen, our law in Virginia lays down that an officer should not interrogate a witness. We don't have the rule which they have in some states, what is called the third degree, and statements or an admission brought out must be brought freely and voluntarily and without any suggestion or persuasion, otherwise it is not admissible." The statement in question, as well as any subsequent statements from Edith, would now be considered tainted evidence.

Judge Skeen's ruling was no doubt a bitter disappointment to the prosecution lawyers, who would try the next day in chambers to get him to reconsider. The defense, in turn, would fight hard to keep the statement out. Throughout the legal tug of war the judge was to remain adamant. "You can't make a witness testify against themselves," he later told the attorneys. "When you call a witness in without her counsel and without anybody to counsel her, and go to popping questions at her to use against her, you had just as well call her down there on the stand if you were to let the admissions go in."

Thus the commonwealth rested around 4 P.M. Monday, having presented its evidence in five hours of testimony by eighteen witnesses. What may have been an important element of Greear's case—Edith's purported confession that she had struck her father with his own shoe—was never revealed to the jury. Judge Skeen had seen to it that in this trial, and in future cases, the prosecution would have to play by the rules. The feisty old judge had proved himself a watchdog for defendants' rights, yet in the process he had ensured that whatever accounting Edith gave to Greear would never become part of the trial record.[7] Skeen's decision would leave future generations to wonder what, exactly, she had said in that most desperate hour.

9   *The Men Decide*

Even without the alleged confession, common-
wealth attorney Fred Greear had managed to rope Edith Maxwell inside
a tight circle of suspicion. But her lawyer, Alfred A. Skeen, had his own
exit strategy. As the defense would later write in instructions to the jury,
"Mere suspicion or probability of guilt however strong is not sufficient to
convict the defendant of any offense . . . but to warrant her conviction
her guilt must be proven so clearly that there remains no theory consistent with her
innocence."

Although Edith, Ann, and even little Mary Katherine had acted suspi-
ciously, Skeen was poised to show that they could explain everything that
happened. They could even reconcile the two apparently contradictory
stories, that of the meat block and of the fight that preceded it. And if
their version *could* be true, the jury would have no choice but to find Edith
innocent.

Beginning Monday afternoon and continuing on Tuesday, November
19, Skeen would call first Ann, then Mary Katherine, and finally Edith to
tell of the events that led to Trigg Maxwell's death. They would weave a
tale remarkable in its consistency, differing in only a few minor details.
Would this be the sign of truth-telling, as is usually assumed? Or would it
be a fable invented by an incredibly well-orchestrated trio, a trio satisfied
that the justice of women had already been served in secret? A mostly
sympathetic press corps waited eagerly to record their words, but the
jury's impression, at least for now, would be all that mattered.

—

July 20 was a typical summer Saturday for forty-nine-year-old Ann Maxwell.
With a husband and three daughters at home, cooking and cleaning always had to be done, and in anticipation of the Sabbath she was cooking
extra. Ann knew she would probably be spending Saturday night alone
except for the company of eleven-year-old Mary Katherine. Her daughter
Anna Ruth, fifteen, would be staying overnight in Wise with relatives, and
Edith, too, intended to go out.

Ann also knew that Trigg would probably be somewhere drinking, as he did most every Saturday night. Many miners liked to get out and make merry on the weekends, to find escape from the harsh conditions of the work week, but she perceived the situation with Trigg to be less benign. In Ann's mind, her relationship with her husband boiled down to simple calculus: drink made Trigg quarrelsome. "He wasn't good to me when he was drinking, but when he was sober he was very good to me," she would tell a packed courtroom.

From the vantage point of thirty-one years of marriage, Ann testified that Trigg "drank principally all his life except about ten months out of one year." That one year, 1933–34, was when his brother, Fred, died suddenly and Trigg had "professed to hope"—an expression that meant he had found salvation. During that time, Ann said, her husband "was lots better than ever in his life." But early in 1935 Ann's hopes had begun to dwindle; Trigg was drinking again, although not quite as often as before. His drinking also brought him into conflict with Edith. When he was high, Ann said, he didn't want Edith to go anywhere. And Edith was equally determined to go. A Saturday night was therefore the most volatile time in the rhythms of the Maxwell family, when tempers could flare as suddenly as a summer thunderstorm.

Yet the very normality of that July day would have dispelled any notion that father and daughter were set on a collision course. Around noon, Ann called Trigg to dinner. He had been working that morning in the rental portion of their building, which had just been occupied the first of the month by their married daughter Gladys Robinson, the village postmaster. Trigg took the meal with his wife, Anna Ruth, and Mary Katherine. Ann had baked a pie from blackberries she picked that morning on Bold Camp, her old homeplace. She would recall that Trigg ate heartily. Only Edith did not eat. About 2 P.M. he caught a ride to Jenkins to attend a funeral. Ann would not see Trigg again until 10:30 that night—a time when all their shared histories would converge to a single irreversible moment, in a place where hope—or redemption—would no longer be possible.

—

Edith had spent most of the day reading at home. After 3 P.M. she walked over to a neighbor's to fetch a bucket of water. On the way home she ran into Archie Vance in front of the beauty shop. They chatted innocently for a moment about a gasoline delivery but made no physical contact. Trigg emerged from Bolling's store and caught up with Edith on the street.

"Come on up to the house," he said.

"There's where I have started," replied Edith.

"What were you talking to him about?" Trigg wanted to know.

"Talking about gas."

"You shouldn't be doing that."

"I can't do anything," was the exasperated reply.

Edith and Trigg parted ways, and Edith continued home with the water bucket. She suspected her father had already been drinking, but she did not intend for this skirmish to affect her evening agenda. Trigg hated for her to go places with her mother's side of the family, so she was planning to go out in the company of Trigg's brother's boy, Vernon Maxwell. That way she figured she would be safe. By sundown, she and Vernon had caught a ride to Wise, some thirteen miles away. She had promised her mother she would be home early.

———

At 6 P.M., Mary Katherine Maxwell entered the Lonesome Pine Cafe with a nickel, intent on buying a bag of potato chips. She noticed her father drinking beer with E. L. Sikes, the village physician who was the Maxwells' next-door neighbor. Just as he had instructed Edith earlier that day, Trigg told Mary Katherine to get home. But the seventh-grader was not a timid child; she would not leave until she had gotten her snack. Trigg paid for the chips out of his own pocket. Mary Katherine went back home and reported her father's whereabouts. She threw her coin down on a table and said, "Mother, you are a nickel to the good."

Trigg did not come home for supper. After the meal Mary Katherine went back out on the sidewalk to play with friends. She was still playing after dark when her father—now clearly drunk, in the little girl's estimation—walked up and again told her to get home. "I told him I was getting but he better come with me," Mary Katherine told the court. Trigg ignored the suggestion, and the child obeyed. She came into the house crying, telling her mother that he was out there drinking and fussing at her, trying to make her come home. Ann and Mary Katherine soon retired to the right front bedroom next to the street.

Mary Katherine was awakened around 10:30 by a light being turned on. From a drowsy place she heard her father saying something about blackberries. She snapped to full attention but lay motionless in the bed she shared with her mother. Trigg was sitting in a rocking chair beside the bed. "How many blackberries did you pick, and where are you going to pick them?" he demanded.

"I've been picking up at the old homeplace," Ann answered, without getting up.

"Well curl your hair and go pick them. I'm just going to give you thirty minutes in the morning to leave."

Ann did not respond to her husband's threat. She told him it was late, that he should go to bed. But Trigg seemed possessed of a restless energy. He said he had to go talk to his brother-in-law. No, Ann said, they'll be in bed. Wait until morning. Trigg stormed out of the bedroom and left the house. Ann got up and turned off the light.

———

In the town of Wise, Shorty's Restaurant was a popular place to be on a Saturday night. Edith was hanging out there with her cousin Vernon and a fellow whose name she wasn't quite sure of, but, as she would later tell the court, there was no romantic interest. She was there "only with Vernon." Edith and her cousin had been one-way hitchhikers coming into Wise. After an evening of visiting friends and relatives—including her mother's half-brother, jailer Jim Dotson—they still had not lined up a ride to Pound. By 11 P.M., her promise to her mother to get back early was proving difficult to keep.

Eventually, Edith spotted a boy she had known all her life, twenty-two-year-old Raymond Meade, a coal miner. Although Meade already had five passengers, he agreed to take Edith home. Vernon did not accompany them, perhaps for reasons of space. So Meade set out down the mountain for Pound with his brother and his brother's girlfriend, a married couple and their baby, and Edith, all sandwiched into his car. Between Wise and Pound, Meade dropped off everyone except Edith. Now he was suggesting that they ride around awhile, maybe go get something to eat.

Edith demurred, telling him she had to get to bed early and go pick berries the next day. But Meade prevailed, and the two young people drove past Edith's house and continued about two miles north of town to a section known to locals as the "Mud Hole." In the days before hard-surfaced roads, the Mud Hole had been a boggy patch where unwary wagoneers often got stuck, requiring double and triple teams of oxen to extricate them. Now it was a place where the venturesome went to get free of their worldly cares, a notorious assortment of joints and speakeasies strung along U.S. Route 23 at the foot of Pine Mountain. Meade pulled in at Oliver Pilkington's place, the Little Ritz.

Once inside, the two young people bypassed the public counter and went into one of several private rooms in the back, each furnished with a table and chairs. An acquaintance of Edith's, Alf Ellison, went with them. Edith told Meade she wanted potato chips and a soft drink. As Edith would later testify, Meade pressured her to order a drink of liquor, but she steadfastly refused. Ellison was not drinking either. "I'm off of it and me and Edith quit," he said in the jocular way one uses to deflect social pressure. Meade left the room and came back with the liquor. He poured Edith a glass anyway.

Somebody called for Meade to come out front; there was a Boggs boy who wanted to talk with him. Edith and Ellison were left alone.

"Alf, I don't want this liquor," she said.

Ellison suggested she pour it out the window and refill her glass with ginger ale. When Meade returned he didn't seem to notice that a switch had been made. As the three talked, Meade downed a couple of drinks of liquor, and Edith munched on her chips.

"I've got to be going," Edith said eventually. "I am going to pick berries tomorrow. I can't stay out and pick berries."

"Wait a few minutes," coaxed Meade.

"We better go now."

Edith went out to the car and waited for Meade to pay the bill. When her impromptu chauffeur came outside, he saw a friend parked next to them and killed perhaps fifteen minutes more in conversation. Finally, they drove straight to her house, arriving at about 12:40 A.M. Raymond Meade had done Edith a favor, and for politeness' sake she had humored him, gone with him to the bar. Now she could only hope to crawl in bed without awakening the others. She had made a promise to her mother that she did not keep.

———

With the blessed ease of children, little Mary Katherine had gone back to sleep after her mother and father's ominous conversation at 10:30. But Ann had been awake ever since, perhaps pondering her husband's threat to run her off in the morning. Around 12:30 A.M., she had heard Trigg coming in again.

Trigg was as drunk as she had seen him in quite awhile. But he did manage to ask a sensible question, Had Edith come home yet? Ann, a Sunday school teacher, might well have been thinking of an old proverb: A soft answer turneth away wrath, but grevious words stir up anger.

"No, she'll be in in a few minutes," was her measured reply.

"A man ought to take a club and break her neck."

For the second time that evening, Ann urged her husband to go to bed. This time he went in his room and sat down on the bed, remaining fully clothed.

———

Edith let herself silently into the living room, careful not to rattle the sprung latch on the door. She turned on the light, took off her dress, and looked under the studio couch, which did double duty as a sofa by day and her bed at night. Not finding her bed covers in the usual place, Edith went into her mother's adjoining bedroom to ask about them. Ann, who was in bed, said the covers were in Trigg's room. Mary Katherine raised up from behind her mother to give Edith a warning. "Don't go in Poppy's room," the little girl said.

"Why?" said Edith.

"Poppy's drunk."

"That doesn't make any difference. It's not the first time."

"I know," said Mary Katherine, "but he said he was going to run Mamma off."

"Forget that, he's not going to run Mamma off."

"Yes, he is," Mary Katherine insisted.

The light was on in the back bedroom, where Trigg was lying down and mumbling to himself. Edith went in and got her covers, paying no attention to her father's rantings. She made up the studio bed and returned to her mother's room to use the chamber pot.

Suddenly, Trigg's voice rang out from the kitchen. "I'm running this house," he said. "If I want to run her off, I will." Trigg apparently had heard every word of the sisters' conversation. Now he was standing just outside the open doorway leading to Ann's room.

Edith took up an opposing position just inside the bedroom door. Father and daughter faced off about three or four feet apart. "Poppy, you are not going to run Mamma off."

"Yes, I will, and I will whip you too."

"You might whip me, but you won't run Mamma off."

Trigg picked up a flat-bottomed kitchen chair that was next to the door. "Don't do that," said Edith. Trigg set the chair down. Next he grabbed a black-handled butcher knife off a small table in the kitchen and started toward Edith.

"Poppy don't stob [stab] me," she yelled. Ann and Mary Katherine jumped out of bed. Trigg dropped the knife, and Edith bent down to see where it landed. Seizing the opportunity, he grabbed her by the hair and began dragging her around the kitchen. Edith kept moving right along with him to keep her hair from being pulled out.

"Trigg, don't do that," said Ann, who along with Mary Katherine apparently had come into the kitchen almost immediately. "You ought to be ashamed of yourself. Come in here. Both of you go to bed." Ann laid a restraining hand on Trigg's shoulder.

"Don't you touch me," he told his wife. Ann quickly stepped back.

Trigg kept his grip on Edith's hair. They careened into a side table, upsetting some pans and a bucket of water. Near the stove, Trigg tripped over a washstand that stood about knee-high. He sat down on it and, perhaps suddenly winded, let Edith go. But as she retreated toward her mother's bedroom, Trigg lunged at her again. "I will show you I can whip her," he said to Ann.

Edith turned to face her father. He grabbed her by the shoulders and began pushing her backwards into her mother's darkened bedroom. Edith would later tell the jury her version of what happened:

> He shoved me over a chair right at the foot of Mamma's bed. When he shoved me over the chair, it hit right in the small of my back and knocked me off the chair and I fell on my right shoulder blade, and there was something under there and it was hurting and I reached back to see what was hurting me and I was trying to keep him off too, and when I pulled it out, I felt it and I knew it was a shoe, and he says, "Edith, I am going to finish you." He was choking me and I didn't know what to do. I wouldn't have hurt him for anything in the world. The only thing I was scared and I was just trying to get loose. I only had on my underclothes, a princess slip, and he had hold of me like this, holding my flesh and underclothes. He had some fingers off and they were bearing down through there and hurting and I began striking to get away. I was afraid he was going to hurt me. I struck at him and I don't know how many licks I struck coming up. I don't know whether I struck him even. After I got up, I knew I had to get away some way or other. I thought he was going to kill me.[1]

With a rip of fabric Edith finally broke loose and threw down the shoe. Her mother and sister were still in the kitchen. She ran outside through the living-room door and started in the direction of Chant Kelly's but suddenly realized that her underclothes were torn half off. Terrified that Trigg would attack again, she decided instead to hide on a rear stairway at her own house, steps that led from the side porch to an above-ground basement underneath. As she reached the second step, little Mary Katherine called out from the lattice door at the front of the porch. "Here comes a man." And that is when Edith told Chant Kelly to go back, that there was, after all, no fire there.

———

With a few choice oaths, Trigg Maxwell picked himself up off the bedroom floor. "Ann, look what she's done," he called out toward the kitchen. His wife came in at once. Edith was gone, and Trigg was standing at the foot of the bed. He wiped some blood from his head with his shirt sleeve. Though Ann had not witnessed the fight in the darkened room, she did not think her husband was badly hurt. He was, however, still cursing and thrashing about. As she helped him into his bedroom, Trigg kicked over a flask of carbide that he used to fuel his lamp at the mines. He even ripped off his bloody shirt with his bare hands and demanded a clean one, which Ann gave him.

Ann fixed a pan of water and got Trigg to sit down. She washed the cut near his hairline and applied Alcorub disinfectant. With Mary Katherine's help, they finally got him in bed. The two pulled off his shoes and tugged at his pant legs to remove his trousers. Then they hid his pants in their own room to keep him from getting out. They left his clean shirt on. Mary Katherine noticed that the spilled water from the kitchen bucket was starting to creep into her and her mother's room. The little girl offered to mop while Ann tended to Trigg. Her mother told her to go ahead.

Trigg by now had settled back against his pillow. Ann dabbed at the wound with a damp rag and noticed it had almost stopped bleeding. Carefully she began to shovel up the carbide and tidy her husband's room. Into the cold fire chamber of the kitchen cookstove she put the carbide, a broken fruit jar, and the tattered, bloody shirt.

———

Edith was sitting on the back steps leading down to the river when Mary Katherine appeared for a second time. "Edith, please come back in the house."

"All right, but not for long." Edith had decided to leave home. But even now, with all that had happened, it would not be easy to tell Ann. She rose and followed her little sister inside.

"Mama," began Edith, "I am twenty-one years old and you know as long as I have been born he has drunk all his life, and when he comes in [drunk] he jumps on us children and you and when he is sober he is all right. He hardly ever speaks. But when he comes in drunk, he jumps on me and I have stood all I can. I can't go out. I can't go to a neighbor's house without he hollers."

"Go on to bed and in the morning he will forget about it." Ann was offering her perennial advice.

"I know it," said Edith. "Then when he gets drunk again, he starts over again." Nobody could argue with her logic. "Mamma," continued Edith, "I know what I'm going to do, I'm going to leave. I can make a living most anywhere I go. I have been to college and everything, and I have got a little money. Let me go."

Ann began to cry, and soon Mary Katherine was crying too. Edith started packing her clothes. Eventually, she noticed that her purse was missing and went into Trigg's room to look for it. She told him, too, that she was leaving. Now it seemed that all the rancor had drained from both of them.

"Edith, don't go. Mind Ann and stay here. If you won't leave, I won't quarrel any more. You had better mind Ann. You've got a good home and you don't know how to appreciate it."

"I know I've got a good mother and father, but I can't stand this all the time. I can't stand it."

Edith could not find her purse in her father's room either. In another part of the house, Ann was still crying and carrying on and begging her not to go. Edith relented. "All right, for you I will stay until in the morning," she told her mother. Edith went into her bedroom and turned on the big floor-model radio, waiting a minute or two for the tubes to warm up. Sound flooded the room.[2] "Edith," hollered Ann from the next room, "turn off the radio. Trigg don't want to hear it."

—

All had been quiet and dark in the Maxwell home for about half an hour when Mary Katherine heard her father stirring in the back room. The light in his room came on, and he started through the kitchen.

"Poppy's leaving again," whispered Mary Katherine.

"He can't leave, we've got his clothes," responded Ann. "He ain't going to get out in his nightclothes."

As before, Trigg had overheard the conversation. "No, I want a drink of water."

"Poppy, I'll get you a drink," offered Mary Katherine.

"No, I want to spit," Trigg said, heading for the porch.

The screen door opened. Mary Katherine and Ann heard the sound of something falling. The little girl's first thought was that her father had knocked over the box containing her baby chicks. The birds were sheltered on the porch to safeguard them from predators of the night. But there was no sound of alarm from the sleeping diddles. Ann sensed that Trigg himself must have fallen. She and Mary Katherine ran to the porch and found him lying with his head against the meat block. Ann cradled his head in her lap and screamed for Edith.

Edith thought Trigg had fainted. She drew a dipperful of water from a bucket on the back porch and threw it in his face. Ann rubbed his face, but he did not respond. She sent Edith next door to awaken Dr. Sikes while Mary Katherine ran to Chant Kelly's, the neighbor on the other side. Within a few minutes, the doctor was telling her that Trigg was gone.

The Associated Press reported that Ann Maxwell, the first defense witness to take the stand, had "told her story of a family row unemotionally but in detail."[3] The United Press, however, had a different spin on Ann's demeanor: "There was no color in her cheeks and she crouched in the chair like a person afraid of the unknown."[4] Ann did have much to lose if her testimony went badly—not only the companionship of her beloved daughter but also, eventually, her own liberty as well. Still awaiting trial on murder charges, the fragile widow had taken a risk by testifying on her daughter's behalf, opening the possibility that prosecutors might use her statements against her in a later proceeding.

If one believed a crime had occurred, Ann by her own testimony had admitted to being an accomplice after the fact. She was the person mainly responsible for washing, sweeping, and straightening—and, some would say, concealing evidence in—the home while Edith was hiding on the back steps. Yet in Ann's telling of the story she was not hiding anything of a criminal nature because her husband had not yet been seriously hurt. She swore she knew nothing about Chant Kelly approaching the house. She was just cleaning up in the aftermath of a family quarrel that she did not want to be reminded of. Nonetheless, her zealous cleansing of the death scene gave prosecutors plenty with which to confront her during cross-examination.

During the trial Ann insisted that her husband was wearing a "yellowish brown work shirt" at the time she found him lying by the meat block. The shirt he supposedly had ripped off after the fight—the bloody one Ann had crammed in the kitchen stove—had been an old white one. Yet at least three prosecution witnesses would testify in rebuttal that Trigg wasn't wearing a shirt at all when he was found dying, just underwear, socks, and men's garters. What was the jury to make of this discrepancy? Why would a man demand a clean shirt to go to bed in? And why was it important for the defense to place Trigg in the yellow shirt?

The answer seems to come from Ann's testimony during cross-examination by Oscar M. Vicars. Fred Greear, while gathering evidence at the Maxwell home on the day of Trigg's death back in July, had asked Ann for the clothes Trigg had been wearing on Saturday night. Ann gave Greear a traveling bag packed with the yellowish shirt and with the pants that Trigg had been wearing during his struggle with Edith. Not until later did she say anything about the *first* shirt, which she had burned on Sunday in the course of perking a pot of coffee. Its incinerated remnants were found by sheriff's deputies during a search of the house.

Similarly, there was conflicting testimony about what the deputies had found in the clothes barrel on the porch. The officers swore that they had found what appeared to be a blood-stained sheet and pillowcase with a wet pillow still inside the case. Ann readily acknowledged that she had placed the sheet and pillowcase there but denied putting in the pillow. The sheet, she explained, had been pinned to an ironing board that was in Trigg's room next to the bed. The pillowcase was the one he had rested his head on after the fight. But at no time was she trying to hide these items; she had simply put them where they belonged.

The prosecutors also pointed out Ann's sins of omission, which to them seemed even more damning than her actions in cleaning up the house. Vicars wanted to know why, when the doctor was finally called, was nothing said about the cut on Trigg's head that had been bleeding earlier? How could the doctor treat him effectively if he wasn't told what had happened? Over and over, Ann could only repeat that she hadn't thought to tell him, she was too excited. "I [al]'lowed he would ask me, and he didn't ask me what was wrong, didn't say a word." So Ann had kept her silence.

Now the elderly prosecutor was ready to flat-out accuse Ann and her two daughters of a cover-up. "You fixed up the tale that he fell against the meat block and that he was drunk and you didn't want the doctor to know that he had been hit?"

"I did not do that."

"You all three blamed it against that?"

"There was not a word between us until the doctor came."

"You never talked to each other about it?"

"No, sir, positively did not."

"Never said a word to each other?"

"No, not one word."

⚊⚊⚊

During the private interrogation session back in July, when Greear had pressured Edith into giving a statement, she found him to be "one of the rudest men I have ever encountered."[5] The commonwealth attorney, however, was more complimentary of the woman in custody, of whom he said, "Her brow suggested a mentality I felt a strong desire to test."[6] Now they would reenact their confrontation in public as Edith wound up her time on the witness stand Tuesday morning with another grilling from Greear—this time under oath.

One of the prosecutor's first objectives during cross-examination was to show that the carefully rouged woman sitting before him in a powder-blue crepe dress had been a disrespectful and disobedient daughter. Edith acknowledged that she had a father who liked to quarrel when he was drinking. But she resolutely maintained that she never quarreled back, never called her father names, and certainly had never hit him. Rather than fight, she told Greear, "Many a time I have walked off from a quarrel with my daddy."

On the night of the fatal encounter, Edith insisted, she did nothing to provoke the attack other than stay out late. Greear suggested that her father intended to whip her for "laying out" and for "the way you acted with that man that afternoon"—a reference to her alleged flirtation with the gas station attendant.

"He didn't name that man to me one time," Edith responded.

"When did you change your mind on that?" asked Greear.

"Never changed my mind," said Edith. "When you had me down in your office—   ."

She was quickly interrupted by Judge Henry Alexander Wise Skeen, who was vigilant in keeping any mention of her prior statement away from the jury. "Don't tell that," he said.

Next Greear focused on the fight in the kitchen, leading Edith through the scenario so many times that Judge Skeen's patience was severely tested. Once again Edith told how her father had picked up the chair and set it down, had advanced on her with the knife and dropped it when she grabbed his arm, how he pulled her around the room by her hair. Suddenly, Greear asked an amazing question, one that, if answered differently, could have substantially altered the theory he was working so hard to prove to the jury.

"When he got you by the hair, your mother came in to help you?"

"No, sir."

"Did she hit him with a hatchet or hammer or anything while he had you by the hair?"

"No sir, my mother certainly did not."

"Was little Mary Katherine hitting him with anything?"

"No sir."

"She didn't hit him either?"

"No sir."

This round of questions revealed a fundamental weakness in Greear's largely circumstantial case. Although he had shown that Edith and her mother had misled investigators about some key facts, Greear still did not know what instrument Trigg had been hit with. And he could not even say with certainty *who* had struck what the doctors believed to be the fatal blow.

Still, the prosecutor pressed on. Why, if she was terrified her father was going to hurt her, did she not let Chant Kelly in to help calm him down? Edith answered as her mother had, that she didn't think it was any honor to let people know they were having a family "racket." Why then, after Kelly left, did Edith turn the radio on at full volume? Was it, Greear said sarcastically, "for one last tune before you left" or was it to drown out Trigg's screams? Edith maintained that Trigg was cursing—not moaning in pain—and that the radio wasn't all that loud.

Greear managed to put Edith on the defensive several times during their exchanges. Most stunning was her denial that she ever told anyone that Trigg fell against a meat block, a denial contradicted by numerous prosecution witnesses. Yet Edith never strayed far from the story told by her mother and little sister, and occasionally she seemed to win Judge Skeen's admiration for her spirited responses. At one point she even went on the attack. "Mr. Greear, you've got some children, don't you? How do you whip your children? Pick up a chair?"

Thus the commonwealth attorney had engaged Edith and found a worthy opponent. As the United Press put it, "Sometimes she was weeping, sometimes storming at . . . Greear, but her brain called up answers quickly and she walked off the stand with her head high."[7] With the conclusion of her testimony just before lunch, Edith's attorneys rested their case. Sitting on the cool, polished surface of the defense table was their main piece of physical evidence—the pair of high-heeled slippers shown to the jury on Monday. Ann had later identified the shoes as her own. She said she had been wearing them on Saturday night, July 20, and left them on her bedroom floor. (Unlike a famous case sixty years later involving a glove, no one asked Ann to try on the shoes in court.)

The defense also introduced a map showing the layout of the Maxwell home, but some other exhibits and witnesses that might have supported the women's testimony seemed to be missing. The butcher knife was not presented, nor was the torn slip that Edith supposedly was wearing during the struggle. Edith also testified that she had scratches on her arms and blue marks on the back of her neck when she was arrested, but she had not shown them to law enforcement, just to her brother and some other women prisoners at the jail. No one else was called to testify about her alleged injuries.

—

The opposing legal teams had prepared sets of instructions to the jury, each side interpreting the law in a manner most favorable to its desired outcome. Judge Skeen granted all ten instructions proposed by the commonwealth and accepted five of seven put forth by the defense. Greear and Alfred A. Skeen then read their respective instructions to the jury. The panel would have the option of finding Edith innocent, guilty of first-degree murder, or guilty of second-degree murder. Curiously, there was no option for manslaughter or some lesser charge; neither side had requested it. Apparently, the prosecution thought it had proved a strong case for premeditated murder, and the defense evidently was gambling that the jury would return a verdict of not guilty on the grounds of self-defense.

The opposing attorneys summed up their cases for four hours on Tuesday afternoon. Their speeches did not become part of the trial record. Only a sentence or two of Greear's argument was captured by news accounts, and none of Alfred A. Skeen's. Greear had invoked the biblical injunction "honor thy father and thy mother." He argued that Edith had deliberately killed Trigg because he "cramped his daughter's style" by forbidding her to "run around" at night. "I don't think the girl should be made a heroine because she killed her daddy," Greear said.[8] Perhaps he was referring to flattering press coverage describing Edith as "a girl who got 'new fangled notions' in the outside world" and "had broken the code of the mountains."[9]

The twelve jurymen retired for deliberations at 6:35 P.M. If they voted for acquittal, Edith would be free to return to her teaching at Pound or, more likely, to start afresh somewhere far away from Wise County. If they found her guilty of first-degree murder, they could recommend a sentence of death or a prison term ranging from twenty-five years to life. Greear was not asking for the death penalty, but it was a wild card that the jury could play, only adding to the dread that Edith and her supporters must have felt.[10]

Although it was suppertime, the crowd in the courtroom had scarcely dwindled at all. All the "big-shot" press sent to cover the story were presumably there, awaiting the verdict as well: Ed Lockett from the International News Service; Harry Ferguson of the United Press, a veteran reporter of high-profile cases like the Lindbergh baby kidnapping and the assassination of Huey Long in Louisiana; Joseph Nettles, a writer from the Associated Press in Richmond; and an AP photographer named Harris who had been dispatched from Louisville.[11] Writers for the detective magazines may have been there as well.

With the jury still out, Judge Skeen took the opportunity to publicly scold some of the visiting journalists for their coverage. The Associated Press was taking a fair and balanced approach, but others had been less circumspect. The judge's warning, given back in August, that correspondents should stick to the facts had been ignored by color writers such as Ferguson, secure in their First Amendment privileges.

Ferguson's cartoonish UP dispatches were painting Judge Skeen's courtroom as an undignified assemblage of country bumpkins; he even wrote that the judge "cut himself a chew of plug tobacco" during the trial, an outrage to those who knew that the judge preferred a more gentlemanly source of nicotine—cigars.[12] The UP had also reported that the jury consisted entirely of men "because women are still considered not quite equal with men here," neglecting to mention that state law, not local custom, barred women from jury service.[13] Of Edith, Ferguson reportedly implied that she had never seen the moon until she went away to college because mountain women were under curfew and not allowed to stay up late.[14] So perhaps it was only natural for Judge Skeen, his tormentors assembled before him, to lash out. As he lambasted the press for their "pack of lies and slanderous stories" the spectators burst into applause.[15]

The jury reappeared in the courtroom after only thirty minutes of deliberation. Edith stood as the court clerk solemnly read the verdict: "We the Jury find the defendant Edith Maxwell guilty of murder in the first degree as charged in the within indictment and fix her punishment by confinement in the penitentiary for a period of twenty-five years."

Earl Maxwell kept a protective arm around Edith as the decision was announced. She appeared dazed and stared at her brother in disbelief. Ann, waiting in a witness room, collapsed when she heard the news. Earl went to his stricken mother and started to carry her out of the building. When Edith caught a glimpse of Ann in Earl's arms, she began screaming and tried to break through the crowd to reach them. She was restrained.

"Oh Lord, somebody take care of my mother," cried Edith hysterically. "I don't care so much about myself."[16]

After several minutes Edith began to calm down and was escorted back to the county jail. Reporters hurried to wire their copy to an awaiting nation. The jurors had voiced their dark judgment of the young school-teacher, but now the press would have its say. And in the court of public opinion, things would be altogether different.

10 A Mouse in a Trap?

Four days after Edith's conviction, reporter Marguerite Mooers Marshall and photographer Clarence Albers found themselves flying blind somewhere over southwest Virginia. Their flight from the New York area to Washington, D.C., on a small private airplane proved uneventful, but on the second leg of the journey they ran into the season's first major snowstorm. Mountain peaks jutted like icebergs through an ocean of clouds as the craft sped westward from Washington over the Blue Ridge and into Appalachia. By the time they approached their destination, Bristol, a small city straddling the Virginia-Tennessee border, the storm had rendered the airport invisible. While the pilot searched for an opening that would allow him to land, the two journalists might have begun to wonder if they would live to complete their mission.

Marshall and Albers were employees of the *New York Journal*, one of a pair of daily newspapers operated by William Randolph Hearst in New York City. Their plan was ambitious yet simple. They would interview and photograph the famous hillbilly girl now lodged in the Wise County Jail. No interviews with Edith Maxwell had been allowed since her trial ended November 19. An Associated Press reporter, peering through the bars of Edith's cell a day later, had described her as "a bit haggard, perhaps, but otherwise bearing up well under the heavy penalty she had not expected."[1] Readers, however, wanted to know more. An interview with Edith would be a pearl of great price. With the right pictures it would be a scoop that would cause widespread gnashing of teeth among Hearst's competitors.

By the time she found herself on this precarious flight, forty-eight-year-old Marshall had been chasing down interviews for more than twenty-five years. A graduate of Tufts College, the New Hampshire native had written features and commentary for the *Boston Herald* and *New York Evening World* before joining the Hearst organization. In 1935 her column "Just Like a Woman" ran not only in the *New York Journal* but was also syndicated in about a hundred other newspapers across the country. Marshall, who was married to a newspaper editor, described herself as "a middle-of-the-road feminist, pro-woman but not anti-man."[2]

The Hearst reporter had an unerring instinct for getting the celebrity interview, having profiled such notables as H. G. Wells and Margot Asquith. She specialized in the "soft" news of the day, such as giving almost-monthly progress reports on the Dionne quintuplets. Tall, somewhat absent-minded, and characteristically dressed in tweeds, Marshall had perfected a flowery writing style that lent itself to prose and verse for magazines such as *Harper's, McCall's,* and *Woman's Home Companion.* She had also shown a flair for fiction and had four novels published, including one whose proofs she corrected while covering the Hauptmann trial in New Jersey. Marshall was well versed in the arts of the sob sister. Now she hoped to bring these talents to bear in interviewing Edith Maxwell—who was, like herself, a former teacher but otherwise an inhabitant of a different world.

First, though, the airplane had to find its way through the roiling skies over Bristol. With the airport still eluding him, the pilot had begun to worry about running out of fuel. The party flew to Greensboro, North Carolina, for refueling and again made the approach to Bristol, this time landing without incident. Albers and Marshall hired a car to take them seventy-five miles into the Lonesome Pine Country, where their quarry was sequestered at Wise.

Arriving in town on Saturday, November 23, Marshall quickly gained access to Edith in the county jail, pouncing on the exclusive interview that other reporters had been denied. She also spent Sunday and Monday at Wise and Pound, interviewing several of the participants in the trial. Her photographer, Albers, was equally successful. According to the *Coalfield Progress,* he "secured pictures of all kinds relative to the recent trial, pictures of Miss Maxwell, of her family, of the defense attorneys, of the jail, of the courthouse, of Main Street of Wise, of the Wise post office, etc."

Marshall and Albers were reported to have paid a quarter apiece to some of Edith's former students to pose for pictures at the Mullins School near Pound. Albers photographed several little boys in overalls, kneeling at their desks with hands clasped in prayer. As a later caption would tell it, the youngsters were "supplicat[ing] heaven for her return" to the classroom.[3]

The photographer left Wise at 8 P.M. on Monday, November 25, his camera kit loaded with what the *Journal* would call "intimate camera studies of Edith Maxwell." Unwilling or unable to fly out of Bristol, Albers drove the mountainous 250–mile stretch to Winston-Salem, North Carolina, in eight hours. There he was able to catch a 4 A.M. flight to the New York area, ensuring that his pictures would appear in Tuesday's *Journal.*

The so-called first photograph of Edith in jail was emblazoned on page 1 beneath a banner headline: "Hill-Billy Girl's Own Story." The picture showed Edith looking out through the bars of her basement cell. Her pale eyes, framed by thin, arched brows, stared straight into the camera in seeming contemplation of her twenty-five-year sentence.[4] Edith posed in a wool coat, velvet hat, silk stockings and high heels for other pictures, looking more like a visiting social worker than an inmate.

In the accompanying interview, Marshall told New York readers of finding Edith in "an almost literal dungeon"—a six-by-eight-foot cubicle containing six bunks stacked in tiers of three.[5] Daylight scarcely penetrated the heavily grated windows in the outside corridor, and a single lightbulb in the cell added little illumination. Still, Marshall had seen that the grimy walls were covered with graffiti and taped-up pictures from old newspapers. There were no mirrors, chairs, tables, chests of drawers, or hooks on the walls. Clothing had to be hung from a line stretched across the cell or kept in suitcases. Among Edith's small comforts, brought in by her family, were a radio and her own quilts and blankets.

Marshall had found the smell "nauseating," adding that the cell "is an appalling place for a sensitive, attractive girl of twenty-one." She noted that Edith's cell held only three other women—two short of its full capacity—yet she implied that these women were of a lower social class, having been imprisoned for "sexual offenses." "I was also told that, in this congested penal institution . . . they do not draw the color line," lamented Marshall. "How, I wondered, could a dainty, well-educated young woman such as Edith Maxwell, the mountain child, has become, endure such intimate associations?"

Marshall had chosen to interview Edith in more pleasant surroundings. "She [Edith] steps from this black-hole-of-Calcutta jail across a cement walk and the main street of Wise, to the book-lined offices of her lawyers and she looks as if she had just arisen from a dainty dressing table in the sort of pretty room which you and I would give our daughters," Marshall wrote in a motherly tone. The writer devoted four more paragraphs to Edith's appearance and mannerisms:

> She is fairly tall—I should say about five feet, seven—with a beautifully shaped face, the brow broad, the chin delicately pointed. Her eyes are hyacinth blue, with brows and curling lashes the warm golden brown of

her hair. She has been described as "black-haired," but her naturally wavy bob is the color of hazelnuts, and grows charmingly about the nape of her neck.

All her features are cleanly and delicately cut, the nose long and straight and shapely, the mouth delicately curved and showing a double row of even white teeth when Edith smiles. The smile is lovely, though usually a little sad. Her cheeks are wild-rose pink, but the whole contour of the face is fine and sharpened by the chiseling of the tools of sleeplessness and pain. She has a slender, pretty figure, with trim ankles and hands that are long and shapely and white.

When I saw her she wore a coat and skirt of some rough material, cream-tone in color; a white silk blouse from which rose her round, white throat; a brown velvet, brimless hat set slightly to one side, a gleaming metallic ornament thrust through its crown. Her silk stockings and suede shoes exactly matched her hat, and the color scheme was most becoming to her fairness and her nut-brown locks.

She sat erect, yet gracefully poised, in the straight-backed chair beside her lawyer's desk, her slender artist's hands were clasped over her brown suede purse; a certain tensity in the grip betrayed her nervous tension. Also revealed by the icy coldness of her fingers which I discovered when she shook hands.

Marshall conducted the interview with Earl Maxwell standing by Edith's side, his hand resting on his sister's shoulder. Perhaps he was there just to offer moral support, but he probably also stood ready to coach Edith through any difficult parts of the session. It is doubtful he ever had to. Marshall, once described as an interviewer who "comes armed with highly probing questions," asked nothing of the sort, openly sympathizing with her subject.[6]

"My dear, I am sorry. . . . It's been terribly hard for you, all this, hasn't it?"

"It shu-ah has," she admitted, in her low, soft Southern voice, with the Southern trick of making a dissyllable of "sure." "I don't think anything could have been much harder. I don't believe any girl ever went through anything much worse."

Marshall continued on in this vein for several lengthy columns but managed to say almost nothing about the case itself. Perhaps this was agreed to in advance, but nothing in the article even hints that the writer made the slightest attempt at balance or objectivity. Instead, she chose to tell readers that Edith had an untreated toothache, was teaching the other prisoners to read and write, and hoped to go to New York to study nursing if set free. She ended the story by calling Edith "that gallant, pitiful young fighter against an incredible cruel destiny."

Like other color writers before her, Marshall insisted on giving Edith the drawl of the Deep South rather than her true mountain speech. It is also likely that she "doctored" Edith's remarks to make them more appealing to a New York audience. Marshall quotes Edith as saying, for example, "The one thing which helps me to bear the terrible ordeal through which I am passing is my conviction of complete innocence. If I had to live with the knowledge that I had actually done the thing of which they accuse me I could not bear it. Knowing that I have done nothing with which to reproach myself is what keeps me going." According to court transcripts, the real Edith Maxwell spoke in a much more conversational style and would never have responded with such twisted syntax.

Articles like Marshall's played on the public's natural sympathy for a woman in trouble, but did nothing to get at the facts of the Maxwell family tragedy. As James Thurber would later note in *The New Yorker,* "The romanticized stories in the Hearst press, dedicated to freeing the 'lovely Trail of the Lonesome Pine Girl,' are of little value."[7] The "Hill-Billy Girl's Own Story" turned out to be not much of a story at all. But what it lacked in narrative it made up in a compelling message. No longer did people have to be born rich or titled to become celebrities. With the burgeoning power of the mass media, the press could bestow celebrity on practically anyone it chose—even ordinary people who, by good luck, good looks, or even tragic circumstances, matched the tenor of the times.

On November 26, 1935, Edith Maxwell became a darling of the Hearst press, much like a Hollywood starlet taken under wing at a major studio. Articles and photographs about her case were destined to shape public opinion far beyond the burroughs of New York. Through Hearst's network of wire services and syndicates, this fairy-tale version of the Maxwell story would tug at the heart strings of millions of readers in eighteen American cities and even overseas.

Reading about Edith Maxwell's plight was, for many, a call to action. Women's clubs, labor unions, foes and supporters of Prohibition, and ordinary citizens were beginning to rally behind the young schoolteacher and demand her freedom. In Knoxville, Tennessee, readers of the Scripps-Howard *News-Sentinel* had learned of the trial through the highly distorted United Press dispatches of Harry Ferguson. Edith Kane Stair, a business-woman in the city, soon proposed that some civic group step forward and start a defense fund. "Unless we in the South do something about it, this case will be spread in papers throughout the country as an example of

Southern backwardness," Stair warned. "Some group in the East probably will start some action in her behalf and another wrong impression of the South will be broadcast."[8]

The Knoxville chapter of the Business and Professional Women's Clubs of America immediately accepted the challenge, and the *Knoxville News-Sentinel* agreed to forward readers' contributions to the club and to print a tally in the newspaper. Within a few days more than $200 had been garnered from well-wishers as far away as California. A woman in Madison, New York, sent a dollar and urged that the case be appealed to President Roosevelt. "I earnestly wish, hope and pray that the whole United States may rise in righteous indignation in behalf of Edith and her family and that that jury may get the punishment they so deserve," she wrote.[9]

Carrying letters such as these, a delegation of four Knoxville women—Edith Stair, club president Mary Elliott, policewoman Mary Allen, and attorney Hattie Love—drove to Wise County on November 27, hoping to meet Edith and offer their group's assistance. The next morning, the women's first stop was at the offices of the *Coalfield Progress* in Norton, where they discussed the case with editor and publisher Pres T. Atkins and a reporter. "My impression after talking with them was that they were both sympathetic toward the girl," Elliott said, "but that she had been tried before an intelligent jury and deserved some sort of a penalty, though not as severe as she got."[10]

Atkins offered to help them obtain an audience with defense attorney Robert P. Bruce, referred to locally as "Senator" Bruce in deference to his years in the state legislature. Atkins telephoned ahead and then accompanied the women to Bruce's office in Wise. When the five visitors arrived, they found a reporter and photographer—whose identities they did not know—seated in an anteroom. Atkins waited with the pair of strangers while the delegation was ushered to an inner office.

Initially, the meeting with Bruce went well. Elliott found him to be "a Virginia gentleman of the old school, a thoroughly delightful man who gave us every courtesy."[11] He and fellow defense attorney Alfred A. Skeen spent an hour and a half with the delegation, going over details of the case. When the women asked to see Edith, however, they were told they could meet her but could not discuss her legal situation.

The four activists must have sensed that their mission was doomed by this unexpected restriction. Bruce nonetheless telephoned the jail to ask that Edith be brought to his office, but the call did not go smoothly. As soon as Bruce hung up, he and Skeen hurriedly left the room.

Skeen returned after a few minutes. He explained that Edith had recently signed an exclusive contract with a newspaper syndicate for all photograph and interview rights. As representatives of Hearst's International News Service (INS), Marguerite Mooers Marshall and Clarence Albers had not only gotten a prime interview and pictures but also put a stranglehold on rival reporters and anyone else who might blab to Hearst's competitors.

Edith's newly minted agreement with the syndicate would effectively block the Knoxville visitors from talking with her in any meaningful way. But as Edith Stair would later tell it, the women were urged to go to Edith's jail cell by one of "two odd reporters who had been sent about four hundred miles and couldn't get a thing" on the Maxwell case. (Presumably, these were the two journalists who had been hovering around Bruce's office, but she did not explicitly say so.) As Stair recalled:

> At first it looked like we would get to talk to the young lady who was in the jail.
> We were then told we could see Miss Maxwell, but could not talk to her. I replied, "Well we surely would not want to humiliate her or ourselves by just looking at her. It would be too much like looking at an animal in a cage, so we will not go—just to look." Then our discouraged new friend whispers, "Oh please go for our sakes" (thinking he would be permitted to go with us). He was not of the syndicate on this particular contract. So for his sake we went over.[12]

A Hearst photographer and reporter met the women at the jail and accompanied them to the basement, where Edith was waiting. One woman asked Edith how old she was when she graduated from high school, and Edith replied, "Eighteen."[13] "We were not permitted to talk with her further—the Hearst man was there to see to that," Elliott recounted. "Mrs. Stair did say, 'Edith, I hope when you get out you can do a lot of good.' We were in the room about four or five minutes but Edith did not talk to us," Elliott continued. "Presumably she had been told not to."[14]

Elliott and her stunned colleagues beat a hasty retreat to Knoxville.

———

In the view of her critics, Edith Maxwell had been "all bought up" by the Hearst news organization. No longer was she a poor, defenseless "girl" facing a monstrous future but a commodity to be carefully packaged and sold to an eager public. How had this transformation occurred?

Knoxville News-Sentinel writer John T. Moutoux was one of the first to find out. A few days before the clubwomen's visit, he had ventured into the coalfields to investigate the Maxwell case. Moutoux's trip was at least partly a response to indignant letters the newspaper had received from Wise County subscribers who had bridled at Harry Ferguson's whimsical descriptions of their homeland—especially his bizarre claim that Edith had never seen the moon before going to Radford.

"Pound isn't growing a gang of backwoodsmen," wrote college student Garcia Cantrell, a high school classmate of Edith's. "The moon is alluring to all, whether or not we are natives of the Lonesome Pine country. . . . Miss Maxwell isn't the only girl in our community who has gone away to college. She isn't the only girl in our community who wears 'store bought' clothes. The days of spinning and weaving have passed. . . . Too, Edith isn't the only girl who wears 'town curled' hair. Other girls have pride and dignity as well as those who are school teachers. We have access to as many things as the citizen in any town in the Appalachian region."[15]

Thus Moutoux was dispatched to Wise County to write a piece that would "tell both sides" of the one-sided story previously reported by Ferguson. He traveled to Pound, where he had a less than enthusiastic reception from Earl Maxwell. Although Earl did grant him an interview, he later confronted Moutoux on Main Street and threatened to give him a black eye for taking exterior pictures of the Maxwells' home "without permission." Even though the reporter was photographing a public street scene, Earl demanded and got Moutoux's film, burning it on the spot.

The chastened reporter then drove to Wise and called on Edith and Earl's uncle, Gernade Dotson, whom Moutoux described as "a kindly old man." Genteel though he was, attorney Dotson had to turn down Moutoux's request to interview Edith in jail. Dotson explained that, so far, Judge Henry Alexander Wise Skeen had barred the press from talking to Edith, but an offer from a newspaper syndicate was being considered.

"The girl's brother (Earl) told me that some newspaper syndicate is willing to pay part of the expense of the trial if it can talk to the girl," Dotson told Moutoux. "If the judge will let it, we may do that. We need money to pay for the record and the clerk's cost. We don't want this money for ourselves but for the expenses of carrying on the fight."[16]

It is not known whether Judge Skeen—given his disdain for the yellow press—approved the publicity arrangement, but a deal evidently was struck between the Hearst organization and Edith's brother and lawyers within a week of her trial. In a pattern that was to leave its imprint on the Maxwell case, Earl clearly was the point man for his family's dealings with the press. Details of how the agreement was negotiated remain a mystery. Marshall and Albers probably knew they had the scoop even before they left New York, but it is also possible that they were able to "muscle in" and secure an agreement only after they arrived in Wise County.

This exercise in what is today called "checkbook journalism" apparently involved an entire team of Hearst writers and photographers. Even before Marshall and Albers left town with their scoop, other Hearst employees had arrived at the jail—not only to shield their newly acquired "property" from the curious but also to begin dredging up Edith's life story for future consumption. According to the *Coalfield Progress,* Fred Menagh of King Features Syndicate and INS photographer Arthur Scott also received full cooperation from Edith's relatives and lawyers.

Had the Knoxville clubwomen not attempted to meet with Edith on November 28, the Hearst connection might have gone unnoticed by almost everyone except the defense attorneys and reporters from competing newspapers. The women's botched mission gave high visibility to the fact that Edith had signed with Hearst; the *Knoxville News-Sentinel* went so far as to say that the syndicate had "taken over [the] defense."

Whether it was a financial necessity or a cynical calculation, Edith Maxwell's contract with the Hearst syndicate was, in some people's eyes, tantamount to a pact with the devil. Her would-be benefactors from the Knoxville Business and Professional Women's Club felt that she and the Maxwell defense team were purposely exploiting a family tragedy. When the delegation returned from Wise, the clubwomen quickly dismantled their defense fund and announced they would return the money.

In a front-page *News-Sentinel* story on November 29, the club gave its reasons for the about-face. The delegation found, first, that Edith was represented by experienced, highly qualified attorneys; second, that she received a fair trial "before an intelligent jury, and a judge whose opinions have seldom been reversed"; third, that her financial needs were being provided for by the news syndicate; and, fourth, that the case had been unnecessarily sensationalized. On the last point the women found:

> That the manifestations of indignant concern from the public are out of all proportion to the actual facts in the case, and that a great injustice has been done to all concerned—the defendant, her attorneys, the jury, the judge, and the people of that splendid community by the distorted and highly colored news reports emanating from sources which would seek to glorify crime from their own selfish purposes.
>
> The kindest thing that can be done under the circumstances, is for the public to allow the orderly processes of the law to take their courses without interference.

The club's reasons for suspending the crusade were to be debated in the press for months afterward. Were the women really convinced Edith had received a fair trial, or were they indignant that the Hearst newspapers had gotten to her first and robbed the club of a golden opportunity to take the spotlight?

Writers sympathetic to the defense were quick to seize the "sour grapes" interpretation. James Thurber, writing in *The New Yorker,* said that the four clubwomen were accompanied by journalists from Knoxville; Hearst's *Daily Mirror* claimed that the women became angry because a Knoxville reporter and photographer were not allowed to go with them inside the jail to interview Edith. Neither of these sources, however, can be judged totally reliable because the *Daily Mirror* had a vested interest in guarding the Hearst exclusive, and Thurber, admittedly, was relying on secondhand information for his analysis.

Although the clubwomen *had* been working closely with the *Knoxville News-Sentinel,* Edith Stair said the two desperate journalists she met in Wise "had been sent about four hundred miles." This statement seems to rebut Thurber's contention that they were from Knoxville, because that city is less than 150 miles from Wise. Still, the seemingly accidental encounter with two of Hearst's competitors—and the women's accommodating attitude toward them—may have cast unwarranted suspicion on the delegation's true motives.

In a letter to Virginia governor George C. Peery written on December 2, 1935, Stair said, "You may rest assured that the unfortunate contract with scandal-mongers was not what influenced our decision." In fact, she characterized Edith as "a poor little mouse caught in a trap—not set by the Courts or even her own people, but the helpless little victim of a vicious, exploiting press."[17]

The issue of whether the Maxwells were exploiting their family tragedy—or whether they themselves were being exploited—was one question. Whether justice had been miscarried was another. How, then, did the Knoxville Business and Professional Women's Club conclude that Edith had been given a fair trial? According to Elliott, they did not consult commonwealth attorney Fred Greear or his assistants, nor could they have read the transcript of the trial, which was not yet available.

Elliott said the committee's interviews with local editor Pres Atkins and defense counsel Robert Bruce had influenced the club's assessment of the Maxwell case. Both community leaders had attested to the basic fairness of the Wise County court system, yet the influence of inflammatory press coverage could not be ruled out. "Senator Bruce told us that he would be willing to be tried by that very same jury and before Judge Skeen," Elliott explained to the *News-Sentinel.* "It was his opinion that what hurt the girl was the colored stories written by some of the newspapermen which incensed the whole countryside."

—

Was nationwide publicity a boon to Edith Maxwell, as her brother Earl evidently believed, or was it a bane, as old Senator Bruce thought? Would the public outcry free the young teacher, or would further dalliance with the Hearst press harm Edith's chances if she got a second trial? Why had the Maxwell defense team agreed to this risky "exclusive"?

In an age when criminal appeals were not automatically funded by the taxpayers, the answer seemed simple enough: Edith's attorneys were expecting more than $1,000 in royalties from the sale of her photograph and interview rights, an amount equivalent to about $13,430 in today's dollars.[18] Letting Edith tell her story to the world and pose for pictures must have seemed a small price to pay for Hearst's largess.

Even in happier times before Trigg Maxwell's death the Maxwells did not have pockets deep enough to pay extensive legal fees had one of the family run into trouble. Trigg and Edith had supported a family of five on combined wages of about $30 a week. Income from rental properties such as the post office provided a thin safety net. No one went hungry in the Maxwell household—there was spare change for the occasional bag of potato chips—yet one relative would later testify that the Maxwells could hardly be described as prosperous.

By late 1935 the *Washington Post* was characterizing Edith's family as "virtually destitute." Aside from the modest rental income, it is unknown how Ann was providing for herself and her two daughters still at home. Months of legal work and court costs lay ahead if Edith were to have any chance of reversing her heavy sentence. A *Post* reporter noted, "What few assets the girl's father had, in the form of insurance and land, are still in custody of the court and may not be used for her defense."[19] The deal with the Hearst syndicate represented a desperately needed infusion to the cash-poor legal team.

Other options, though, surely existed. The practice of appointing lawyers to represent indigent clients charged with serious offenses was fairly widespread in American courts by the early 1930s, and Wise County, Virginia, was no exception. In August 1935, for example, two local lawyers appointed by Judge Skeen won an acquittal for Ida Baldwin, the Norton woman who had been charged with murdering her husband on the same day that Trigg Maxwell died.

Edith had appeared before Judge Skeen the same week as Baldwin, but instead of asking for a court-appointed lawyer she sought (and was granted) more time to raise money for her own defense team. Apparently, Earl Maxwell had decided early on to go the private route, enlisting the services of Alfred A. Skeen and Senator Bruce. Now that the jury had condemned Edith to spend her youth in prison, perhaps it was time to consider the idea of a court-appointed attorney—or even a volunteer one—to carry forward an appeal. According to press reports, Edith had received several offers of assistance from lawyers, at least one of whom was willing to represent her pro bono.

There was also the question of taste to be considered. Even some of Edith's sympathizers believed that the syndicate deal had compromised her image of an innocent woman caught up in family tragedy. Associations with "scandal-mongers" tended to obscure the real issue of a woman's right to defend herself from a brutal attack. For others with harsher views, like the Knoxville activists, the arrangement was simply a glorification of crime.

The spurned clubwomen were not the only ones to question the wisdom of this course of action. Howard C. Miller, a former Wise County newspaper editor, expressed his misgivings in a December 1935 letter to the *News-Sentinel.* Although Miller denounced the verdict as "extreme," he went on to issue a grim prediction:

> It is to be regretted that defense counsel, according to report, have given one of the Hearst organizations exclusive publicity rights to and about Edith Maxwell. The excuse given, according to the same report, is to raise money for the defense of the unfortunate girl. It would have been much better and more in keeping with the proprieties of the situation if this money had been raised by private subscription, as the Knoxville Business and Professional Women's Club has proved it can be done. No such a contract should have been made, particularly with such a scum-gatherer as William Randolph Hearst and his various publicity bureaus. It will be dear money in the end—the Hearst money—and counsel for the defense and the entire citizenship of Wise County, I predict, will live to regret it.

From November 1935 on, Edith's fortunes and those of the Hearst organization would intertwine in a mutual search for "justice" and—at least in the case of the chain—for profit and glory.

Fred Bonham Greear, commonwealth attorney of Wise County, won two hard-fought convictions against Edith Maxwell in Wise County Circuit Court. Despite the trials' notoriety and allegations of political influence, he maintained that the prosecution was "simply another murder case." A graduate of the University of Virginia Law School, Greear went on to help establish a campus of the university at Wise. (Photo from *Actual Detective Stories*)

Maine state senator Gail Laughlin was a veteran attorney and dedicated advocate for women's rights. At the behest of the National Woman's Party, she questioned the constitutionality of the all-male jury pool at the Maxwell trials, becoming the first woman to plead a case before the Wise County court. (Photo courtesy of the Historic National Woman's Party, Sewall-Belmont House and Museum, Washington, D.C.)

Edith smiles from the stairs of the Lee County Jail in Jonesville, Virginia, where she was housed briefly in the summer of 1936. Visitors seeking a glimpse of the celebrity prisoner poured into the jail by the hundreds each week. Admirers sent Edith cards and money—and even a parakeet as a gift. (© *Richmond Times-Dispatch;* used with permission)

A cow strolls down Main Street in front of the Wise County Courthouse where Edith Maxwell was tried in 1935 and 1936. Photos such as this one, which appeared in a detective magazine, dismayed some local residents who felt the images reinforced negative stereotypes of Appalachian culture. The backlash against the "outside" press may have influenced the two local juries that meted out heavy sentences to Maxwell. (Photo from *True Detective*)

The twelve male jurors hearing evidence at the second Maxwell trial strike a
solemn pose in front of the Colonial Hotel. Edith's lawyers later appealed her
conviction on the grounds that Virginia's law prohibiting women from serving
on juries violated the Fourteenth Amendment. Front row, left to right, foreman Lewis Estes, D. F. Hensley, Owen Carter, G. W. Pennington, John Lambert,
and W. H. Umbarger; (back) unidentified man, W. M. Bond, Rush Horne, F. P.
Gardner, Eldridge Christian, R. L. Hilton, and John Roller. (AP Photo)

Chief prosecution witness Chant Kelly, second from left, testifies about a diagram of the Maxwell home at the December 1936 retrial. On the right are prosecutor Oscar M. Vicars (holding pencil) and defense attorney Charles Henry
Smith; the man on the far left is unidentified; and jurors are in the foreground.
(AP/Wide World Photos)

Long before she became involved in the Maxwell case, First Lady Eleanor Roosevelt had taken an active interest in living conditions in Appalachia and visited mountain communities in several states. Here she is shown at White Top Mountain, Grayson County, Virginia, in 1933. (Photo courtesy of the Franklin D. Roosevelt Library)

Just days after the second guilty verdict in December 1936, Edith and Mary Katherine decorate a small Christmas tree at their home in Chesterfield County, Virginia. Edith had just been hired as a restaurant hostess in nearby Richmond. (AP/Wide World Photos)

The grave of H. Trigg Maxwell, Bolling Cemetery, Pound, Virginia. The inscription on the stone reads, "After night comes the morn." (Photo taken in May 1994 by Curtiss M. Ellison; used with permission.)

11 Trading Places

Two days after the clubwomen's November 27 visit, at the other end of Wise County police found the body of Lelborne N. Falin sprawled in the front room of the restaurant/gas station he operated in the Wildcat community south of Big Stone Gap. Still clothed in his overcoat, Falin, fifty-nine, was lying face down in his own blood. He had been felled by two blasts from a double-barreled 12–gauge shotgun, one of which struck him just above the heart. In his right hand was a pistol, and in his left pocket was a nearly empty bottle of whiskey.

The police knew without even checking the till that this was no robbery. The perpetrator, who had already admitted firing the shotgun, was in custody, awaiting transport to the Wise County Jail. It was Falin's sixteen-year-old son, Haugeman. Over the next twenty-four hours he would pour out a story of horrifying parental brutality to all who would listen, telling how he had been pistol-whipped, stomped, and threatened with death by his drunken father, whom he ultimately was forced to shoot. Although the boy's tale sounded highly believable, it fell to Big Stone Gap officers to interview witnesses who could provide an independent account of Lelborne Falin's final hours. As they began piecing together a scenario, the undertaker went about the work of removing the body.

The Falin family, which also included a two-year-old girl and boys fourteen and eight, had only just moved to the Wildcat Valley the previous summer, having spent about five years in Rogersville, Tennessee. But the parents were known in Norton, where Lelborne Falin had worked as a boilermaker for the Norfolk and Western Railroad in the 1920s. Ironically, the family had been victimized by a break-in at their new business sometime in late 1935, an incident that prompted Falin, his wife, Margaret, and Haugeman to drive to the Wise County Courthouse on Friday, November 29, seeking justice. It is unclear what happened to the breaking and entering case, but Lelborne Falin was not called to testify before the grand jury then in session—possibly because, as Margaret would later tell police, he had "been drinking continuously since Thursday."[1]

The trip home from Wise, a distance of about twenty miles, began pleasantly enough, with the Falins stopping in the Ramsey section of Norton to visit their old neighborhood. But, as Margaret would later tell it, the atmosphere soured as they continued and their car broke down in the middle of a city street in Norton. They successfully restarted it but not before the father had lashed out at Haugeman, cursing him and accusing him of letting the car run dry of water. The teenager contended that the problem lay with the spark plugs.

About fifteen miles down the road—and just one mile shy of the Falins' home and business—the car quit for good. Lelborne again blamed his son and began slapping him around. Haugeman sprang out of the disabled vehicle and started walking toward home, his parents following at a slower pace. When Margaret and Lelborne arrived, the sixteen-year-old was sitting in the restaurant, drinking a ginger ale. The two younger boys and their toddler sister were nearby.

Still incensed after his walk, Lelborne Falin was apparently not about to let the argument subside. According to Margaret, he began waving a pistol and hit Haugeman over the head with it, knocking him to the floor and kicking him. When she tried to interfere, Lelborne kicked her in the knee. Terrified, Margaret picked up her baby and ran across a creek toward a neighbor's house, dropping the little girl once in the water due to nervousness and fright. Suddenly she heard two shots. She assumed that her son was dying or dead.

But Haugeman had somehow managed to make it into the kitchen and arm himself with the shotgun. He ran out a side door and around to the front of the restaurant, which faced the road. Lelborne came to the front doorway and spotted Haugeman outside. He raised the pistol. "[And] so I shot," the youth explained to police.[2]

Later that evening, Haugeman presented himself at a Big Stone Gap doctor's office for treatment of a deep gash on the front of his head, apparently the result of the pistol blow his father had administered. The town sergeant arrested him there and took him to a local lockup, where he remained for a few hours before transfer to the Wise County Jail. While in custody Haugeman gave detailed statements about what had happened. The boy clearly felt he had taken a life to spare his own—precisely the same argument Edith Maxwell had made unsuccessfully to a Wise County jury just ten days earlier.

Word of the Falin shooting electrified the out-of-town press corps still encamped in Wise in the days following Edith's trial. In addition to numerous Hearst reporters, a writer from the *Washington Post* was now on hand as well. Like a rare conjunction of planets, the presence of the reporters at this pivotal moment in Haugeman Falin's life guaranteed that he, too, would have his brief moment of fame. Within days the story of the "Second Wise County Patricide" was front-page news in Washington and elsewhere.

A photograph of Haugeman, taken in jail and more portrait than mug shot, revealed a well-built young man dressed in a zippered jacket. His brows were heavy and dark, and his eyes were set in an almond-shaped face. His tousled, ebony hair, cut short over the ears and kept longer on top, gave him an air of vulnerability, as if he needed someone to reach inside the photograph and smooth the strands for him. His quiescent features hinted that he had just emerged from sleep or else was still in shock, not fully connecting with the awfulness of recent events.

Although Haugeman was not allowed out on bond, his stay in jail promised to be a short one. Virtually everyone—including commonwealth attorney Fred Greear—seemed to readily accept his plea of self-defense.

At a juvenile court hearing in the town of Appalachia on December 9, Margaret Falin and nine other witnesses corroborated the youth's story, although Haugeman himself did not wish to testify. According to the *Washington Post,* the teenager did not have a lawyer present, but his witnesses were "gently treated" by the commonwealth attorney. After hearing the evidence, trial justice J. T. Hamilton acquitted the boy of the charge of patricide but ordered him to report monthly to a probation officer for one year.

Despite his sympathetic treatment in court, reporters had not heard the last of Haugeman Falin. He had been on probation less than a month when he was arrested and jailed on a charge of attempting to shoot his mother. She and some neighbors had complained to police that Haugeman "was intoxicated, was acting queerly and was shooting at everyone in sight."[3]

E. P. Boyden, Wise County's superintendent of public welfare, was Falin's probation officer. He investigated the second shooting incident and learned that Haugeman had been "mentally upset" since his father's death. Margaret Falin also told authorities that her son was still bothered by a skull fracture sustained when he was run over by a car at age three. In the quaint language of the day, the *Coalfield Progress* reported that Boyden recommended sending Haugeman to the child welfare clinic in Richmond "for study by alienists"—as psychiatrists then were called. Boyden said local mental health facilities were too limited to be able to diagnose the case. "I do feel, though, that the difficulties Haugeman is at present in is [*sic*] in part due to the influence of his father who had a considerable reputation as a gunman," he added.[4]

Boyden took his charge to Richmond in early January 1936 for a mental evaluation, and the story quickly faded from the headlines. What is clear, however, is that Wise County authorities initially took a progressive—rather than punitive—approach by trying to help this troubled youth break the cycle of abusive behavior that threatened to overwhelm him.

The two apparent patricides—and their radically different legal outcomes—gave reporters a ready opening to question the even-handedness of Wise County justice. Fred Greear was asked why the two apparently similar cases were treated so differently. But the commonwealth attorney insisted that the cases, despite appearances, were not alike. Responding with a candor that few prosecutors would allow themselves today, Greear said the past behavior of the two victims had caused a difference in public sentiment. "Trigg Maxwell was a good citizen and always has been," he said. "Falin had always been a bad actor." Greear also lashed out at the secrecy and dissembling that had surrounded Trigg Maxwell's death. "The thing that turned folks against the Maxwell girl," he continued, "was the way she tried to cover up the crime. At first the family claimed Trigg Maxwell hurt his head by hitting it against a meat block as he fell while he was drunk. It was two or three days before she or anyone else in the family would admit she'd hit him with a slipper."[5]

That was the reason, some believed, that a Wise County jury had thrown the book at Edith Maxwell. Now, with the first posttrial hearing in the Maxwell case just days away, Greear was determined to make sure that verdict would stand.

In Richmond, nearly four hundred miles from Wise County, Virginia governor George C. Peery could feel the strong aftershocks that had followed the recent Maxwell trial. Coverage by the yellow press—coverage that in many instances ignored the commonwealth's evidence almost entirely—convinced readers throughout the country that Edith Maxwell was the victim of persecution by a barbaric society. Outraged citizens from all over America flooded Peery's desk with letters and newspaper clippings, demanding that he take immediate action. So far, he had done nothing except to keep his ear to the ground.

"Clemency being refused to Edith Maxwell, and the mountaineers being upheld in their savagery of murderous and cruel laws, is comparable only to Christ before Pilate when Pilate washed his hands of the matter and let the innocent be put to death," a New York City woman wrote to Peery on November 22.[6]

Although Peery may have been concerned with the state's national image, his background had prepared him to place his trust in the beleaguered Wise County justice system. A native of Tazewell County in southwest Virginia, Peery not only had the Scots-Irish heritage common to many Wise County leaders but he also knew Judge Henry Alexander Wise Skeen personally. Around the turn of the century, when he was a young attorney just two years out of Washington and Lee University Law School, Peery had struck out for the town of Wise and found work representing several coal and land-holding companies. The future governor practiced law in Wise County for about thirteen years, during which time he married, built a twenty-room mansion on Wise's Main Street, and partnered with a group of local businessmen to construct the Colonial Hotel.

Peery had moved back to his native Tazewell County in 1915 and soon became a key figure in state Democratic circles. His political career was rooted in the "Fightin' Ninth," a congressional district that included thirteen mountain counties—Wise and Tazewell among them—and the city of Bristol. A longtime political associate of Harry Byrd, Peery went on to serve three terms in the U.S. House of Representatives from 1923 to 1929. In 1933 he won the governor's race by a three-to-one margin over his Republican opponent.

Historians would characterize the tall, silver-haired Peery as prudent, cautious, and conservative—an able governor yet one not given to social activism. Throughout his years in Richmond and Washington he had kept strong ties to the land west of the Blue Ridge, preferring the life of riding, hunting, and playing horseshoes to formal receptions and teas. Confronted with the Maxwell case midway through his term, the sixty-two-year-old Peery evidently had no compelling reason to question the Wise County institutions in which he had once been a player. Within days of Edith's conviction the governor had decided to take a noninterventionist tack.

Responding to letters critical of Judge Skeen, Peery typically answered that the elderly jurist "is in every way a Christian gentleman. I feel that he will give every consideration to the arguments that are presented for and on behalf of this unfortunate woman. She has been ably defended and no doubt they will preserve every right to which she is entitled."[7]

Peery forwarded some of his mail on the Maxwell case, along with his standard response, to Judge Skeen in late November as the judge was preparing to rule on whether to set aside the jury's verdict. "I know you well enough to know that you will appreciate my position," the governor said in a cover letter. "I do not send them [the letters] to influence your decision in the matter one way or the other—I merely give you this indication of what the newspapers are carrying and the letters that are being written."[8]

Even if Peery had been inclined to intervene, he probably had no legal justification for doing so in December 1935. Edith Maxwell was just beginning the appeals process that ideally would correct any miscarriage of justice that might have occurred. The hour was early, the governor might have reasoned—far too early for anyone in this unfolding drama to wear the robes of Pontius Pilate.

Silence fell like an early twilight in the Wise County Circuit Courtroom as soon as lawyers for Edith Maxwell and the commonwealth wound up their lengthy arguments on December 12. Although the hour was 1 P.M., Judge Skeen had declined to declare a lunch break, preferring to press on with the hearing that would decide whether Edith got a new trial. Now, nearly everyone was leaning forward in the wooden pews, waiting intently for Judge Skeen to rule on the defense's motion to set aside the jury verdict handed down on November 19.

To be sure, the lawyers had given him plenty to think about in the three hours they had argued before him in their blustery, old-fashioned, oratorical style. Defense attorneys Alfred A. Skeen and Robert P. Bruce had produced a list of seven assignments of error—alleged defects in the trial that could be remedied only by throwing out the verdict: improper evidence admitted, improper instructions given to the jury, jurors not given the option of finding the defendant guilty of lesser degrees of homicide, a verdict contrary to the law and the evidence, no evidence to support the verdict, the improper remarks of the commonwealth attorney, and failure of the evidence to establish the commission of a crime.

Alfred A. Skeen had emphasized the problem with the instructions to the jury, which forced the twelve men to declare Edith either guilty or innocent of murder without considering the option of manslaughter. His partner had focused on what he considered a lack of evidence to support a verdict of premeditated murder. "The prosecution has made mountains out of mole hills," shouted Bruce. "It has tried to make every act of these poor people an indication of guilt."[9]

But Oscar M. Vicars, arguing for the commonwealth, had forcefully rebutted the points made by the two veteran defense lawyers. He reminded the judge of the threats Edith had made against her father, how she had turned Chant Kelly away from the door as Trigg lay dying, and how her mother had burned Trigg's bloody shirt in the cookstove. This evidence, Vicars asserted, showed premeditation as well as an attempt to conceal the crime.

With all these points to digest, Judge Skeen could easily have taken the motion under advisement, yet he had decided to rule without delay. Edith's eyes were riveted on him as he announced his decision. Skeen began by saying that he had carefully studied the trial testimony and could find only one instance in which he had erred in admitting evidence—that error being in favor of the defense. Further, he said, he was not obliged to offer jury instructions that the defense lawyers themselves had not asked for.

"The main issue," Skeen declared, "is whether this verdict is against the evidence." He declined to comment on the testimony of specific witnesses, citing other cases pending in his court, but maintained that the jury was "the sole judge of the facts. . . . The jury judges both the credibility of each witness and the weight to be given to the evidence," he continued. "If there is any conflict in the evidence on a material point, this court's hands are tied. Under the limited powers of this court I find there is evidence to support the verdict."[10]

For the second time in less than a month Edith found herself reaching for the steadying support of Earl Maxwell. On this day, Ann and the younger girls had stayed home in Pound, leaving Earl as the only immediate family member present at the hearing. Earl tried to console Edith while her body shook with sobs, the reality of her twenty-five-year prison term now all too apparent. Finally she pulled herself together to ask, "Then there is no further chance?"[11]

Edith was quickly assured that her appeal would be taken to a higher court. Judge Skeen granted a sixty-day stay of her sentence so that her attorneys could petition the Virginia Supreme Court of Appeals to hear the case. She could remain in her uncle's jail at Wise and would not have to go to state prison just yet. This small bit of news offered some consolation to Edith on an otherwise disastrous day. "I want to stay here," she said, "so I can be near mama."[12]

As Edith was being escorted the few short steps from the courthouse to the jail next door, she crossed paths with waiting news photographers. With an approving Earl by her side, she stopped to pose for the cameras. Her cooperation drew a rebuke from Uncle Jim Dotson, who disapproved of the photo op. A family squabble flared up in front of the press.

"I'll do anything my brother says is all right," Edith told her uncle.

"And a lot he'll help you," said Dotson sarcastically.

Now Earl jumped into the fray. "You're right, I'll help her and I won't advise her to sign a first-degree murder confession like you did," he retorted.[13]

Possibly, Earl was referring to the statement, later suppressed, that Edith had given to Fred Greear back in July. In any case it was clear that Earl and his uncle, although both well-intentioned, fundamentally disagreed on strategy. Unlike jailer Dotson, Earl apparently believed that crusaders in the press—rather than the Maxwells' own lawyers—were becoming the most effective advocates for his besieged sister.

———

Over at the jail, N. F. Hix, the county coroner and jail physician, liked to kid around with Edith, whom he found more educated than the average prisoner. The two had a running joke. Dr. Hix would offer to swap photographs with Edith so that he, too, could sell a picture to the newspapers for $500. Edith would laugh and agree that they could swap photos, but there was a catch: The good doctor would also have to trade places with her and serve her sentence.[14]

12   *"Country People without Much Money"*

William Randolph Hearst's New York tabloid, the *Daily Mirror,* was once described by a former editor as a "hopeless sheet full of half-baked features, handicapped by lack of news service, inaccurate in its stories, and surviving solely through the flabbergasting information of Walter Winchell."[1] Although the $1,000–a-week gossip columnist and radio personality did command a vast following, the *Mirror* seemed forever destined to be a nag running several lengths behind the established tabloid frontrunner, the *New York Daily News.*

Hearst's exclusive deal with Edith Maxwell and her family in late 1935 must have been welcomed like a division of fresh troops arriving to help the *Mirror* in the circulation war with its archrival. Even though several Hearst reporters had already combed the mountains of southwest Virginia, the tabloid dispatched its own men to the area to mine for material—dark veins of scandal that the Hearst dailies perhaps dared not use. Under the headline "More Hearst Men in Wise County," the *Coalfield Progress* noted on December 5 that reporter Arthur Mefford and photographer Fred Must, both of the *Daily Mirror* staff, were "the latest arrivals." Their visit came just three days after representatives of two other Hearst enterprises, King Features Syndicate and International News Photo Service, had wound up a week-long stay in the county.

Although based in New York City, Arthur Mefford was no stranger to exotic assignments. In 1932 he had been involved in a bizarre attempt to rescue aviator Charles Lindbergh's infant son, whose abduction from the family home in rural New Jersey had saddened and outraged the nation. The management of the *Mirror,* hoping to boost daily readership to the million mark by recovering the child, had sent Mefford and editor Emile Gauvreau to Canada to meet with rumrunners who allegedly knew the child's whereabouts. The plan was to pay a $50,000 ransom, photograph the baby on the steps of New York City Hall, and *then* return him to his frantic mother. Although Mefford and Gauvreau were briefly held hostage while "negotiations" took place between groups of gangsters, the scheme—like so many others—came to naught. The little boy's body was eventually found in a wooded area, and a German immigrant, Bruno Richard Hauptmann, was convicted of the crime and sentenced to death.

Now, three years after the Canadian expedition, Mefford had come to Wise County to uncover Edith Maxwell's life story. He would later mention visiting Edith in her cell, but Earl, rather than the defendant, was quoted extensively in articles that Mefford ultimately produced. The tabloid writer spent several days in the Wise County area, apparently interviewing local people and even setting up a "mock jury" of women at Pound to comment on the case. Whatever information he collected, however, seems only to have kindled his imagination. In true tabloid fashion, Mefford's New York City readers were about to be treated to some of the wildest distortions ever printed about mountain people or the Maxwell case.

On December 11, 1935, the tabloid began serializing the Mefford epic, which he called "a transcript of Edith Maxwell's short life, it's [*sic*] few hours of happiness and its many, many hours of misery."[2] Before it was over, no fewer than twenty-three installments would appear under Mefford's byline. The Maxwell stories were featured only slightly less prominently than those about Bruno Hauptmann, who was providing the *Mirror* with his jailhouse memoirs while awaiting execution.

Sprinkled amid the stories of victims and villains were numerous photographs of Edith. Although she was an accomplished athlete who carried herself with considerable grace, Edith apparently had been asked by the Hearst photographer to strike some awkward poses. The camera had snapped away as she clutched the bars of her cell, put her hands together in prayer, or rolled her eyes toward heaven. Only occasionally was she seen in a more natural setting, helping cellmates polish up on the three R's or listening to one of them strum a guitar.

Far more interesting than these cardboard cutouts were pictures of the actual places where Edith had lived. There was the old homeplace on Bold Camp where she was born; the Little Ritz beer joint, where, the caption said, "Edith made innocent whoopee"; and, finally, the old, four-story, brick house-turned-jail, with its steeply pitched roofs and gloomy atmospherics. The *Mirror* also printed a few snapshots apparently obtained from Edith, her family, or acquaintances—most likely the pictures that Dr. Hix had teased her about selling. One showed Edith looking school-marmish in a polkadot dress. At the bottom, it carried a handwritten question, "Do I still remind you of Singing John?" possibly a reference to John Gilliam, Edith's grandmother's brother. The tabloid also unearthed a rare portrait of Trigg Maxwell dressed in his Sunday best and posing with his wife and daughters.

But none of the pictures, whether hokey or authentic, could match the sensational quality of Mefford's writing. He described Wise County as "a weird land of howling hound dogs, screeching bobcats and moonshine whiskey, where more than 12 percent of the white population are illiterate." He frequently expressed contempt for the locals, who in his view were "taught from earliest infancy to hate furriners"; were superstitious yet possessed of an "inbred telepathy"; and, as parents, were "not particularly interested in education." Moreover, "Girl children, instead of being a blessing, are considered 'pesty critters' by the illiterate, swaggering hill-billy males, who, according to tradition, are born with the inherent right to dominate, body and soul, every action of their meek and fearful women."

Mefford emphasized that Edith and Earl were of a class apart from their neighbors. He admiringly described Earl as "a hill-billy who had courage and ambition to pull himself out of the rut." And although about four hundred Wise Countians were attending college in the mid–1930s,

Mefford decreed that Edith was "virtually a furriner" by virtue of having spent two years at Radford. As he saw it, Edith's alienation from her home environment was bound to produce conflict:

> Edith had acquired a certain polish; a culture which could not be quite hidden. It made her stand out over the frowsy girls and loutish boys among whom she had spent her unhappy childhood. . . .
>
> Old Trigg, like the average resident in the primitive "Land of the Lonesome Pine" and stronghold of the "Blue Ridge moonshiners" made famous in John Fox, Jr.'s immortal novel, "Trail of the Lonesome Pine," professed to believe that the modern generation was headed "straight for Hell," and that their youthful ideas were "the thoughts of Old Scratch,"—meaning the devil. . . .
>
> And so he tried in every way to impress his attractive, brown-haired school-teacher daughter with his own importance as ruler of the domain of which his own riverside shack was the throne, and his Hill-Billy sceptre of mountain law, the direct appointment of God. . . .
>
> Only the constant intervention of his wife, the toil-worn and scrawny, aged-beyond-her-years mate who'd countenanced his mistreatment for "more'n thutty year," stood between Edith and violence.
>
> And Edith, complimented in letters from her brother for her "spunk," invariably stood her own ground when the illiterate mountain women of her acquaintance trod too heavily upon her slim toes. . . .
>
> In such an environment, no wonder, then, that Edith Maxwell with her taste of "book-l'arnin" acquired in Teachers' College, rebelled against the unbridled fury of her father's tongue and his fists when he took her to task for her acquired habit of "always goin' places," where she could mingle with persons of her own intelligence.

Mefford reported that one such run-in between Edith and Trigg happened on a night in April 1935, shortly after Edith's twenty-first birthday. According to his account, Trigg came home one evening and found that Edith had gone to Norton to spend the weekend with a girlfriend. He was upset that she had gone without his permission. Ann took up for Edith, making Trigg so angry that he twisted her arms. When Edith returned home, having cut short a double date at the movies, Trigg shoved her over a bed and beat her. "So, he himself, by his ignorance—his lack of understanding of modern youth—thus set the stage for his own execution, whether it was by his daughter's slipper heel or by a stroke," Mefford dramatically concluded. He embellished the tale by claiming that Edith was keeping the identity of her date a secret because "Pappy's relatives might kill him."

This alleged episode eerily foreshadowed Trigg's death about three months later, but did it really happen? If it did, it is strange that it did not surface in court testimony despite its seeming significance. The prosecution never used it to show premeditation, but perhaps it could be argued that they didn't want to put the deceased in a bad light before the jury. For the defense, however, it would have offered a key piece of evidence to prove a repeated pattern of abuse.

Even though the story seems reasonable enough—given the fractious nature of Ann, Edith, and Trigg's relationship—Mefford's narrative cannot be taken at face value. His remark that Trigg's relatives would attempt to harm the man who took Edith to the movies surely is nonsense. It was not the last outrageous claim that Mefford would make. Two days later, he told readers that Earl Maxwell, upon hearing of his father's death in July 1935, was duty-bound by the mountain code to go to the Wise County Jail and kill Edith for vengeance. Mefford claimed that the jailer barred Earl from visiting Edith "for several days" for fear Earl would serve as "official executioner" of his sister, when in fact he paid her a sympathetic visit on the very day he arrived from New York.

Somehow these stories trickled down to Wise County, leaving some people to feel that they had been hoodwinked by city slickers. Mefford's credibility was challenged by a Bristol, Virginia, woman who was quoted in the *Mirror* series. In a letter to the *Coalfield Progress,* the woman claimed she had never met or spoken with Mefford but instead had received a visit from Marguerite Mooers Marshall of the Hearst-owned *New York Journal.* Marshall told her she was there to raise funds for Edith Maxwell, and the woman had no idea she was being interviewed for publication. Creed Bruce, chair of the Wise County School Board, was visited at home by a man and a woman (the latter believed to be Marshall) who asked him for an interview. Although quotes from both Bruce and his wife appeared in Mefford's series, Bruce would later swear under oath that neither had made any such comments to the visitors.

As Mefford's series wore on throughout December, prosecutor Fred Greear, too, was chafing under the outlandish accusations and misrepresentations. He wrote a private letter to Harter Wright, an attorney friend in New York City, in which he gave the prosecution's side of the case. "I trust that we will never descend to the point where we will make heroes and heroines out of criminals," Greear wrote. "We think our section has been pictured in a most unjust manner and we are very anxious to have it corrected."

The *Mirror* obtained Greear's letter and incorporated parts of it into Mefford's series. For every key point offered by the commonwealth attorney, Mefford followed up with a tart rebuttal. Peeved over Greear's refusal to allow the *Mirror* access to a transcript of the trial, Mefford claimed that the prosecutor's summary of the evidence was inconsistent with recollections of reporters at the trial. Perhaps had Greear released the transcript—clearly a public record—it could have shed light on the matter, but given the *Mirror*'s lack of regard for the facts, it might have merely provided more grist for the distortion mill.

Another Wise Countian, Big Stone Gap *Post* editor Carl Knight, also found that a letter of his had made its way to Mefford's pages. Formerly a stockbroker in New York, Knight had written to Walter Winchell to try to correct negative impressions of southwest Virginia, which Winchell apparently had put forth in a radio commentary:

Dear Walter:

I always thought you were a pretty wise guy until you fell for this Edith Maxwell case. Your listeners down here in the Land of the Lonesome Pine Country are giving you a big Bronx razz since that Sunday night broadcast. They're even saying Mrs. Winchell's boy, Walter, has gone soft on them.

The natives along the Trail of the Lonesome Pine have gotten many a laugh since one of the service news hounds unearthed a dust-covered copy of neighbor John Fox's imaginative best seller and concocted a story of mountain codes as foreign to us as the Bowery would be to you in its heydey of fashion parades. Most of the news stories on the Maxwell case have been written in hotel rooms with a bottle of "corn" in one hand and "Trail of the Lonesome Pine" in the other.

The Edith Maxwell case is just another of those sordid murder trials. You can find dozens of them any day in your own New York. If the Virginia mountains have a curfew, I've yet to hear of it. We have our quota of night clubs; maybe not as pretentious as the Hollywood or the French Casino, but you can always find them full of young bloods and laughing lassies, who go home when, if and as they please.

The Knoxville, Tenn., club women who investigated the Maxwell case only to return all donations, did so, not as you say, because Miss Maxwell could not be interviewed, but because the facts did not substantiate the news stories they had been reading. As one news hound to another, I do not hesitate to say it was the worst example of news reporting I have ever seen. The wire reporters were espe-

cially guilty of distorting facts. The Knoxville ladies found that much
of the so-called "store bought" clothes worn by mountaineer lassies
came from your own New York department stores.

If that cowpath called Broadway continues to bore you and you
desire to cover the new trial Miss Maxwell is certain to get, then
come down to the "Land of the Lonesome Pine" as guest of my
paper. But be sure to bring your tuxedo.

And I'll promise to protect you from any enterprising native who
tries to sell you the all-famed "Trail of the Lonesome Pine." Frater-
nally, etc.

Mefford dismissed Knight's letter with a single phrase—"sour grapes."
He said he "strongly suspects" Knight of being a correspondent for "a
certain Knoxville, Tenn., newspaper" who had failed to break the ironclad
exclusive so jealously guarded by the Hearst correspondents at the Wise
County Jail. In Mefford's analysis, Knight's witty critique of the news coverage is nothing more than the whining of a reporter beaten on a story.

By early January, Mefford apparently had answered all his critics in
print and had milked the Maxwell story for all it was worth—at least for the
time-being. Throughout his nearly two dozen columns he had consistently
sounded the theme of escape: how Earl had begged his mother to leave
Trigg, to move up north and bring the three girls with her. It was Ann's
stubborn refusal to do so, and Edith's refusal to leave her, that ultimately
had yoked them all together in tragedy.

Mefford further argued that the problem was not just Ann's inability to
leave a bad marriage; it was the culture of Appalachia that had prevented
her from doing so. "The lore and the law and the traditions of the mountains was 'dead set agin' a woman leaving her husband," he wrote. And in
another place he quoted Earl as saying, "I guess my father was no worse
than most of the other men down in this hill country—the backwoods,
anyhow—for they all drink and they all consider themselves God so far
as their womenfolks are concerned."

There may have been a hidden autobiographical strain running
through Mefford's harsh indictment of the culture. In his next-to-last
installment, he surprisingly revealed that he, too, was of Appalachian
origin—"a hillbilly himself, born and raised in Eastern Kentucky in just
such a community as Wise." Although he was not a "New Yorker," clearly
he set himself apart from his native culture, where "passion and fury"
are the "dominant traits." For Mefford, both he and Earl managed to
escape physically and psychologically, but Edith lost her chance. She had

become "just another victim of the rage which sweeps over these primitive mountain folk."

—

On a bitterly cold morning in early December, a late-model Ford coupe cautiously maneuvered through the middle of Pound.[3] At the wheel sat a skinny reporter in an overcoat, his blaze of sandy red hair extinguished by a dark felt hat. The driver quickly summed up the town: five or six stores backed up against the Pound River, the high school on the opposite bank, and a handful of houses scattered about. On Main Street—really, the only street—he saw a group of men putting up a new store building while twenty or thirty others loafed in front of existing businesses. Their eyes bored into his District of Columbia license plate as he parked.[4]

The visitor was admittedly skittish. The *Washington Post* had reported that Pound was a "hard, suspicious place." But he got out anyway and approached an elderly carpenter named Lee Greear. "I've heard that Pound isn't a very friendly place for reporters," he said. "But here I am, so go ahead and shoot if you must."

Much to the stranger's relief, the deadpan humor found its mark. The old man took off his cloth mitten and extended a hand. "Yes sir, we'll be glad to talk to you," Greear said. "We'll be glad to. I'd like for you to talk to a lot of people around here."

Within minutes the reporter had attracted a friendly crowd of a dozen men. He was Ernie Pyle, a roving columnist for Scripps-Howard newspapers. Just a few months before, Pyle had quit his post as managing editor of Scripps-Howard's *Washington Daily News*, a desk job he hated, and struck out across the country to report on whatever caught his eye. His six columns a week were published regularly in the *Washington Daily News* and made available to twenty-three other Scripps-Howard newspapers across the nation. Just two days earlier he had arrived in Wise County, he wrote, "to see if the mountains have a 'code' that allows a man to beat his grown-up children; a 'code' that says all girls must be in after dark; to see if people are ignorant and mean; to see if their minds are closed to everything modern; and to see what Wise County actually thinks about the Maxwell case."

Now this bunch of rough-looking men, poorly dressed and mostly unshaven, was telling Pyle that the characterizations of Wise County in the national press had been untrue. "It's terrible what they wrote about us," complained Greear. "You'd think we had never had a haircut in our lives. It's bad for us. It hurts the county's credit. And it will hurt our children. When they go away, people will say, 'Oh, you're from that terrible place.'" One of the worst of the misrepresentations, Greear said, was that people with an education (like Edith Maxwell) were held in contempt. "Why, that's the one thing that every man around here works the hardest for, to educate his children."

After the crowd had its say—"their sincerity was intense, unquestionable" Pyle later wrote—he visited with more than a dozen other people in Pound, including physician E. L. Sikes, high school principal Earl Morris, and Mrs. Phillips, the wife of a missionary. All assured him that the "mountain code" played up in the Hearst press did not exist, a curfew for women did not exist, and people in Wise County "were anxious for everything modern they can get."

"Maybe it's just a strange old hillbilly custom," Pyle wrote in his December 13 column, "but I was asked to stay for lunch at three different places. I mentioned that to somebody later. He said you could go to the poorest log cabin in the farthest hills and ask to stay all night, and they'd make room for you."

Had he stopped to analyze it, Pyle might have traced his success in connecting with the people of Pound to his own beginnings in rural Indiana. Born in 1900 and reared on an eighty-acre farm, he had been stung by the taunts of "town kids" who liked to lord it over farm boys in school. Although Pyle decided early in life to escape the monotony of farm living, he had never lost appreciation for the struggles of ordinary working people. Now his recent decision to travel the depression-stricken country—a journey that would eventually take him to all forty-eight states, Alaska, Hawaii, and beyond—gave him a chance to reconnect with the energy and vitality of life outside the city.

Pyle's trip to Wise County in December 1935 probably began in Washington, D.C. If so, he likely made his approach from the east via Route 58 after getting off the Lee Highway at Abingdon. Of his trip to the town of Wise, he wrote, "This is mountain country all right. The last sixty miles in here is so crooked it makes you dizzy." Pyle drove in through a snowstorm that gave the sharp mountain peaks emphatic definition, an effect he found beautiful. (Always physically distressed by cold weather, Pyle would spend at least one night of his trip sleeping in his overcoat while at a hotel.) At the lower elevations he saw prosperous-looking farmhouses and trucks laden with tobacco on their way to market. But the landscape as well as the economy began to change as the climb began: "As you get closer to Wise, things get poorer," he wrote. "One and two-room cabins and shacks are frequent. There is no level place, and they are perched on hillsides and down in valleys. You see poor-looking, cold-looking men on the road. You see women in red calico chopping wood."

Arriving in the county seat, Pyle found a small mountain community of about 1,100, which, he said, "looked smaller." The two blocks of stores, which along with the courthouse and Colonial Hotel formed the town center, were surrounded by open countryside. The lay of the land—and the absence of laws requiring fences—meant that an occasional cow could be seen walking down Main Street amid the shiny new cars that Pyle noticed parked on both sides of the road.

Pyle would later tell readers that he had seen bovine pedestrians on the main streets of towns in Illinois, too. And the townspeople, he reported, "were dressed in fashion, not rube-like at all." It was mostly in the halls of the courthouse that he encountered the poor—countrymen loafing in their overalls and "thin old scraps of clothing." To Pyle, it was a demographic he had seen repeated many times:

> Maybe I know small towns and their people too well to appreciate the theatrical qualities of a place like Wise. To me there is nothing strange here. It's just another small town. And the people are just some more small-towners. America is full of them.
>
> The trouble is, in making a national story out of Wise, the reporters may have taken the poorest form of life here and made it the common denominator.
>
> There are people in Wise County like those in the cartoons; people who say "pappy" and stay drunk on moonshine, and never smile, and are suspicious of "furriners" and beat their grown-up children, and live like chickens, but they don't seem to be numerous.
>
> There are people here with Master's degrees, who think and speak better than we do, who have been all over the world, who have polish and city personalities, who drink cocktails instead of moonshine. They are a minority too.
>
> The great majority are just folks. They're fairly intelligent, pretty good-hearted, not very backward. They work hard, don't get much money for it, and live the best they can on what they have.
>
> They're poor, and they dress and talk like poor people. I believe some of the reporters have confused rural poverty with quaintness. If I didn't already know, I couldn't tell you from looking whether Wise was in Vermont or Iowa. Country people without much money have a way of being alike all over America.

Armed with these perceptions, Pyle spent at least four days talking not only with citizens of Wise and Pound but also with people "out in the hills between the two towns." Just as Wise Countians had strong opinions about media representation, they also had definite opinions about Edith's

guilt or innocence. "People say that two thirds of Wise County thinks her
twenty-five-year sentence for killing her father was just," Pyle reported.
Although Edith's attorney, Robert P. Bruce, thought the numbers weren't
quite that high, Pyle himself spoke with only "two or three" people who
were for her.

The reason, Pyle found, was that the public perception of Trigg Maxwell was radically different from the image of him presented at trial by
the defense. Trigg was regarded as "completely harmless," a henpecked
man with no control over his own family. Folks would tell how Trigg had
to go to work at the mines without breakfast, packing only a cold potato
in his dinner bucket, because the women of the house refused to cook
for him. Many people also believed that Trigg had reformed his drinking
habits after the death of his brother, swearing off hard liquor and leading
a more sober life. Some remembered him as good-humored when under
the influence, not the mean drunk he was made out to be in court.

According to Pyle, the majority of people simply did not believe Edith's
story of self-defense. "They think Trigg Maxwell was killed in bed," Pyle
wrote. (And although he did not say so, this same scenario was hinted at
in Edith's "confession," which was never revealed in court.) The thing
that infuriated people most, he said, was that neighbors were turned away
from the door after they heard Trigg moaning.

Nowhere in Wise County could Pyle find anyone who supported the
idea that Edith had been persecuted for violating a supposed "mountain
code." Many thought Judge Henry Alexander Wise Skeen had ruled consistently in Edith's favor. And, these sources told Pyle, the prosecution
was considered "very decent," having declined to use information "that
would have blackened Edith's character."

"The people generally don't seem violent in their feeling against
Edith," he added. "They simply think she was guilty and the law will do
the punishing. They don't blame her for causing all this unfavorable
'mountain code' and 'hillbilly' publicity. They blame the newspapers."

Outside of Edith's family, even her supporters believed "she should
probably have a sentence," according to Pyle. But they further believed
twenty-five years was draconian, especially in a case where the evidence
was largely circumstantial. The pro-Edith sources had also pointed out
what they considered two missing elements in the prosecution's case: the
absence of a murder weapon and the absence of a motive. "If Maxwell
was so mild and so badly under his family's thumb," wrote Pyle, "what was
the point of killing him? Even those against Edith haven't a satisfactory
answer for that."

The columnist had several conversations with "Senator" Bruce, who kept an office in Wise across the street from the courthouse. Like other visitors before him, Pyle was impressed with the defense attorney's gentlemanly demeanor. "He is in late middle age, a nice looking man of considerable culture, and he is extremely well thought of around here," Pyle wrote. "He is tolerant of the mass of public opinion against Edith. He understands it, and is sorry for it."

In Bruce's view, the trial was conducted fairly, but the verdict was not supported by the evidence. (He, too, found the tales of the mountain code to be distressing nonsense.) After listening to Bruce's analysis of the case, Pyle wrote, "The whole murder case boils down to this: The unsupported story of the family against a lot of circumstantial evidence. Both sides are weak. And when there's doubt—twenty-five years seems a long time if there's even a possibility you might be mistaken."

Among the people Pyle did *not* mention talking to were Earl and Ann Maxwell. The family had already cast its lot with the Hearst organization, a reality that Pyle, a Hearst competitor, understood all too well. Nonetheless, the Scripps-Howard reporter evidently believed that his visit to Wise County would not be complete without an audience with the famous prisoner herself. A couple of days before the hearing to request a new trial, Pyle sent word to the jail that he would like to meet Edith. It was 9:45 A.M. when the message reached her. Edith, who typically slept late and had just gotten up, said for him to wait until she combed her hair.

A jailer escorted Pyle to the basement where Edith was confined in a cell with several other women. She walked through the open door of the cell into a wide corridor and approached a barred gate where Pyle was standing. He was immediately impressed by Edith's beauty:

> She is medium tall. Her face is thin, and sensitive looking. She is much younger and more boyish than in her pictures. I thought she would appear older than twenty-one, but she doesn't. She looks right at you when she talks. She has a good countenance.
>
> She had on a navy blue zipper jacket, the kind boys wear, and she kept her hands in the slit breast pockets as you do when you are cold. I have an idea this is the way she looks best; not dressed up.
>
> Knowing that she was signed up with a newspaper service, I asked her if she were permitted to talk to me at all. She said she was sorry, but she wasn't supposed to talk about the case. She was quite decent and friendly about it, and willing to talk about anything else.
>
> If I could have thought of anything to say outside of the case, we could have had a long chat. But I never was good at making small talk, so after a couple of minutes I wished her luck, and left.

As his parting words to Edith suggested, Pyle held no animosity toward her for not giving him an interview. In fact, he devoted part of his last column on the Maxwell case to explaining why, after reviewing the evidence, he was squarely on Edith's side. Pyle argued that Edith had "lost on past performance." She had a reputation for being hot-tempered. She came from a family where fighting was the norm. And had it not been for a capricious turn of fate the fight that ended Trigg Maxwell's life on July 21, 1935, would have been no different from many others that had preceded it over the years.

The difference this time, Pyle said, was that the blow to the head that Trigg sustained caused a blood clot that killed him. Otherwise, the injury to the head would have been slight. "It was a freak death, like falling out of a chair and breaking your neck," he wrote. "If the gods were against you, you might kill a man by tapping him on the head with a pencil."

Pyle concluded that Edith was "the sad victim of circumstances" and deserved a new trial. "For even though there may be some consolation in being a national figure at the moment, five years from now not one person in a dozen would know who Edith Maxwell is," he predicted. "And twenty-five years from now, when the gates open, she will be a middle-aged woman—even an old woman. So why not take a chance?"

With these words Ernie Pyle ended his dispatches on the Maxwell case. He would move on to east Tennessee by Christmastime, continuing the odyssey that would eventually make him one of America's most beloved journalists. Through his canny observations of the people of Wise County and of the defendant herself, Pyle had proved himself the rare outsider who could understand the plight of Edith Maxwell without demonizing the community that had both nurtured and judged her. He had taken to heart the plea of a man in Pound, who said to Pyle, "Try and write the truth about us."

13   *"The East" Steps In*

In the closing weeks of 1935 Edith Maxwell was riding high in the popular imagination. A cowboy singer in the Richmond area had written a song on her behalf and was playing it live over the radio.[1] About fifteen letters arrived daily in her cell—some with dollar bills enclosed—and by Christmas her supporters would send five hundred pounds of candy. So many people trudged through the corridors of the Wise County Jail to see Edith that jailers finally had to restrict the flow of visitors. Even so, well-wishers and the merely curious flocked to Wise in such numbers that the Colonial Hotel and other establishments near the courthouse were profiting from what one newspaper called "Edith's mushroom fame."[2] At B. F.'s Cafe, formerly called Shorty's, visitors could eat beef stew and drink coffee in one of the high-backed green and white booths, wondering all the while if they were sitting in the exact same spot that *she* had occupied just hours before killing her father.

It all might have seemed like a winter carnival to tourists and shop-keepers, but one whose ending date was well defined. Wise's magnetic attraction would be gone to the state pen before Valentine's Day, barring some reversal of fortune. The clock was running on Edith's sixty-day stay of sentence, a fact that was galvanizing many far-away organizations to rally support for the embattled teacher. Just as Edith Kane Stair, the Knoxville clubwoman, had predicted, "the East" was about to step in.

In Washington, D.C., the city's two morning newspapers—the *Post* and its bitter rival, the *Herald*—were giving the story almost daily page-one attention. The *Herald* had been on the story almost from the beginning, thanks to Fulton Lewis's splashy series in the summer of 1935, but the *Post* had since managed to play a respectable game of catch-up, sending correspondent Virginia Lee Warren to Wise County. Now both newspapers were ready to cross the line from journalism to activism by helping the defense raise money for an appeal.

The *Post* announced the creation of its Edith Maxwell defense fund on November 26. "Still tired and haggard from the ordeal of her trial, this mountain girl who defied the customs of the ancient dwellers of the high places, brightened perceptably [*sic*] when told of *The Post*'s move," Warren reported in almost biblical language. The *Herald* followed a day later, telling readers that it would begin accepting money on Edith's be-half. Both started publishing coupons that readers were asked to fill out and send in with their contributions.

In New York City, a *World-Telegram* columnist called on the National Woman's Party, the American Civil Liberties Union, and "all other groups that care about justice without regard to sex" to help secure a new trial for Edith Maxwell.[3] ACLU officials, although sympathetic, said it was not a civil rights case. Leaders of the National Woman's Party, however, saw Edith's conviction as a clear symbol of women's oppression—and as a case that could spotlight their own cherished causes.

Founded by New Jersey activist Alice Paul, the National Woman's Party

(NWP) had begun more than twenty years earlier as a militant wing of the main suffragist organization, the National American Woman Suffrage Association (NAWSA). Paul's splinter group later broke with NAWSA completely, formed the NWP, and adopted a strategy of campaigning against whichever political party held power. In 1917 that meant holding Woodrow Wilson and the Democratic Party responsible for women being denied the vote.

Paul and her comrades boldly took their case to Pennsylvania Avenue, standing silently in front of the White House gates with signs and banners. Although the women protested peacefully over the course of several months, they eventually were arrested and charged with blocking public traffic on the sidewalk. Of 218 women detained, nearly a hundred drew prison terms.[4] Some hunger strikers, like Paul, endured painful force-feedings and solitary confinement. The resulting bad publicity for the Wilson administration led to the pickets' release and helped turn the tide in favor of suffrage. Women finally got the vote with the ratification of the Nineteenth Amendment in 1920.

By 1923, Paul and the Woman's Party activists had a new vision. They would seek enactment of the federal Equal Rights Amendment, a sword that would cut at the very heart of economic discrimination. The ERA, introduced in Congress that same year, said simply, "Men and women shall have equal rights throughout the United States and every place subject to its jurisdiction." But the more conservative NAWSA, which would eventually become the League of Women Voters, opposed the amendment, fearing that it would erase the special benefits that had been carved out for working women—protectionist legislation that limited the hours and conditions under which they could work.[5] The NWP opposed such measures, reasoning that special laws meant to protect women would actually give employers an excuse not to hire them or to pay them less than men.

Campaigning for the ERA would prove to be a very lonely course as the 1920s wore on, but Paul had managed to attract a talented and committed group who worked tirelessly to gain women's equality through political advocacy and public education. As Susan Becker observes, "The NWP activists were generally upper middle-class, but also included a number of wealthy and socially prominent women. They were well-educated and often had a background of settlement work, urban reform movements during the Progressive period, or unusual achievement in the professions. Many were related by birth or marriage, nearly all lived their adult lives in the northeastern United States, and most had been involved in the militant phase of the struggle for the Nineteenth Amendment."[6] Bluebloods like Florence Bayard Hilles, the daughter of Grover Cleveland's secretary of state, held positions of power, and other women of achievement such as Amelia Earhart could be counted among the members.

By the 1930s the NWP leadership had long since abandoned its strategy of militant confrontation, preferring to methodically lobby Congress from its headquarters at Belmont House in Washington, not far from Capitol Hill. But if the 1920s had been inhospitable to the ERA campaign, prospects in the 1930s were even more dismal. Feminism was considered increasingly out of style by a younger generation of women who had not shared the camaraderie of the suffrage campaign. Worse still, the crush of the Great Depression fell more heavily on women. The prevailing public attitude was that men—the traditional breadwinners—should not have to compete with women for the precious few jobs that remained. The Woman's Party particularly opposed the so-called married persons' law, a New Deal measure that resulted in the layoffs of several hundred female federal workers whose husbands were also employed by the government. And even though feminists found much to admire in independent, forthright Eleanor Roosevelt, who supported the right of married women to work, they were dismayed that this influential First Lady was opposed to the ERA.

Within the Woman's Party, leaders debated whether to devote party resources to campaigning nationally for the ERA or to tackling women's problems at the state level. Several eastern states had NWP chapters that had worked for many years to repeal or overturn state laws restricting women's rights in the areas of inheritance, divorce, custody of children, and employment. The NWP legal staff also had undertaken an ambitious research project to catalog the legal status of women in each state.

In Virginia, NWP researchers had learned, the post–World War I era had seen a blossoming of opportunity for women. In 1918 the law was amended to allow females to apply for medical licenses, and a similar change two years later allowed women to practice law. By 1925 all professions regulated by state law were open to women—at least in theory. In reality, the practical obstacles remained high. Women seeking to enter the University of Virginia, for example, had to pass much stricter entrance requirements than male applicants did.

Although women had long held jobs as teachers, the custom in Virginia and elsewhere dictated that female educators like Edith Maxwell had to resign their positions upon marrying. An April 11, 1935, editorial in the *Coalfield Progress* declared that a court ruling in Bedford County, Virginia, allowing married women to serve as teachers would have little effect locally. In Wise County, teachers who married during the school year had to notify the school board and were allowed to work only through the end of that school year. Noting that all Wise County teachers were hired on a year-to-year basis anyway, the editorial said that the ruling "promises no practical assurance to those who would marry and continue their jobs as teachers."

Virginia women working in factory jobs also faced certain restrictions, no doubt imposed "for their own good" by well-intended male legislators. Female industrial workers could work no longer than ten hours a day, although exceptions existed in the food- and tobacco-processing industries. In southwest Virginia, the age-old superstition that females brought bad luck to coal mines was actually underpinned by state law. Women were forbidden to mine coal, with violators facing a maximum penalty of ninety days in jail or a $500 fine.

Just as women could not hope to compete as equals in the workplace, neither could they find equal footing in the justice system. The courtroom was still a male preserve in Virginia and most other states in the 1930s; female attorneys were rare, and women could not serve as jurors. Standards of a bygone era required that women be protected from hearing the sometimes graphic testimony presented on the witness stand, and some men worried about wives and daughters being in close proximity with male jurors over the course of a trial. Thus the power of a jury to define socially acceptable behavior was, in most locales, reserved exclusively for men.

A May 2, 1936, editorial in an NWP newspaper, *Equal Rights Independent Feminist Weekly,* lamented that it was particularly difficult for women to obtain justice in cases of a sexual nature, where men were often the "transgressors." When a woman appeared in court to charge a man with rape, to establish paternity, or to defend herself on prostitution charges, a female viewpoint was especially needed on the jury. "Men have a natural sympathy toward one another, understand too well the difficulty of resisting temptation," said the editorial. "They have blamed the woman and exonerated themselves ever since the days of Eve."

Years of organizing and editorializing by the NWP and other women's groups had yielded disappointing results on the jury service question. By the mid-1930s, only the District of Columbia and twenty-one states, mostly in the Midwest and Far West, allowed women to serve as jurors. Along the East Coast, the all-male jury states stretched in a nearly unbroken line from Florida to New Hampshire, with Pennsylvania, Rhode Island, Maine, and the District of Columbia being the exceptions. In the South, only Arkansas and Louisiana afforded jury service to women. Feminists had not been able to claim a single statehouse victory on the issue since 1927, despite a lack of organized opposition. It appeared that hardly anyone—including most women—considered jury service a pressing issue.

———

As Woman's Party lobbyists knew all too well, getting a law enacted could be boring business to an apathetic public. But seeing how laws were enforced—how they played out in the criminal justice system—was another matter entirely. Trials had been a staple item of public fascination since the days of the Greeks and Romans. In more recent times, Bruno Richard Hauptmann's 1935 trial for the kidnap-murder of the Lindbergh baby had held an entire nation in thrall.

Thus the NWP legal staff kept a watchful eye on court cases that might galvanize the public on women's issues. Such cases could potentially demonstrate the basic injustice of the system; better still, they might actually result in women's rights being expanded. In 1932 the party had challenged the all-male jury system in Massachusetts by defending a woman who was convicted of illegally selling whiskey, but to its regret the U.S. Supreme Court had refused to hear her appeal. As news accounts of Edith Maxwell's murder trial reverberated throughout the country in late November 1935, party strategists instantly realized that this Virginia case presented another chance to advance the legal status of women.

Elsie M. Graff of Richmond, chair of the NWP in Virginia, pounced on the Maxwell case. Her chapter was working to introduce a woman juror bill into the Virginia legislature, which was due to convene in January 1936.[7] Although the General Assembly had repeatedly nixed such measures over the years, the plight of Edith Maxwell could call attention to the issue in a dramatic way. Just a few days after the verdict, the Virginia chapter issued a statement calling Edith's prison sentence "cruel and unusual punishment" and recommending that an appeal be taken to the Supreme Court.[8] Thus the party could benefit from all the fuss about Edith Maxwell in two ways, either through the legislature or through the federal courts, finally freeing Virginia juries of all-male domination.

With the NWP's national conference due to be held in Columbus, Ohio, on November 30, the timing was propitious for Graff to take her case directly to the party's leadership. She outlined the Maxwell case to the NWP's governing body, the National Council, which was meeting at the Deshler-Wallick Hotel. A resolution denouncing the Maxwell verdict was hastily penciled in on the conference agenda. The following day, delegates declared that "the National Woman's Party is greatly aroused because Edith Maxwell was not tried by a jury of her peers, since women are denied the right to sit on juries in Virginia." The resolution called for passage of an equal rights amendment to the U.S. Constitution to ensure that women could serve on juries in every state.[9]

As publicity about the Maxwell case mounted, the NWP national office in Washington received a flood of letters urging the party to do more than simply pass a resolution. A woman in Haymarket, Virginia, for example, asked NWP attorney Rebekah S. Greathouse to come to Edith's defense. "I thought if you could interview her she would want you as her counsel, for her all-men trial failed," the woman wrote. "Then you might put at least one woman on the jury and she couldn't be sentenced if I were on [it]."[10]

The Maxwell case did hold considerable promise for the Woman's Party agenda, but apparently opinions varied among the NWP membership as to how and when to get involved. Even before the conference, Greathouse had written to one of Edith's attorneys, suggesting that *he* bring up the question of the legality of all-male juries when filing the appeal, but now there was strong pressure for the NWP to act.[11] Some feminists believed that the party should wait and file a "friend of the court" brief when, and if, the case reached the U.S. Supreme Court; others argued that the case would never get that far without the party's vigorous financial and legal support.[12]

Greathouse, who was also the NWP national secretary, responded to the woman in Haymarket with a thoughtful letter outlining the Woman's Party's position:

> We have been very much stirred by the Maxwell case and wish very much there were something we could do. However, I understand that offers of assistance by other women's organizations have been refused.
>
> It would not be possible to have a woman on the jury except by going to the Supreme Court and possibly having them rule that keeping women off the juries is unconstitutional. . . . It would be necessary for Edith Maxwell's lawyer to make the request and then appeal from the ruling. This organization is chiefly interested in securing an amendment to the Constitution which would provide equal rights for women and among other things the right to serve on the jury in every state.
>
> Of course you understand that neither as an individual nor an organization could I help in the case without the request of Miss Maxwell and her attorney.[13]

In a similar vein, Greathouse had told Elsie Graff on December 3 that little else besides enacting the resolution could be done until the NWP was sure its help would be welcome. With a bow to depression-era frugality, she advised Graff to go ahead and cautiously sound out Edith's position. "If [*sic*] would be fine if you could get a reliable report as to the intentions of Miss Maxwell's lawyers and their attitude toward possible assistance from us," Greathouse wrote. "Probably the only way this could be done would be to send a person to call on the lawyers and, of course, I do not know whether this would be worth the expense involved."[14]

By December 6, Greathouse had gone public, telling the *Washington Herald* that she had asked Edith's lawyers to bring up the question of women's exclusion from juries when they filed a motion for a new trial. "Of course we have fought this in the Virginia legislature for many years as we have in other States," Greathouse said. "Now we are concentrating on the Equal Rights Amendment, which will make it mandatory in every State for women to be given an equal chance with men to serve on juries. Regardless of what the outcome may have been in the Edith Maxwell case, women everywhere would have been more satisfied with the verdict, if they knew the girl had been heard by her peers."

Back in Richmond, Elsie Graff apparently felt she had a green light from the national leadership to move forward, even though she was misinformed about the details of the Maxwell case and apparently had some misconceptions about Appalachian culture. She reportedly told the NWP's Virginia members, for example, that Edith "was attacked with a whip because she had returned home later than 9 o'clock, the hour regarded by the simple people of her neighborhood as the curfew hour."[15] Graff evidently did not follow Greathouse's lukewarm suggestion to send an envoy to Wise to meet Edith's lawyers but decided that a letter would do. According to *Equal Rights Independent Feminist Weekly*, Graff on December 15 "communicated with Miss Maxwell, promising funds and the services of counsel." She soon received the following letter signed by Edith:

> I wish to take this opportunity of thanking you for your letter of the 15th instant offering to assist me in every possible way and to employ counsel to help me secure vindication from an offense which is charged against me, providing I desire you to do so.
> I do want all the assistance you can render, and will greatly appreciate it. I would desire whomever you may employ as counsel to immediately confer with my present counsel here, Hon. A. A. Skeen, of Clintwood, Va., and Hon. R. P. Bruce, of Wise, Va., and render all legal services they

possibly can to bring about my acquittal. I can assure you of my complete innocence, and the fact that I have been wrongfully convicted.

I will ask my brother, Mr. Earl Maxwell, to confer with you and give you all the facts and information which you may desire. As soon as possible I would like for you to arrange a conference with my counsel and to render all the aid possible in preparing for my trial and asking for reversal of my case, but act as quickly as possible due to the fact that we have very little time in which to act.

Again, thanking you for your kind interest and great help, I remain. Edith Maxwell.[16]

With Edith's acceptance in hand, Graff swiftly arranged for a Richmond bank to administer her Edith Maxwell defense fund and began shopping for a lawyer. Her chapter would need to raise at least $1,500 to cover the cost of an appeal, including money for travel, printing, typing, telephone calls, and court fees. An urgent message went out to Woman's Party members and the general public, asking them to "dispatch a contribution, large or small, to Mrs. Graff immediately." In turn, Graff promised a receipt to each donor and, eventually, a full report of how the funds were spent.[17]

Two days before Christmas, newspapers announced that Edith had accepted an offer of legal assistance from the Virginia chapter of the NWP. The *Richmond News Leader* conceded in a December 27 editorial that the Maxwell case might indeed bring about an appeals court decision that would open the jury room to women. The newspaper, however, seemed skeptical of the new alliance between a criminal defendant and a radical political group: "If the Maxwell case develops [into] a struggle for woman's rights, it will have one more sensational angle. It is doubtful, however, if this phase of the contest will throw any further light upon the main question: Is the young woman guilty of murder?"

14   *Big Shots in Town*

Outsiders who had never set foot in Wise County were now convinced that Edith Maxwell had been unjustly convicted by a "mountain code" and were determined to save her. "If we were to take such sentiments seriously," said one satirical letter about the Maxwell case, "it would cause us to wonder why our social, welfare, missionary and religious organizations have spent so much time, in all the years past, soliciting funds and workers for the uplift for the heathen of the Orient or the savage of Africa, when for less effort and expense they could have gone to Wise County, Va., and found a county full of them!"[1]

In fact, missionary fervor was a phenomenon already well known to residents of Appalachia. Scores of well-meaning preachers and school-marms—many from the Northeast—had come to live and work in the mountains in the decades since the Civil War. These outsiders had built schools and colleges, improved public health, and made other civic contributions. But in many cases they also had regarded the locals as specimens for anthropological study—or worse, targets of social improvement. Their efforts to impose "proper" customs of speech, dress, and behavior on the population had often set the stage for hillbilly intransigence.

Gov. George C. Peery, himself a native of the mountains, now had to uphold for Wise County, whose justice system was under attack. On December 17 he made his first public statement on the Maxwell case. "The kindest thing that can be done," he said, "is to leave the matter to the orderly processes of the courts without outside interference."[2] The *Roanoke Times* editorially praised the governor for his stance, calling him "a man who would never think of usurping the powers of the courts either directly or by subterfuge." And, the *Times* added pointedly, "Others might profit by his example."[3]

The advice of the newspaper and the governor, however, was destined to go largely unheeded. Whether one regarded outsiders as meddlesome demons or rescuing angels, powerful forces were fast converging on Wise. Edith's attorneys Robert P. Bruce and Alfred A. Skeen, although competent, had thus far failed to win her a new trial. Rumors had swirled for weeks that big-shot lawyers were coming to join the big-shot reporters already in town. In murmured conversations at the courthouse, over table-talk at the Colonial Hotel, and in the pages of the newspapers, people wondered who these luminaries would be.

No less a figure than Clarence Darrow, the renowned attorney who had humiliated William Jennings Bryan at the 1925 Scopes trial, had been mentioned by the *Washington Herald* as a possible attorney to lead Edith's appeal. "If Darrow should undertake the defense of Edith Maxwell, who probably never dreamed that the greatest criminal lawyer of his age would become interested in her case, he would enter a courtroom in the South for the first time since the Scopes trial at Dayton," noted the *Herald*, clearly relishing the prospect of recreating history.[4]

The newspaper's efforts to woo the seventy-eight-year-old Darrow out of retirement in Chicago apparently were thwarted by his wife, who said he was too frail to undertake such an arduous assignment. Darrow did offer his weighty moral support, however, by speaking out publicly about the Wise County trial. "The [jury's] decision was one belonging to the dark ages and the State twenty-five years from now will be ashamed of the verdict," he said.[5]

The *Coalfield Progress*, however, told readers that Bruno Richard Hauptmann's "famous New York attorney"—undoubtedly the flamboyant Edward J. Reilly—reportedly had offered his services to Edith Maxwell. In a colorful career spanning a quarter century, Reilly made a name for himself in Brooklyn by representing bootleggers and "female killers," particularly women who allegedly had suffered at the hands of abusive husbands before finally doing them in.

He was hired in 1934 by the Hearst-owned *New York Journal* to defend Bruno Richard Hauptmann on charges of kidnapping and killing the Lindbergh baby; in return, Hauptmann's wife had agreed to give the *Journal* her exclusive story. Because Edith, too, had negotiated an exclusive with the *Journal*, there was speculation that Reilly might once more be pressed into service. The Hauptmann verdict, however, had been only one in a series of recent courtroom losses for the veteran lawyer. Although Reilly had provided good newspaper copy at the January 1935 trial—and collected a $25,000 fee from the *Journal*—he had failed to save his client from a death sentence. "In view of his success in defending Hauptmann, we can not imagine that any one would be enthusiastic about his assistance," jibed the *Coalfield Progress*.[6]

When the new lawyer's name was finally announced in late December, the choice was Minitree Jones Fulton, a well-connected Richmond attorney in his late sixties. Elsie Graff had moved swiftly after receiving Edith's letter, retaining Fulton on behalf of the Virginia NWP. A Grayson County native and graduate of Washington and Lee University Law School, Fulton had served in the General Assembly and had practiced law with Richard E. Byrd, father of Virginia senator Harry F. Byrd. Fulton was also well known in Washington, D.C., where he had successfully defended Ada Burroughs, the secretary of Bishop James Cannon Jr. on a charge of conspiring to violate federal election laws.

Fulton tantalized reporters with hints of "new evidence of a very material nature" that could lead to a new trial for his client.[7] Shortly after Christmas, he traveled to Wise to confer with Earl Maxwell and the local defense team. From this confab emerged a new strategy that would profoundly transform the architecture of the defense. At Edith's trial in November, Bruce and Skeen had tried to prove that the shoe Edith allegedly used as a weapon *could* have caused her father's death, and therefore her claim of self-defense was true. Now, the defense would argue that the blow from the shoe *could not* have caused his death, which therefore must have been due to natural causes. The reason this was not evident at trial, the defense now maintained, was because the autopsy had been hopelessly botched. Therefore, Fulton and his fellow lawyers decided to return once again to Judge Henry Alexander Wise Skeen to persuade him to consider a plea of newly discovered evidence. As Hearst writer Fulton Lewis Jr. had eerily predicted six months earlier, "modern medical science" might hold the key to unlocking Edith's predicament.

On December 31, 1935, the defense filed a second motion for a new trial in Wise County Circuit Court, thereby unveiling a radical new strategy to an eager press and public. Edith's lawyers asked Judge Skeen to consider whether exhumation of Trigg Maxwell's body and a microscopic examination of his brain might yield new evidence about the cause of death. And, not surprisingly, the defense questioned the constitutionality of the Virginia statute that permitted only men to serve on grand juries and trial juries. Another constitutional point related to the use of a short form of indictment, one that charges guilt but does not go into detail about the alleged crime.

The defense maneuver may have surprised some observers who were expecting Edith's attorneys to proceed at once to a higher court. It also might have come as a shock to Judge Skeen, who perhaps thought his involvement in this troublesome case had ended on December 12. A defense attorney explained the reason for trying once again to resolve the case in Wise County: "This is a somewhat more favorable situation than if it were an appeal to a higher court. In such an appeal, only questions of law could be presented, and they would be limited by the exceptions taken by the defense at trial. Apparently the most important errors were not excepted to at the trial. Therefore it seems as though there is more likelihood of getting a new trial . . . [in Wise] than in a hearing on appeal."[8] Essentially, the defense was asking Judge Skeen to re-open the case upon which he had already ruled.

Although New Year's Eve was the last day of the court term, Judge Skeen obligingly agreed to extend the session into the new year so that the motion could be heard. He asked both sides to submit briefs and set oral arguments for January 15, 1936. The defense was quick to claim victory. In the meantime, more legal reinforcements from "the East" would be on their way.

—

In Portland, Maine, attorney Gail Laughlin was preparing for her 1,500–mile journey to Wise, Virginia. A devout feminist and vice chair of the National Woman's Party, Laughlin had been outraged when she read about Edith Maxwell's plight. Not only did the trial have the flavor of an all-male inquisition but the tale of the young woman attacked by a drunken father also resonated with Laughlin's own deep aversion to alcohol.

Laughlin was not a criminal lawyer like M. J. Fulton, but Elsie Graff had invited her to contribute her considerable expertise in constitutional law to help win a new trial, laying the legal groundwork that would allow women to serve on juries. Laughlin announced on January 5 that she, too, would join the defense at the request of the NWP. Within forty-eight hours she caught a southbound train.

Laughlin, then sixty-seven, had devoted her adult life to breaking down barriers for women. Reared in Maine and Canada by a widowed mother with several children to support, Laughlin by age twelve had already perceived the vast inequalities in men's and women's lives. She decided to make her mark in a man's world by becoming a lawyer. In 1890 she entered Wellesley College in Massachusetts as a "calico girl" (a student who paid her own way) and went on to graduate from Cornell Law School, where she was one of three women in a class of 128.

In 1902 Laughlin went west as an organizer for the National American Woman Suffrage Association, and for the next four years she lived the life of a stagecoach-riding preacher, exhorting women to demand the vote. Several years later in San Francisco, she drafted and saw the enactment of a state law permitting women to serve on juries. She also joined the National Woman's Party and was elected the first president of the National Federation of Business and Professional Women.[9]

Laughlin moved back to Portland, Maine, in 1924 and set up a law office with her brother, but, as usual, feminist politics remained front and center. She gained national attention in 1927 when she led a motorcade to President Calvin Coolidge's summer vacation spot in the Black Hills of South Dakota. The convoy of seven hundred women breached the president' s privacy long enough to ask for his help in getting the Equal Rights Amendment passed by Congress. Such antics apparently endeared her to the clubwomen of Maine, who asked her to run for the legislature in 1929. Laughlin campaigned as a Republican and won handily; she served three terms before being elected to the state senate in 1935.

The Maine lawyer in many ways fit the stereotype that some people still associate with the word *feminist*. Early in her career she discovered that frilly blouses and sweeping skirts were a nuisance. From the 1920s on, tailor-made black trouser suits with neckties were her workaday "uniform." She kept her hair short and combed it back. For leisure activities, as in her professional life, she favored traditionally male pursuits such as golf, fishing, and flying small private airplanes.[10] She never married. This unconventional lifestyle, coupled with her tendency to say exactly what was on her mind, made Laughlin a natural target for criticism. Mumbled asides about Laughlin's mannish ways, however, had seldom deterred her from doing what she thought was important—like tackling the Maxwell case.

Laughlin's journey down the eastern seaboard took her first to the Woman's Party headquarters in Washington, D.C., on January 7. Her next stop was Richmond, where she stayed for several days as the guest of Elsie Graff and conferred with the other Woman's Party lawyer, M. J. Fulton, about the upcoming January 15 hearing. Fulton had already been working on the constitutional aspects of the case and had sent Governor Peery a draft copy of a document called "Assignment of Error No. 10," in which the defense asserted that Edith Maxwell had been denied equal protection under the law because women could not serve as jurors at her trial.

"If Hon. H. A. W. Skeen should set aside the verdict in this case and grant a new trial on this or other grounds, or should overrule the motion, it would not cure the defect in our laws, and their Constitutionality may be raised in every case in the Courts of this State and would result in going to the Supreme Court of the United States," Fulton wrote to Peery. "This in my opinion merits most serious consideration, and as the General Assembly is now in session, their attention should be called to it so that they may have an opportunity to remedy this omission."[11] Peery answered swiftly and impassively with a two-sentence form letter, saying he would "be glad to look into the matter," but no legislation was forthcoming.[12]

Aside from his unsuccessful lobbying effort, Fulton was fretting because a copy of the trial transcript he was expecting from Wise County had not yet arrived. Finally, on January 10, the prosecution's portion of the trial record came in the mail, giving Fulton and Laughlin just five days to peruse it, travel nearly four hundred miles to Wise, and be ready for court.

Edith Maxwell took her by-now-familiar place at the defense table in Judge Skeen's courtroom on Wednesday, January 15, with Earl and Ann Maxwell seated nearby. It was becoming apparent, however, that the table might now need a leaf. Yet another lawyer had surfaced in court that morning, swelling the ranks of the defense to no fewer than six attorneys.

While the National Woman's Party Virginia chapter was busy recruiting Fulton and Laughlin, the *Washington Post*—which had its own thriving defense fund for Edith—had not been content to see its role eclipsed. Purchased in 1933 at a bankruptcy auction by Eugene Meyer, the *Post* was decades away from being the newspaper that would bring down a dissembling president and win the respect of the nation. Its reporting of the Maxwell case was heavily biased in Edith's favor, and some of its writers referred to the infamous mountain code as if it really existed.

However lopsided and incomplete its stories, the *Post*'s coverage was still a rung above that of Hearst's *Washington Herald*. It even seemed that the *Post* had been able to maneuver past the Hearst exclusive that had kept other competitors away from Maxwell case. The newspaper had lined up a list of prominent Virginia lawyers to submit to the Maxwells for consideration, and Earl Maxwell, perhaps in turn, had begun writing front-page, bylined articles that appeared in the *Post*. By the end of 1935 it had raised $741 in defense funds (valued at about $10,000 today).

In early January 1936 the newspaper announced that it had retained Charles Henry Smith, an Alexandria, Virginia, trial attorney, to represent Edith. From Edith's uncle, Gernade Dotson, had come the invitation for Smith to enter the case. Smith had served three terms in the Virginia House of Delegates from 1922 to 1927, so it is possible that he knew Dotson, who also was a Democratic delegate during most of the same period.

The *Post* boasted that Smith, forty-two, had a "brilliant record of accomplishments before the Virginia bar," having obtained acquittals in thirty out of thirty-four first-degree murder cases. Smith was expected to handle the criminal law aspects of the appeal, while Fulton and Laughlin would concentrate on questions of constitutional law. Edith's local attorneys—Dotson, Skeen, and Bruce—apparently would have no public role in the drama about to unfold.

As the hearing began, Smith and Laughlin—both newcomers to the Wise County courtroom—first had to state their qualifications to practice law, and then they formally took the oath making them officers of the court. A crowd quickly filled the room as the out-of-town lawyers began presenting arguments in favor of a new trial. Never before had a woman pleaded a case before the Wise County bar.

Laughlin had carefully studied the famous Scottsboro trials from Alabama, which promised to serve as a road map for the Maxwell case in the event it ever reached the federal courts. In 1931, two white women riding as hoboes on a train had accused nine black teenagers of gang-raping them. All the youths except one were swiftly convicted and sentenced to death on questionable evidence, provoking outrage among many who believed them innocent. Prominent writers and intellectuals such as Theodore Dreiser publicized the case, and legal assistance poured in from the American Communist Party and other groups. In April 1935, in the landmark decision *Norris v. Alabama,* the U.S. Supreme Court had overturned one defendant's conviction on the grounds that no blacks had been included in the jury pool at his trial.

If Edith's state-level appeals proved unsuccessful, the Woman's Party was poised to carry her case to the high court as well. One important distinction between Edith's case and that of the Scottsboro Boys is that it was not illegal for black men to serve as jurors in Alabama, although they were seldom, if ever, called because of racial discrimination. In Virginia, women were not allowed *by law* to serve. But the heart of the argument was still the same: The Scottsboro Boys had been denied equal protection of the law guaranteed by the Fourteenth Amendment and so, reasoned Fulton and Laughlin, had Edith Maxwell. Taking the Maxwell case to the Supreme Court could result in women being included in the jury pools of *all* states.

One weakness to this approach, Laughlin realized, was the fact that defense attorneys Skeen and Bruce had not objected to the makeup of the jury pool *before* the November 1935 trial—a tactic that probably would have seemed to them exotic to say the least. Still, Fulton and Laughlin had thought it important to raise the issue to get it on the record. If a new trial were granted for any reason, they would have an opportunity to object to the calling of an all-male jury pool, just as one of the Scottsboro defense attorneys had successfully challenged an all-white jury.

"The Scottsboro case is hardly more noted than this case, judging by the flood of letters, written by inadvised persons, to me and the papers," Judge Skeen told an amused courtroom audience, "but they have no influence over me, not a bit in the world." According to the *Coalfield Progress,* the judge then "launched into a comparison of the two cases."[13] By day's end, however, he would remain unswayed on the question of women jurors, ruling that jury service was an obligation and duty rather than a privilege of citizenship.

Fulton also used a second constitutional argument to chip away at the guilty verdict, questioning the adequacy of the "short form" indictment. This document had charged Ann and Edith with murdering Trigg but did not set forth any specific allegations about the role each woman may have played. "Where does it charge willful, deliberate, premeditated murder, with malice aforethought?" Fulton asked.[14]

As the morning wore on it was becoming increasingly apparent that constitutional arguments alone were not going to persuade Judge Skeen to toss out the jury's verdict. It was time for the defense to play its trump card—the plea of newly discovered evidence.

Charles Henry Smith, armed with affidavits from three eminent East Coast coroners, declared that the state had failed to establish the cause of Trigg Maxwell's death at the trial—and therefore no proof of a murder existed. Drs. James M. Whitfield of Richmond, A. MacGruder MacDonald of Washington, and Thomas A. Gonzales of New York had submitted sworn statements criticizing the autopsy performed in Norton by Drs. T. J. Tudor and G. T. Foust. The original autopsy report concluded that Trigg died from blood clots in the brain resulting from blows to the head. The defense's medical experts, however, alleged that the autopsy report did not contain enough evidence to support that conclusion.

According to Dr. Gonzalez's affidavit, the autopsy was incomplete because no examination of the heart, stomach, and other organs had been performed. Neither had the brain been chemically or microscopically examined. Similarly, Dr. Whitfield had found nothing in the report sufficient to explain Trigg's death.

This new medical opinion apparently had been solicited by Earl Maxwell and a *Post* reporter in the weeks following the November trial. On December 19, Earl had traveled to Richmond to have specialists examine the autopsy report, but they reportedly had said they could not form an opinion without studying the head of the deceased. Since his return Earl had been seeking permission to have his father's body exhumed from a Pound cemetery in the hope that a more complete autopsy might be performed, but he had not met with success. Earl wrote in the *Post* that he expected Judge Skeen to rule on the defense's petition to exhume the body at the January 15 hearing, but, strangely, the matter apparently wasn't discussed in open court.

For the time-being at least, the defense would have to content itself with raising doubts about the validity of the autopsy report prepared by

Drs. Tudor and Foust. Smith baited the prosecution lawyers by yelling at them, "If you're so sure of your case why don't you recall these witnesses? You surely have something to conceal."[15] Smith told Judge Skeen that he planned to put expert medical witnesses on the stand to substantiate the coroners' affidavits if a new trial were granted.

The defense finished its presentation around noon Wednesday, but Judge Skeen decided to press on without a lunch break. After listening to the prosecution's rebuttals during the afternoon, the judge still had not completely made up his mind. He quickly rejected all the constitutional arguments set forth by Laughlin and Fulton but decided to reserve judgment on the question of newly discovered evidence until the commonwealth's physicians could be recalled. Judge Skeen ordered commonwealth attorney Fred B. Greear to have the doctors in court the next morning, clearing the way for Smith to cross examine them. The medical affidavits—although hardly a dramatic piece of evidence—had gotten his attention. "This is the most encouragement that we have had in months," said Edith.[16]

On Thursday, Judge Skeen listened to an hour and a half of testimony from the Wise County doctors who had performed the autopsy. Tudor and Foust both stood by their original conclusion: Trigg had been killed by blows to the head. Dr. Tudor testified that microscopes had been available to him at the time of the autopsy but that the brain injury had been readily apparent to the naked eye. He also said he had not thought it necessary to "mutilate" the body by examining the heart and other organs.

Judge Skeen was now ready to make a decision. "The judgment again of this court is that the verdict of the jury be carried out by the officers of the law," he said.[17]

Edith's face flushed as she heard the words. She turned to Earl, who was sitting beside her, and laid her head on his shoulder. Edith dabbed at her eyes with a handkerchief as Judge Skeen formally pronounced the sentence of twenty-five years in prison.

The best efforts of the outside lawyers—and Earl's tireless legwork—had failed to produce results. Nonetheless, at least some of the defense lawyers believed that a more solid basis for Edith's appeal had been established. On Friday, Fulton announced that a petition would be filed with the Virginia Supreme Court of Appeals. The clock was now reset. Judge Skeen had granted the augmented defense team sixty more days before Edith's sentence would be imposed.

Gail Laughlin, returning to Richmond after the hearing, put an optimistic spin on the defense's prospects. In a newspaper interview she

declared that the Wise County commonwealth attorney had been unable
to cite a single state case that held that the exclusion of women from
juries does not violate the Constitution. The U.S. Supreme Court had
never ruled on the question, she said, but their ruling on "the position
of Negroes" made it clear that a fair trial by jury must be "trial by one's
peers. Unless one goes against the ruling of the Supreme Court," she asserted confidently, "Edith Maxwell is entitled to a trial by a new jury."[18]

Edith, however, was said to be "bitterly disappointed" by the judge's
decision. Her hopes had run so high in the days before the hearing that
she even made a "date" with her lawyers to see a movie in Norton on
January 15 if the judge decided to release her. For the price of a twenty-
five-cent ticket Edith could have lost herself in a John Wayne adventure
or a romantic comedy, perhaps even imagining herself up there on the
screen of the Bolling Theatre. Now, that means of escape would have to
wait indefinitely.

15   Let's Have a Show

On Sunday evening, February 16, several hun-
dred New Yorkers ventured out into the drizzly dark to catch a show at
the Majestic Theater on Forty-fifth Street west of Broadway.[1] The occasion, however, was not the usual song-and-dance. In fact, the star of the
production was not even backstage but was instead sequestered hundreds
of miles away in the Wise County Jail. The theater-goers had turned out
for a benefit performance for Edith Maxwell, the imprisoned mountain
teacher whom they had read about so often in Hearst newspapers.[2]

As is frequently the case with amateur productions, the show was late.
By 8:15 nobody had claimed the stage. Twelve straight-backed chairs va-
cantly greeted the audience. A small boy peeped from the wings and
withdrew his head. A big woman in a coat and hat came out briefly and
beat a retreat. The crowd began to fidget and stir. A playful member of
the audience earned a few laughs when he stood and offered to sing.
Finally, a man came from backstage and set up a microphone near the
footlights.

The large woman reappeared with another man and two girls in tow.

She was Louise Gross, head of the Women's Moderation Union, a group that had successfully lobbied for the repeal of Prohibition. Gross explained that the purpose of the gathering was to raise money to defend Edith, otherwise known, she said, "as the Trail of the Lonesome Pine Girl." She then turned to introduce her companions, Earl Maxwell and his sisters, Anna Ruth, sixteen, and Mary Katherine, twelve.

The Maxwells sat quietly in the hard-backed chairs for the next ninety minutes as a variety show unfolded before them. A dozen or more children—ranging from toddlers to teenagers—danced, sang, and did imitations. Then Nick Kenny, radio editor for the *Mirror,* recited poetry and sang original compositions such as "Love Letters in the Sand" while his brother played the violin. The musical portion of the rally ended with the whole crowd joining in a rousing popular song, "The Trail of the Lonesome Pine."

Then it was little Mary Katherine's turn to perform. Although she told the *New York Times* she had never "spoken before strangers" except at Edith's trial, the thin, blond youngster stood before the microphone with Gross and flawlessly repeated her half of a rehearsed conversation.[3]

"How do you like New York?" Gross asked the child.

"Fine," answered Mary Katherine.

"Did you see your sister in the jail before you left home?"

"Yes," said Mary Katherine. "She wants me to bring her back a purse, a pair of gloves, and a watch."

"Have you seen the Statue of Liberty?

"Yes, I have," the little girl said gravely. "She looked very hopeful and I hope she brings freedom to my sister."

Her final line delivered, Mary Katherine left the stage. Anna Ruth did not speak to the crowd. Being the shyer of the two girls, and having been away from home on the night of the tragedy, she was destined to remain mostly out of the limelight. She merely curtsied to the audience and made her way off-stage behind Mary Katherine.

Earl stepped to the microphone next. The thirty-one-year-old salesman evidently felt at home before this friendly crowd in his adopted city. No trace of a mountain accent lingered in his voice as he told the by-now-familiar story of how Edith had been attacked by her father and seized the only weapon at hand, a shoe.

While petitions destined for Virginia authorities circulated through the crowd, Earl talked about recent developments in Edith's case. He said that the defense was trying to establish that Trigg had died of apoplexy rather than the blows from the slipper. His efforts to exhume his father's body, now seven months in the grave, thus far had been blocked in Wise County. "Let him rest in peace," Earl had been told bluntly by one unnamed official. The meeting ended with a plea for funds to help the Maxwells. Although the total amount raised is unknown, it is likely that the New York audience opened their wallets as well as their hearts to the Maxwells' stirring appeal.

James Thurber, *The New Yorker* columnist who reveled in digging up true-crime stories, was in the crowd that night. Thurber was finding it maddeningly difficult to learn the facts of the case because a trial transcript was not available to the New York media, and the Hearst newspaper accounts were dubious at best. "One of the most interesting trials since the Scopes case was left largely in the hands of the sob sisters and brothers," he would later lament.

But the columnist walked away from the meeting clearly swayed by Earl's story. "One can only reconstruct the scene [in Wise County] from the saner news stories, such as they are, and from Earl Maxwell's admittedly biased but nevertheless calm and convincing recital," Thurber wrote. "He impressed his audience with a quiet and straightforward account of his mother's and Edith's and Mary Cathryn's version (they're all one) of the night his father died, a night on which occurred what has been variously been described as 'just another sordid murder' and 'one of the worst miscarriages of justice in the proud history of Virginia.'" Regrettably, Thurber's three-page *New Yorker* article on February 29 would be his only published word on the case. The gifted reporter would leave it to other journalists, in other places and times, to fully comb through what he called "the tangle of mountain family life, custom, prejudice and pride" that bound up the Maxwell story.

On March 9, 1936, defense attorney Alfred A. Skeen was back in court, once again holding the leather slipper he had displayed to the jury at Wise the previous November. This time he was in Richmond, passing the shoe to members of the Virginia Supreme Court. In his youth, Skeen had belonged to a debating society in a remote backwoods community called Middle of the World, where he and his fellow students would eagerly walk eight or ten miles for the chance to outshine an opponent at the finer points of rhetoric. Now, half a century later, the veteran attorney was calling on those youthful gifts of persuasion to convince the justices to review Edith's case.

Unlike the packed Wise County courtroom where Skeen had labored earlier, the hearing before the justices took place in a conference room with only a few spectators present. Edith remained in jail. M. J. Fulton and Charles Henry Smith both attended, but Skeen—one of the original trial lawyers—was the only member of the defense team to address the court. Although the constitutional arguments so dear to the Woman's Party were part of the defense petition, Skeen made little mention of them in his thirty-minute argument. Instead, the Dickenson County lawyer contended that Circuit Court Judge Henry Alexander Wise Skeen had improperly instructed the Wise County jury by failing to mention second-degree murder and manslaughter as possible verdicts. The defense could have asked the court to include these instructions but did not do so, Alfred Skeen said, because it "would have forced abandonment of our plea of self-defense."[4]

Skeen next turned to what he called "the one vital point" of his argument—insufficiency of evidence. In his view, the commonwealth had failed to prove beyond a reasonable doubt that Edith intended to kill her father or that the blows she had wielded resulted in his death. He relied on Ann Maxwell's shoe to bolster his argument. Skeen had to admit that it had not been kept securely in a chain of evidence—and had, in fact, been worn for several days after Trigg's death. Such wear and tear could have obliterated any traces of blood on the shoe's heel, had they been present in the first place.[5] Even so, the defense attorney argued that the slipper was a most unlikely choice of weapon for premeditated murder, noting that a hatchet was kept just outside the Maxwell's kitchen on the porch. (Ironically, had commonwealth attorney Fred Greear been in court he would have agreed completely with the defense attorney on this point. He did not believe the shoe had been used.)

"I am not unmindful of the weight which attaches to the verdict of a jury upheld by a court," Skeen said, "but when this court has considered this record, it will be at a loss to account for the returning of a verdict of first-degree murder, and it will be equally surprised how a jury could find against this girl for anything."

The defense attorney also acknowledged that time was running out for his client, who had been granted a sixty-day reprieve from her impending prison sentence on January 16, 1936. Just a week remained to win a new trial. Skeen told the court that the defense's slowness in filing the appeal papers had been due "to circumstances beyond our control." Just what those circumstances were remains a mystery, yet expectations for the new, citified defense team were very high. If Edith lost there would be plenty of blame to go around.

The justices took just nine days to act on Skeen's request. On March 18—two days after the actual prison deadline—the Virginia Supreme Court of Appeals granted a writ of error, formally expressing its intention to review the case. The *Roanoke Times* voiced its approval in a March 19 editorial:

> In view of the widespread hue and cry over the verdict in the Maxwell case, and the quite unnecessary clamor raised by persons who in most instances know nothing of the case except incorrect reports of the trial carried in sensational newspapers published hundreds of miles distant, there will be very general satisfaction among the people of Virginia that the highest tribunal of the State has been able to see its way to review the case. No one wishes to see this young woman martyred to local prejudices and on the other hand no one wishes to see the ends of justice thwarted and set at naught.
>
> All that Miss Maxwell or her lawyers have a right to ask is justice at the hands of the law. This they are now assured of receiving.

Emboldened by victory, the defense team decided to press for Edith's release on bond. Earl Maxwell quickly filed an application for bail with the Wise County court. Judge Skeen, however, remained adamantly opposed, telling bail commissioner J. M. McLemore that he never permitted the release of anyone convicted of first-degree murder. McLemore denied the application on March 24.

The defense tried again a month later. This time Edith was represented by her cousin, Allen Thurman Dotson, a Richmond attorney who was the son of her uncle Gernade. On April 24—Edith's twenty-second birthday—she appeared in Wise County Circuit Court to request bail. The commonwealth offered no evidence opposing Dotson's motion, but Judge Skeen, citing his long-established policy, ruled against it. The only good news for the defense that day was that Ann's trial was postponed, which allowed the Maxwells' lawyers to concentrate their resources on Edith's appeal.

Smith, Fulton, and Dotson then turned to the Virginia Supreme Court on the bail question. In briefs filed with the court they noted that state law gives the trial judge discretion in releasing prisoners during the course of an appeal. They also argued that Judge Skeen, by his blanket policy, had ruled in an arbitrary fashion. Although the supreme court apparently was in recess, Edith's lawyers were able to convince Justice E. W. Hudgins to issue a writ of error on the bail issue on May 7.[6] The entire court would hear arguments on the motions for a new trial and for release on bail during its June 1936 term at Wytheville.

⸻

On July 21, 1936, Edith observed the passing of her first year in the Wise County Jail. Home, she told a reporter, now seemed like "a dream."[7] Edith was in the custody of the new sheriff, Clyde Bolling, a Democrat from Pound who had taken office on January 1. Other than court appearances, she had been out of the jail twice in 1936—once to have a tooth pulled at the dentist and once to get a permanent.[8] She recalled, with perhaps a trace of amusement, that Bolling himself guarded her at the beauty shop and had to wait three or four hours while she had her hair done.

Waiting was an exercise in which Edith herself was becoming well schooled. Arguments before the Virginia Supreme Court had taken place as expected in early June, with M. J. Fulton and Charles Henry Smith pleading for the defendant and Attorney General A. P. Staples representing the commonwealth. A decision, however, was not likely until September at the earliest—possibly not until the March 1937 term of the high court. In the meantime, the prosecution of Edith's mother was again delayed, pending the outcome of the daughter's case.

Nothing much was happening on the legal front, but Edith's living quarters, which she jokingly referred to as her "apartment," had been improved. Upon taking office, one of Sheriff Bolling's first actions had been to move women prisoners out of the basement and into cells on the first floor. Renovations soon began on the old jail, which had been roundly criticized by visiting journalists for its dilapidated conditions. In early August, authorities transferred Edith and the other women prisoners to Jonesville, forty miles from Wise, to wait out the remodeling.

Jonesville was the seat of Lee County, Wise County's older and tamer neighbor to the southwest. Named for Henry "Lighthorse Harry" Lee—a Virginia governor and father of the revered Robert E. Lee—the county was formed in 1792. More than sixty years later it gave up a chunk of land to be included in the new county of Wise. In rugged Wise, farming was largely confined to ribbons of bottomland or high mountain tableland, but Lee County's gentler terrain naturally lent itself to widespread agriculture. The broad expanse of the Powell River Valley that fanned out westward toward Cumberland Gap—the route followed 170 years earlier by Daniel Boone—sustained a placid mixture of tobacco and cattle farms framed against the spectacular Cumberland Mountains.

Midway down the valley sat Jonesville, a town of four hundred dominated by an almost-brand-new courthouse of buff brick. A hotel, bank, and several general stores made up a tiny business district. The jail sat back behind the courthouse. Here Edith was placed in the custody of Sheriff R. F. Giles. Displaying the prejudiced attitudes of the times, the *Washington Post* noted regretfully that Edith was forced to share a cell block with a "thief," a "drunkard," and "an epileptic awaiting transfer to an asylum," but she continued to receive the extra privileges she enjoyed at Wise. In her cell was an electric percolator, hot plate, and toaster with which she prepared snacks to supplement the two daily meals the jailer provided. Edith stocked her "kitchen" with coffee, eggs, ham, and bread—paid for by well-wishers who sent money.

Unlike her relatively cloistered existence in Wise, Edith's sojourn at the Lee County Jail was enlivened by a steady stream of visitors and autograph seekers—usually about eighty a day but peaking one day at two hundred. Sheriff Giles once took a group of schoolchildren on a tour of the jail, cautioning them beforehand not to stare at Edith as they filed past.[9] According to the *Washington Post*, "They come here in droves almost as great as those which flock to Canada to see the Dionne quintuplets."[10] Admirers who could not travel to Jonesville wrote to Edith or sent telegrams and gifts.

All these distractions likely had begun to pall as the goldenrod touched the fields with the first signs of autumn. By early September, the Virginia Supreme Court still had not issued a ruling on Edith's motion for a new trial, although word filtered down that a decision was near. Edith spent the evening of Friday, September 11, nervously pacing about her cell.

On Saturday morning, justice of the peace W. B. Merriman hurried over to Edith's cell to tell her that the court had reached a decision. Perhaps it was too early for the usual throng of visitors, for he found her quietly staring out the window. Bars of sunlight divided and reformed on the cell floor as her eyes searched out the distant rim of the Cumberlands. A prison pallor had settled on her face during her one year and fifty-one days in jail. The melancholy tableau, however, was quickly shattered by Merriman's news. The justices had overturned her first-degree murder conviction and ordered a new trial on a five-to-two vote. "I certainly am happy. I certainly am happy," Edith kept telling Merriman over and over.[11]

Once the shock had begun to subside, Edith's first question to the Lee County authorities was, "How much longer will I have to stay here?" Although the appellate court had awarded her a new trial, it declined to order her release on bail. The justices said the issue was now moot. The case would be remanded to Judge Skeen's court, where he would have another chance to rule on the bail question under different circumstances. Edith was no longer a convicted murderer but, once again, a defendant presumed to be innocent. Her supporters sensed that freedom—or at least a respite from jail—was just around the corner.

As the day—unlike so many others—unfolded quickly, Edith was allowed to take telephone calls from the news media. She told a reporter that she couldn't wait to phone her mother in Pound. "I hope I will be the first to give her the news," Edith said.[12] She did eventually reach Ann, who was reported to be "tickled to death" by her daughter's good fortune.

Meanwhile, in Richmond and Alexandria, defense attorneys M. J. Fulton and Charles Henry Smith were preparing to travel to southwest Virginia to secure Edith's release on bond. Earl Maxwell, back in New York City, was likewise getting ready for the trip south. The *Roanoke Times* reported on September 15 that Edith was "upbeat" and expecting the arrival of her attorneys and brother the following week. Over the weekend she hovered near the cell door, listening to radio news broadcasts describing her victory. According to the *Times*, "Visitors continued to enter the jail by the score" while courthouse watchers eagerly debated the likelihood of Edith's new trial being moved to Lee County. Like Sisyphus, the legendary king of Corinth, the defense attorneys had been pushing a stone up a hill since November 1935, only to watch it roll down again. Now, it seemed that gravity had shifted in their favor.

———

The reversal of Edith's conviction by the Virginia Supreme Court did *not* depend on any of the defense's ambitious constitutional challenges, which the court curtly termed "without merit."[13] Neither were the justices interested in newly discovered evidence, which the commonwealth insisted could have been ascertained *before* the November 1935 trial. Instead, it turned out that Alfred Skeen's instincts had been correct. What he called "the vital point" of his argument—insufficiency of evidence—was exactly the issue the court had cited in overturning the verdict.

Writing for the majority, Justice John W. Eggleston noted that except for the question of whether Trigg was drunk, the evidence of the commonwealth and the defense was basically in agreement. Yet prosecutors believed that the defendant had fashioned a false story to fit the facts. "The Commonwealth lays great stress on certain additional circumstances as showing that the testimony of Mrs. Maxwell and her two daughters was unworthy of belief and as demonstrating that the accused was guilty of first degree murder."

As the majority of the court interpreted the evidence, though, they did not believe that Edith had actively plotted to kill her father. In their opinion, the threats she had made against Trigg were uttered in the heat of an argument or even sometimes made as gestures of bravado in front of friends. Analyzing the father-daughter relationship, Eggleston wrote:

> There is testimony that the father had frequently reprimanded her for what he considered to be her improper conduct in staying out late at night with men. At times he even threatened to whip her for such acts. All of this she resented, and not entirely without cause since the evidence does not disclose she was guilty of any more reprehensible conduct than keeping late hours with young men. When these occasions arose the accused undoubtedly, as the evidence shows, assumed a defiant attitude toward her father and even gave vent to her feelings in what may be termed wild and unguarded remarks. But the chances are that such were soon forgotten by both the accused and her father.

Eggleston also addressed the commonwealth's contention that it was "highly improbable" that Trigg's head wounds were caused by the heel of a shoe. Despite the prosecutors' insinuation that a heavier weapon had been used and possibly thrown into the river behind the Maxwells' home, they had not been able to prove it. "Except for the nature and extent of the fatal wound itself there is not ground for these suggestions," wrote Eggleston. "No other weapon of any kind was in any way connected with the killing. No hammer or hatchet was found. The smoothing iron was in evidence at the trial and bore no marks of suspicion." Evidently, the justices did not believe the rusty substance on the iron was really blood. Further, the commonwealth's own medical evidence did not rule out the shoe as the weapon.

Nonetheless, Eggleston continued, the commonwealth *had* proved that the blows Edith struck did cause Trigg Maxwell's death. This happened either in the way she said it did or "in some other way which is unexplained." He noted that the question of whether the homicide was justified was properly a question for the jury—and that the jurors had not believed Edith's story of self-defense. But, said Eggleston, "If there is reasonable doubt as to whether the accused is guilty of murder in the first or second degree, that doubt must be resolved in her favor." Thus the jury did not have the right to find her guilty of "willful, deliberate and premeditated killing" because of the insufficiency of the evidence.

In a thoughtful editorial on the Virginia Supreme Court decision, the *Coalfield Progress* on September 17 tried to discern what may have been going on the jurors' minds when they cast their votes for first-degree murder. Although admitting that he had not interviewed the twelve men, the editorial writer (presumably Pres Atkins) said that once the jurors decided Edith was guilty, they probably gave little thought to the degree of homicide. The jury did, however, have some leeway in sentencing. The editorial speculated that the men, in deciding upon twenty-five years, probably believed that "under the Virginia practice [she] would not serve more than half of the time fixed by verdict"—an effective sentence of twelve and a half years.

The Wise County jury's verdict was endorsed by the two justices of the Virginia Supreme Court who had issued a vigorous dissent. Henry W. Holt, joined by Preston W. Campbell, disagreed with the majority's conclusion that premeditated murder had not been proven. Citing the many threats Edith had made against Trigg, Justice Holt argued, "Plainly the jury had ample reason to believe that Edith disliked her father and resented his attempts to control her."

Holt also believed that the "meat block" episode was invented to cover up a murder. "Upon reflection, the accused reached the conclusion that her first account of her father's death put an undue strain upon credulity. One could not seriously ask a jury to believe that a trail of blood from the kitchen to the porch and body wounds in divers [*sic*] places were the results of stumbling against a meat block, and so this story manifestly false has been abandoned in toto. Not only was it false, but it was a product of a conference between mother and daughter, who proceeded to drill this made-up story into the young sister." The trial, Holt added, was "no backwoods inquisition" but a fair proceeding in which Edith had been represented by "eminently competent" counsel.

Even though the justices' decision had not been unanimous—and did nothing whatsoever to put women on the next jury—the ruling was widely regarded as a vindication for Edith and her supporters in the East. The *Washington Post* ran a triple-decker, front-page headline proclaiming the Virginia Supreme Court action and reprinted the entire text of the majority opinion. Not only was it a victory for Edith, said the newspaper, but "it was also a victory for *The Washington Post* and hundreds of its subscribers, who sent money, more than $1,000 in all, to the Edith Maxwell Defense Fund."

The September 17 *Coalfield Progress* editorial, however, declared the justices' decision a triumph for the process of law—*despite*, rather than *because of*—the "outside" press:

> Wise County does not begrudge Edith Maxwell a new trial. Its only hope is that it may conduct the trial in due time, in the usual manner, without volunteer assistance of any of the lurid "gentlemen of the press," who

flooded the county immediately preceding, during and after the former trial, with so much "color" that it befogged the issue and maligned an entire community. . . . Nor do we believe that this fanfare of publicity has helped her one bit in securing for her a new trial. The Virginia courts, in their regular routine, have taken up and passed on the case exactly the same as they have handled thousands of others.

Whether the powers of "the East" were responsible or not, the young schoolteacher and her lawyers now would have another chance to persuade a jury of her innocence. Charles Henry Smith told reporters that he expected the case to come to trial within two months. But no sooner had the retrial been won than Edith's champions found a new locus of worry.

"Ahead of her is another trial," observed the *Post* on September 13. "Will it, like the first one, be held in Wise, where the people dislike her? That is up to the court which, in sentencing her to twenty-five years, caused men and women in thirteen foreign countries and forty-eight states to take up their pens in protest."

Any motion for a change of venue would have to come before Judge Henry Alexander Wise Skeen. Whether he would want to keep the world-famous case in Wise or be shut of it was a question on which even the pundits dared not place their bets.

16   *"A Change of Scenery"*

On the afternoon of September 19, 1936, Edith Maxwell stood outside the Wise County Courthouse with her lawyer, seemingly bewildered by her first minutes of freedom after fourteen months in jail.[1] She compulsively glanced over her shoulder and twisted her felt hat aimlessly in her hands.

"What are you looking for?" Charles Henry Smith finally asked.

"I was looking for the law," Edith responded. "I just can't get used to the idea that they're gone."

Events had moved with surprising speed since the Virginia Supreme Court decided eight days earlier to overturn her first-degree murder conviction and grant a new trial. The justices had tossed the question of bail squarely back in Judge Henry Alexander Wise Skeen's court, and Edith's defense team lost no time in pressing for her release. A bond hearing had been hastily scheduled for the morning of September 19 at Judge Skeen's house in Big Stone Gap. In the meantime, rumors circulating through the courthouse suggested that Robert P. Bruce and Alfred A. Skeen, two of the three original defense attorneys, were no longer associated with the case. Bruce and Skeen made no public comment, but they apparently had nothing to do with the bond hearing about to take place on their home turf.

Perhaps smarting from his loss in state court, commonwealth attorney Fred Greear said it "made no difference" to him whether Edith got bail.[2] He did not appear at the hearing in Big Stone Gap, and Edith, still incarcerated in Jonesville, likewise did not attend. Judge Skeen, acting on a motion from defense attorney A. T. Dotson, readily agreed to release Edith on bond. Even though it was a Saturday, the judge drove to Wise immediately to take care of the paperwork. Two other defense attorneys, Smith and M. J. Fulton, were reportedly en route from Bristol when the 10 A.M. hearing took place.

Wise County deputy sheriff Pat H. Kennedy was dispatched to pick up the celebrity prisoner at the Lee County Jail, where his arrival caused quite a stir. Newspapers had been predicting Edith's release, but for some reason she seemed as surprised as anyone else that the hour was finally upon her. Edith hastily packed her belongings for the return trip to Wise while her cellmates took turns hugging her and wishing her well.

No sooner had Edith left the jail than she rushed back in as if she had forgotten something. She returned carrying a canary in a cage. The singing inhabitant, named Bing Crosby, was a gift from a man in Connecticut. "Edith, feeling pretty much like an uncaged bird herself, toyed with the idea of giving the canary his freedom," reported the *Washington Post.* "Reminded, however, that the bird was essentially a pet and might perish if freed, she abandoned the idea."[3]

Earl was waiting when Edith and Deputy Kennedy drove into Wise on Saturday afternoon, presumably with their twittering companion. Smith and Fulton had by now arrived, finally catching up with their fast-moving case. Brother and sister embraced and then trailed the lawyers into the courthouse. Judge Skeen set bond at $6,000, the same amount he had fixed at the time of Edith's arrest in July 1935. Edith's lawyer-cousin, A. T. Dotson, and Dotson's father-in-law, M. B. Taylor of Norton, pledged their real estate as security. Once formalities were over, Judge Skeen told Edith, "You are free, young lady. Your new trial will start November 16."[4]

When Edith, Earl, and Charles Henry Smith emerged from the courthouse they were accompanied by a crack reporter from the *Washington Post*. Thirty-seven-year-old Edward T. Folliard—destined to win the Pulitzer Prize in 1947—was a veteran journalist who had witnessed many of the major events of his time, such as the arrival of "Lucky Lindy" from Paris in 1927 and, nearly a decade later, the execution of Bruno Richard Hauptmann. The tall, lanky reporter had come to southwest Virginia to cover breaking developments in the case of yet another of America's most famous prisoners.

As Edith stood with the three men in front of the courthouse, scarcely able to comprehend the absence of the jailers, a friend asked her to walk to the drugstore for a chocolate soda. Edith accepted with a flash of humor and perhaps defiance. "I sure am glad to go," she said with a smile, "and happy that I don't have to ask the law for permission."[5]

Once the celebratory soda was finished, Edith (probably accompanied by Earl) struck out for her emotional "true north." Sometime in the afternoon she arrived at her mother's house in Pound—the same quarters where Trigg had died and from which she had been hauled off to jail some fifteen months before.

Ann's eyes welled with tears when Edith walked in. "Oh, my baby," she cried, wrapping her arms around her daughter's slender frame. "Mummy," Edith replied. Virtually nothing else was recorded of the reunion, but they probably talked excitedly of moving with Anna Ruth and Mary Katherine to the Richmond area, where the family planned to live while awaiting the next trial. After an hour Edith took her leave, saying she was "going away with Earl to get a rest."[6] Time and distance had done nothing to loosen the extraordinary bond between Edith and her mother. If anything, their shared troubles had only cemented their devotion.

⸺

Edith's release from jail had been accomplished with surprisingly little fanfare, probably because Judge Skeen's order had been carried out so quickly—and on a weekend, when the courthouse was virtually empty. The quiet, though, would not last long. When Edith, Earl, Smith, and Folliard stopped at the Liberty Cafe in Norton for dinner on Saturday evening, Edith began to learn firsthand what it means to be famous.

Word had gotten out that she was in town. A curious crowd gathered around the Liberty, hoping for a glimpse of "the girl who killed her daddy." According to Folliard's eyewitness account, "Not all of those who stared meant to be rude. A number of them came forward to offer a friendly hand and wish her well."[7] Edith said she didn't mind the attention, but her appetite quickly disappeared. As the crowd continued to swell, police were called in to clear the sidewalk and protect the glass windows at the front of the cafe.

This episode no doubt reinforced Edith's intention to stay hundreds of miles away from Wise County until her new trial, which was two months away. Newspaper accounts suggest that she and Earl, accompanied by Smith and probably Folliard, either flew or took an overnight train to the East Coast soon after the chaotic dinner at the Liberty Cafe. On Sunday, September 20—her first full day of freedom—Edith went on a sightseeing tour of Washington, D.C., following Smith's advice to get "a change of scenery."[8] Twenty-two-year-old Edith caught her first glimpse of the White House, Capitol Hill, and other landmarks before taking in a downtown movie—a pastime she bitterly had been forced to forego after the hearing before Judge Skeen in January 1936. The *Washington Post* gave front-page coverage to her arrival and ran her picture on page 12, noting without a trace of irony that "her greatest thrill came from being able to move about the city without being stared at."[9]

Newspapers continued to have access to Edith but apparently agreed to keep her exact whereabouts a secret. After touring Washington, she visited some friends in nearby northern Virginia, but their names were not reported. The following Thursday, September 24, her photograph appeared on the front page of the *Richmond News Leader* under the headline "Edith Maxwell at Farm Near Here Begs Quiet." The owner of the farm, which was said to be in Henrico County, was merely identified as "an older woman."[10] Edith herself looked the part of a lovely yet unlikely milkmaid as she sat holding a bucket under the udder of a cow and glancing back over her shoulder toward the camera. She wore a light-colored dress and a pair of high-heeled, t-strap shoes not so unlike those that were displayed in court as a defense exhibit. As if to emphasize her desire for privacy, a second headline under the photograph advised "Confident of Acquittal, Wants to Be Free of Prying Eyes while Awaiting Trial."

———

By mid-October, Earl had installed his mother and sisters on a forty-five-acre farm in neighboring Chesterfield County, about nine miles from Richmond. The farm, situated in the Drewrys Bluff community, reportedly belonged to Edith's first cousin, A. T. Dotson, although there is some mystery about the actual ownership.[11] The *News Leader* said the family had left Pound "bag and baggage," taking their furniture with them, and was expecting "to make their home permanently" in Chesterfield County.[12]

Later that month, Edward T. Folliard came down from the *Washington*

Post to document the Maxwells' daily activities as tenant farmers. The resulting feature stories—accompanied by striking photographs of Edith and her sisters—were printed in the *Post* alongside renewed appeals for Edith's defense fund. The newspaper implored readers to send in another $1,000 for the next trial, explaining that although Charles Henry Smith was donating his services the money was needed to interview witnesses, pay their expenses, and obtain medical depositions and court transcripts.

Folliard found Edith living in a "comparative heaven," having been reunited with her family. Edith, Ann, and Earl tended the farm while Anna Ruth, sixteen, and Mary Katherine, thirteen, made a fresh start at nearby Chester High School.[13] Earl—with the assistance of two black field hands—was preparing a ten-acre section of ground for planting winter wheat. Edith's chores included milking two cows, harvesting tomatoes, feeding a pig and some Plymouth Rock chickens, and helping her mother with the housework and cooking.

In Folliard's estimation, Edith "looked neither like a school teacher nor a killer" as she went about her chores in a pair of blue pants and an old coat. The sunshine of Chesterfield County had chased away her prison pallor, adding a smattering of freckles across her nose. She was also said to be regaining some of the weight she had lost during her long confinement.

It is not known whether Edith enjoyed any kind of social life during this period. According to Folliard, the former teacher spent many evenings helping Anna Ruth and Mary Katherine with their homework. He reported on October 21 that the Maxwells "go to bed at an hour when Washington is heading for F street and the movies, and they are up with the cock's crow."

The photographs and dispatches from Chesterfield County paint a picture of tranquility and refuge: the Maxwell teenagers gathering hickory nuts in the autumn leaves or frolicking with puppies born to Spot, the rat terrier, and a boyish-looking Edith waving gaily from the bed of a haywagon. The idyll, however, could only have been bittersweet. The Maxwells, after all, were not simple farmers. They were complex people caught up in a web of history and—some might have said by now—more than a little self-invention.

Life on this sunny farm was clouded by inevitable thoughts of the upcoming trial. The question uppermost in the Maxwells' minds was where the proceeding would be held. Even though the *Post* reported that there had been a "noticeable change of attitude" toward Edith in Wise County since the Virginia Supreme Court decision, they knew Smith was planning to push hard for a change of venue—perhaps to Jonesville—while Greear was equally opposed to moving the trial. When the prospects of a second trial in Wise were mentioned, a look of fear invariably would cross Edith's face.

———

For reasons never quite explained, defense attorneys Alfred Skeen and Robert Bruce had dropped out—or had been nudged out—of the Maxwell case in the spring or summer of 1936. Charles Henry Smith, the lawyer for the *Washington Post,* had by now emerged as Edith's principal attorney, although M. J. Fulton of the Woman's Party was still an active participant. A. T. Dotson, the Richmond attorney who had helped engineer his cousin's release on bond, was also helping prepare for the retrial. And Gail Laughlin was planning to come down from Maine, determined as ever to make history with the Maxwell case. Edith's uncle Gernade Dotson, the third original counsel, was still associated with the defense but only in an advisory role. The out-of-town lawyers would largely be on their own with a mountain jury.

Edith's attorneys undoubtedly were aware of Fred Greear's uncanny ability to endear himself to each and every member of a jury. He seldom needed to conduct voir dire—the questioning of potential jurors—during jury selection. Thanks to his vigorous door-to-door campaigning and excellent recall, he already knew what church they belonged to, what their likes and dislikes were, and whether any black sheep were in their families.

Of course, it could be argued that Gernade Dotson, who had practiced law in Wise since before Greear was born, could provide similar intelligence for the defense. But Greear, the master orator, would be talking directly to the jury while Dotson would not. Edith's lawyers probably hoped that changing the location of the trial would strip Greear of his built-in familiarity with the jurors—and perhaps offer up a venire, or jury pool, more sympathetic to the defense. First, though, they would have to convince Judge Skeen to move the proceedings. If that failed, they might even ask for a jury to be brought into the county.

Smith, Fulton, and A. T. Dotson appeared in Wise County Circuit Court on Saturday, November 7, ostensibly to argue the change-of-venue motion. Edith remained on the farm. Perhaps fearful that Judge Skeen would rule against them, they now planned to drop what one wag called "a loudly detonating bomb" into the Maxwell case.[14] Unbeknown to the judge, Edith's lawyers had been conducting a thorough search of his family tree. Now, with just nine days left to go before trial, the defense presented him with the startling fruits of its discovery. The judge was a distant cousin of Trigg and Edith Maxwell.

Judge Skeen's grandfather, John Skeen, had been a brother to Trigg Maxwell's great-great-grandfather, Stephen Skeen. The brothers both had lived in the East Stone Gap community in pioneer days, but their lineages had spread out over much of Wise County during the nineteenth century. As the *Coalfield Progress* put it, "Little did he [Judge Skeen] suspect that Trigg Maxwell's mother, before her marriage, was the granddaughter of his grandfather's brother."[15]

Upon receiving the news, the seventy-seven-year-old jurist immediately halted the hearing and removed himself from the case. Judge Skeen maintained that he could have ruled fairly on the motion but said that he was bowing out to avoid any appearance of a conflict of interest. As he had a wide circle of relatives in the county, it seems doubtful that this distant kinship would have in any way affected his impartiality. This surprising exercise in genealogy did, however, bring about the desired result for the defense. A new judge would have to be appointed, one who might prove more amenable to their desires.

The *Coalfield Progress* sympathized with Judge Skeen's sudden dilemma and praised him for promptly disqualifying himself. "Let Edith have her trial under a new judge, in a new county if she insists," said an editorial, "not that she could not have a fair trial in Wise county, as fair as in any county, but because the case has attracted such national attention that Virginia's court administration, Virginia's determination to do justice, is at stake now, even more than Edith's guilt or innocence."[16]

No sooner had a copy of Judge Skeen's decision hit Gov. George C. Peery's desk than the governor named his replacement. Six-foot-four-inch Ezra T. Carter, described by the Associated Press as a "towering, kind-faced jurist," was handed the reins of the Maxwell case on November 9.[17] Carter, sixty, was in many ways a logical choice, having presided since 1922 over the Twenty-fourth Judicial Circuit that covered neighboring Lee and Scott counties. He was a native of the Scott County town of Rye Cove, which the Carter Family musical trio had chronicled in a folk song about a devastating cyclone that struck the village school in 1929. Carter had studied law at the College of William and Mary in Williamsburg, Virginia, and had been a member of the Scott County bar since 1906.

With his white hair and patrician features, Carter epitomized the southern gentleman. A person of great warmth, he was known throughout the southwestern corner of the state for his sense of humor and love of conversation. In Jonesville in 1933, his judicial decorum was severely tested when the commonwealth attorney interrupted a breaking and entering case to announce, "Your honor, the courthouse seems to be on fire!" The blaze, which had started in the cupola, consumed the Lee County courthouse, but everyone escaped and most of the records were saved.[18]

Judge Carter's fourteen-year record on the circuit court bench earned him the reputation of seldom being reversed by a higher court. He had imposed the death sentence only once, in the case of a convict who was electrocuted for killing a Scott County prison camp guard. Although the commonwealth was not asking for the death penalty in the Maxwell case, some court observers saw this fact as evidence that Carter was certainly not a "hanging judge." His appointment brought generally favorable reviews.

Carter got word of his new assignment while presiding over the fall term of circuit court at Jonesville. He obligingly offered to postpone his regular cases to hear the Maxwell change of venue motion, which had been in limbo since his diminutive predecessor had abruptly departed the case. Yet the change of judges meant an inevitable delay in the start of the next trial. Edith, still in Chesterfield County, would have a few extra days of freedom.

—

Linked arm-in-arm with her brother Earl, Edith appeared at the Wise County Courthouse on the morning of November 23, smartly outfitted in a maroon dress topped by a grey cloth coat and accented by a black hat and matching slippers. Although the skies were dull and foreboding, perhaps the two had just walked the short distance from Uncle Gernade Dotson's house, where Edith had spent the night. They made their way to the now-familiar second-story courtroom, which was only about two-thirds full. One spectator who had claimed a front-row seat was none other than the recently deposed Judge Skeen, who would listen ardently to every word spoken over the next several hours. Taking Skeen's usual place on the high bench was his visiting judicial colleague, Ezra T. Carter. A bailiff solemnly brought the change-of-venue hearing to order at twenty past 9.

In an effort to show that Edith could not receive a fair trial in her home county, defense lawyers Smith, Fulton, and A. T. Dotson presented the court with sixty-nine identical affidavits signed by local residents.[19] Commonwealth attorney Fred Greear and special prosecutor Oscar M.

Vicars, joined at the counsel table by Trigg's brother-in-law, the former sheriff Lee Skeen, had no affidavits but instead had summoned a host of opposing witnesses. Greear objected to the introduction of the statements, saying he thought the court wanted to hear oral testimony. Judge Carter calmly asked Smith to read one of them aloud:

> I am a citizen of Wise, County, Virginia, residing at ____, Virginia, and have been for ____ years; that I am well acquainted with the people living in and around my section, and on frequent occasions I have heard numbers of them discussing the case of the Commonwealth vs. Edith Maxwell, both before and after her trial, and it is my opinion, based on these discussions, and on the scurrilous and slanderous statements published by the press and magazines about the habits, manners and customs of the people of Wise County that the minds of the people of my section have become prejudiced and inflamed against Edith Maxwell to such an extent that it would be impossible for her to have a fair and impartial trial at their hands.[20]

Carter responded that he would like to hear testimony from the people who had signed the affidavits. He declared a recess so Smith could round up some witnesses. When court resumed, the defense called seven men who had widespread contact with the public and had heard numerous discussions of the Maxwell case.

Smith quickly elicited testimony that most people in Wise County held opinions about Edith Maxwell, some believing her guilty and others convinced of her innocence. John Fisher, an ice-cream salesman, testified that it would be impossible to find a local jury that had not formed an opinion about the case. Fisher's sentiments were echoed by Henry Cantrell, a middle-aged farmer who had been one of Trigg's neighbors. Cantrell said he had heard "quite a bit of talk" about the Maxwell case over the past year and a half and that it would be "pretty hard to find a large number [of potential jurors] but what had expressed their opinion in some way."

Defense witnesses also testified about the impact of the negative press coverage of Wise County by newspapers far distant. The men unanimously agreed that the sensationalism and ridicule had offended many people in the community. Smith tried to present evidence that the resentment had extended to his client as well as to the press, but the responses from his own witnesses were sometimes contradictory.

G. D. Jenkins, a local photographer hired by the Hearst organization to shoot pictures at the first trial, agreed with Smith that there could be "unconscious resentment" against Edith as a result of the articles. Other defense witnesses, however, maintained that the ill feeling was *not* directed against her. "I heard more talk against the reporters than against Edith," said Henry Cantrell on cross-examination.

The defense saved its most powerful witness—former sheriff Preston Adams—until last. Adams testified about the overt hostility he had encountered in July 1935 during his ill-fated attempt to escort Edith to her father's funeral. A group of strangers, apparently union miners who had worked with Trigg in Kentucky, had approached his car in a threatening manner and demanded that he take Edith away. (Also among the group of hecklers, Adams later learned, were a brother and sister of Trigg Maxwell.) The sheriff had stepped out of the car and warned his opponents to leave.

"If nothing else is going to do and you are going to give trouble, you may as well begin here," Adams recalled telling the miners. "You are not going to put your hand on the girl, or on me or on the car, or somebody is going to get hurt." The hecklers backed down from the confrontation, but Adams decided to return Edith to jail anyway because "it looked at the time like we might have trouble."

On cross-examination, Greear tried to soften the impact of Adams's testimony by noting that the funeral was fifteen or sixteen months past and suggesting that Edith had recently visited Pound without incident after being granted bond. When Greear asked if he knew of anything that would prevent Edith from having a fair trial in Wise County, Adams carefully replied, "I couldn't make any statement for or against that. I don't know."

Smith rested his case when Adams left the stand. The defense attorney had shown that many people held fixed opinions as to Edith's guilt or innocence, thereby raising doubts that there would be enough unbiased people from which to draw a jury. The majority of Smith's own witnesses, however, had failed to support the primary allegation stated in the affidavits—that people throughout the county were prejudiced *against* Edith Maxwell.

The prosecution, in turn, produced fifteen witnesses who maintained that Edith could indeed get a fair trial in Wise County. Calling on prominent men from several localities, Greear and Vicars questioned traveling salesmen, merchants, bankers, a Baptist minister, the school board chair, and the editor of the *Big Stone Gap Post*. The men testified almost uniformly that no local prejudice existed toward Edith Maxwell. One said that most of the comments he had heard had been "very favorable" toward her; another said there was "considerable sympathy" for her situation.

Most prosecution witnesses also testified that they had never heard about the threats of mob violence directed toward Edith on the day of her father's funeral. A Norton man told the court that Edith could get an impartial trial because the great majority of the men he knew "would not be party to anything that was not based on absolute fairness."

On cross-examination, Smith and Fulton tried to poke holes in the commonwealth's seemingly impenetrable front. They were able to establish that four of the prosecution witnesses were friendly with, or at least had met, former sheriff Lee Skeen—hardly a damning indictment. On the issue of press coverage, some of those testifying said the Hearst articles had offended local residents, whereas others, such as the newspaper editor, said it was merely amusing "that daily newspapers should be so gullible."

Seven hours into the hearing, Greear completed his evidence. Twenty-two witnesses—all male—had been heard in a single day. Over the course of the afternoon the courtroom had gradually filled up. As the *Washington Post*'s Folliard observed, "There were coal miners present, some with grimy faces. There were old men whose chins frequently fell on their beards as they took cat naps. There were a half dozen women with infants in their arms" (and, he could not resist adding, "cows wandered on the streets outside").[21]

Perhaps the vehement arguments of the attorneys woke the old men from their slumbers. "Everyone in the county has formed a definite opinion about the case," M. J. Fulton declared. "There is deep feeling between both sides of the Maxwell family."[22] He called upon the judge to move the trial to a county where Edith had no kinfolk and where there "may be no feeling as to the rights of parents and children."[23]

Greear countered that widespread discussion of the case by county residents was not grounds to move the trial; the defense attorneys had to prove actual prejudice. In discussing what he termed "erroneous" news reports of the 1935 trial, the commonwealth attorney argued that hostility was directed at the writers of the articles rather than at Edith herself. "I do not know of a county in Virginia where we could secure as fair a trial as right here in Wise County," he said.[24]

By 5 P.M. Judge Carter was ready to bring the long, often monotonous proceeding to an end. Edith sat nervously, twisting a handkerchief as Carter began reviewing the evidence put on by the defense. The most serious, he said, was the threat of violence directed at Edith before her father's funeral. "I think that Sheriff Adams acted with extreme prudence and good judgment, and some little resentment by the deceased's relatives and friends was only to be expected," Carter told the audience, "but this was not a matured prejudice or hostility which, I think, would interfere with her trial." He also discounted the effects of alleged prejudicial publicity, saying that the exaggerated news reports and color stories had little impact in Wise County.[25]

"It's been my experience that we have very few juries in Virginia that we have to fear," Carter continued. "I don't say that juries don't commit errors, nor do I say that courts don't commit errors as long as cases are decided by human instrumentalities. All we can do is to reduce errors to a minimum. But has the defense shown hostility, prejudice and bias which would render a fair and impartial trial impossible?"[26]

Carter decided that the defense had failed to meet the necessary burden of proof to overcome the presumption that "a crime shall be tried in the community where it was committed." He said, "The duty of the court, it seems to me, is clear: to overrule the motion for a change of venue." After conferring with the attorneys he set a trial date of Wednesday, December 9.

The *Coalfield Progress* reported that Edith—surrounded by her brother, her lawyers and a maternal aunt—"accepted the decision gamely," chatting with supporters in the aftermath of the hearing. And despite her attorneys' wails about publicity, before leaving the room she took time to smile and pose once more for the flashing cameras, as if drawing sustenance from each radiant particle of light. Had it not been for press coverage, the *Washington Post* had recently congratulated itself, Edith by now "probably would be nothing but a number in the state penitentiary."[27] Instead, she was a woman walking out the courthouse door, heading for an automobile and the open road that led, in some way yet unfathomable, from her past.

17   *"Roman Holiday"*

To the soothsayers in the National Woman's Party, Judge Ezra T. Carter's refusal to move the trial could only be "an ill omen" for Edith Maxwell. "We deplore the court's decision and are apprehensive of its results, but even the darkest cloud has a silver lining," said a party journal. "Women in ever increasing numbers are coming to Edith Maxwell's defense and if it becomes necessary to carry the case to the Supreme Court of the United States there appears to be hope that the essential support will be forthcoming."[1]

If that day ever came, Gail Laughlin was determined to be ready. By Tuesday, December 8, 1936—the eve of the new trial—the Woman's Party lawyer was back in Wise County, preparing to lay the groundwork for a successful federal appeal. Edith, Ann, Earl, and Mary Katherine had arrived from Richmond the day before and were staying at Uncle Gernade Dotson's house in Wise. On Tuesday night Laughlin met with Edith and members of the Maxwell family in her hotel room, likely at the Colonial Hotel, which was buzzing with out-of-town visitors.

Laughlin was immediately struck by how twenty-two-year-old Edith had changed since their last meeting in January 1936. Although her features were still pleasing, stress had drained any hint of vitality and youthful high spirits from her face. Edith's mother, Laughlin noticed, was in even worse shape, "crazed with the anxiety and suspense."[2]

The Maine lawyer felt a certain pity edged with contempt for Ann Maxwell, whom she thought had a "worn, cowed look" from years of abuse. Perhaps forgetting her own humble beginnings, Laughlin would later tell a reporter that the Maxwells' house was "nothing but a hovel" and "fit only for hogs." In fact, she regarded Ann as typical of a whole generation of mountain women: "Their status is three hundred years behind the times. If they have the privilege of voting they do not know it. They have accepted the community's stand that women are of no account except to do the drudgery and wait upon the menfolks. Husbands and fathers regard the women of their families as much their personal property as they do their animals."

For Ann's children, though, Laughlin had nothing but admiration. She would speak approvingly of Earl's decision to leave home as a teenager and would even repeat the absurd tabloid tale that he had gone against hillbilly custom in 1935 by refusing to kill Edith to avenge his father's death. She saluted Edith's "brains and ambition" and considered little Mary Katherine "as bright and smart a girl as you would find anywhere." But personalities aside, Laughlin was taking the long view. It was not just for her client but for thousands of women yet unborn that she would make her case before Judge Carter and those she regarded as the gawking rubes of Wise County.

As if to compensate for commonwealth attorney Fred Greear's superior knowledge of potential jurors, Edith's lead attorney, Charles Henry Smith, took a tour through the county on Tuesday. He even crossed over into Kentucky, where Trigg had worked with a tightly knit group of union men, and told the press he was "encouraged at the change in public feeling since last year." The Alexandria lawyer believed that people had calmed down, but still he admitted the upcoming trial was "not going to be a picnic."[3]

Facing off against Smith and his associates would be the same prosecution team that had won a conviction at the 1935 trial—Greear and his assistants, Oscar M. Vicars and Lewis McCormick. Unlike before, much was now being made in the press of Vicars's participation in the trial. The *Richmond News Leader* on December 3 described the tall, grey-haired attorney as "one of the outstanding criminal lawyers of the Lonesome Pine country." He was said to have been hired by Lee Skeen, the former Wise County sheriff and husband of Trigg Maxwell's sister, Clora.

Skeen's involvement, said the *News Leader,* "is interpreted in most quarters as emphasizing the bitter family feud between Trigg Maxwell's people and the Dotsons, kinfolk of Edith's mother, the former Anna Dotson." The *Washington Post* also weighed in on the same day: "There is nothing unusual about private interests hiring lawyers to assist the Commonwealth. In this instance, however, it is one of many strange aspects to a strange case that has aroused interest all over the world."

A little saying, only half made in jest, circulated among the citizens of Wise on Tuesday morning. Neighbors urged one another to pen up all livestock for the duration of the trial lest an unfettered cow should wander down Main Street and into the stories and pictures of visiting correspondents. "Thirteen newsmen and photographers are on the job at Wise, to tell the world of the second Edith Maxwell trial," said the *Coalfield Progress.* "That thirteen is going to be unlucky for someone. Some of the 'newsmen' are women. But all of them here, perhaps, to picture the trial, to their metropolitan readers, as another Roman holiday trial, contrasting sharply with what Commonwealth Attorney Fred B. Greear describes as just another murder case. We just are hoping," added the newspaper, "[that] the newspapers let the court conduct the trial."[4]

With seventy-five witnesses summoned to testify—some of them said to be harboring "new and startling" evidence—the journalists from the United Press, Associated Press, several daily newspapers, and at least one tabloid were assured of a big story.[5] The Western Union telegraph office was gearing up for an unprecedented transmission boom—a cornucopia that was expected to total more than a hundred thousand words. This time around, the *Washington Post* was the dominant news organization, apparently having assumed the role that the Hearst syndicate played at the first trial.

In Edward T. Folliard's polished accounts, *Post* readers would find few if any references to the "mountain code" and women's "curfew" that had so enraged southwest Virginia residents. But like the Hearst correspondents before him, Folliard was unabashedly for Edith and did not hesitate to report the defense's allegations as the unvarnished truth. On November 6, a *Richmond Times-Dispatch* editorial had taken to task "at least one supposedly reputable newspaper"—undoubtedly the *Post*—for reporting only the defense's side of the story "time after time." By the time the trial opened, the *Post* not only had raised more than $600 for the new Edith Maxwell defense fund but also heavily invested its own reputation in the case.

The *Coalfield Progress* also reported that the two Hearst papers in Washington—the *Times* and the *Herald*—nonetheless dispatched three writers to Wise "to keep step with the *Post*." One of them was Washington socialite Anne Hamilton Gordon Suydam. Nicknamed "Wallie" by fellow reporters, the Sorbonne-educated Suydam was reported to be a cousin of Wallis Warfield Simpson, the American divorcee whose romance with the Prince of Wales was creating turmoil within the British royal family.

Suydam served as a special correspondent for Washington newspapers (in this case the *Herald*) and also wrote poetry. Her highly descriptive, often florid prose would range from the deeply insightful (of Mary Katherine, she wrote, "She . . . has a grimness and an agelessness that should be no part of a child") to the banal (of Edith's students she noted, "Their ages range from seven to seventeen, and their mentalities ranged from who knows where").[6]

Suydam and her colleagues no doubt found much on the streets of Wise that did resemble a Roman holiday, for the trial held the prospect of riveting entertainment for those not directly touched by the Maxwell tragedy. The *Washington Post* said that a "carnival spirit" pervaded the town as the trial opened Wednesday morning. Parked automobiles were wedged wheel to wheel along the street, and hundreds of people milled about in the sunny courthouse yard. A blind street musician strummed his guitar and sang "Oh, Susanna, Don't You Cry for Me." A hawker peddling a cure for nosebleed called out to passersby, while soap and baking powder salesmen handed out free samples of their wares. "Farther down the street a star-gazer and fortune-teller was prophesying that an American girl would be sitting on the throne of England inside of six months," reported the *Herald*. "He did a brisk business in printed horoscopes."[7]

Those lucky enough to actually make it into the courtroom—which was built to hold perhaps two hundred—anxiously vied for seats. Even the deep sills of the high windows were covered with spectators by the time Judge Carter appeared. Reporters had to work standing during the morning session, bracing their notebooks on other people's backs until an extra table was eventually brought in. Unlike Judge Henry Alexander Wise Skeen (who was back as a spectator), Judge Carter allowed photographers to roam freely. Children played in the aisle separating the attorneys' tables from the crowd, "but despite the crush, matters proceeded in an orderly fashion," the *Herald* reported.[8]

All eyes were on Edith as she took her place at the counsel table, with Earl and Mary Katherine resting on the arms of her chair and her mother and Mrs. A. T. Dotson seated nearby. Another woman in the courtroom, however, soon drew even more attention than the accused. Gail Laughlin was preparing to press the constitutional argument so dear to the National Woman's Party: Women had a right, under the Fourteenth Amendment, to serve on grand and trial juries.

Although she had appeared before Judge Skeen the previous January to assist with Edith's appeal—a historic "first" in the Wise County courts—Laughlin was back, this time before a much larger audience. Few had ever seen the spectacle of a woman operating on the same footing as male lawyers, judges, and bailiffs. The crowd strained to get a better look as the short, stocky stranger rose to offer her pretrial motions.

On this day Laughlin had forsaken her customary black wool suit for a blue smock dress, but her brows were dark and heavy and her expression typically severe. The words she was about to utter in her "loud, husky" voice were revolutionary, yet her brassy demeanor alone would have been enough to mesmerize the onlookers. "Even her bristling gray bobbed hair was belligerent," wrote Anne Suydam, "and the South is not yet quite used to Yankee boldness in women."[9]

Laughlin was not at all impressed with Judge Carter despite his Lincolnesque stature. She regarded him not as a gentleman but as a "large, coarse-looking individual continually pulling out a plug of tobacco and taking a bite."[10] Neither was she impressed by the dignity of his court. Especially bothersome were the swarming children who invaded her space and clawed at her back. Nonetheless, the feminist, sixty-eight, proceeded to offer her arguments.

Laughlin first attacked Edith's murder indictment on the ground that no women had been eligible to serve on the grand jury that indicted her. She also questioned the makeup of the all-male jury pool (the venire) called to try the present case, because women could not legally be sum-moned as potential jurors. "When under the Bill of Rights, a woman could sit as judge of this court, it is certainly an anomaly to say she could not sit on this jury," Laughlin asserted. "[Or] suppose that a jury of twelve women sat in judgment of a man here. Would that be regarded as constitutional, as just, as an equal protection of the law?"[11]

Greear responded that Virginia appellate courts had repeatedly re-fused to support Laughlin's argument. Playing to the crowd, he gave a theatrical bow and added patronizingly that Laughlin's convictions were admirable "no matter how silly her argument sounded." The audience howled its appreciation.[12]

Laughlin and the other Woman's Party lawyer, M. J. Fulton, made several motions to quash the indictment and the venire on various legal grounds, but Judge Carter quickly overruled them all. He politely told Laughlin, "If there's anything wrong with the law, it wouldn't have been overlooked in Virginia all these years."[13]

The state senator from Maine had lost a battle she could scarcely have expected to win even if she had been a man. By noting an exception to the judge's ruling, however, the defense had sown the seeds of an appeal to the U.S. Supreme Court—if that drastic step should ever prove necessary. Just as she intended, Laughlin had played the legal gladiator. She had run a gauntlet of patriarchal slings and arrows, coming clear, doing the job she came south to do. Yet she left the courtroom with her prejudices firmly intact.

—

While the Maine legislator made her passionate appeal for women's rights, one of her male colleagues was not listening. The *Washington Post* reported that Charles Henry Smith, the lead defense counsel, "walked out of the courtroom when Miss Laughlin arose to talk and did not return until she had finished."[14] It is unknown whether Smith disliked Laughlin personally or whether he did not want to work with female colleagues in general. Probably he felt that Laughlin's radical feminist rhetoric—not to men-tion her abrasive style—would alienate the locals, and thus, he sought to distance himself from her. As everybody in the mountains knew, you could catch more flies with honey than with vinegar.

Beyond questions of style, there was the matter of strategy: Smith's goal was to win an acquittal now, and if the glory accrued to his newspaper backers as well as to him, all the better. Laughlin's goal, however, was to effect sweeping social change. Edith's personal vindication (and that of the Woman's Party's efforts) might have to wait months or years but would ultimately be all the sweeter. Whatever view prevailed might ultimately depend on who had the most to offer the Maxwell family.

In an exercise of perhaps wishful thinking, the *Washington Post* reported that Laughlin, "having made her point," was leaving town that evening—even though the trial had barely begun. But Laughlin did not take the bait. She stayed on, posed with Edith for the Hearst photographers, and suffered the trifling deprivations of life in the hinterlands. ("There wasn't a store or stand where a newspaper or magazine could be bought," she later complained. "If we had the daily papers we had to order them of a boy and order early.") Smith continued to work with Fulton on the criminal law aspects of the case. With feminist concerns safely brushed aside, the proceeding would become, as the prosecutors liked to call it, simply a murder trial.

———

Jury selection began shortly before noon, the morning hours mostly having been consumed by Laughlin and Fulton's futile constitutional arguments. An unusually large number of veniremen—sixty-five—had been ordered to report for possible jury duty. Of thirty-one potential jurors questioned, eleven were discharged for having knowledge or opinions about the case.[15] The remaining group of twenty soon was whittled down to twelve after the defense and prosecution each took four "strikes." The whole process took less than two hours, much to the surprise of court-watchers who had assumed it might take up to two days to seat an unbiased jury.

None of the twelve men chosen hailed from Pound or even from Wise; many lived in the western end of the county at least thirty miles from the Maxwell home. The panel included Owen Carter and W. H. Umbarger of Stonega; F. P. Gardner of Dorchester; Lewis Estes, S. Rush Horne, W. M. Bond, and D. F. Hensley of Coeburn; Eldridge Christian of Inman; John Roller of East Stone Gap; and George Pennington, John Lambert, and R. L. Hilton of Big Stone Gap. Judge Carter took the unusual step of ordering the jury to be sequestered this time around.

Once the jury was empaneled, the clerk of the court explained the range of options to be considered if Edith were found guilty. If convicted of first-degree murder, she could be given the electric chair or a minimum of twenty years in prison. On the other end of the spectrum, a conviction for involuntary manslaughter would carry a penalty of one to five years and/or a $1,000 fine.

Defense attorney Smith was pleased with the makeup of the panel, which included four farmers, a grocer, a road worker, an insurance agent, two miners, a carpenter, a railroad section hand, and Estes the undertaker, who was chosen as foreman. The *Washington Post* noted that this group "is not nearly so grim-looking" as the jury at Edith's previous trial. W. A. S. Douglas of the *Herald* expounded a popular theory that the more sophisticated "town" jurors (he counted six) would vote to acquit, while the remaining rural men would favor a guilty verdict, resulting in a hung jury and mistrial. Anne Suydam was even more optimistic: "Those who have her interest most deeply at heart believe that she has a fortunate jury."[16] But none, of course, could overestimate the rhetorical powers of Fred Greear.

———

"The scene will be the same, the cast almost the same, but the indications are . . . that the plot (at least, as written by the defense) will be vastly different," Edward T. Folliard had predicted on the eve of the trial.[17] Fred Greear, by contrast, had little reason to change the prosecution's longstanding theory of the Maxwell case. Greear's hard-won conviction had been thrown out on appeal, but that cloud over the prosecution also contained a silver lining. A very careful reading of the Virginia Supreme Court decision seemed to say that even though the commonwealth had failed to prove premeditation, it made a credible case for second-degree murder. Greear and his assistant prosecutors therefore might have felt reasonably safe in following the same game plan they used in 1935. Nonetheless, they were not content to try this time for a second-degree murder conviction. They had spent the past several months seeking out new witnesses and eliciting more information from those who had already testified.

In his opening statement to the jury on late Wednesday afternoon, the slender, balding Greear began by downplaying the historic significance of the Maxwell trial, saying, "It is no more important than any other murder case."[18] Speaking in a "low, conversational tone," he said he would offer testimony to document Edith's long-standing enmity toward her father. "She said that the happiest day of her life would be when she saw him lowered into the grave," the prosecutor said.[19] Greear told the jury that she had repeatedly threatened to kill Trigg and had once "laid her father low with a poker." "It's a lie," Edith immediately hissed. She was quickly shushed by her attorneys.[20]

Continuing, Greear said Edith refused to heed Trigg's wishes when it came to her socializing with men, shouting at him on one occasion, "Well, what are you going to do about it?" The prosecutor said Trigg led "a dog's life" and slept in the "junkroom" of the Maxwell home, adding that the victim was in the process of building a two-room shanty in which to "live in peace and perhaps in safety" when he was killed. Authorities investigating Trigg's death found an electric iron stained with what appeared to be blood, and his carpenter tools had disappeared as well. Greear was forced to add, however, "The Commonwealth does not know with what instrument Trigg Maxwell was struck."[21]

Greear also emphasized that Edith had twice changed her story of how Trigg died. The defendant first said her father had "killed himself" by falling against the meat block, but she later admitted striking him with a shoe during his alleged drunken attack. According to Greear, Edith first said the shoe was her father's rubber-soled shoe but later described it as her mother's slipper. The tall, distinguished Smith then took his turn, pausing before the brass rail of the jury box with one hand tucked in a pocket of his dark suit. The jurors listened intently as he unveiled the defense's stunning new plot twist, challenging Greear to prove that a murder had even been committed. "Gentlemen," Smith said, "we will show that the wound inflicted by the slipper in this defendant's hand could never have caused Trigg Maxwell's death. We will call eminent medical authorities to show that he died of natural causes."[22]

Smith's idea was not new, at least not to anyone who followed the story in the Washington newspapers. Earl Maxwell had long been telling anyone who would listen that his father suffered from heart trouble and had been denied life insurance a few days before his death. Press reports sympathetic to the defense had suggested that members of Trigg Maxwell's family also had died sudden deaths.

Nonetheless, Smith's mundane-sounding strategy of relying on the experts—a radical departure from the defense's position at the first trial—was risky. He was asking the jury to believe that the wounds to Trigg's head were a red herring that drew attention away from a heart attack, stroke, or some other fatal malady. In other words, Smith was suggesting that although Edith's scuffle with her father might have helped induce some sort of medical crisis, Trigg's death was just an unlucky coincidence for his client. "Edith was the first one to run for a doctor," Smith said.[23]

With opening arguments concluded, court adjourned until 9 A.M. Thursday, yet speculation about Smith's position spilled over onto the street corners of Wise. "To some of the natives who followed Edith's first trial, news of Attorney Smith's plan of battle seemed fantastic," reported Folliard. "The truth is, however, this has been Smith's plan from the time he took over the case last January."[24]

It was almost as if Smith had taken a page from the great Clarence Darrow's book, trusting in science and rationality as the final arbiter of truth. Or would he use his fancy experts simply to obscure the truth? In the days to come, jurors would have to decide between Smith's carefully cultivated batch of outside scientific testimony and Greear's folksy patchwork of evidence from local doctors and people who knew the Maxwells well. Who could say which would prove more persuasive?

18   *Coma Tiller's Axe*

His cast of characters now greatly expanded, Fred Greear planned to show that Ann and Edith had long been allied against Trigg Maxwell in a kind of domestic warfare. The prosecutor had lined up a Greek chorus of the Maxwells' neighbors, friends, and relatives—nearly twenty strong—to tell how *Trigg* had been on the receiving end of insults, threats, and physical violence.

Greear's case nonetheless got off to a bumpy start Thursday morning as defense attorneys M. J. Fulton and Charles Henry Smith objected to almost every one of these witnesses' stories. They argued that the incidents were either too far in the past to make a difference or were simply irrelevant. But Greear and Oscar M. Vicars proved effective in persuading a reluctant Judge Ezra T. Carter to allow most of the testimony to go before the jury.

The first witness, Leonard Hill, had been the Maxwells' neighbor on Bold Camp near Pound more than fifteen years earlier and later worked in the mines with Trigg. Hill testified about hearing Ann frequently quarreling at Trigg. "I have heard Ann call him bad names—old rascal, old dog and things like that. I heard her call him old rascal, old sorry face and he wasn't any account," Hill said. Hill, however, said he did not remember Edith (who only would have been five or six years old) saying anything to her father.[1]

On cross-examination, A. T. Dotson asked Hill, "How many times have you been on drunks with Trigg Maxwell in your life?"

"I have been on several of them, when Trigg was drinking," Hill responded. "He got so he didn't drink any since Fred died, he didn't drink."

Greear also had lined up three tenants who lived in the partitioned-off apartment at the Maxwells' home in Pound in the years leading up to Trigg's death. Flora Mullins Branham, a homemaker and former high school teacher at Pound, testified that Edith had visited the apartment during the 1929–30 school year and told of an upcoming family trip to Chicago to see Earl. When Branham asked if Trigg was going with them, Edith responded, "What do you think? Do you think we would take him? No, we wouldn't take him. He would disgrace us."[2]

Branham also testified that she was often awakened late at night and in the predawn hours by the Maxwells' quarreling. Branham said that Ann Maxwell would use epithets such as "old dog" and would refuse Trigg's requests to get up and cook breakfast. Eventually, Branham reported, "He wouldn't call on anyone to get his breakfast. He would just get up and leave."[3]

Greear's next witness was schoolteacher Mabel Maxwell Mullins, whom a reporter described as "a little wisp of a blond-red girl."[4] Mullins, the daughter of Trigg's late brother, Fred, lived in the apartment with her husband, Zemery, around 1933. They, too, were disturbed by loud quarrels that pierced the thin plank dividing wall. Mullins started to tell about an episode in which Trigg had a black eye, but she only knew by hearsay how he had gotten it. Her testimony was quickly cut off by objections. Judge Carter told the jury to ignore the remark about Trigg's injury.

Mabel's brother, Vernon Maxwell, took the stand next. Interest in this witness was no doubt considerable because "Little Vernon" was a family intimate. Not only had he ridden with Trigg to work for a two-year period but he also was the young cousin whom Edith had accompanied to Wise on the night of Trigg's death. Vernon Maxwell testifed that Trigg and Ann "lived more or less separate" under the same roof, with Edith taking her mother's side in family arguments. Greear tried to question Vernon about how the Maxwell home was furnished, but Smith objected that such details were irrelevant.

"I don't know how it could have been otherwise, when a man [is] browbeaten and put in a junk room to sleep," Greear responded. Defense attorney Fulton immediately demanded a mistrial, saying Greear's remarks were improper. He was overruled by Judge Carter, and the questioning continued.

Vernon testified that in 1935 Trigg was building a house on the road to Clintwood, a location within a mile of the Maxwell family home on Main Street. He gave the dimensions of the uncompleted structure as twenty feet wide by twenty-five or thirty feet long. Vernon said his Uncle Trigg had told him why he was building the house, but he was not allowed to repeat the deceased's remarks in court. Another witness, Herbert Huey, described the structure as "very small," about twelve feet by sixteen feet. Although the estimates varied, the implication was that Trigg was *not* planning to move his wife and daughters into the new house.

With these first few witnesses the prosecution had sought to portray a family deep at odds, long steeped in alienation and finally on the verge of physical separation. With the next group, Greear planned to show threats that Edith and Ann allegedly made against Trigg's life.

Some witnesses repeated their testimony from the first trial. Conrad Bolling, a twenty-nine-year-old teacher, recounted the chilling story of how he had been car-riding with Edith and how she had said she "would kill" Trigg if he ever tried to whip her. Everett Holyfield, a former Pound taxi driver, again testified that he and his wife gave Edith a ride from Jenkins to Pound one evening, during which Edith said she "hated him [Trigg] cause she couldn't keep from laughing at him to see him laid out dead."

This time Mrs. Holyfield, who was reluctant to testify at the first trial, took the stand and corroborated her husband's story. Another new witness was W. Z. "Zemery" Mullins, a Pound grocer and car salesman who was the husband of Mabel Maxwell Mullins. Zemery Mullins similarly testified that he had heard Edith say "her happiest moment would be when she saw him laid in his grave."

As in 1935, some of the most damaging testimony came from Ruth Baker, a teacher whose mother was Trigg's sister. Edith's last year at Radford State Teachers College coincided with Baker's first year. Baker testified that she roomed with her cousin Edith for one and a half quarters, during which time she frequently heard Edith say, "I will kill him," referring to Trigg. Baker also mentioned a previously undisclosed incident in which Edith, while still in high school, had become physically violent with her father. "I laid him out with a poker and he had to tell that a hornet stung him," Baker quoted the defendant as telling her.

Defense attorney Smith, on cross-examination, asked Baker why she had not testified about the poker at the first trial. "The other time I wasn't asked to tell all I knew," Baker responded. She told Smith that she resented some of the testimony at the first trial that "wasn't true" and therefore now had decided to be more forthcoming with the prosecutors.

The next witness was Helen Gilliam Moles, who lived in the Maxwells' apartment until just a few weeks before Trigg's death. (She had moved out in June 1935 to make way for the new post office, which opened there in July.) During her seven months in the building, Moles—like previous tenants—could overhear conversations through the wall.

When asked to characterize the Maxwell family's interactions, Moles said, "They talked very mean at times, and at other times they talked good to each other." During the bad times, Moles recalled, Edith called Trigg "a God-damned son of a bitch" and threatened to kill him. On one occasion, Edith dared her father to come out of his room and fight her. "If you don't you are an old coward," Moles quoted Edith as saying. "And if you don't I will get out and broadcast that I got an old coward for a daddy." The Maxwells' tenant also testified that Ann did not participate in these arguments between Edith and Trigg, although she did sometimes quarrel with her husband.

Having established that Edith threatened her father over a period of several years, Greear was ready to move the lens of memory closer. His focus shifted to Saturday afternoon, July 20, 1935, less than twelve hours before Trigg Maxwell's death. Once again, the prosecution constructed the spectacle of Edith defying her father—this time in the very public arena of Pound's main street.

Restaurant manager J. L. Sowards told the now-familiar story of Edith and a gas station attendant flirting in the middle of the street around 4:30 or 5 P.M., in view of Trigg Maxwell. This time in court, three new witnesses supported Sowards's observation that Edith and Trigg appeared to argue immediately afterward. The bystanders testified that Edith said to her father, "If you don't like it, what are you going to do about it?" But—as before—none could say what Edith referred to.

What Edith did after returning home from Sowards's was not brought out at the trial. One can only assume that she prepared herself for a Saturday evening out, although it is not known exactly what she had intended to do. Vernon Maxwell was recalled to the stand to tell how he encountered Edith at Pound around 9 P.M. From the testimony of Little Vernon (once described as "a handsome man about the county") it is clear that he had plans for the evening that did not include his cousin Edith. "I came [to Wise] on personal business of my own," he said. "I was waiting on the car I was coming here with. While I was standing there she came up and asked me if she could come with me. I said, 'Yes.' We stood there until the car came along the road and she rode in the seat with me."

Vernon was never asked to name the driver who brought them to Wise. He testified that he did not accompany Edith around town, although he did run into her at Shorty's Cafe around 10:30 or 11 P.M. The next time Vernon saw Edith, his Uncle Trigg was dead.

One person who had never before given testimony in the Maxwell case was Raymond Meade—the young man often described in the Hearst tabloids as Edith's "beau" and "own true love"—the man for whom she supposedly had risked her father's wrath. In reality, though, the tale of Raymond and Edith seemed a bit more prosaic than that of star-crossed lovers. Of his relationship with Edith, Meade would merely say, "I knowed her all my life." Although the two probably were not involved in a serious romantic relationship, Meade was thought to be sympathetic to Edith. In fact, Earl Maxwell at one time had even pegged the strapping coal miner as a potential witness for the defense, but he was in court on Thursday morning as Fred Greear's witness.

Now court-watchers could hear Meade—whether willing or reluctant—give firsthand the story they had thus far heard only from Edith's lips, how the two young people had gone, unchaperoned, to the Little Ritz bar near midnight on Saturday, July 20, 1935. As Meade told it, he had been driving back from Norton with a married couple and their child when they decided to stop for ice cream at Shorty's in Wise. Meade spotted Edith standing on the corner and offered her a ride home. She accepted. Meade dropped off the others at their place between Wise and Pound, then drove Edith about a mile and half beyond her home to the Little Ritz. The couple had retired to a private dining room in the back.

Meade's testimony up to this point had closely mirrored what Edith herself had said at the 1935 trial, but now it was about to take a surprising turn.

"What did you do when you got in the private dining room?" Greear asked.

"I got a drink of liquor and a chaser, and got her a bottle of ginger ale and potato chips."

"Did you just get one glass of liquor?" the prosecutor queried.

"No," Meade responded. "I got two. I got one for her and one for myself."

Meade's revelation apparently rocked the courtroom. Judge Carter interrupted the questioning to bark: "I want order in this court, or you will have to get out."

Greear then got Meade to repeat that he had bought the liquor for Edith. The witness, however, said he didn't know whether Edith drank hers, leaving open the possibility that she had thrown it out the window as she had sworn. But the next exchange cast more doubt on Edith's claim of abstinence.

"Had you drunk any liquor before with her?" Greear asked.

"Yes, I had took a drink with her," Meade replied.

Fulton quickly objected and asked that Meade's remark be stricken from the record. He was overruled.

Meade further testified that he and Edith stayed at the Ritz about a half hour and that he dropped her off at her doorstep around 12:30 A.M. Although his evidence did not shed any direct light on what had happened after Edith got home, it broached a disturbing possibility. If Edith—as well as Trigg—had been drinking, it could only have fueled the antagonisms they could already scarcely control.

Worse still, Meade's bombshell was damaging to the teacher's reputation, even as it did nothing to harm his own. If there were proper young ladies drinking liquor in Pound, they kept that fact well hidden. After all, conventional wisdom still held that a woman who would take a drink "would do anything."

When Greear finished with his witness, the defense declined to cross-examine Meade.

It was no accident that Greear, in his opening statement, had alleged that Trigg Maxwell's mining and carpenter tools turned up missing on the morning after his death. Soon after Edith's arrest in the summer of 1935 he had privately accused her of striking her father with a broadaxe—an allegation she had bitterly denied while admitting in a written statement (later suppressed) that she hit him with an iron.

For some reason Greear now had decided to revive the candidacy of the axe. The commonwealth attorney was no longer willing to rely solely on the electric iron he previously had trumpeted as the likely instrument of death, but neither would he forsake it. In the absence of hard facts, the prosecutors had decided on an "either/or" approach that would allow them to offer the jury an expanded menu of possible murder weapons.

Greear and his team set the plan in motion shortly before noon by calling Pound civic leader Chant Branham Kelly—the commonwealth's next best thing to an eyewitness. Under questioning from Vicars, Kelly repeated his story from the first trial—how he had been reading in bed just after 1 A.M. when he heard a "racket" next door and Trigg Maxwell hollering "Oh Lordy" for about five minutes, and how he was turned away by Edith from the latticed-in porch when he offered to help.

"[Edith] told me that it wasn't any fire over there and for me to go back," he told the packed courtroom.

Kelly's story up to this point had been a fairly consistent retelling of his previous testimony, but with the next question Vicars interjected an entirely new element. The prosecutor asked Kelly why he had acquiesced to Edith's wishes instead of forcing his way into the Maxwell home, surely a strange question by today's standards of civil liberty.

"Really, since you ask me the question, I was afraid to go in," the witness responded.

"Why? What caused you to be afraid?"

"She [Edith] was located out on the porch where Trigg kept all the tools and in a position where she could get hold of most any kind of an instrument I wouldn't be able to combat."

With this response, Kelly had put a different slant on his state of mind during the encounter. Whereas his previous testimony showed nothing more than bewildered frustration over not being allowed to help, Kelly now was saying that he had feared for his own safety. With the new testimony, Vicars was able to portray Edith not only as secretive and maybe a bit snooty but also willing to do violence to anyone trying to find out what was going on inside. The prosecutor also planted the idea that a carpenter's tool might have been a deadly weapon in Edith's hands.

Fulton strenuously objected, calling Vicars's strategy "an attempt to inject something into this case by a witness who knows nothing of the actual fact." He argued that Kelly's response should be stricken from the record because Kelly did not actually see any tools on the porch that night. Judge Carter overruled the objection, and Vicars was able to establish that Trigg Maxwell owned an assortment of saws, hammers, hatchets, and mining axes, which he sometimes kept on the porch where Edith had been standing.

Continuing his story, Kelly testified that he reluctantly returned home, only to be called back an hour or so later by Mary Katherine. He told of his futile attempts to resuscitate the dying man and recalled how Ann and Edith said repeatedly that Trigg had fallen and struck his head against a meat block. Kelly, however, could find no blood or hair on the wooden block. His attention was drawn to several strange wet spots, one underneath Trigg's head and three others in the kitchen, that "apparently had been washed up." Vicars then asked if he found "any tools or anything." Kelly said he did not notice any inside the house that night, but he did see a mining axe on the porch the next morning.

The remainder of Kelly's direct testimony mostly related to the floor plan of the Maxwell home and the building's proximity to the Pound River. After a lunch break, the prosecution introduced "Kelly Exhibit No. 1," a drawing of the Maxwell residence. Kelly explained that the supporting pillars at the rear of the home were positioned only about two feet from the river. He testified that it would have been possible for a person to take a back stairway from the porch down into a partially enclosed basement and gain access to the river.

On the morning after Trigg's death, police officers searched under the house for a murder weapon and tried to comb the river, but the water was too muddy. According to Kelly, the mud in the river bottom was nine to ten feet thick near the Maxwell home. The implication was that a heavy instrument, dropped into the thin, gummy substrate, would be enfolded, concealed forever. But no one had seen Edith, or Ann or Mary Katherine, perform such an act.

Now it was time for Charles Henry Smith to try to punch a few holes in Kelly's story—or at least try to pin on him the persona of a nosy, intrusive neighbor. Smith asked Kelly how he interpreted Edith's remark, "There's no fire here."

"I took it as a flatter," the witness responded.

"As what?"

"As being flattered."

"It is a fact that she and other people had kidded you around the neighborhood, hadn't they, about going to fires and things of that sort?"

"The first thing I knew anything about it was when I saw it in the newspapers."

"But you had never been kidded before that?"

"I think not."

"You had had a fire sometime prior to this?"

"Yes, sir."

"And you naturally were a little uneasy about fires, were you not?"

"Not any more than usual."

"You don't subscribe to the doctrine that a burnt child fears the fire?"

Kelly made no answer to this final rhetorical question, and Smith let the subject finally die. The defense attorney was unable to shake Kelly's direct testimony.

The prosecution then called others who lived in the Kelly building to corroborate the now-familiar scenario of Edith arriving home, an argument erupting, Trigg hollering "Oh Lordy," and the radio playing loudly before neighbors finally were allowed in. Kelly's sisters-in-law, Verna Hubbard and Martha Strange, again confirmed parts of his testimony. Hubbard testified that she, too, heard scuffling next door and subsequently heard Trigg groaning, "Oh, Lordy." She also reported seeing Edith standing between the Maxwell and Kelly buildings and hearing Mary Katherine say, "Edith, come back, your daddy has got blood all over his head." Hubbard did not venture to the Maxwell house that night, but Strange testified about going next door and hearing the Maxwell women explain that Trigg had fallen upon the meat block. A boarder at the rooming house, plumber Clarence "Chick" Groschen, also backed up portions of Kelly's story.

Another of Kelly's tenants, J. L. Sowards, who had testified that morning about seeing Edith flirting in front of his hot dog stand, was recalled to offer crucial details about an electric iron. Awakened by Mary Katherine's screams, Sowards had hurried next door and assisted Dr. E. L. Sikes and Kelly as they worked over the prostrate form of Trigg Maxwell. When Dr. Sikes decided that Trigg "needed heat," someone had plugged the Maxwells' electric iron into an overhead socket in the front room, leaving the iron sitting on the linoleum floor. (How the cord could have reached from ceiling to floor was never explained.)

Sowards testified that he went to get the iron twice, but it remained cold and was never used in the resuscitation attempt. This bit of evidence was important because it contradicted the defense's claim that the iron *had* heated up and melted the linoleum rug, producing telltale red spots on the iron that the police mistook for blood.

Greear showed Sowards an iron and asked if it was the one he had seen that night. Sowards said it was "just about like that, about the same size." The prosecutor offered the iron in evidence, drawing a swift objection from Charles Henry Smith. Judge Carter agreed to admit the iron but said he expected the commonwealth to "follow it with something to connect it up."

Now it was Fulton's turn to cross-examine. He got Sowards to admit to selling Trigg three bottles of beer on that fateful Saturday at about 5 P.M., 7 P.M., and midnight. But Sowards insisted that Trigg was not intoxicated and that he "hadn't seen Trigg drunk in two years." Fulton also accused Sowards of illegally selling liquor at the restaurant, but the witness denied it.

With Kelly and four of his associates having concluded their testimony, the prosecution was now ready to hear from the police officers who investigated the case. Former deputy sheriff R. S. Hubbard testified that he went to the house on the morning after the slaying to help Sheriff J. P. Adams take Edith and Ann into custody. A search of the premises was apparently already in progress.

Hubbard said the women seemed "greatly surprised" but managed to repeat the story they had been telling for the previous nine hours—that

Trigg had fallen against the meat block. They said nothing about the fight that Edith would later describe so graphically in her testimony at the 1935 trial. They merely told Adams and Hubbard that "it was a sight to be accused of something like that" and that they "didn't know anything about it."

Hubbard and former county policeman Ed DeLong both testified about their search of the Maxwells' porch. A sheet, blanket, and pillow with pillowcase—all wet and stained with what appeared to be blood—were found in a laundry basket with other clothes on top of them. Some women were standing nearby as the deputies recovered the linens, which were believed to have come from Trigg Maxwell's bed. DeLong recalled hearing a woman's voice behind him—which sounded to him like Edith's—saying, "You ain't no blood specialist, are you?"

On cross-examination, Smith questioned Hubbard closely about the sheet and pillowcase, which had been brought into court as prosecution exhibits. Hubbard conceded that the stains on the pillowcase appeared lighter than they had previously but said they otherwise looked the same. Smith suggested that the sheet, which had pins fastened to it, might have been used to cover an ironing board and could have acquired "iron stains." Hubbard countered that the sheet was wet the day he found it and that he thought it was stained with blood.

Prosecutor Vicars also produced the electric iron that had been shown to Sowards. DeLong would later testify that he had found the iron, marked with "red splotches, like blood" in a box on top of a cabinet inside the Maxwell home. But Vicars first asked the other police officer, Hubbard, to identify it and point out the areas that resembled blood spots. Then the iron was passed to the jury.

Smith regarded the spots on the iron with skepticism, quickly establishing that no chemical analysis had been made. As with the pillowcase, Hubbard maintained that the stains appeared to be fresh blood in July 1935 but were less evident after more than a year had passed.

Toward the end of the police testimony, Fulton broke in with a belated objection. He argued that the objects found by Hubbard and DeLong could not be used as evidence against Edith unless it were shown that she had actually touched the iron or placed the bedclothes in the basket herself. Greear countered that they were seized from the house in which the dead body was found and that Edith and Ann were present. Judge Carter allowed the items to remain in evidence.

In recounting his search of the porch, DeLong also mentioned finding a "pole axe" near the meat block. The instrument had a handle twelve inches long and a single blade about five by three by one and a half inches. "There was some kind of an ice box or refrigerator sitting where the meat block was and I kind of stuck it up under that," he said. DeLong was not asked to explain why he did not seize the axe as evidence.

As the day's proceedings drew to a close the commonwealth presented some provocative—but hardly conclusive—evidence that had not been brought forth at the previous trial. Coma Tiller, a woman who had lived three doors down from the Maxwells, testified that she frequently loaned the Maxwell family a hatchet used for chopping kindling.

"I show you here a small axe," Greear said, "and ask you if that is the kind of axe you had there?"

Tiller responded that the axe in the prosecutor's hand was not hers but was similar in size. She related that she and her husband, Carter, had been visiting in Norton for a week before Trigg's death. They returned home on the evening of Sunday, July 21, to find the hatchet missing. Mrs. Tiller testified that she had not seen it since.

Smith quickly jumped to his feet. "It serves no purpose in the world except that it gives, by innuendo and implications, a suggestion of evidence before this jury that cannot be gotten to any other way," he protested. "It is highly prejudicial." Smith added, "There might have been thousands of people in Wise County who lost axes during that week," but "that does not prove Edith Maxwell stole them."

Greear responded that the defendant was not charged with stealing an axe. Coma Tiller's evidence, he said, showed that the Maxwells had access to an axe and "were in the habit of using it."

Fulton joined the fray, maintaining that Tiller's testimony in no way implicated Edith. After considerable wrangling by the attorneys, Judge Carter ruled in favor of the prosecution, paving the way for the commonwealth's final witness of the day, Carter Tiller.

Over the objections of defense counsel, Carter Tiller confirmed his wife's story about the missing pole axe, which he had bought at Pound Hardware where he worked. Their axe, he said, was the same brand and size as the one Greear displayed in court except the Tillers' axe was not new.

Greear then moved to introduce the axe as evidence, although he had never really established where the new tool had come from. Reportedly, he purchased it at a hardware store.

"We object to that," Fulton said.

"All you are trying to do is to get before the jury as near as you can, the kind of axe he is dealing with," Judge Carter commented, perhaps thinking out loud.

"Your honor," responded Charles Henry Smith, "we are not dealing with an axe is the point."

"I think we are," the judge said.

"He is getting something before the jury that is not in the case and we except," Smith noted.

Fulton then moved for a mistrial on the ground that Judge Carter had prejudiced the jury by appearing to side with the prosecution. The jurist swiftly overruled the motion, bringing the first day of testimony to a tumultuous close.

———

"Everything considered, this was a bad day for Edith Maxwell," concluded the *Washington Post*'s Edward T. Folliard in his account of Thursday's proceedings. "Neighbors, erstwhile playmates, even relatives took the stand to paint Edith as a hot-tempered, willful girl who always was threatening to kill her father or 'wishing' he were dead."[5]

The long parade of prosecution witnesses *had* taken its toll. According to Folliard, Edith at one point during the testimony began sobbing loudly and gave way to "an attack of nerves." The wife of A. T. Dotson rushed out to a nearby drugstore, procured ammonia, and helped Edith regain her composure. The Associated Press reported that "the muscles of her face twitched nervously during the proceedings, but occasionally she smiled and chatted."[6]

The biggest news of the day was, of course, the shiny new axe the commonwealth had introduced as a facsimile of the possible murder weapon. Folliard could scarcely conceal his outrage over its admission, noting that "there was no evidence she had stolen it, nothing whatever to connect her with the hatchet." Even the more dispassionate Associated Press reporter Carter Lowance observed that the Tillers' testimony "did not name Edith as the borrower or specify that she used the axe for any purpose, but was offered by the state as one circumstance concerning the death of the fifty-two-year-old miner." Although the commonwealth had prevailed, defense attorneys were hopeful that the furor over the axe—and Judge Carter's comment—would engender another successful appeal should the verdict go against Edith.[7]

Neither defense nor prosecution lawyers, however, had much time to celebrate victories or mull over defeats that Thursday evening. They had to prepare for the next day's battle. Greear and his associates were expected to wind up their case sometime on Friday. Charles Henry Smith placed a telephone call to his star witness in Washington, telling him to catch a midnight train.

19 "The Least Said, the Least Mended"

"Now, Doctor," intoned special prosecutor Oscar M. Vicars, "tell the condition in which you found the body, the wounds you saw, and what you did."[1] With this question to Norton physician T. J. Tudor on Friday morning, Vicars inched into what would soon become a quagmire of conflicting medical testimony over the cause of Trigg Maxwell's death. For the next few days jurors would be asked to sift through layers of verbiage about brain anatomy and physiology—all without the benefit of simple blood tests or x-rays that would have made their task more comprehensible. In the end, the question would come down to whether they believed Tudor and the other local doctor who had performed the autopsy on Trigg Maxwell or the eminent eastern medical authorities who had come to discredit these findings.

Before Dr. Tudor could fashion a reply to Vicars's question, defense attorneys moved to have his entire testimony—indeed, all of the prosecution's medical evidence—excluded as irrelevant. M. J. Fulton argued that the commonwealth had failed to prove the corpus delicti, a legal term literally meaning "body of the crime." "Corpus delicti" refers to material evidence that a crime has been committed. "They [the commonwealth] have not proved this defendant has so much as laid her finger on Trigg Maxwell," Fulton said. If the evidence did not show that Edith caused his death, then the cause of his death was irrelevant, the defense attorney claimed. After a lengthy debate among the lawyers, Judge Carter overruled the motion and allowed Dr. Tudor to continue.

Mirroring his testimony at the first trial, the doctor said he found a deep cut on the top of the victim's head, one inch back from the hairline. Bruises were found on each side of the head wound and on the back of the left forearm and left hand. Bluish, darkened areas around the victim's eyes and nose had led Tudor to expect a skull fracture, but none was found. Instead, the autopsy revealed small clots in the upper part of the brain and at the base of the brain near the spinal cord. In Tudor's opinion the blows to the top of the head had caused a severe concussion, rupturing blood vessels and resulting in death.

The doctor's testimony up to this point had followed a well-worn path, but soon it was to make a startling detour. Over the objections of the defense, Vicars showed Dr. Tudor the hand axe and asked if it could have made the wound on Trigg's head. "Well it could if the right size," he responded. Dr. Tudor proceeded to measure the axe blade and decided it was a bit too wide to have caused the fatal wound. Vicars hastily extricated himself from that line of questioning, but the *Washington Post* could not resist a gleeful comment: "The two prosecutors . . . looked as if the ax had jumped up and nicked them."[2]

When Charles Henry Smith's turn came, he demanded to know why Tudor—a private physician hired by Clora and Lee Skeen—had performed the autopsy rather than county coroner Nicholas F. Hix. Tudor replied that he had assumed Skeen, being a Maxwell in-law, had the authority to arrange for the autopsy.

Smith then led Tudor back over his testimony about the cause of death, through a lengthy discussion of the embalming process, and on to a discourse on his medical qualifications. The Alexandria attorney repeatedly attacked the autopsy procedure. Why had Drs. Tudor and G. T. Foust concluded the autopsy after examining the brain but not the rest of the body? Tudor said they felt they had found the cause of death in the brain hemorrhages and "out of respect to the dead and living we didn't go farther."

The long cross-examination did, however, yield one moment of levity. Smith asked Tudor if the opinion of medical experts "offers room for disagreement."

"Oh yes, we doctors disagree," the witness conceded.

"Almost as much as lawyers, don't you?"

"Hardly as much."

"If you do, you don't make as much fuss about it?"

"We don't make as much money out of our disagreements."

Undertaker Fred H. King took the stand next. King testified that he brought the body from the Maxwell home to Norton around 4 or 5 A.M., embalmed it, and observed the noontime autopsy, which he said was arranged by Vernon Maxwell, Clay Robinson, and Lee Skeen.[3] King said he saw several clots of blood on the top of the brain and two clots at the base. He testified that the embalming process would not leave large clots at the base of the brain "unless they were there previously."

King was followed by Dr. Foust, whose testimony basically seconded that of his colleague Tudor except in one important respect. When asked if the axe could have caused Trigg's head wound, Foust said it was possible that it was an axe "of this type."

Dr. E. L. Sikes, the Maxwells' next-door neighbor and longtime family physician, testified that Trigg had never complained of any symptoms and appeared to be in good health on the afternoon preceding his death. Sikes said he and Trigg drank "one or two bottles of beer" together at Sowards' place, but Trigg remained sober. Late that night, Edith came to his door and told him Trigg was dying. Sikes hurried next door and found him unconscious on the floor. When Chant Kelly pointed out the wound on Trigg's head, the doctor thought it appeared to be a depressed fracture. "I found that he was dying. I went to my room to dress. I told Kelly to do what he could," Sikes testified.

The prosecution then recalled both Foust and Tudor for further questioning. Tudor admitted that no microscopic examination of the brain had been made but said the blood clots were clearly visible to the naked eye.

Having presented evidence that Trigg Maxwell died from a blow to the head, commonwealth attorney Fred Bonham Greear and his team were now ready to counter defense attorney Fulton's claim that "They [the commonwealth] have not proved this defendant has so much as laid her finger on Trigg Maxwell." Attorneys for both sides very well knew that Edith had said she hit her father with a shoe in testimony at the November 1935 trial, and both Greear and Smith had mentioned the fact in their opening statements at *this* trial.

But courtroom pronouncements of lawyers did not count as evidence. Thus the prosecution recalled R. S. Hubbard, the former deputy sheriff who had testified earlier about the arrest of Ann and Edith.[4] Hubbard, who had attended the first trial as Edith's guard, was asked to tell what she had said on the witness stand. Smith was instantly on his feet, objecting in what one writer called "the loudest tones he has used so far."[5] The jury was sent from the courtroom.

In presenting his motion to exclude Edith's previous testimony Smith was forced to reveal his defense strategy. "It is quite possible, your honor, that we may decide not to call the defendant to the stand," he said. "In that case any previous testimony in a previous trial given by her is not permissible either under the laws of Virginia or those of the United States." The lawyers argued Smith's motion at great length, but Judge Carter's decision was not immediately forthcoming. Carter said he would take the matter under advisement, setting aside several law books he planned to study that evening.

Determined to pressure the defense into putting Edith on the stand, Greear then called Bill Fortner, a twenty-six-year-old St. Paul bootlegger who had served about six months in the Wise County Jail while Edith was held there. Fortner had worked as a "trusty" or jail helper and visited the women's section of the jail, where he claimed to have spoken with Edith on several occasions. Fortner said he repeatedly told Edith to "keep her mouth shut" but that she sometimes couldn't resist talking. He quoted Edith as saying, "I hit him [Trigg] with a slipper is all I hit him with and you couldn't kill him with that."[6]

Judge Carter adjourned court at 4:45 P.M., leaving both sides to wonder whether he would allow any mention of Edith's prior testimony. The prosecution's case would spill over into Saturday.

———

Half a world away from Wise County, another drama was rapidly unfolding that December day. Judge Carter had closed his courtroom fifteen minutes early so he could hurry across the street to catch the news on the radio at Shorty Gilliam's cafe. Edward Windsor, who until a few hours before had been king of England, was now delivering his abdication speech. Not only the judge but also Edith and several of the courtroom spectators jammed into Shorty's to catch the historic address. According to Anne Suydam, the Wise County crowd found the love story of the former king and Wallis Simpson even more enthralling than the celebrated murder case now being tried.

"Booted and gumshoed, lumberjacketed and miner clad, all gasped as Edward uttered his closing words: 'God bless you all. God save the King,'" she reported. But Suydam could not resist comparing Edith to Wallis Simpson: "One stands accused of murdering of her father. The other stands accused of murdering tradition."[7] The fortuneteller who had seen Simpson on the throne had it wrong. As with many predictions, it had proved merely to be wishful thinking.

———

Now three days old, the Maxwell trial was, without doubt, the greatest show this side of the Atlantic. Spectators had refused to go out for lunch lest they lose prized courtroom seating, so the entrepreneurial Shorty Gilliam brought baskets of sandwiches from his restaurant and sold them on the spot. But according to *Coalfield Progress* editor Pres Atkins, those who absorbed only the daily courtroom scene were missing half the action. Equally entertaining, in Atkins's view, were the "off-stage moods and activities" of the thirteen members of the out-of-town press corps who spent their evenings at the Colonial Hotel, second-guessing the day's events.

"The hotel sessions of the press group were more active, and perhaps more enlightening, than the court proceedings," Atkins would write at the trial's conclusion. "They discussed and analyzed every bit of testimony and every move by commonwealth and defense counsel, studied and outlined what they if they had been the attorneys, would have done on the morrow, and as the case neared its close, they became an informal, unorganized and unofficial jury, a cross section of their views being a quite accurate reflection of the jury's verdict."[8]

It was snowing in Wise on Saturday morning, but the blind troubadour outside the courthouse kept to his usual business, a tin cup strung from his guitar. Back in court, and before the largest crowd of the week, Judge Carter announced that he would not allow R. S. Hubbard (or anyone) to testify about Edith's sworn statements at the first trial. This was a major victory for Charles Henry Smith, who now was under much less pressure to call Edith to the stand. But the prosecution, still trying to get her statements before the jury, called on Wise County deputy jailer James Cantrell to tell what he had heard *outside* the courtroom.

Over Smith's objections, Cantrell testified that while Edith was in jail he repeatedly told her "the least said, the least mended," but she sometimes talked about her case anyway. The jailer said Edith had told how she had hit Trigg with a slipper during a struggle. Cantrell quoted Edith as saying that Trigg "had her by the hair of her head" and shoved or knocked her down before she hit him, which was consistent with her story of self-defense.

Following the jailer's testimony, Greear announced that the commonwealth had only one remaining witness, but that person had not yet arrived in court. A recess was taken, but the mystery witness never showed up. The prosecution had no choice but to rest its case around 10:30 A.M.[9]

With the jury out of the courtroom, Smith and Fulton then argued the customary defense motion to strike the commonwealth's evidence, asking Judge Carter to set Edith free on the basis of insufficient proof. Such a motion is almost never granted except in the very weakest of cases. Judge Carter, after summarizing the prosecution's evidence, declined to dismiss the murder charge. To no one's surprise, he was allowing the jury to decide the facts of the case.

Just as reporter Fulton Lewis Jr. had predicted back in July 1935, "modern medical science" was the white horse upon which Edith Maxwell would ride free—assuming the defense strategy proved effective. With the prosecution's case completed, Edith's lawyers immediately began calling physicians to raise questions about the cause of Trigg's death.

The first defense witness was Edith's pal Nicholas F. Hix, the Wise County coroner bypassed by Lee Skeen when the private autopsy was performed. If Dr. Hix felt aggrieved by this slight, he did not directly say so, but he did testify that he could not determine what caused the victim's death from reading the autopsy report prepared by Foust and Tudor. (Cleverly, Greear had not offered the report in evidence this time, preferring to use the much more detailed testimony of the doctors themselves.)

On cross-examination, Greear found himself in the unusual position of grilling a fellow county official, one with whom he presumably had worked amicably on other occasions. The exchange revealed, more than anything else, the casualness with which some of the edicts of the General Assembly were regarded outside Richmond. Wise Countians were unaccustomed to having an official coroner, and apparently a recently enacted state law requiring one had not made much impact—even on the kindly, stoop-shouldered Dr. Hix. He told Greear he could not recall how long he had been county coroner, estimating "three or four years, possibly longer." Hix did not know whether those who arranged the autospy were aware of his position.

On a more substantive matter, Dr. Hix maintained that Trigg might have died of heart failure, saying the brain injuries mentioned in the report would not have been severe enough to kill him. Greear asked if brain damage could cause the heart to stop. Dr. Hix agreed that it might but admitted he was "kind of rusty as to which section [of the brain] controls the heart action."

Next came a far more formidable witness—the one whom Charles Henry Smith had summoned to take a midnight train to the Virginia mountains. He was Dr. A. MacGruder MacDonald, a graduate of Georgetown University Medical School and coroner for the District of Columbia. First as deputy coroner and then as coroner, MacDonald had performed or supervised about seven thousand autopsies over a sixteen-year period. The D.C. official had had ample opportunity to study Trigg Maxwell's autopsy report, which had been furnished to him by a *Washington Post* reporter a year earlier. Now, he was about to spend the next four hours pointing out its deficiencies.

With Foust and Tudor's report in hand, the doctor told Smith that he found "no sign of brain injury" on the basis of what he had read. MacDonald said the small blood clots were caused by the pressure used to inject the embalming fluid, and in any event there was insufficient hemorrhage to have caused death. He noted that it is possible for a concussion to be fatal, even without a skull fracture, but that the victim loses consciousness immediately upon receiving the blow to the head—a scenario that did not seem consistent with Trigg's symptoms during the last hour of his life. MacDonald also testified that there are "many causes of sudden" death and that an autopsy should have included examination of all body organs. Winding up his direct testimony, MacDonald swore that the lacerated wound on Trigg's head could not have killed him.

Shortly after lunch, Vicars began his cross-examination of this important witness. In what the *Washington Post* called "an effort to embarrass" MacDonald, Vicars asked him to name every organ of the human body that would be examined in a complete autopsy. MacDonald did so without hesitation, beginning with the skin and ending with the lower extremities.

Vicars quickly seized another tack. In an effort to appeal to the jury's common sense, he sketched a hypothetical situation in which a man is seen at midnight, apparently healthy, and two hours later is found dead with a gunshot wound to the head. "Would you examine his pelvis to see what caused his death?" Vicars asked skeptically. The doctor answered in the affirmative, saying he would examine the entire body "as a matter of routine."

The special prosecutor then moved on to what is today standard procedure in cross-examining experts, making sure the jury understood that MacDonald was, in Vicars's words, "a professional witness." MacDonald explained that he was testifying "at the instigation of the *Washington Post*," which had advanced him money for expenses. He said his usual fee was $100 per day—an enormous sum in those days—but he had not reached an agreement with the *Post* as to what he would charge in this case. Vicars then stated that he believed the *Post* was owned by the Hearst syndicate, but MacDonald corrected him, naming the publisher as Eugene Meyer. (It is unknown whether Vicars had not done his homework or whether he intended to get the Hearst name before the jury.)

After Vicars's lengthy examination of Dr. MacDonald, Smith arose to ask his witness a few more questions. Smith brought up Trigg Maxwell's family history, suggesting that his parents and brother had died sudden deaths. MacDonald agreed that a predisposition for certain diseases runs in families and may have been a factor in Trigg's death, yet he gave no specifics to support the theory.

The defense next called Richmond city coroner J. H. Scherer, whose testimony closely followed that of Dr. MacDonald. "I see nothing in this autopsy that could possibly account for the cause of his death," Scherer said flatly. On cross-examination, Greear tried to tar Scherer with the same brush Vicars had used on MacDonald, but with less success. The Richmond pathologist admitted being an expert witness but pointed out that he routinely testified for the commonwealth and this was his first time speaking for the defense.

With these two accomplished medical authorities, Smith had convincingly demonstrated the shortcomings of Tudor and Foust's report—and of the autopsy itself. He also had raised the important issue of whether the embalming process had skewed the results. Still, neither MacDonald nor Scherer had been able to determine a cause of death. The Wise County doctors, although much less experienced with autopsies than their eastern colleagues, had the advantage of examining the brain of the deceased, and they had relied on their considerable experience in treating head injuries suffered by the scores of miners mutilated by roof falls and other accidents.

As court adjourned late Saturday afternoon, these conflicting medical opinions only deepened the mystery of Trigg Maxwell's death. Whether the uncertainty would translate into reasonable doubt in the minds of the jurors was still an open question. But when the trial resumed on Monday the defense was promising to present its own cause of death: compelling evidence that Trigg Maxwell's mother, brother, and father all died of heart attacks. "This testimony," said the *Post,* "is vital to the defense."

After four punishing days in the courtroom the sequestered jurors were taking Sunday off at the Colonial Hotel under the vigilant eye of the sheriff, Clyde Bolling. Unfortunately, the out-of-town press corps had chosen the hotel for its base of operations as well, and the sheriff was finding the more rambunctious members hard to control. In the chandeliered lobby, a writer for a New York tabloid was carrying on loudly about the case being tried, either not knowing or caring that jurors were nearby.

"You say another word about that trial here," Bolling warned the offender, "and I'll lock you up."

"It's a public place, isn't it?" the woman shot back.

"Surely," the sheriff answered, "but the jury's eating and sleeping here. I can't keep them locked in one little room all the time."[10]

Bolling did not deny the men their Sunday papers but screened them carefully beforehand, snipping out all references to the Maxwell case.

—

The first thing on Monday morning, Judge Carter was about to make a surprising reversal. With the jury absent, he revealed that he had had second thoughts about allowing into evidence the axe purchased by the prosecution at a hardware store. Carter said he had decided to exclude testimony that the Tillers' axe—frequently borrowed by the Maxwells—had turned up missing around the time of Trigg's death. Therefore, the "replica" axe would have to go. "The matter, I think, is rather remote," Judge Carter told the assembled lawyers. "I don't want to take any chances on it. I am going to exclude it." When the jury returned, he asked the men "to wipe from your mind any evidence whatever relative to the Tiller axe."

The defense then called Dr. J. B. Hopkins, described by the *Washington Post* as a "brilliant" twenty-seven-year-old graduate of the Medical College of Virginia at Richmond. Hopkins had been practicing medicine for three years and had moved his practice to Pound in August 1936. Under questioning by Smith, Dr. Hopkins testified that in order for a concussion to be fatal, it would have to be so severe as to cause hemorrhages throughout the entire brain. He suggested that the brain injuries listed in the autopsy report could have been inadvertently caused by Foust and Tudor as they sawed and chiseled the skull. Like the other physicians testifying for the defense, Dr. Hopkins said that nothing in the autopsy report explained Trigg's death.

On cross-examination, Greear downplayed the significance of the report, reminding Hopkins that it was not in evidence and that the commonwealth's medical experts had testified to a "good deal more" than was written in the document. Hopkins agreed with the prosecutor, calling the report "worthless," but the two agreed on little else.

The doctor insisted that the head wounds were consistent with a man falling and striking his head on a piece of wood. He told Greear it would be "impossible" for a woman to kill a man with a lightweight lady's slipper. The stroke of a hammer or hatchet—administered with sufficient force—could kill, but such a blow typically would depress the skull.

Dr. Hopkins testified that "one of the most interesting things" about Trigg's condition was that the area around the eyes was discolored. "This discoloration was perhaps due to the basal fracture that wasn't found," he said, adding that many other things could have caused the "black eyes." When Greear pressed him on this point, he reversed himself somewhat. A first-year medical student could have found such a fracture, had it existed.

The defense next turned to Norton insurance agent Isaac Walker Bush, who had spoken with Trigg at the Rendezvous Cafe in Pound two nights before his death. When Bush started to relate their conversation, Greear immediately objected on the grounds of hearsay. The jury was sent from the room, and Judge Carter asked Bush to tell what had been said. Bush said Trigg mentioned "two reasons why he couldn't talk to me about getting insurance in my company." The first was that he couldn't afford the high premium at age fifty-two, and the second, that he had either heart trouble or high blood pressure and feared he could not pass a physical examination.

After a lengthy argument by counsel, Judge Carter ruled to exclude Bush's testimony. An impassioned Vicars began cross-examining the insurance man anyway, despite the victory the prosecution had just won. Didn't Bush know that Trigg had carried a $1,200 life insurance policy with Equitable Life Insurance Company, which had already been collected? And wasn't it true that a person might say he couldn't pass an examination just to get rid of an insurance agent? Bush coolly responded that he was merely giving Trigg advice. The skirmish over, the jury returned and Bush stepped down.

With its medical testimony virtually over, the defense still had not presented any evidence about members of the Maxwell family dying of heart attacks—and as the roll call of defense witnesses continued, no one ever did.[11] Edith's lawyers now turned to Maxwell friends and family who could tell about the relationships between Trigg, Ann, and Edith. One of these was Edith's brother-in-law Clay Robinson, whose wife, Gladys, was the postmaster at the Maxwell building.

Although sympathetic to the defense, Robinson clearly was uneasy about discussing family matters in public. On direct examination by Fulton he testified that the Maxwells got along "about [like] the average family." They quarreled at times, but never had he heard anyone utter threats against Trigg. Moreover, he said Trigg spoke well of Edith and had borrowed money to send her to college. "I never heard him say anything to the contrary that she wasn't good to him," Robinson testified.

Robinson also distanced himself from the now-controversial autopsy, contradicting previous testimony that he, along with Vernon Maxwell and Lee Skeen, had arranged for the procedure. He swore he had never met Drs. Tudor and Foust and did not authorize them to do an autopsy. Robinson maintained that his wife had arranged for the body to be taken to Norton.

The Maxwell son-in-law also testified about briefly visiting Trigg's home shortly after his death. Robinson saw a blood spot in the front room but did not ask other family members what had happened. He said Dr. Sikes told him "it looked like he had a lick on the head," but again, he did not inquire further. "I didn't want to get mixed up in any family affairs," he testified.

Robinson did admit he had heard rumors about Trigg's having been killed with either a hammer or hatchet. Soon after the slaying, he went into the post office and searched for a hatchet that he and Trigg had been using that Saturday morning while doing carpentry work. "At first I went to the office and looked for the hatchet and didn't find it," he testified. "Somebody had put a piece of wallboard there and the hatchet was lying against the wall." Robinson found the implement on the Sunday afternoon following Trigg's death but did not share his find with the police. He said he still had the hatchet at his home and "they can have it any time they want it."

Vicars also questioned Robinson about how much insurance Trigg carried. Robinson said that he did not know, although he also said he had been administrator of Trigg's estate.[12] He testified that Trigg had been insured by his employer, Consolidated [*sic*] Coal Company, but that he had not had to take a physical examination when first hired. Robinson confirmed that Trigg was missing part of a hand but said he did not know why he was allowed to skip the examination. Waving a piece of paper, Vicars said company records indicated that Trigg *had* been examined and that his only disability was a missing thumb and right ring finger. Smith objected on the basis that the records had not been properly identified and introduced as evidence.

Vicars also used the cross-examination to uncover tantalizing details about the house Trigg had begun building. Robinson testified he was in the process of selling his father-in-law a small plot of land near Robinson's own home. On the afternoon before his death, Trigg told him that he "was selling the building to get the house and move there," according to Robinson's testimony. (This was an apparent reference to selling the Maxwell family home and rental unit on Main Street.)

The son-in-law said that Trigg was going to cook for himself at the new house. Robinson said he was "confident" that Trigg would have invited

Martha Maxwell to live there if she chose because Trigg had always thought highly of his mother. By telling Vicars these details, however, Robinson seemed to be suggesting that Trigg was planning to move there alone, the very opposite of what the defense wanted to establish.

When the cross-examination concluded, Smith rose to rescue his witness. "Do you recall having a conversation with Mr. Maxwell that afternoon before he died about this place, closing it up, when he said Ann, meaning his wife, would sign the deal; that she was willing to sell the place because it was so old and sell the furniture and move up in that house?" asked Smith.

"I believe they did mention something about that," Robinson responded. Smith soon released the witness, who no doubt was glad to step down.

State Trooper Warren Edison Orr, the next witness, found himself in the somewhat unusual position of being called to testify for the defense. Orr, who hailed from Lee County, had been patrolling the Pound area on the night of July 20–21, 1935. The trooper went to the Maxwell home around 5 A.M. after being summoned by Mary Katherine. As Orr approached, he saw Edith and Ann standing in the road in front of the house. "They were apparently heartbroken, consoling themselves as best they could over the death of Mr. Maxwell," he testified. Orr went inside, introduced himself to Dr. Sikes, and asked what had happened. He testified that the doctor told him Trigg had died "a natural death," of heart failure.

Greear immediately moved to strike this evidence on the grounds of hearsay. Smith countered that Dr. Sikes had made a "contrary statement" when he testified earlier in the trial about finding what he thought was a depressed fracture in Trigg's skull. The prosecutors argued that Smith did not cross-examine Dr. Sikes about the alleged conversation with Orr and therefore could not use Orr's testimony to contradict Sikes. Judge Carter ruled to exclude this part of Orr's story.

The defense next called a trio of Edith's friends who flatly denied Conrad Bolling's story about Edith threatening her father while on a drive. According to Bolling, he teased Edith about her father whipping her, and she had responded defiantly, "I'd like for him to try it. If he did I would kill him." The three young women riding in the car that day—Oma Craft, Ruth Craft, and Thelma Mullins—all swore that the telltale conversation never took place.

The Craft sisters lived less than a mile from the Maxwells and frequently stopped in to visit after checking their mail at the post office.

They described Trigg Maxwell as a quiet man who had little to say unless he was drinking. Oma Craft, a teacher, testified that Trigg "seemed harsh with his family when he drank." Her sister, Ruth, who had attended school with Edith, said he "would cuss and fuss around" when he had been drinking.

Both Craft women disputed the prosecution's contention that Trigg had stopped getting drunk when he got religion. According to Ruth Craft's testimony, sometime after Trigg's conversion she and her sister met him staggering down the street in Pound. "He asked if we had started to his home," Ruth recalled. "He always liked us and was interested in us and we told him we [had] started to their home and he said to go on there, he would be looking for us. He had all the appearances of a drunk man."

Ruth Craft also testified about a conversation she allegedly had with Ruth Baker at Trigg's funeral. Baker was Edith's first cousin and former college roommate who had testified that Edith threatened her father on numerous occasions and once had struck him with a poker. According to Ruth Craft, Baker told her privately at Trigg's funeral that she would "get even" with Edith, presumably for her uncle's death.

Another sympathetic witness was Katherine Green Jessee, the young woman described in a New York tabloid as a "gorgeous blonde" with a "delicious Southern drawl."[13] Jessee had gone to Radford State Teachers College when Edith was in her second year. Shortly after school started, Edith began staying in Jessee's room, and the two became close friends. Jessee testified that sometimes she and Edith would spend the night across the hall in Ruth Baker's room.

Jessee testified that she had never heard Edith threaten her father or speak of him "in a disparaging manner." According to Jessee, Edith spoke little of her home life except to say that "her father drank right much and it was really no pleasure to go home." She said Edith did tell her about receiving a letter from Ann Maxwell around Thanksgiving in 1933, which reported that Trigg had quit drinking. Edith had remarked that it would be "more pleasant" to go home in the future.

Jessee apparently married soon after the 1933–34 school year and did not return to Radford. Edith graduated that year and began teaching school in Pound, but the two kept in touch. Jessee continued to socialize with Edith after her marriage—and visited even after Edith was arrested. On cross-examination, Greear quizzed Jessee about her talks with Edith at the Wise County Jail. Jessee denied that she and Edith had ever discussed Trigg's death. She also denied telling her landlady in Norton, Mrs. R. H. Bolling, that Edith had admitted killing her father.

Jessee was followed on the witness stand by Carl Hillman, one of Edith's Dotson cousins. Hillman, whose mother, Cora, was a sister to Ann Dotson Maxwell, had lived with Trigg and Ann for about six months in 1934.[14] Like the Craft sisters, Hillman pinpointed Trigg's drinking as the source of family disagreements. He testified that the Maxwells "got along just like everybody else" when Trigg was sober, but when he came in drinking there would be "rackets."

Under questioning by Vicars, Hillman explained that the drinking episodes he had referred to took place before Fred Maxwell's death in 1933. Hillman testified that Trigg had quit drinking for at least a year after his brother died but had resumed shortly before his own death and was, in fact, drinking on Saturday, July 20, just hours before he died.

On Monday afternoon the defense recalled I. W. Bush, the insurance agent who allegedly had spoken with Trigg two days before he died. During the lunch break, Judge Carter had second thoughts about excluding Bush's story as hearsay. When court reconvened, Carter reversed himself and permitted Bush to repeat the conversation to the jury. Bush testified that Trigg had asked him for advice about an insurance policy another agent had been trying to sell him. Trigg told Bush he had either heart trouble or high blood pressure. Bush said he could not recall which one.

Judge Carter's ruling on the Bush testimony—following on the heels of his decision to throw out the axe—was the second victory of the day for the defense. And now, their best witness was waiting to tell her story.

20 *"The Little Sister with the Golden Curls"*

By the time of the December 1936 trial, Mary Katherine Maxwell had turned thirteen. She now lived in the Richmond metropolitan area, a world apart from the tiny mountain village she had always known. Her photograph had appeared countless times in the *Washington Post* and other publications, and she had performed admirably before five hundred people at the fundraiser in New York. As she took the witness seat in the Wise County courtroom on Monday, December 14, her feet did not dangle quite so high above the floor as they had the previous year. Still, "the little sister with the golden curls" (as Edward T. Folliard called her) managed to retain the qualities that made her such an appealing witness at the earlier trial. Her small stature and Dresden-doll looks belied a scrappy survival instinct that already had served her well.

Mary Katherine once again was being called upon to recite her family's anguish for the benefit of strangers. Unlike her November 1935 court appearance, where she had merely corroborated her mother's and sister's accounts, she would be going it alone this time. Charles Henry Smith was about to decide (if he hadn't already) not to call Edith to testify. Both Edith and Ann would remain silent as part of an apparent strategy to keep the jury from hearing about their evidence at the first trial.

During her own previous testimony, Mary Katherine had spoken coherently and sometimes eloquently, earning the title of "star witness" from members of the press. Despite her popular appeal, Mary Katherine was a girl under considerable strain. She was dreading a rematch with seventy-four-year-old Oscar M. Vicars, who had reduced her to tears thirteen months before in a most ungrandfatherly cross-examination. Since that time, someone no less than a justice of the Virginia Supreme Court of Appeals, in his dissenting opinion, had accused Edith and Ann of making up a story and "drilling" it into Mary Katherine. If that were the case, she'd had plenty of time to perfect her script. Others, however, believed in her complete sincerity—and that no child could possibly keep such an elaborate story straight unless it were true. In any case, Mary Katherine must have felt that she herself was on trial. Just one misstatement might be enough to cast her beloved sister into prison or worse.

Wearing a blue felt hat that set off her heart-shaped face, Mary Katherine gamely began the ordeal. Smith gently led her through the events of July 20–21, 1935, beginning with Ann, Mary Katherine, and Edith picking blackberries on Saturday morning and leading up to Trigg's death in the kitchen doorway. The most crucial testimony, of course, was her eyewitness account of what had transpired in the privacy of the Maxwell home. Although her recitation varied little from her story at the first trial, the spectacle of a child on the stand was highly dramatic. Here is what she told the enthralled listeners:

Trigg, after an evening of drinking, had come home around 10:30 and awakened his wife and eleven-year-old daughter. He began questioning Ann about where she had been that day. Trigg sarcastically told his wife to "powder and paint and curl her hair and go out and pick berries" as if she had had a romantic encounter in the thickets of Bold Camp or had been somewhere else entirely. He told Ann he was going to give her thirty minutes to leave the house the next morning and then stormed out, setting the stage for the unfolding tragedy.

Mary Katherine was awakened a second time by Trigg coming in, demanding to know where Edith was. After Ann told him that Edith had not yet returned from Wise, Trigg remarked that "a man ought to break her God damned neck" and went to his room. Edith arrived ten minutes later, walked into the room where Ann and Mary Katherine were in bed, and learned that Trigg had threatened to run off their mother the next morning. "Go on back to sleep, Mary Katherine," Edith said. "Mama is not going to leave, because I know where she has been picking blackberries."

Trigg then appeared in the bedroom doorway and said not only would he throw Ann out in the morning but he was also going to whip Edith right now. Edith told her father he could whip her but that Ann was not leaving. Mary Katherine then heard Edith say, "Don't stab me with that knife, Poppie." Ann and Mary Katherine jumped out of bed and found Edith and Trigg scuffling in the kitchen. Mary Katherine picked up the knife from the floor and hid it behind a clock. Edith momentarily got loose from Trigg's grasp and ran into Ann's room. Trigg followed her.

Soon Mary Katherine heard Trigg saying, "Ann, look what she has done to me." But Trigg told his wife he was not hurt and soon retired to his room. Ann went to Trigg's room and washed his head. Mary Katherine said she did not see Trigg's head bleeding but did notice blood spots as she was mopping up some water that had spilled in the kitchen during the struggle.

In the meantime, Edith—dressed only in a princess slip—had gone outside and was sitting on the steps leading under the house. Mary Katherine joined her. They could hear Trigg inside, "kicking and cursing Jesus Christ." Edith cried and said she was leaving.

Mary Katherine walked back inside and helped her mother put Trigg to bed. Edith soon came in and started packing her clothes, but Mary Katherine hid Edith's purse under a mattress, figuring she could not leave without money. Just as the little girl had hoped, Edith could not find her pocketbook and finally went to bed. Edith turned on the radio when she lay down but cut it off in less than two minutes after her mother protested.

A little later that night, Mary Katherine heard Trigg get up, and "just a breath after that" she heard something fall. She and her mother jumped up and found him collapsed in the kitchen doorway. Ann splashed water on Trigg's face. She sent Edith after Dr. Sikes. And Mary Katherine ran out in the road, screaming for help.

As she told the courtroom audience of Trigg's final moments, Mary Katherine broke down sobbing. Edith began crying, too, and even some of the jurors had tears in their eyes. "Take your time, no hurry," Smith soothingly told the girl. But Mary Katherine continued to cry and had difficulty answering the next few questions. She eventually recovered herself, and Smith finished questioning his star witness.

The shadows had begun to lengthen when Vicars began his cross-examination. Wearing a black suit, white wing collar, and spectacles that dangled on the end of his nose, the six-foot-two Vicars appeared to the visiting reporters as a "picturesque character." His style was to glare over his glasses and hurl questions in a voice dripping with sarcasm. Mary Katherine, however, dried her tears and began to sass the elderly lawyer as the exchange proceeded. Sometimes she would respond to Vicars as if *he* were the child—correcting him, lobbing his own queries back at him, and displaying a ready wit and nimble tongue. When he once admonished her for guessing at the answer to a question, she shot back, "Well, common sense would teach you that." By 5:10 P.M.—when court adjourned for the day—Vicars seemingly had failed to trip up the witness on a single point.

Mary Katherine ran from the witness stand and hugged Edith, thinking it was over. But in an anteroom a few minutes later the girl learned that she would have to return to the stand the next morning to complete the cross-examination. She cried hysterically, begging Smith, "Oh, don't let them be mean to me."[1]

In the morning, Vicars renewed his attack. Perhaps he had spent the previous evening comparing Mary Katherine's testimony from the first trial with the story she had told on Monday. Armed with transcripts of her earlier statements, he alternately loomed over the tiny witness or slouched in a chair opposite her, firing off question after question.

The lawyer referred to Mary Katherine's testimony at the first trial in which she recalled her father fussing at her mother around 10:30. At that trial Mary Katherine denied that Trigg had offered to buy sugar for Ann to use in canning the blackberries she was planning to pick. She also said that Trigg did not argue with her mother for more than five minutes. Yesterday afternoon, however, she had sworn that Trigg *had* offered to buy the sugar during an argument that lasted twenty to thirty minutes. Hadn't Mary Katherine forgotten part of her story from the first time around?

Like a champion speller puzzling over an unfamiliar word, Mary Katherine showed great presence of mind. She asked to read the transcript of her previous testimony. She still was not able to resolve the contradiction but quickly went on the attack. "You know, nearly two years is a pretty long time to remember the minutes and seconds of things," Mary Katherine said, adding that Vicars had "scared [her] to death" in 1935.

"Scared you to death?" repeated the prosecutor.

"It certainly did."

"You are not easily scared, are you?"

"No, but the way you question me, who wouldn't be scared?"

"Nothing in these questions to scare you, is there?"

"No, but when I look at you."

The audience howled appreciatively at the girl's wit. The bailiff rapped for order.

Vicars continued to pore over Mary Katherine's previous statements but found only slight discrepancies in an otherwise airtight story. As the cross-examination neared its end, the prosecutor posed his most damning series of questions:

"As a matter of fact you and your mother and Edith had talked this all over and mopped the house up?"

"No, sir, I mopped the house up."

"You mopped the house up?"

"Yes, sir."

"And removed all signs of blood you could and after all that was done, while your father was unconscious and dying you let them all come in and you all in one chorus said 'he fell against the meat block; he fell against the meat block; he fell against the meat block,' and neither of you ever told anybody that night or the next day that he had been into a difficulty and had got hit in the head, did you?"

Mary Katherine denied that Edith and Ann had concocted a story. She swore that she had seen Trigg's head lying against the meat block. As for the earlier altercation, she said: "I thought it was just a little scrap in the family and wasn't going to run over the country telling the news."

While claiming not to know what had happened to the bloody shirt that Ann burned in the stove, Mary Katherine identified a second shirt and pair of pants she said her father had been wearing on the night he died. With that, she was allowed to step down.

The defense rested. A chorus of groans rose from the spectators, who, had they been in a theater, might have stomped and catcalled until the leading lady was forced to take the stage. But Edith would not be speaking. Smith was gambling that the golden-haired youngster had carried the day, her spunky presence filling the space left by Edith and Ann's silence.

As Fred Greear would tell a detective magazine, he, too, was disappointed by Smith's strategy, for he had been "most anxious" to cross-examine Edith. But Greear was back on the offensive by early Tuesday afternoon, ready to counter the defense testimony with a string of rebuttal witnesses. Former deputy R. S. Hubbard, jailer J. M. Cantrell, and Pound resident Vie Horne all testified that they observed no scratches on Edith in the hours following Trigg's alleged attack. Three of Trigg's co-workers and union buddies maintained that he had not been drinking in Jenkins on the afternoon before his death. Several others, including one convicted bootlegger, swore that they had seen Trigg around Pound that night and that he was not drunk. Edith's first cousin, Ruth Baker, took the stand to deny that she had ever vowed to "get even" with Edith, contradicting Edith's friend Ruth Craft.

Greear, as usual, saved his most dramatic testimony until last. It came from three young Norton women acquainted with Katherine Jessee, Edith's former college chum. In 1935 Jessee was living in an apartment built in the yard of the R. H. Bolling mansion in Norton. The Bollings' daughter, Louise, recalled a conversation with Jessee that took place shortly after Edith's arrest.

"I got the morning paper and called over there and told her that Edith had confessed to killing her father," Louise Bolling testified. "She came over and said she already knew that. She said that she [Edith] had told her Sunday when she was up to see her and she said she killed him with an iron but she didn't mean to do it, but wouldn't confess unless they brought her mother into it."

Pauline Hutchinson, a young woman who lived at the Bollings, corroborated Louise's story. A third woman, Lucille Blevins, testified that she had heard Katherine Jessee talking in the library of the Bolling home about the Maxwell case on another occasion. According to Blevins, Jessee quoted Edith as saying she had "picked up an iron and threw at her father but didn't intend to kill him."

Defense attorneys asked Judge Ezra T. Carter to instruct the jury that the women's testimony could only be used to rebut Jessee's earlier testimony, not to prove anything against Edith. When Greear had cross-examined her, Jessee had denied under oath that she and Edith had ever talked about the circumstances of Trigg's death during visits at the Wise County Jail. She also had denied speaking with the Bolling woman about the case.

Judge Carter agreed that the testimony could only be used to impeach Jessee, but nonetheless the three new witnesses from Norton had made a considerable impact on the jurors. According to the *Herald*'s W. A. S. Douglas, they "gave their testimony unwillingly and later bewailed the lack of discretion which had set them to gossiping about the tragedy in hot-dog stands, barbeque pits and lunch counters—the usual gathering places of flaming youth in these parts. . . . The testimony seemed more damaging because of the evident sincerity and reluctance of the girls. It bolsters, if the jury considers it that way, the theory of the prosecution that Trigg was killed by a blow from either an axe or a flat iron."[2]

Fred Greear must have rejoiced when Katherine Jessee took the witness stand earlier in the trial. Her presence there, although intended to help Edith, had allowed him to spring a carefully devised trap.

———

Wednesday, December 16, promised to be another day of intense drama. All witnesses having spoken; it was now the attorneys' chance to mold the previous five days of testimony into an approximation of truth. Three hours had been allotted to each side. Reared with a deep appreciation of storytelling—a favorite pastime in the mountains—miners and farmers were laying off work and school children playing hooky to hear the attorneys' closing speeches. Some people speculated that the case might even go to the jury the same day.

After an early-morning conference with counsel, Judge Carter opened the proceedings with about twenty minutes of instructions to the jury. Unlike the jury at the first trial, this panel had a wide range of charges and punishments to consider. The jurors' options included: innocent; guilty of first-degree murder, punishable by twenty years to life imprisonment or death; guilty of second-degree murder, punishable by five to twenty years' imprisonment; guilty of voluntary manslaughter, punishable by one to five years; and guilty of involuntary manslaughter, punishable by up to five years or a minor fine. The *Herald* reported that the judge's instructions "brought confidence" to the defense. Edith's lawyers, for example, had gotten Carter to agree that a slipper could not be considered a deadly weapon. With the jury thus instructed, the show could begin.

As the lawyers prepared to trade barbs and accusations over the next several hours, they were about to play to a divided house. Edith was seated at the defense table with Ann, Earl, and members of the Dotson family. She held Mary Katherine on her knee. Across the room and behind the prosecution table sat her father's family—Trigg's brother Vernon Maxwell and other relatives. "The two sides of the family didn't so much as bow a nod of recognition as they listened intently to the contradictory views attorneys presented," reported the Associated Press.[3]

Lewis McCormick was the first prosecutor to speak. He suggested that there had been no struggle at all, that Edith had struck Trigg with a heavy object "probably while he slept."[4] Defense attorneys A. T. Dotson, M. J. Fulton, and Smith would each take a turn later in the day, as would Commonwealth Attorney Greear. But it was for the elderly Oscar Vicars that Hearst writer Anne Suydam reserved her most fulsome praise:

> In the quavering tones of the old school of oratory, Oscar Vicars denounced the girl whose case has aroused the interest of the entire country. Ranging from tones pitched so high as to be almost hysterical, he dropped to hushed whispers of dire solemnity as he enjoined upon the jury their inescapable duty of charging Edith with the premediated [sic] murder of her father. Stalking up and down before the jury, he frequently paused to glare accusingly at Edith, who, sitting within her brother's arm, returned his gaze unmoved. . . . Murmurs of admiration circulated around the court room as Vicars, in the best revivalist manner, hit the saw-dust trail for the sanctity of the home and the dignity of fatherhood. Trigg Maxwell was a martyr when Vicars finished with him.[5]

Not only did Vicars uphold the character of the deceased but he also ridiculed the opinion of the eminent physicians recruited by the defense. "They bring doctors in here to say he died of heart failure," he thundered. "To say Maxwell died of heart failure, why it's ridiculous. . . . Why, gentlemen, I don't know what was used to kill Trigg Maxwell. It may have been an ax or it may have been something else. But this poor man was beaten to death. I haven't any time to waste on these experts who talk about heart failure. It's your duty to convict this girl of first-degree murder."[6]

Defense attorney Fulton, roughly the same age as Vicars, spoke in "equally flowery" language, trying to tear down the martyr Vicars had just created.[7] Fulton told the jury that Trigg ultimately had brought his fate upon himself by excessive drinking. On the night of his death he had been to several beer joints—including one suspected of selling moonshine—and his intoxicated state had fueled the attack on Edith.

Fulton frequently referred to the tall, athletic Edith as "this little girl" and "this frail little defendant," obviously hoping to provoke stirrings of chivalry from the all-male jury. He argued that Edith had acted in self-defense during the fight with Trigg and that her behavior afterward was that of an innocent person.

"They tell you that he was killed in bed, and they carried him to the kitchen."

"If Edith killed him, would she run out to get the doctor? He was dying then. No. she would have waited until the breath had left him before she ran for the doctor."

"Gentleman, if I had been beating my daughter as Trigg Maxwell was beating Edith, I would expect her to hit me over the head with a slipper. So would you," concluded Fulton.[8]

As the day of speech-making wore on, the cries of infants in close quarters became an increasing irritant. Twice Judge Carter had to halt the proceedings to demand quiet. According to Anne Suydam, "Several women, threatened with being thrown out of court because of their wailing babies, openly nursed them. Others, according to local report, stupefied them with paregoric [an opium-laced medication], to insure themselves permanent seats."[9]

Charles Henry Smith was the last defense attorney to speak. He began by asking the jury not to regard him as a "foreigner." Medical testimony, Smith asserted, "is the very basis of this trial." He reminded the jurors that four doctors testifying for the defense had said that Trigg Maxwell did not die of a blow to the head. "In the name of God, how can the prosecution ask you for a conviction?" he roared. "The court has told you that if there is a reasonable doubt in your minds, you must not convict."[10]

Smith talked for an hour and a half, discussing his theory of an alleged conspiracy involving Lee Skeen and the two Norton doctors who had performed the autopsy. "If Trigg's body had not been whisked off to Norton by Lee Skeen, there to be examined by physicians who contented themselves with a history of the case as told them by Skeen, but instead had been handed over to the duly elected coroner, Dr. Hix, there would have been no murder trial here today," he told the panel.[11]

Smith also downplayed the threats Edith had made against Trigg by humorously referring to a recent article by Eleanor Roosevelt. "She wrote about some newspaper reporter, 'I could have slain him,'" Smith said. "Now if that reporter should die mysteriously, I suppose Mrs. Roosevelt will be indicted for murder." The Alexandria attorney closed his presentation by emphasizing the testimony of his child witness. "Little Mary Katherine has come here and told you how her daddy died, but the prosecution asks you to forget her testimony. They ask you to believe a fantastic story about Edith killing her father with a mysterious ax. May the God you worship help you do the right thing," he solemnly told the jury.[12]

Now the spotlight was on the commonwealth attorney, who by tradition would give the final oration. Greear used inferences from the evidence to construct his vision of what had happened on the night of July 20–21, 1935: After Edith returned home from a round of cafes and learned that Trigg had threatened to run her mother off, she became furious. "She said to Mary Katherine, 'I'll go right in and kill the son of a bitch.' And she did, with what weapon I don't know—."

Greear's argument was cut short by an outburst from defense attorney Fulton. "Your honor," he shouted, "I move for the discharge of the jury because of the misconduct of the Commonwealth's Attorney. He is arguing on matters which were never in the evidence."

All eyes turned to Judge Carter, who was surrounded by a great throng of spectators around his bench. He thought for a moment and then denied the motion for a mistrial. The defense noted an exception.

"Women's voices were heard raised loud," continued Greear. "She advanced to the bed. There was blood on the bed."

Another objection was raised and quickly overruled.

"He threw up his hands to ward off the blows—."

The defense objected a third time, but the judge let Greear finish.

Greear told the jury that Edith had then taken the murder weapon and gone to the back steps of the house, throwing the instrument in the river.[13]

"Gentlemen," the prosecutor said, "this is just another murder—a cold-blooded murder. Some regard victory as greater than the truth. I don't. Take the case and decide. The responsibility is yours."[14] With Greear's charge upon them, the twelve men retired to the hotel to spend the night. On the morrow, formal deliberations would begin.

Anticipation swept through the crowded Wise County courtroom as the twelve jurors filed in at 11:37 A.M. on Thursday. They had been deliberating the case for approximately an hour and a half.[15] Surprise over the quickness of the decision turned to "mingled murmurs of approval and dismay" as the verdict was announced.[16] The jury had found Edith guilty of second-degree murder and recommended the maximum sentence of twenty years.

Edith had been expecting an acquittal until she saw the look on the jury foreman's face. Now her knees were buckling. Earl grabbed her and held her close as she began to cry. Edith looked over Earl's shoulder at the twelve men leaving the room. "Them jurors know I am not guilty," she exclaimed bitterly.[17]

A *Herald* reporter followed jury foreman Lewis Estes to a coatroom and pressed him for answers. The "smartly clad, clean-cut" undertaker explained that there had been no disagreement among the twelve men as to Edith's guilt. To arrive at a verdict, they had relied on the third article of Judge Carter's instructions: "The court instructs the jury that every unlawful homicide is presumed to be murder in the second degree. In order to elevate a murder to first degree, the burden of proof is on the Commonwealth. To reduce to manslaughter, the burden is on the prisoner."

Although the jurors did not go on record explaining *why* they thought Edith was guilty, a gray-haired cab driver later gave a reporter what might have been an opinion reflecting their views. "Edith—she's always been wild and willful," he said. "She just couldn't stand to have anybody say to her what she should do. And her mother always favored her when she was afighting with her dad. There was always bad blood between them, with Trigg on the taking end since the girl got grown up."[18]

The panel's only real deliberation had been on the degree of punishment. Ten jurors had initially favored the twenty-year sentence, while one advocated fifteen years and another eighteen years. The two more lenient jurors were convinced to join the majority, and the twenty-year sentence was unanimously recommended. The jurors could have given her as little as five years for second-degree murder.

"The verdict not only stunned Edith, but her counsel as well," reported the *Coalfield Progress* on December 17. "Charles Henry Smith, chief counsel, had difficulty framing any statement for the newspaper boys." Even so, Edith's attorneys had not quite finished their day's work. Smith immediately filed notice of his intention to appeal, and Fulton petitioned Judge Carter to release Edith on bail.

At first the judge was reluctant to let Edith go, stating that it was against his practice to allow bond for felons with sentences greater than ten years. Once defense attorneys furnished legal authority for the bail motion, Judge Carter decided to allow bond but raised it from $6,000 to $15,000. One report said that people in the audience were now "swayed in sympathy" for Edith and had "literally crowded over one another to go her bail."[19] A farmer and a real estate agent joined her two original bondsmen in pledging their property.

Minutes after her release, Edith laughingly told a companion, "I could have made it for $25,000 just as easy. . . . I have some friends left."[20] But as Edith was returning to her Uncle Gernade's house in Wise, probably to gather up her belongings, gloom settled over her again. "This whole thing is keeping me from getting married," she told Anne Suydam. "I'm like most other women—I'd like to get married. But if they make me out to be a murderess, I don't think there's a man in these United States would have me—not if I wear high heeled slippers, anyway. I get a lot of crank proposals by fan mail, but that's about all."

"Her family hooted in derision," reported Suydam, "and assured me that there was more than one young man of her acquaintance anxious to marry her."[21]

———

Edith was back home in Chesterfield County a few days before Christmas, decorating a miniature tree for the benefit of her two younger sisters. Her mother, who had cried through the closing arguments of the trial, was still crying, and Edith—her own spirits somewhat recovered—was trying to cheer her up as well. With Mary Katherine and Earl, they had driven back to the farm immediately after the verdict, rejoining Anna Ruth, who apparently had stayed in the Richmond area. Here Edith planned to remain until her sentencing hearing in Wise on March 1, 1937, when her lawyers, once again, would argue a motion to set aside the verdict. The murder case against Ann Maxwell also had been delayed until the March term of circuit court. But whatever anxieties the Maxwells may have felt over future court battles were soon superseded by a more immediate concern.

The press reported that the family was living "in impoverished circumstances," unable even to buy enough coal to heat the two-story farmhouse.[22] Earl was said to be seeking work, having given up his job in New York and spent his savings. "It'll cost us about $1,000 for just the stenographic record of Edith's last trial, but we've got to have it in order to go through with our appeal," he told a reporter. "And that appeal is going through, right up to the Supreme Court, if I have to sell myself into slavery to do it."[23]

On December 18 Edith announced that she, too, would like to get a job. Within twenty-four hours she had accepted a position as hostess and cashier at the Richmond Inn, a posh "cabaret" restaurant frequented by legislators who transacted the state's business at the capitol just across the street. The proprietor, Walter Kirsch, did not disclose Edith's salary but told reporters that she would be well paid "and won't have to do anything she doesn't want to do."[24]

After a lunchtime meeting with Kirsch on the nineteenth, Edith went Christmas shopping with her cousin, Lucille Bryington. The two women had plans to join Earl for dinner at Edith's new place of employment. They arrived at the Richmond Inn before he did and hid out in an alcove, escaping the notice of the affluent clientele but not of the press. Edith uncharacteristically announced that she was "not at home" to photographers. When a cameraman insisted on taking her picture, she refused to allow it without Earl's okay. When her brother finally arrived, he told the assembled newshounds to "let the poor girl get a little rest."[25]

Edith began working at the Richmond Inn the next evening. Given the fact that her celebrity had brought several job offers, it seems odd that she chose so public a position as that of restaurant hostess. Like protective mother hens, both the *Roanoke Times* and the *Richmond News Leader* seemed anxious to deflect the withering gaze of public curiosity that Edith's presence was sure to invite—an interest the newspapers, ironically, had helped perpetuate. "The dark-haired, blue eyed girl, who has faced two sets of jurymen and has spent more than a year in jail may find it slightly difficult at first to face the crowds of curious diners," noted the *News Leader,* "but she will come through in flying colors, her employer believes, for Edith honestly wants to work and work hard." Similarly, the *Times* hoped patrons of the Richmond Inn would not gawk at Edith. "Doubtless she will be grateful if people will eat their meals and depart without staring at her as though she were an animal on exhibition in a circus menagerie," advised an editorial.[26]

Edith's notoriety nonetheless followed her to the restaurant. One day after the Virginia press voted the Maxwell case the top news story in the state for 1936, she rang in the New Year with admiring patrons. According to the Associated Press, Edith "sat with a party of merry-makers and told incidents of her life to misses who said they were 'just too thrilled' to talk to the Edith Maxwell they had read so much about. They hung on Edith's every word as she told them incidents of her life before and after the alleged slaying of her blacksmith-miner father."[27]

Had she been inclined to reflect on the year just past, she might have judged it both cruel and kind. She had begun 1936 among the unfortunates in the Wise County Jail; now she found herself pampered by fans in most luxurious surroundings. Yet in some ways she was little better off. After months of legal work and thousands spent, the result was only a five-year reduction in sentence. "No wonder Edith wept bitterly when she heard the verdict," said the *Roanoke Times* on December 18. "Her case rests with the Virginia courts, where it rightly should rest, and not with the newspapers of Washington, Chicago, New York and other Northern cities." One fact alone might have served as a balm to gloomy thoughts: Edith's popularity was undiminished. Perhaps, in the new year, she was counting on celebrity to see her through.

21 *Marry in Haste,*
Repent at Leisure

To the true believer, Edith Maxwell's second murder conviction had plucked her from the ranks of ordinary mortals and set her in the firmament of feminist martyrs. Soon after the trial, the National Woman's Party journal published a year-old closeup photograph of Edith staring wide-eyed through cell bars. "Edith Maxwell symbolizes the position in which women find themselves today, the world around," read the caption. "In all countries, including the United States, the liberties of women have been encompassed by man-made bars, which, while perhaps not so obvious as in the picture, are equally effective. Let women greet the New Year with a challenge, and free themselves in 1937 by writing the Equal Rights Amendment into the United States Constitution."[1]

Gail Laughlin, back home in Maine, burned with a holy anger that fairly sizzled off the columns of the *Lewiston Evening Journal,* which published a lengthy interview on January 14. Declaring the second trial "a travesty of justice," Laughlin flatly stated her belief that Trigg had died of natural causes and Edith had been framed. It was all an act of revenge by the Maxwells against the Dotsons, she said, a family feud brought on by Ann Dotson's marrying out of her class. Finally the Maxwells had seen their chance to get back at uppity Ann and her daughter. "That girl was practically convicted before the trial opened in December," Laughlin declared. "If her innocence had been written across the sky in letters of fire by the hand of God Almighty, the court's verdict would have been the same." The article gave no specifics about the alleged frame-up except to say that the political influence of Lee Skeen played a role.

"I don't think I should care to go down there now alone and unprotected," she added. "I might very likely be shot down from ambush by one of the girl's enemies. That seems to be the prevailing custom down there—accident of course."

Although her invective was unusual for an attorney in an ongoing case, Laughlin still considered herself part of the defense team. She expected the appeals to drag on in the Virginia courts for about another year. According to her scenario, Judge Ezra T. Carter would "undoubtedly" refuse to set aside the jury verdict at the hearing in March. Another appeal to state court would be made, and—if Edith's lawyers were successful—Laughlin (despite her fear of ambush) anticipated returning for a third trial the following December. Each setback at the local or state level, however, inevitably moved the case closer to the U.S. Supreme Court and to a possible landmark decision outlawing all-male juries. If the state refused to give Edith another trial, the stage was set for Laughlin—and the Woman's Party—to land a place in history.

In Richmond, the head of the Virginia NWP chapter seemed equally determined to see the case through. "We will continue the fight until justice is rendered, provided of course ample additional funds can be secured," wrote the ever-practical Elsie Graff on New Year's Day, 1937.[2] Graff soon announced that the Virginia branch of the National Woman's Party would sponsor a series of six galas in Washington, Philadelphia, and other cities to raise money for Edith's defense.

The NWP's first benefit ball was to be held at Hotel Washington on January 15. In advance publicity, the *Herald* informed readers that "Washington is going to have a chance to meet Edith Maxwell in person." The newspaper coupled the announcement with a photograph of Edith wearing dark lipstick and a jaunty hat, adding the curious notation that Edith "has new personality."

Although some capitol socialites may have regarded the upcoming affair as just another charity ball, NWP members scarcely needed reminding of the serious purpose at hand. Proceeds from the dance would be used to pay for printing the transcript of Edith's second trial—a document essential to carrying an appeal to a higher court. Helena Hill Weed, a Vassar graduate and geologist who had served jail time during the suffrage battles nearly twenty years before, was one of the NWP members coordinating the event. According to Weed's correspondence, Edith's supporters had been told to raise more than $1,600 (about $21,500 in today's dollars) by March 1, 1937. Otherwise Edith would miss the chance to appeal her twenty-year sentence.[3]

Weed and her cohorts put their organizing skills to work. To keep overhead low, they secured bargain rates for printing the invitations and persuaded the hotel management to make the Hall of Nations ballroom available for a minimum charge. A local women's orchestra, the Thelma Schilling Cadets, agreed to play for free. The NWP also enlisted an impressive group of "patronesses" for the dance, prominent East Coast women whose stamp of approval could help make the fundraiser a success. Among these were Gail Laughlin and Harriet Stanton Blatch, daughter of the revered Elizabeth Cady Stanton and a feminist leader in her own right.

Edith apparently had quit her cashier's job at the Richmond Inn very early in the New Year. By January 6 she was reported to be "living in seclusion" in Washington.[4] On January 8, Edith began selling tickets from the lobby of the hotel where the dance was to be held.

That evening, she and Earl attended a reception at the Alva Belmont House on 144 B Street N.E., the chandeliered headquarters of the National Woman's Party. The three-story, red-brick building, acquired by the NWP in 1929, was a historic residence that had figured in the War of 1812. In recent times its stable and carriage house had been converted to a handsome library. Elaborate mantels and woodwork provided a backdrop for exquisite colonial furniture, including desks reportedly owned by Susan B. Anthony and Andrew Jackson. Even the door locks were plated with silver.[5]

Here the upper echelons of capitol society—some three hundred members of Congress, admirals, diplomats, and their spouses, along with an actress from the hit play *The Children's Hour*—were paying tribute to Sarah Thompson Pell, the NWP's new national chair.[6] Sarah Pell was a tall, moneyed New Yorker who owned her own little piece of American history. Her husband had inherited Fort Ticonderoga, the strategic Revolutionary War fortress, and the couple had transformed it into a popular museum. Pell was described in social columns as a Washington "favorite."[7] She was using her connections to campaign for passage of the Equal Rights Amendment, which had been reintroduced into the then-current session of Congress as Joint Resolution Number 1.

Even among these symbols of power and privilege, Edith was cloaked in an aura of celebrity that others found irresistible. The NWP reception was an opportunity for many party members—who had been raising money for Edith for more than a year—to hear her story in her own words. She soon became the focus of an admiring group. "Among the indignantly sympathetic women who were impressed anew with the personality of the sad-faced, slender girl, whose quiet dignity and poise under painfully trying circumstances were the subject of favorable comment by all, were Mrs. Charles McNary, wife of Senator McNary, and Mrs. Raymond Gram Swing of New York," reported *Equal Rights* on January 15.

At least one party insider, however, thought all the attention made Edith uncomfortable. "I'm frank to say it was odd to shake hands with her," the woman wrote after the reception. "She is a fragile, delicate little creature, rather pretty and very shy. Told me she was not used to all this and did not know how to act. Said she was not used to people. But she stayed too, till the last minute, like everyone else."[8]

—

Sharp-eyed Anne Suydam, the *Herald* reporter who had written the "color stories" on Edith's second trial, was on hand to record the benefit ball in her usual florid style. The men and women whirling across the floor at the Hotel Washington seemed to defy the usual taxonomies of a society crowd. Suydam found "couples clad in dinner coats and street clothes, couples from Washington streets and Virginia hills," even a few from Wise County.[9] Among the contingent of Woman's Party attendees was the tireless Elsie Graff, who was said to be chaperoning Edith. Earl was collecting tickets.

Edith herself did not dance. Suydam chronicled her behavior as one of quiet dignity. "Dressed in a deep blue rough crepe, long-sleeved street frock, she stood among the patronesses of her benefit, and greeted friends and strangers. She wore a small shoulder corsage of sweetheart roses, brought to her by a young man and woman hitherto unknown to her."

A photograph from that evening shows Edith standing in a receiving line flanked by Graff, Weed, and several other women. At twenty-two, she is a head taller and perhaps thirty years younger than most of the women attending her—a sweet bird of youth among nurturing silver owls. Edith is smiling, extending her hand to a man in black tie. In another, more innocent time, it could have been a scene from a wedding or graduation party, but later events reminded everybody how different it really was.

As the night (and perhaps the champagne) flowed on, Edith's fans became bolder. Near midnight she found herself besieged, crowded up against a pillar in the ballroom by autograph-seekers. Before the night was over more than forty patrons would take home Edith's signature, trophies wooed not from a politician, home-run king, or movie star but from a woman who had—or maybe hadn't—killed her daddy.

—

In addition to ticket sales, the hoopla surrounding the ball had attracted several sizable donations, including checks from a U.S. senator and from wealthy Washington hostess Evalyn Walsh McLean. The next day, Helena Hill Weed wrote to thank McLean for contributing $50, promising to send her a detailed statement of receipts and expenditures as soon as a financial report could be compiled.[10] Weed noted that the money had been sent directly to a Richmond bank and deposited in a defense fund account controlled by Elsie Graff, the NWP state chair. Weed emphasized that Graff was relying on advice from a Woman's Party lawyer [most likely M. J. Fulton] to make sure the funds would be used only for expenses that were "actual and proper" for Edith's defense.

"I make this explicit statement," Weed wrote, "because our committee has been somewhat embarrassed by the overly-enthusiastic and unauthorized activities of her brother Earle [*sic*] in connection with raising this fund, of which our committee is sponsor and trustee." Weed did not tell her patron just what Earl's "overly-enthusiastic" and "unauthorized" fundraising ventures were, but clearly a struggle for control of the money—and Edith's future—was under way. And Edith, for her part, had always said she would do exactly as Earl wanted her to do.

Whether by accident or design, Edith and Earl Maxwell stayed out of the headlines from mid-January through late February 1937. On the surface, it was a fallow news period in this year-and-a-half-old case. Journalists connecting the dots of each court appearance must have anticipated that the next big story would fall on March 1, when Edith's lawyers planned to appear before Judge Carter in Wise. Behind the scenes, however, a story of a different ilk was brewing, and by Tuesday, February 23, one newspaper had printed it.

"EDITH MAXWELL REPUDIATES AID OF NATIONAL WOMAN'S PARTY," declared an eight-column banner headline topping the front page of the *Washington Times*. The *Times* said it had "learned exclusively" that Edith had written to the NWP, asking them to stop working on her case and demanding an accounting of all funds raised on her behalf. The letter gave the boot to M. J. Fulton—the prominent Richmond lawyer who had played an important role at her second trial—and also to Gail Laughlin because she, too, had been ushered into the case by the Woman's Party.

Edith reportedly stated that only the *Washington Post*'s lawyer, Charles Henry Smith, and her cousin, A. T. Dotson, were authorized to represent her. But the *Washington Times* said Dotson was quitting because "he was not in accord with the new proceedings and that he regretted this new turn in the case." Dotson later amended this statement, saying that he was still quite willing to assist Edith, but his job in Richmond at the state comptroller's office would prevent him from doing so.

Elsie Graff publicly maintained that the decision to part company was mutual, but in reality the activists had little choice. Graff gave this statement—gracious yet unenlightening—to the press:

The work of the Virginia Branch in behalf of Edith Maxwell was started on December 19, 1935, following a written request to render help and legal services to bring about her acquittal. Miss Maxwell said little time was left in which to act and urged us to proceed with as much speed as possible. The Virginia Branch employed counsel and has been continuously active in raising funds for Miss Maxwell's defense.

On Friday, February 19th, the Chairman of the Virginia branch and counsel decided it would be in the interest of all concerned for this organization to withdraw from further participation in the case. On Saturday, February 20, a letter was received from Miss Maxwell withdrawing the authorization to represent her.

The Virginia Branch is as much interested now as ever before to see Miss Maxwell acquitted of the charge against her, and hopes the new defense arrangements will result in establishing her innocence.[11]

Although Graff's remarks struck an even tone, the *Times* reported that Edith's letter had "thrown a bombshell into her defense" and "caused a furor in the Woman's Party." The repudiation was not only a stunning setback to the NWP's political agenda but also a public embarrassment. Now the party had no case to take to the Supreme Court—and the memory of all the resolutions, teas, editorials, and "Dime-for-Justice" boxes must have made the activists feel slightly foolish.

The Washington headquarters of the National Woman's Party swiftly distanced itself from its erstwhile cause celebre. In a less than candid statement, the NWP declared that there had been a "misunderstanding" and that the party had "never taken any action in the Maxwell case."[12] Although it was true that Elsie Graff and the Virginia branch had initiated and directed fundraising activities for Edith, they did so with the blessing of the NWP's national council, which not only had contributed money and staff time but also wagered its public standing. *Equal Rights,* the party journal that had put Edith on its cover less than two months earlier, would make no mention of her again. Some NWP officials now complained that the focus on "individual issues" by state chapters was hurting the party's image and draining away resources from the Equal Rights Amendment campaign.[13] The NWP had been quick to marry itself to Edith's cause. Now it could repent at leisure.

———

Guarded pronouncements about Edith's divorce from the NWP did little to satisfy public curiosity. Had the party's radical politics become an albatross to the defense, or were the feminists merely a convenient scapegoat? Had Charles Henry Smith delivered an ultimatum to the Maxwells demanding sole authority over the case? Did Edith really believe that the

Woman's Party was exploiting her for its own political or financial purposes? Had the dispute with Earl over the money been the final straw? Or had Edith (or Earl) secured other, more influential backers? When pressed by reporters, neither Elsie Graff nor NWP lawyer M. J. Fulton would explain. Commonwealth attorney Fred Greear, who received letters from Fulton and A. T. Dotson confirming their withdrawal, likewise remained mum.

Finding the clues required a close reading of certain newspapers. The *Washington Herald,* long sympathetic to Edith's cause, downplayed the incident but did report the views of "Miss Maxwell's friends," who were not identified:

> Decision by Miss Maxwell to go ahead with her fight under the direction of one lawyer is said to have been due to advice of friends who have interested themselves in her plight and have agreed to furnish funds with which to fight for her liberty to the end.
>
> At the second trial, with a large group of attorneys around her, there was reported to have been a series of conflicts on the matter of procedure. The Virginia branch of the National Women's Party has been interested in the Maxwell case from the political angle, considering it a fertile field for bringing national notice to their contention that a constitutional amendment should be enacted making conviction of women by all-men juries illegal.
>
> Miss Maxwell's friends consider the important thing is to hue [*sic*] to the line along the evidence and leave political angles out, except as they might be brought in on a Federal question, should the case ever reach the Supreme Court of the United States. Another matter objected to by the defendant's friends was that Edith was being shown around at dances and other get-togethers in order to raise the money for the fees of attorneys appearing for the Virginia branch of the Women's Party.[14]

The victor of all the infighting, Charles Henry Smith, may have shed a few crocodile tears as he spoke with a *Herald* reporter about the new defense arrangement. "Naturally, I have nothing to do with elimination of other counsel from the Maxwell case," he said. "I have been retained by people whose sympathies for Edith have been aroused and have been asked to work alone." Smith went on to say with evident sincerity that he would do all in his power to free Edith, while noting that "the tragedy which has enveloped her can never be entirely lifted."

Still, one question cried out to answer: Exactly who were "Miss Maxwell's friends"?

On February 24, just one day after the *Washington Times* broke the NWP story, the *Richmond News Leader* came up with its own explanation for the split. Quoting reliable sources, the Virginia newspaper offered a surprising assertion: Edith had spurned the NWP's further assistance because she had "made profitable financial arrangements with a motion picture firm." Ann Maxwell refused to confirm that a contract had been signed, but she admitted that her daughter "would like to sign up with the movies" if she remained free on bail or eventually was acquitted. According to the *News Leader,* "It was rumored that Edith would be given a contract, if she escaped the prison sentence, to appear in a movie based on the story of her crime."

Echoing the rationale given for the 1935 Hearst newspaper deal, Ann Maxwell said the new financial arrangement was necessary to fund Edith's continuing legal appeals. According to Ann, Edith held no resentment toward the Woman's Party, but "she had no choice. She had to decline the help of the Woman's Party or give up the other." Her mother did not say, however, who "the other" was.

Warner Brothers, the Hollywood studio reportedly involved in the negotiations, said it "had no contract with Edith and contemplated none," according to the article. The *News Leader,* however, said that Edith intended to make personal appearances at theaters to support screenings of *Mountain Justice,* a soon-to-be-released film version of the Maxwell tragedy. The alleged plan would depend on Judge Carter's willingness to continue her bond at a hearing the following Monday in Wise.

With this turn of events Edith began to deviate from the script that had been written for her by a sympathetic press. The woman portrayed as a humble teacher of mountain children, fighting to clear her name of the horrible stigma of patricide, was now apparently bent on a career in show business—unless the law inconveniently interfered. According to Earl Maxwell, Edith had received an offer to perform in vaudeville as early as January 1936. Earl, however, had told the *Washington Post* at that time, "You can be sure of one thing, if she's ever acquitted she's not going to appear in vaudeville or go in the movies or anything like that. We're not going to capitalize on this affair. All we want is to have Edith with us again." Yet by 1937 the temptations perhaps were proving irresistible to both Edith and Earl.

22   *Six Coonhounds from Kentucky*

Although rumors about Edith and show business deals did not surface in the eastern press until February 1937, at least one film inspired by her case had been quietly in development for well over a year. Wise County Court clerk E. B. McElroy, months earlier, had received a letter with an unusual request: Would he be so kind as to forward a diagram of the courtroom to Hollywood? At the Warner Brothers studio in Burbank, Luci Ward, a secretary and aspiring screenwriter, was fashioning a film script based on the much-publicized story. McElroy promptly responded with a hand-drawn sketch showing where Edith and Earl Maxwell, the judge, the attorneys, and the jury had been seated.

It was not surprising that Warner Brothers, of all the major studios in Hollywood's Golden Age, would tackle a subject as controversial as the Maxwell case. Known as the "workingman's studio," Warner tended to avoid high-society films; it preferred the seamier side of life. By 1930, sensing America's obsession with organized crime and social upheaval, studio executives had shrewdly embarked upon a "torn-from-the-headlines" policy, adapting stories of crime and corruption drawn from newspaper accounts. This realistic formula worked, and Warner scored some major successes with gangster movies and social protest films.

One of the studio's riskiest ventures in this genre was *I Am a Fugitive from a Chain Gang* (1932), an exposé of conditions in the Georgia prison system. Real-life escaped prisoner Robert E. Burns had lived in Hollywood under an alias while the screenplay based on his memoirs was being developed, serving as a technical advisor to a team of Warner Brothers writers. The subsequent public outcry when the movie was released set in motion a reform movement that eventually forced Georgia officials to remove chains from prisoners throughout the state. *Fugitive* won critical acclaim but reaped condemnation from Georgia lawmakers, even though the setting was heavily disguised. Two prison wardens sued Warner Brothers and its affiliate, the Vitaphone Corporation, for defamation. According to author Charles Higham, the case was eventually settled out of court, and *Fugitive* went on to become a film classic.[1]

The Maxwell case, coming just three years later, was prime Warner material. Its overtones of family violence, subjugation of women, and lynch-mob action had the makings of another electrifying script. Perhaps the studio could do for women in Appalachia what it had done for prisoners in Georgia.

Scriptwriter Ward completed the first draft of her screenplay about three months after Edith's first trial. With Edith far away in the Wise County Jail, Ward had to rely almost exclusively on newspaper stories as research material. Thanks to the wire services, there were hundreds—if not thousands—from which to choose by the end of 1935. Ward filled several scrapbooks with clippings from the Los Angeles and New York City press, notably from the often unreliable Hearst newspapers.

Although she consulted a few other publications, Ward generally used print sources that fed her a steady diet of the "mountain code" material she uncritically wove into her script. Conspicuously absent were accounts of the trial from the Virginia newspapers—which would have given more balance and perspective to the complicated case—or a trial transcript, which probably would not have been available.[2] The resulting screenplay, eventually given the ironic title *Mountain Justice,* was a bitter denouncement of the "Appalachian culture" that Ward had come to view through the warped perspectives of the yellow press.

Not surprisingly, her original draft contained several obvious parallels with real-life events. The Edith Maxwell character (Ruth Harkins) is a beleaguered teacher who graduates from "East State Normal College." Her little sister, "Bethie," speaks passionately on her behalf at her murder trial. And her mother, "Meg," faints and is carried out of the courtroom when the guilty verdict is read.

Studio executives had problems with Ward's screenplay, however, possibly because it was close enough to real life to invite lawsuits. They brought in another writer, Norman Reilly Raine, to help rewrite the script. By July 25, 1936, Raine and Ward had created another version in which the Edith character was a nurse instead of a teacher. Exactly one month later the writers delivered a finished draft of *Mountain Justice,* and casting could begin.

Rumor had it that the leading female role would go to Warner star Bette Davis. Some in the studio, however, feared that the grim melodrama of *Mountain Justice* would not be an appropriate vehicle for the sophisticated Davis, so the part went to a lesser-known actress, Josephine

Hutchinson, who had spent most of her professional life on the stage. She had made the switch to movies only a couple of years earlier, playing in *Oil for the Lamps of China* (Warner, 1935) and *The Story of Louis Pasteur* (Warner, 1936).

Irish-born actor George Brent was cast as Hutchinson's suave leading man, the New York lawyer who saves the fictional Ruth Harkins from hillbilly justice. Robert Barratt, a ubiqitous screen heavy who had been "knocked out" or "killed" twenty-four times in his previous three years of film work, was chosen to play Ruth's father. Comedic actors Fuzzy Knight and Margaret Hamilton would supply the movie's lighter moments as they wrangled over the attentions of Doc Barnard (Guy Kibbee), an affable country physician.

The task of directing went to Michael Curtiz, the Hungarian-born filmmaker who would make motion picture history in 1942 with the release of *Casablanca*. Curtiz began his show business career as a teenaged strong man in a Hungarian circus. After becoming a successful stage and screen director in Europe, he set his sights on Hollywood and became a "workhorse" director for Warner Brothers, turning out forty-four films between 1930 and 1939. His knack for action was perfectly suited to the Errol Flynn epics *Captain Blood* (1935) and *The Charge of the Light Brigade* (1936).

It was an era of studio set design, when shooting on location was virtually unheard of. Although the picture was to be filmed mostly in southern California, the meticulous Curtiz went to considerable lengths to make his film look authentic. His (and Luci Ward's) lust for true-life detail was no doubt behind the studio's request for a sketch of the Wise County courtroom where the Maxwell case had been tried in 1935.

Warner Brothers also hired Kentucky schoolteacher Elizabeth Hearst to serve as technical advisor. According to the *Mountain Justice* press book, Hearst was on the set every day, "working with Curtiz to ensure authenticity in speech, customs and costumes of America's forgotten people." She was also called upon to whip up an occasional batch of cornpone or to teach the Hollywood actors to spit melted licorice candy as if it were streams of tobacco. Presumably on her advice, the studio "imported" six coonhounds from Kentucky, along with thirty corncob pipes, forty-three plugs of chewing tobacco, fifteen long and short gourds, twenty-seven jars of preserves, and 1,400 yards of calico. Two dozen watermelons were forwarded to the set from Hope, Arkansas. The coonhounds would later be seen lying about the fictional Wise County courtroom.

On September 10, 1936, as Edith was anxiously waiting for news of her appeal to the Virginia Supreme Court, Curtiz began shooting *Mountain Justice* on Stage Number 6 of the First National lot in Burbank. The film was to be shot in just thirty working days—an astonishingly ambitious deadline of October 14—but the production ran behind schedule almost from the beginning. The filming was not completed until November 6, 1936, nearly three weeks late.

On November 20, Twentieth-Century Fox beat Warner Brothers to the box office with *Career Woman,* its own film inspired by the Maxwell case.[3] Having been scooped by a rival production, Curtiz apparently decided to take his time with editing and finishing *Mountain Justice.* Movie-goers would have to wait several months to see his screen version of the Maxwell story. In the meantime, Warner Brothers would consistently disavow any connection between the film and the real Edith Maxwell, even as E. B. McElroy's sketch of the Wise County courtroom lay nestled in the studio's files.

On January 29, 1937—just two weeks after the Woman's Party benefit ball in Washington—Edith and Earl Maxwell had quietly paid a visit to the New York office of lawyer Morris Ebenstein. The Warner Brothers attorney was on the verge of closing a deal with the Maxwells: Edith's endorsement of *Mountain Justice* (which was in the editing stage) in exchange for a cash payment. As one Warner executive put it, the Maxwell endorsement would be a "great publicity stunt."[4] The studio was in a ticklish position, however. How could it use Edith to promote the movie when it publicly maintained that the film had no connection to her real-life story? In any case, Ebenstein had thought it prudent to settle with the Maxwells lest they at some future time seek a financial claim on *Mountain Justice.*

The day before Earl and Edith's visit, Ebenstein had telegrammed Warner Brothers' West Coast offices, trying to get a rough cut of *Mountain Justice* sent to New York for Earl and his attorney to preview. The Burbank office was against it. "Definitely adverse [*sic*] to anyone seeing picture until it arrives NY for exploitation," came the reply from California.[5] They would have to content themselves with merely reading the script.

Edward Amron, the New York attorney who had been handling negotiations for the Maxwells, was tied up in court on January 29 and could not attend the meeting with Ebenstein. Earl proceeded to close the deal on his own. After several draft statements had been considered, Edith signed off on a letter endorsing *Mountain Justice.*

In the document she first acknowledges having read the script and then notes that the plot of the film, although "quite different" from her own case, offers a "vividly accurate" portrayal of life in the mountains. "Your script dramatizes the intense human struggle resulting from the opposition of certain of the mountain people towards those in their community who are trying to bring into it education, hygiene and higher living standards and ideals," the letter concluded. "I endorse your picture as a stirring plea for progress and enlightenment of our mountain people."[6]

Edith signed a second letter acknowledging receipt of $1,000 for endorsing a movie she had not yet seen. Warner Brothers also agreed to pay her an additional $250 if the studio decided to make her statement public—perhaps this was the "publicity stunt" that was being considered.

Nothing was said in either letter about Edith traveling to theaters to promote the film, as the *News-Leader* had reported, but the studio's option to pay her the additional amount seemed to leave open such a possibility. Later, Earl's lawyer, Edward Amron, placed a claim on the hypothetical $250, complaining in a letter to Ebenstein that "the Maxwells unceremoniously left the city without paying me my fee of $250.00."[7]

Edith and Earl did walk away from the Warner office with the equivalent of about $13,430 in current dollars—not a great deal of money by the standards of today's entertainment industry. Seen in another light, however, the $1,000 contract must have seemed enormous to a woman who had made about $70 a month teaching school. In any case, Edith was not in control of the purse strings. "Kindly pay all sums hereunder to my brother, Earl Maxwell," she instructed the studio in her letter.

Returning to Virginia with the Warner deal concluded, Edith soon would dismiss the Woman's Party attorneys and cast her fate solely with Charles Henry Smith. The $1,000 in movie money and support from her mysterious benefactors in Washington now guaranteed funds for the next appeal.[8] If only she could "come clear," glittering possibilities lay ahead.

23 *Smith Redux*

Although few people knew about it in 1937, one of the most powerful women in Washington, D.C., had long been toiling behind the scenes as a friend of Edith Maxwell. Eleanor "Cissy" Patterson, the headstrong, red-haired editor of the *Washington Herald*, had lived a life of privilege far removed from the coal camps and mountain farms from which Edith had sprung, yet she empathized strongly with the teacher's predicament.

Patterson was born in Chicago in 1881 to a wealthy newspaper family; her grandfather founded the *Chicago Tribune*. The product of elite boarding schools, she married a Polish count at age nineteen and gave birth to a daughter, but the marriage did not last. Her way smoothed by a custom-built private railway car, Patterson spent most of her twenties, thirties, and forties as a socialite commuting between Chicago, New York, and Washington, D.C., where her family had a mansion on Dupont Circle.

In 1928, after writing two modestly successful novels, Patterson surprisingly decided to enter journalism. By 1930 she had coaxed her friend William Randolph Hearst into naming her editor and publisher of the *Herald,* one of a pair of newspapers he owned in Washington. Not only was the *Herald* losing money but it was also not considered a respectable purveyor of news. Patterson immediately set about imprinting her own personality on the newspaper despite having to bow to what she called "the rock-bottom fact" of Hearst's ultimate editorial control.[1] With that gutsy move she would make her mark as the first woman to head a major American newspaper.

Patterson became known as an activist editor—doubling the newspaper's circulation by 1936—yet the *Herald*'s journalistic reputation remained checkered at best. She championed humane treatment of animals, environmental cleanup, and hot lunches for schoolchildren, but the paper remained, as one historian would later put it, "exciting, gossipy, unpredictable" and "operating on the standards of yellow journalism and regressive politics."[2] Patterson's political views, which were said to be "isolationist, and apparently, pro-Nazi" brought her into conflict with columnist Walter Winchell, a leading opponent of Hitler in the 1930s.[3] The *Herald* also became a soapbox for Patterson's personal gripes as she carried on a bitter circulation war and public feud with *Washington Post* publisher Eugene Meyer.

Two specialities of the *Herald* were women and crime, topics that neatly intersected in the case of Edith Maxwell. Patterson's coverage of women's issues—although often in sob-sister style—had earned her the gratitude of the National Woman's Party, and her hiring of female reporters prompted *Time* magazine to dub the *Herald* "Cissy's Henhouse." Cissy's writers were adept in obtaining crime scoops, but at times they seemed to take on the personas of gangsters themselves, carrying guns and hiring bodyguards with the management's approval. In the 1935 Lyddane murder conspiracy case, for instance, the *Herald* was fined $5,000 by a Maryland court for obstructing the administration of justice, yet it continued to aggressively pursue the crime news its readers craved—even if it meant traveling to faraway spots like southwest Virginia.

The *Herald*, of course, had been the first newspaper to bring the Maxwell case to national attention, beginning with Fulton Lewis Jr.'s sensational series in the summer of 1935. After its intensive coverage of the first trial—and the packaging of Edith's "life story" as a serial that ran in the Hearst newspapers—the *Herald* inexplicably had appeared to yield the spotlight to its enemy, the *Washington Post*. Why? In a letter written to Eleanor Roosevelt in 1941, Patterson would reveal her secret role in the Maxwell case. "We engaged and paid for the services of Charles Henry Smith, Edith's counsel in her last trial," she wrote. "And because of the disastrous reaction caused by the interference of 'outlanders' at Edith's first trial, the . . . *Herald* kept completely in the background during this second period."[4]

This statement, if true, explains why Smith was publicly identified as the attorney hired by the *Washington Post* rather than by the *Herald*. Patterson's revelation, however, raises some disturbing questions. The *Post* reported that Smith was *its* lawyer and was volunteering his services. If the *Post* knew and failed to report that the Hearst interests were financing the defense all along—even as it solicited funds from *Post* readers—then the newspaper had acted in bad faith. Is it possible, then, that Smith did not tell the editors, or they did not learn, about the Hearst connection? That seems unlikely. Yet why would such bitter rivals as the *Post* and the *Herald* agree to this rare moment of on-the-sly cooperation? And when Smith secured the 1936 affidavits that railed against certain "scurrilous" newspapers, were they, in fact, his employers?

Curious reporters wanting to find out about Edith's new backers in 1937 were not able to completely unravel this behind-the-scenes scenario either. Within a few days of the Woman's Party's dismissal, news reports did say that a Washington group headed by W. A. S. Douglas, the *Herald* writer who had covered the second trial, now planned to finance Edith's next appeal. Douglas was identified as the "representative of a Hearst newspaper syndicate," possibly the same one that had signed the "exclusive" with Edith at the Wise County Jail back in 1935.

Douglas's group had agreed to back Edith on the condition that she refuse all other assistance, including that of the Woman's Party. This was apparently what Ann Maxwell was referring to when she told a Richmond newspaper that Edith had to refuse further aid from the Woman's Party or give up "the other." Evidently, the condition imposed by the Washington group, rather than Edith's movie contract, was the true reason for the NWP's ouster.

Except for Douglas, the other members of the private circle were not identified in news reports in 1937. Cissy Patterson was able to operate just below the public radar screen, playing a role that, over time, would resemble that of Edith's fairy godmother. It is not known whether the *Washington Post* had any further involvement with funding the defense. The other "friends of Edith Maxwell" remain a mystery to this day.

At the very least, the Maxwell case had come full circle. Edith had been crowned a celebrity by the Hearst sob sisters and color writers; she had been wooed by the feminists; tarried awhile in the camp of the *Washington Post;* and now was once more securely in the Hearst fold for the final chapter in her legal battle.

The long train ride between Washington, D.C., and Abingdon, Virginia—the jumping-off point for car travel to Wise County—probably had lost its novelty for Charles Henry Smith by March 1937. But the western odysseys, if nothing else, gave him time to think. Whether his habit of mind favored the future, present, or past is not known. With his long string of wins as a defense attorney, Smith may not have had much occasion to second-guess his legal decisions. Yet, as he prepared to revisit the Wise County court to challenge the twenty-year prison term handed to his famous client, he might have been tempted to relive the preamble to his stunning defeat three months earlier.

Of course there were those like Gail Laughlin (and probably Smith himself) who thought the trial was warped by local politics and in some way rigged, who believed that nothing the defense could have done would have made any difference. But there were also those among Edith's sympathizers who believed that Smith had mishandled the defense strategy. One of these was a man claiming to be a former commonwealth attorney of Lee County, Virginia, where Edith had been briefly jailed in 1936.

Writing to the *Washington Post* under the pen name "George," the lawyer maintained that a fair trial *was* possible in Wise County. He took the defense to task for failing to call Edith and her mother to the stand. "Edith and her mother knew more about this case than anyone else," he wrote. "Why did they not testify? So thought the jury, and in my opinion that was the deciding factor."

Other Monday morning quarterbacks pointed to Smith's overreliance on the testimony of his medical experts from Richmond and Washington. The *Roanoke Times* noted, somewhat ironically, that "time has effaced much of the bitterness of Wise county folk against Edith Maxwell," but others associated with the defense had fared less well: "Although not professing to believe her innocent, many people who were once resentful have changed their attitude, and the only resentment held now seems to be against certain newspapermen who have misrepresented the Wise county people, and against outside lawyers, but above all against the 'physicians' from the outside who came here to refute testimony of Dr. Fouts [*sic*] and Dr. Tudor, 'hill doctors' of Norton."[5]

Smith, for his part, probably at least partially blamed the Woman's Party and the injection of radical politics. Now that problem was gone, but the danger of backlash against outsiders was likely to remain. Smith believed that a different venue at the next trial was essential.[6] First, however, he had to cross the enormous hurdle of *getting* that trial. Of course, Smith, and the tireless Earl Maxwell, had been working on that.

—

Although a snow or two could still be expected in Wise County, by now Jack Frost had largely abdicated his rule. Springtime rituals were about to unfurl like the first green shoots punching through the crusted ground. Nine raccoons—fine breeding specimens lately arrived from Vermont— soon would find release from the pens of the county game warden. Over at Pound, Edith had been sewing and helping her sister Gladys prepare a garden. Her court hearing had been pushed back a week, giving her time to ramble. She had just spent an enjoyable ten days renewing ties with old friends and relatives, dividing her time between her sister's home and that of her aunt, Mrs. W. R. Bryington, in Big Stone Gap. On March 7, the eve of her court date, Edith spoke with a *Washington Post* reporter at Gladys's house. "It seems so good to be back in the mountains," she said. "I do so want to be free." But, Edith acknowledged, should Judge Carter's rulings go against her, she soon might be confined once again.

—

Commonwealth attorney Fred Greear and his co-counsel Oscar M. Vicars entered the Wise County courtroom at 11 A.M. on Monday, March 8, for Edith's sentencing hearing. To these veteran prosecutors the day probably held nothing more threatening than the task of countering Charles Henry Smith's motion to set aside the verdict—an exercise in which they were expected to prevail. But Smith had a surprise waiting for Greear and

Vicars as the hearing opened—new defense affidavits whose contents they had never seen and thus were ill-prepared to rebut.

The week leading up to the court appearance, which had been postponed from March 1 at Smith's request, had been one of frenetic activity for Smith and Earl Maxwell. The defendant's brother had spent the time gathering nine affidavits that—if believable—contained explosive new information to support Smith's impending motion for a new trial. On the strength of the affidavits, the defense was claiming that three members of the jury that convicted Edith in December 1936 had been prejudiced against her. The often-repeated slurs against mountain justice—claims that Edith Maxwell could not get a fair trial in Wise County—would receive an airing in court at last.

Vicars and Greear were amazed by Smith's gambit. After studying the maverick documents for about an hour, they objected to their having been filed without proper notice to the prosecution. They asked Judge Carter to give them until Friday to investigate, but he would only agree to recess the hearing until Tuesday at 1 P.M. Over the next twenty-four hours Greear would scour his bailiwick for witnesses who could mount a counterattack.

Smith's tainted juror allegations formed just one part of a voluminous written motion to set aside the verdict. The defense was asking Judge Carter to consider nearly forty other alleged flaws in the previous trial, including Carter's refusal to move the trial, misconduct by Greear in his closing argument, improper admission of evidence by Carter, and the commonwealth's failure to prove that a crime had been committed (corpus delicti). Especially objectionable to the defense were Carter's admission (although temporary) of testimony concerning the Tiller axe and his controversial courtroom statement that "I think we are" dealing with an axe.

None of these other allegations, however, was nearly as sensational as the charge of juror prejudice. "The affidavits threaten to bring perjury in the case, inasmuch as these men were under oath when they stated they had no opinions or prejudices when they were sworn in for the second trial in December," intimated a March 9 *Washington Post* article that carried the headline "Lawyer Hints at Perjury."

By Tuesday afternoon, word had spread through the community of Smith's spectacular charges, and the courtroom was packed. "There were miners in overalls, coal grime on their faces, taking the day off for court," reported the *Post*. "There were old bearded men who chewed tobacco. There were dignified gentlemen here and there in winged collars. In one of the rows near the front were several young women about the age of Edith, who eyed her curiously, and interspersed in the crowd were little old ladies in bonnets and calico."

Smith began calling witnesses to support his allegations that George Pennington, Eldridge Christian, and John Lambert, *prior to* serving on the jury, had all said that Edith was guilty. Pennington and Lambert were described as "elderly men with white hair and unshaven stubble," while Christian was evidently somewhat younger.[7] The three jurors in question all lived in the western end of Wise County, far from the locale of Trigg Maxwell's death—Pennington and Lambert in the town of Big Stone Gap, and Christian in a mining camp called Inman. It was in this area of the county that the defense had collected the vast majority of its affidavits in 1936 to bolster its motion for a change of venue. That suggested two things: Edith had considerable support there, and the case was discussed in western Wise County as much as everywhere else.

Although Edith's attorneys often claimed that the entire county was against her, testimony arising from the March 9 hearing would dramatically illustrate how deeply the Maxwell case had divided local opinion. Testimony concerning former juror Eldridge Christian was a case in point. Three of his co-workers at the Virginia Iron, Coal and Coke mining operation recalled instances in which Christian allegedly had commented on the twenty-five-year prison sentence handed down at the first trial. One of these miners, defense witness Charlie Roberts, quoted Christian as saying that "her and her mammy both ought to have twenty-five years." Others—including an ordained Baptist minister—testified about occasions where Christian allegedly had said "she ought to have had fifty," or "she didn't get half as much as she ought to have."[8]

Another defense witness, electrician George W. Willis, recalled how he had teased Christian on his first day back at work after being sequestered at the December 1936 trial. "Eldridge, she liked to have beat you back home," Willis had said, alluding to the fact that Edith had been allowed bond despite the second murder conviction.

In Willis's recollection Christian responded by saying, "I figure she will get a new trial."

"Eldridge, why do you believe that?" asked Willis.

"I believe they will pick a flaw in the jury," was the mysterious reply.

The mood had turned sour in front of the "lamp house" later that day when Charlie Roberts confronted Christian over the guilty verdict just rendered. Roberts angrily questioned how Christian could vote to convict on the evidence presented, and the former juror responded that he had heard all the testimony and Roberts had not. They continued to argue until the mine superintendent showed up and intervened.

Bad blood had flared up again shortly before the March 9, 1937, hearing, when Christian learned that Roberts and the others had supplied the defense with sworn statements questioning his objectivity. According to Roberts, Christian confronted him at a local store, called him a "son of a bitch," and tried unsuccessfully to pick a fight. The black-bearded Christian, however, denied under oath that he had made the prejudicial pretrial statements. Greear suggested that Christian's recent successful bid for the much-prized Inman postmaster's job had made him the target of vengeful defense witnesses.

The alleged pretrial statements of former juror George Pennington were also scrutinized by the defense. Coal hauler Richard H. Collins related an incident that allegedly took place at the Liberty Cafe in Big Stone Gap a short time before the December 1936 trial. Collins had engaged in a conversation with the proprietor about the Maxwell case. According to Collins, juror-to-be Pennington joined in and said that Edith Maxwell "was guilty and if he had anything to do with it that he would give her life or all he could."

On cross-examination, Greear elicited the fact that Collins had once served time in prison for involuntary manslaughter. But as Collins explained it, he had been convicted on the basis of perjured testimony and was pardoned by the governor of Tennessee once the perjury was discovered. (In a curious parallel with Earl Maxwell, Collins's brother, a lawyer in Kingsport, Tennessee, allegedly had arranged for the affidavits that had helped free him.)

Smith later called cafe owner Robert Edens and Robert Holly "Bud" Ruth, a sometime-employee at the cafe. Both men corroborated Collins's account and stood by their stories on cross-examination. Greear was able to establish only that Edens had previously been convicted of bootlegging and that he was a neighbor and acquaintance of Ann Maxwell's half-sister, Mrs. Bryington. Ruth, too, had a previous conviction for violating liquor laws.

Pennington in turn testified that he had "no recollection" of ever having talked with Edens, Ruth, and Collins about the Maxwell case. "I never spoke to the gentleman [Collins] in my life," Pennington said.

In the third case—this one again pitting neighbor against neighbor— Fayette "Mack" Haynes testified about statements allegedly made by former juror John Lambert. Haynes, a Big Stone Gap carpenter, said that he had encountered Lambert on a mountain road shortly after the first trial, and the two discussed the verdict. According to Haynes, Lambert said Edith deserved thirty-five years, while he (Haynes) argued that she was innocent.

Haynes further testified that he went to the Lambert home the following year to borrow a tool and learned that John Lambert was away, having been called as a potential juror at the second Maxwell trial. Thenia Lambert mentioned that she was not well and hoped her husband would not have to stay. According to Haynes, he told her that her husband was certain to be released from jury duty because he had already expressed his opinion.

Both John and Thenia Lambert took the stand to contradict Haynes's story. John Lambert denied that the conversation on the mountain had taken place. Thenia Lambert, who had to be brought into the courtroom on a deputy's arm, confirmed that Haynes had visited her house in December 1936 but testified that nothing was mentioned about her husband's fitness to serve on the jury. The Lamberts' daughter-in-law, Sarah, who had been staying with the ailing Thenia Lambert, confirmed her mother-in-law's account.

In addition to Christian, Pennington, and the Lambert family, Greear called more than a dozen witnesses who represented the cream of the political and law enforcement establishment in the Big Stone Gap area. In many cases their mission was twofold: to cast doubt on the veracity of the accusing witnesses and to vouch for the good character of the three beleaguered jurors. Greear's witnesses included a bank president, the former mayor of Big Stone Gap, a prominent merchant, company officials from the mining operation at Inman, two deputy sheriffs, a postmaster, a constable, and a chief of police.

Through their testimony the prosecution attempted to paint several of the defense witnesses as men of questionable reputation within the community. Smith, however, hinted that at least two of the jurors were dutiful underlings in the local Democratic power structure. Smith's cross-examination of Wise County treasurer J. B. Wampler—who had just testified in support of Lambert and Pennington—brought a colorful exchange.

"Mr. Lambert and Mr. Pennington are both Democrats?" Smith asked Wampler.

"Yes, sir."

"You are a Democrat, too, aren't you?" Smith continued.

"Yes, sir."

"We don't have too many of the other kind, do we?" interjected Greear.

"No," Wampler responded. "We don't let them stay down there."

After hours of testimony, the tangle over the affidavits had produced several conflicting stories, much ill-will, and no clear picture of what was actually said by the three jurors before the trial.

The light was beginning to fade outside the arched courtroom windows when Judge Carter rendered his decision. With evening chores to attend to, most spectators had already gone home. The judge told the few remaining onlookers that he had decided to let the jury's verdict stand. Smith's motion for a new trial was hereby denied.

In commenting on his ruling, Carter made no mention of the defense's affidavits concerning the three jurors, nor did he allude to the alleged prosecutor misconduct. "There were a great number of objections, but I do not think they are tenable," Carter said. "The important thing is whether the commonwealth proved *corpus delicti.*"[9]

Edith sat at the defense table with a tight-lipped, perhaps stoic, expression. Her gaze bounced back and forth between Judge Carter and the audience as he began a detailed review of the evidence. Terming the verdict "fair," he mentioned several factors that supported the jury's decision. There had been a fight in the Maxwell home on the night of July 20–21; Edith had previously threatened her father; and the victim received head injuries. "The conduct of the three women in the home immediately after the injury was such that the jury was within its bounds in concluding that the blow was administered by the defendant," Carter said.[10] The judge also spoke of Edith's "conflicting stories" about how Trigg Maxwell had sustained the head injuries.[11] Further, he deemed all the evidence admitted at the second trial to be proper.

Darkness had filled the corners of the dimly lit room by the time Judge Carter finished his hour-and-forty-five-minute analysis. Edith then stood while Carter formally sentenced her to twenty years in prison. Smith immediately noted an appeal and was granted ninety days to file motions with a higher court. He also asked the judge to renew the bond that had kept his client out of jail for the past six months. But Greear, who had not opposed Edith's bond in 1936, now raised an objection. The commonwealth attorney—perhaps smarting over the recent news of Edith's movie contract—said he "saw no reason for allowing the girl to run about the country exploiting the people in her interests."[12] Carter nonetheless ruled that the bond would be renewed.

No doubt schooled by her lawyer to expect bad news, Edith remained calm and "chatted with friends after the adverse ruling."[13] A correspondent for the *Post* interviewed her in Wise the next day and reported that she "was assured of only eighty-nine more days of freedom" yet planned to return to Chesterfield County to look again for work.

The *Roanoke Times* took Judge Carter's ruling as another opportunity to vouch for the Virginia justice system and lament the sensational press coverage. Its editorial of March 11 said, in part:

> The hysterical hullaballoo caused by the excited efforts of people and organizations at a distance to "rescue" Edith from fancied mountain intolerance and "persecution" has done the girl's case more harm than good, undoubtedly. She will get justice from the Virginia courts. More than that she is not entitled to, less than that the strong sense of justice of the people of Virginia would not tolerate.
>
> What happened in the Maxwell cabin on the night Trigg Maxwell met his death has not been definitely established. Edith herself has told conflicting versions of the manner in which her father was killed; opinion differs as to whether she has yet told the truth about what actually took place. The Court of Appeals will give her every consideration to which she is entitled when in due time her appeal from her second conviction comes before that tribunal.
>
> People at a distance will do well to understand that the State of Virginia will never send a young woman to prison for twenty years for a crime of which she is innocent. That she has failed to establish innocence to the satisfaction of two juries is a point that ought not to be overlooked.

The fairness or depravity of mountain justice, then, would continue to exist largely in the eye of the beholder. And if two trials had failed to uncover the truth about Trigg's Maxwell's death, when would it ever be known? Only in the movies, where things were neat and tidy, could reality be ascertained.

24   *"The Wishing Book"*

The marquee above the Rialto Theater in Times Square invited New Yorkers to see the new Warner film *Mountain Justice*, "A Gripping Melodrama of Lust and Lash."[1] The official release date—April 24, 1937—coincided with Edith Maxwell's twenty-third birthday. Warner Brothers, however, apparently had decided not to exercise its option of "going public" with Edith's endorsement, and nothing in the New York press indicated that the celebrity defendant was even in the city.[2] The *Mountain Justice* premiere was described as "just a simple opening" in contrast to the lavish unveiling of MGM's *Captains Courageous* on the same day.[3]

A *New York Times* reviewer would call *Mountain Justice* a "hillbilly anthology," by which he meant that it contained the most Gothic headlines taken from Appalachia and the South in the 1920s and 1930s—child marriage, a near-lynching by a Klan-like mob, and even a courtroom scene reminiscent of the Scopes monkey trial.[4] Grafted onto this dark landscape was the highly fictionalized story of Edith, who as nurse Ruth Harkins was attempting to bring progress and enlightenment to her backward mountain community, which trusts granny women more than modern medicine.

"Even in this age of advanced civilization, there are still some communities which cling grimly to the stern, unbending principles of our ancestors," warned the foreword amid blaring horns. "And sometimes the defiance of Youth against the old implacable tribal laws results in tragedy."

A melodramatic, brooding atmosphere was immediately established through the death of a mother in childbirth, but *Mountain Justice* soon failed to live up to the marquee's promise of "lust and lash." The lash was clearly visible, but the only lust in evidence was the filmmakers' appetite for stereotyping. Midway through the film, Ruth Harkins is taking a lashing with a bullwhip from her father, Jeff. Her crime: refusing to wed the odious Todd Miller, the redneck of her father's choice, and instead falling for a "furriner," New York city lawyer Paul Cameron, whom she has met while clowning before the funhouse mirrors at the county fair. Even though he has prosecuted her father and briefly sent him to jail for shooting a surveyor on Harkins's property (using Ruth as his witness), Paul wants to marry Ruth and "rescue" her from her benighted home and community.

Ruth's character was merely reenacting what by then had already become a cliche in writings about Appalachia—the plight of a hillbilly lass who "betrays" her kin for the love of an outsider. The audience is also made to understand that the educated Ruth is being punished for having modern ideas that are inconsistent with an appreciation of mountain culture. "I can no longer be satisfied with things in the wishing book [mail-order catalog]," she tells Paul. What *was* novel to 1937 audiences, however, was the graphic depiction of domestic violence. So shocking was the whipping scene that Curtiz—no doubt to escape the censors—had projected only the shadow of the whip as Jeff systematically raises and lowers it over Ruth.

After the brutal attack, Ruth's mother, Meg, who has been bullied and defeated by her husband, insists that her daughter escape a similar fate by leaving the mountains for further nurse's training. Ruth goes to New York to work at a settlement house, where she meets Evelyn, a wealthy woman who is also a nurse. Ruth resumes her romance with Paul but continues to spurn his offer of marriage because she wants to start a health service in the mountains. Evelyn agrees both to fund the project and to go with Ruth, commenting privately to Paul that "maybe these hillbillies are human. . . . It'll be fun to find out."

Over Paul's dire warnings, Ruth returns to "Durley County" with Evelyn, and the two launch a string of successful health clinics. Ruth remains estranged from Jeff despite her attempts at reconciliation. She is barred from the family home and lives in an elegantly furnished apartment at one of the clinics.

Late one night, little sister Bethie appears at Ruth's window, terrified. She has run away from home because her father is trying to marry *her* off to Todd Miller. Suddenly Jeff appears, whip in hand. He pushes Bethie aside and attacks Ruth. As they struggle inside the apartment, Ruth is pinned to the floor. She manages to grab the wooden handle of the whip and cracks her father several times in the head. He gets off her, staggers outside, and dies.

Ruth is arrested for murder, and Paul arrives to defend her. For the first time in the film she recants her faith in hillbillies. "You were so right about these people, everything you said," she tells Paul during a jailhouse visit.

Her trial takes place on the courthouse lawn in summer, a carnival-like scene that echoes the Scopes trial held in Dayton, Tennessee, in 1925. Paul contends that Jeff died from heart failure—not from blows to the head—but the all-male jury doesn't buy it. Ruth is quickly found guilty and given twenty-five years in prison.

Local vigilantes, however, aren't satisfied with this "light" sentence. They don burlap hoods and begin agitating outside the jail for a lynching. Ruth's friends disguise themselves as part of the mob and manage to break her out of jail that night. Paul and Ruth fly away in a small airplane just as the villains arrive. She is whisked to safety in New York, where a kindly governor who resembles F.D.R. refuses to extradite her back to the scene of the trouble.

Then Paul gets out *his* wishing book—which contains a marriage license, a wedding ring, a picture of his Long Island mansion, and cruise ship tickets for their honeymoon. Hillbillies be damned! The music comes up, and they live happily ever after.

According to the *Motion Picture Herald,* the eighty-two-minute black and white film "seemed to satisfy the close-packed audience" at the Rialto, but many reviewers were less kind. *Mountain Justice* was largely dismissed as a minor melodrama, "a waste of talent on [a] doomed enterprise."[5] Time would prove this work to be a forgettable footnote in the long and distinguished career of director Michael Curtiz.

"The point it makes, if any," said the *New York Times,* "is that mountain men are an ornery lot, especially Jeff Harkins, who used to assemble his family for Bible readings every night, shoot a "furriner' on sight and whale the daylights out of his daughter when she sold her acre to help Doc Barnard establish a health clinic in the hills."[6]

In addition to its cartoonish characterizations of mountain people, the film was criticized for its unbelievable plot twists in the second half. After all, the foreword to *Mountain Justice* promised tragedy to those—like Ruth Harkins—who violate the alleged mountain code, but the script didn't deliver. According to *Film Daily,* "the business of forcing a happy ending led into absurdities that destroyed all the fine and powerful illusion so cleverly built up."[7]

Good acting, gauntly beautiful cinematography and Elizabeth Hearst's realistic touches could not help the film overcome these difficulties. And although *Mountain Justice* made a strong statement about the oppression of women, it implied that domestic violence could never occur anywhere but in a "backward" place—certainly not in New York City. Except for a few "enlightened" ones, the men and women of Ruth Harkins's Appalachia were depicted as spiteful, ignorant, and deluded by the mountain code into persecuting anyone with progressive values. Even the urbane Fred Greear was parodied as a dowdy, redneck lawyer who feeds slices of an apple to jurors as he makes his summation.

"The picture is stirring and unbelievable tripe," said one of the harshest reviews. "Doubtless the theory behind such an outspoken portrayal of mountaineers is that mountaineers seldom, if ever, attend movies."[8]

Contrary to the critic's words, Warner Brothers studio executives were quite aware that hillbillies not only attended movies but also were capable of suing for libel. Morris Ebenstein, the meticulous lawyer in the studio's New York office, had worried about that prospect almost from the beginning. "The people involved are hardly to be considered ordinary hillbillies," he wrote in an internal document. Noting that about two-thirds of them were college-educated, he regarded the risk of a libel action "pretty grave."[9]

It was an open secret in the press that the "avowedly fictional" story was really the Maxwell case in disguise. Alarm bells had rung through the Warner studio in September 1936 after a *Daily Mirror* reporter visited the *Mountain Justice* set during production and revealed that a book of photographs from the Maxwell case was lying about. "Even the casual newspaper reader will identify the plight of red-headed Josephine Hutchinson with that of the Southern girl, Virginia [*sic*] Maxwell, who was recently tried for slaying her father with a high-heeled shoe," wrote the *Mirror*'s Harrison Carroll on September 30. The article sparked frantic correspondence and a flurry of script changes even though shooting was well under way.[10]

Perhaps Ebenstein's worries stemmed from the controversial yet rewarding case of *I Am a Fugitive on a Chain Gang*, in which Georgia prison wardens had sued for defamation. More intriguingly, it also appears that Edith and Earl told Ebenstein something during their January 1937 meeting that made him even more wary of Warner being sued. Not only was he fretting over the film's possible libeling of the prosecutor or the jurors but he was also concerned about the portrayal of the judge. "Of one thing I am fairly certain," Ebenstein wrote, "and that is that it will not be advisable for us to release the film in the State of Virginia."[11]

The studio had ninety-five theater contracts within the state, and projected revenues from Virginia screenings of *Mountain Justice* at $3958.50— more than $54,000 in today's dollars.[12] Given the film's harsh indictment of the legal system in a certain mountain community, however, Warner lawyers must have shuddered at the prospect of having to defend a libel suit in Virginia courts. They also worried that showing the movie in Virginia might prejudice Edith's case if she succeeded in getting a third trial.

On March 22, 1937, Ebenstein notified other staff that a decision had been reached concerning the film's distribution: "We will not release the film in the state of Virginia and we will also keep it out of the city of Bristol which is in both in Tennessee and Virginia. Otherwise, we will release it throughout the United States."[13] Although *Mountain Justice* would never become the box-office success its creators had hoped, it was eventually distributed overseas. "The yarn will live on the screens of the world," wrote a Virginia journalist. "In mystic Java, before gaily dressed Orientals in Shanghai, in the diamond regions of South Africa, the world will learn the film story of the Blue Ridge Mountain Girl and her sinister high-heel shoe."[14]

Warner had made its decision for sound business reasons, and possibly out of concern for Edith, but the effect was to hide from the people of Wise County what Hollywood was broadcasting to the world. As with the Hearst reporting in 1935, the county's cultural images had been appropriated and twisted. They had, once again, become a badge of shame. It would not be until 1994, more than a half century after its premiere, that *Mountain Justice* was finally shown in Wise County.

⸺

Very little is known about how Edith spent the spring and summer of 1937. Her prospects for publicity work around the release of *Mountain Justice* apparently had fizzled although perhaps she still harbored dreams of some day "signing up with the movies." The job hunt she had announced in March also seemed to evaporate. She continued to live on the farm in Chesterfield County, but the photographers and writers who recorded her every move in 1936 now had turned to other stories. If Edith wore a pretty dress and milked a cow while her case dragged on, nobody was paying much attention.

One Maxwell story, however, did make the headlines that June. After nine months on bond, Edith abruptly found herself back in the Wise County Jail. T. S. Tate, one of the four people who signed Edith's bond after the December 1936 trial, had notified Earl and Edith sometime earlier in June that he wished to be relieved of this responsibility. According to Earl, Tate wanted to sell some real estate that was part of the security arrangement for Edith's bond.

Edith and Earl had returned to Wise County from Chesterfield County on Saturday, June 12, to deal with Tate's request. But while Earl was in neighboring Scott County trying to line up a new bond arrangement, an evidently impatient Tate swore out a warrant for Edith's arrest. Deputy Sheriff Byrl Bolling, son of Sheriff Clyde Bolling, took Edith into custody at the Pound home of her sister, Gladys, that evening.

Earl succeeded in lining up three new bondsmen by Monday morning. The previous sureties—A. T. Dotson and M. B. Taylor, both of Richmond, and C. D. Lay of Coeburn—were joined by Edith's brother-in-law, Clay Robinson, and Malinda Gilliam and Carl Hillman, both of Wise. The new bond, still set at $15,000, was executed before Judge Carter in Fred

Greear's office on the afternoon of Tuesday, June 15. Edith thanked her supporters and immediately went back to Pound to visit relatives. That same day she got some very good news from her lawyer.

___

Charles Henry Smith had been doggedly retracing the legal steps that had led to Edith's new trial the previous year. With Judge Carter's refusal in March to set aside the verdict, Smith had moved on up the judicial ladder. On May 21, 1937, he had presented Justice George Landon Browning of the Supreme Court of Appeals with a petition for a writ of error. The petition, which contained seventeen assignments of error, was delivered to the justice's home at Orange.

Browning had the option of acting on the petition individually or waiting for the full court to convene on June 1 at Wytheville. If any justice, or the court as a whole, granted the writ of error, the case would be put on the docket for review. If not, Smith would have to turn to the U.S. Supreme Court or plead with the governor for executive clemency. Browning apparently decided to postpone any action until the full court could rule. On June 15 the Virginia Supreme Court of Appeals granted Smith's petition to review the case a second time. Oral arguments were scheduled for September 1937. Like a cat with nine lives, Edith's appeal had been resurrected once more.

___

In the fall of 1937 the Chicago-based magazine *Actual Detective Stories* began running a series of detailed articles about the Maxwell case. Sandwiched between large photographs and lurid headlines such as "Crimes of Malignant Love" were supposed first-person accounts of the two-year legal saga from both Fred Greear and Edith herself. Edith's story, "I Am Innocent," was ghostwritten by Walden B. Snell, whereas Greear's "She Is Guilty" carried only his own byline. Both accounts had factual errors (probably due to the magazine's editing), but Edith's was especially revealing about her state of mind:

> The physical hardships and mental anguish I have been compelled to suffer for the past two years have exacted from my youthful body a terrific toll. I have aged. My nerves are wrecked. I have become embittered toward life.
>
> Yet I remain hopeful, more so today than ever before, even though I have the ordeal of a third trial facing me. Across the distant horizon a brighter, happier dawn is breaking—days of sunshine and happiness that

are mine, and that I soon hope to enjoy. I am confident I will enjoy them if Virginia justice will take my destiny out of the hands of that prejudiced mountain country and place it with a group of just and true men elsewhere.[15]

———

Charles Henry Smith and his counterpart, Assistant Attorney General Joseph L. Kelly, presented their arguments to the arbiters of "Virginia justice" on September 14, 1937, the opening day of the Supreme Court of Appeals session at Staunton. Less than a month later, on November 11, the high court unanimously affirmed the judgment of the Wise County Circuit Court. Edith was not entitled to a third trial and would have to begin serving her prison term. Justice E. W. Hudgins, in a brief written opinion, divided Smith's seventeen assignments of error into three broad areas: whether the evidence was sufficient to sustain the verdict; whether Judge Carter erred in refusing to grant a change of venue; and whether improper evidence or statements were permitted at the trial.

On the first point, Smith was relying on his expert medical testimony to argue that the commonwealth had failed to establish the real cause of Trigg Maxwell's death and thus had failed to establish the corpus delicti. But Hudgins disagreed, writing that "Drs. T. J. Tudor and G. T. Foust . . . appear to be unbiased and both well qualified by training and experience to determine the cause of death." Both doctors gave their unqualified opinions that Trigg had died of head injuries, and the jury had believed them rather than Smith's experts. According to the court, Drs. Tudor and Foust, having performed the autopsy, "were in a better position than the experts for the accused to form a more accurate opinion as to the cause of death," and thus "it was for the jury to determine whether the corpus delictic has been established."[16]

On the question of whether prejudicial pretrial publicity had made a fair trial in Wise County impossible, the court concluded that public opinion "seemed to be about equally divided" rather than generally hostile to Edith:

> There was no evidence indicating that the opinions expressed were anything more than casual opinions which laymen usually form from newspapers and other second hand reports of an important or unusual case.
>
> The accused contends in her petitions and brief that opinion was bitter against her because of newspaper accounts reflecting on the community. The evidence, however, affirmatively shows that if the published accounts of the killing and trial did arouse any indignation in the county, such in-

dignation did not react against the accused, but against the newspapers and magazines that published them.

The court also addressed the issue of whether the three jurors at the 1936 trial had previously expressed opinions about her guilt.[17] Some of Edith's witnesses who testified in March 1937 about hearing the alleged opinions admittedly had criminal records, and some of the other defense witnesses' reputation for truth and veracity "was proven to be bad." The accused jurors, however, had denied the charges, and their good reputations had been "fully established" by Greear's numerous character witnesses. Therefore, the opinion said, it was within Judge Carter's discretion not to overturn the verdict on the basis of the defense allegations.

The opinion did not go into detail about Judge Carter's and Greear's remarks at trial. The justices concluded by saying that they had "carefully considered each exception and assignment separately and together, and have reached the definite conclusion that there is no reversible error in this record."[18]

Smith immediately announced that he planned no further appeals. He said the two-year legal battle had cost about $3,500 (more than $47,000 in today's dollars), exhausting the financial resources of Edith's family and friends. There was no money left to carry the fight to the U.S. Supreme Court.

The Maxwell family probably did not have much money left, but Smith's explanation rings hollow when one considers the great wealth of Edith's backers. Although the Hearst publishing empire was suffering a serious financial reversal in 1937, it would successfully survive corporate downsizing, and William Randolph Hearst would remain a wealthy man all his life. Evalyn Walsh McLean and Cissy Patterson, two of Edith's most ardent supporters in Washington, both had considerable personal fortunes. Any one of these individuals, had he or she been so inclined, could easily have spared a few more thousand dollars to continue the appeal. Lack of money apparently was not the primary reason for quitting. Had Edith become old news, less valuable to her newspaper backers? Had she (or Earl or Smith) simply grown tired? Or was another strategy in the works?

One can only wonder whether Edith had regrets about repudiating the Woman's Party eight months earlier. Although the NWP's membership dwindled as the 1930s wore on, these feminists had deep pockets and iron wills. Had Edith not fired Gail Laughlin the previous February, Laughlin probably would have hopped a train south immediately, spoiling for her fight before the U.S. Supreme Court.

But that day would never come. Through the fracture of a relation-ship that had always seemed tenuous at best, opportunistic at worst, the Woman's Party had lost the perfect vehicle for testing the constitutionality of all-male juries. Edith, in turn, had lost not only a last, desperate bid for freedom but also a chance to shape history. In Wise County the reign of the "twelve good men and true" would last until the 1950s, and it would not be until 1975 that the U.S. Supreme Court finally decreed that men and women must be treated equally in the process of jury selection.[19] The federal Equal Rights Amendment, of which Edith was a symbol, has never become law.

25   *Goochland*

     Ann and Edith Maxwell sat listening to the radio in the red-roofed farmhouse in Chesterfield County. A morning news program suddenly dominated the room. "The Virginia Supreme Court of Appeals has refused to grant Edith Maxwell a new trial," came the news flash.[1]

Edith had steeled herself for just such a moment—even pumping herself up with a little gallows humor. The week before, her mother had encouraged her to buy a new hat, but Edith had refused. "It would be foolish," she told Ann. "A hat wouldn't do me any good in the peniten-tiary."

Now with the verdict finally upon her, Edith did not even cry. Ann, however, fainted dead away and had to remain lying down for the next several hours. Charles Henry Smith, who apparently heard the decision announced live at the Supreme Court in Richmond, drove over to the farm to console his client. Smith was shocked by Edith's haggard look. She had dropped from 130 pounds to 112 in just a few months.

"Well, we lost," said Smith.

"You couldn't help that," Edith replied.

According to Edward T. Folliard, who was once again on hand to record the scene for the *Washington Post,* "Edith appeared resigned to a long period behind the bars. A girl quick to adapt herself, she even began thinking of what she might do in the penitentiary and of what she might do to rehabilitate herself afterward. She said that if it were possible, she would try to learn office work or nursing while in prison. She is convinced that she can never teach school again, although plenty of men and women have written her to say they would help her in such a role whenever she is free."

A journalist visiting the Maxwells a few days later filed a much darker story. Roy C. Flannagan of the *Richmond News Leader* paid an unannounced call at the farmhouse and found it "a place of hysterical despair."[2] The reporter talked with Earl for more than an hour before Edith, dressed in a brown skirt and sweater, finally entered the living room. She shrank into a corner of the couch. Although she "accepted a cigarette, which she obviously did not want, in order to be sociable," Edith appeared stunned and volunteered little in the way of conversation.

"The smile which has been on nearly every front page in America was not in evidence," wrote Flannagan. "Her face, sunburned from her work on the farm, was thin to the point of emaciation. She seemed to be utterly exhausted in nerve and body. Even in her efforts to be pleasant to a visitor, her features and her whole figure displayed the most abject melancholy."

Both Edith and Earl were worrying about the prospect of their mother being tried at Wise in the coming spring. No representation had yet been lined up for Ann, and Earl said the family had no money left to pay lawyers. "If I had been able to get clear, then they would not be talking about trying mother," Edith said.

Edith's final chance of avoiding prison was to appeal to Gov. George C. Peery for clemency. The governor had received more letters about the Maxwell case than any other in Virginia history—the tally reached five hundred soon after the second trial, and about a hundred more had arrived since the Virginia Supreme Court ruling. But Peery probably recognized that most of the political heat radiated from distant states rather than hotbeds of protest at home. Moreover, he was in the final weeks of his administration and apparently saw no reason to bow to pressure from Edith's supporters. On November 27 he announced that unless "unusual" facts surfaced in the case, he would not consider executive clemency until Edith had served at least part of her sentence. And by that time, he would likely be out of office.

With clemency all but ruled out, certain practical realities had to be faced. Edith was adamant about not wanting to return to Wise County for her formal surrender, fearing that people would point and laugh. Her cousin A. T. Dotson made arrangements for her to wait in Chesterfield

County while a court order was forwarded from Richmond to Staunton to Wise County, where commitment papers would be prepared and sent back to Richmond. The process took about two weeks, but finally the paper trail ended at the door of the Maxwell farmhouse—and the wait was over.

On Tuesday, November 30, Earl accompanied his twenty-three-year-old sister to the gates of the state penitentiary in Richmond, formally identified her, and was gone. Edith went through the customary commitment procedure—fingerprinting, photographing, and medical examination—before taking her place in the women's ward. Virginia had no parole law, but with half time off for anticipated good behavior and credit for time served in the county jail, her release date was expected to be June 6, 1947. She would be thirty-three years old.

The population of the penitentiary being at an all-time high, most new prisoners were processed quickly and funneled to work venues throughout the state. Edith was transferred on December 9, 1937, to the State Industrial Farm for Women in Goochland County, some thirty miles westward in the hilly country near Charlottesville. This new prison, built in 1933, was probably a welcome change from the overcrowded conditions at the Richmond facility. And Edith must have been pleased by her work assignment: a job in the prison office, where she would learn bookkeeping, typing, and stenography.

In February 1938 Ann Maxwell received word from Fred Greear that he did not plan to prosecute her for her husband's death. Greear said he would recommend to the court that all charges against her be dropped when the case was called on April 5. The prosecutor said he lacked sufficient evidence to connect her with the crime. (If Greear was quoted correctly, this is a rather surprising admission. How did he obtain his indictment without this evidence? Had Ann Maxwell been used as leverage against Edith in bad faith? Or did Greear simply decide in 1938 that punishing Edith was enough?)

The news apparently gave an ailing Ann Maxwell the will to live. She soon checked into a Richmond hospital for what has been described as an "abdominal operation" that she had been avoiding for some time. According to the *News Leader* of March 10, doctors had given Ann, fifty-three, only a year or two to live without the surgery, yet she had consistently refused it. "If I must undergo trial for the murder of my husband I do not expect to live through it and it would be useless to have an operation designed to prolong my life," Ann reportedly had said.

Ann was critically ill after the surgery but eventually recovered. True to his promise, Greear recommended dropping charges against her, and the Wise County court agreed. By late April 1938, Ann was once again living at Pound with eighteen-year-old Anna Ruth and Mary Katherine, fourteen. "Mrs. Maxwell has entered into the life of the community, going to church and Sunday school and attending meetings pertaining to civic betterment of the town," reported the *Roanoke Times* on April 22.

The specter of prosecution that Trigg Maxwell's widow had endured for nearly two years was now erased. Ann would live out her days without further threat of legal action, but suspicions that she had colluded with Edith would be harder to overcome. In some quarters of Pound, suspicions about Ann's role in the tragic events of July 21, 1935, would crystalize into firm beliefs that persist to this day. Yet in the eyes of the law, she is innocent.

—

Long rebuffed by Governor Peery, Edith Maxwell's supporters had set great store by the election of James Hubert Price, who assumed office in January 1938. Price had a modest, informal manner that belied his great, dark brows, serious brown eyes, and the dignified touches of silver at his temples. He usually introduced himself over the telephone as "Jim Price down at the governor's office" rather than "Governor Price." And had the times allowed it, he might have exchanged his trademark gray and blue double-breasted suits for a more populist uniform—perhaps jeans and a cardigan à la Jimmy Carter.

Price was a New Deal Democrat who actively campaigned for Franklin D. Roosevelt and was now trying to bring those policies to a socially conservative state. The fifty-nine-year-old native of Greenbriar, West Virginia, was thought to be more liberal and amenable to persuasion than his predecessor. Beyond that, there were those who spied a darker meaning in Peery's refusal to intervene in the Maxwell case and, by contrast, thought Price was just the man to give Edith a pardon.

A key difference between the two governors derived from their relationships with that titan of Virginia politics Sen. Harry F. Byrd, whose machine traditionally had dominated the state's political landscape. Peery has been described as a "charter member of the Byrd organization" who tirelessly worked his way up through the party ranks and waited until the appointed time to run for governor.[3] Price, however, was "an anomaly in twentieth-century Virginia politics," an immensely popular politician operating outside the confines of the Byrd machine. After representing Richmond for seven terms in the House of Delegates and serving two terms as lieutenant governor, he had launched a maverick bid for governor without the initial go-ahead from Senator Byrd. Party regulars eventually had closed ranks behind him, but Price was beholden only to the voters, who gave him majorities in every county except two.[4]

For those who believed that Edith's prosecution was swayed by sinister political influences, Price's renegade victory in November 1937 had been sweet news indeed. One such conspiracy buff anonymously sent a poem to Governor Price, two pages of rhyming verse that purported to outline the *real* reason that Edith Maxwell had been dealt with so severely by two Wise County juries. Edith, so the theory went, was a hapless victim of her Uncle Gernade Dotson's fateful decision, back in 1927, to run as an independent candidate for commonwealth attorney and challenge the nominee of the Democratic Party. Dotson's political enemies, waiting for a chance to avenge his unorthodox victory at the polls, allegedly had found the perfect opportunity when Trigg Maxwell died a mysterious death.

According to the amateur poet, "The political machine in the state of Va / Decided they must put Edith aWay / Edith is not guilty you may be sure / But the machine decided they'd use her to make a cure." Now that Uncle Nade was aging and vulnerable, the machine would "just keep Nade's family eating humble pie right along / until the day they die."[5]

Neither the poem nor the short cover letter—both typewritten—was dated, but a line of doggerel referring to the charges still pending against Ann Maxwell suggests that the poem was sent very early in Price's term. Price had been inaugurated January 12, 1938, and Fred Greear had announced in February that he planned to drop the charges when court convened in the spring. The communication offered virtually no clues as to the sender's identity except to say he "did not go to College hardly a bit." Even the signature, which said merely "a friend," was typed.

The writer—possibly a Wise County Republican—had made a powerful case as to why Gernade Dotson may have offended the Democratic elite but offered no specifics as to how the "machine" could have twice had Edith convicted and the second verdict upheld by a higher court. (If the Wise County Democratic Party held some sway over the two different sets of jurors, the mechanism by which it could have exerted this influence remains a mystery.) The poet just maintained that Uncle Nade's political insurrection "is one of many reasons why Edith is not out." The missive concluded with a challenge to the new governor: "If there must be a boss to carry the big stick, / why not you grab it and use it quick."

Price, in the opening months of his term, would concern himself with shepherding an ambitious package of progressive social legislation through the General Assembly. He was not yet ready to deal with the Maxwell case.

———

One fey observer of the shifting political winds in Richmond was the Washington, D.C., multimillionaire Evalyn Walsh McLean, heir to a vast Colorado mining fortune. Accustomed to a privileged life that most citizens in the depression could scarcely imagine, McLean was considered the Capitol's premiere hostess. In 1908 she had married Edward B. McLean, whose father, John, owned the *Washington Post* and the *Cincinnati Enquirer.* (Given a wedding present of $200,000, the couple spent it all during their European honeymoon.) By 1933 the marriage had long since disintegrated and the *Post* had passed out of the McLean family, but Evalyn Walsh McLean continued to maintain a bejeweled profile among the city's elite. Her most famous possession was the mysterious Hope Diamond, an enormous, light-blue stone said to have brought misfortune to several previous owners. Guests who received her coveted invitations flocked to her estate, Friendship, as much to gawk at the diamond as to partake of food and conversation.

At her 1936 New Year's Eve party for six hundred guests—rumored to have cost more than $50,000—McLean did not disappoint them. The *Herald,* in a gushing account of the evening, noted, "She wore the famous Hope diamond, blue and gleaming on its diamond chain, and the huge white Star of the East, almost as famous and valuable, pendant from a diamond necklace which fell almost to the waist line. Diamonds were in her ears, a diamond tiara in her hair, and she wore wide diamond bracelets, two or three on each arm."

Despite her love of jewels, parties, and exotic animals, McLean also had a serious and often generous side that she expressed by writing newspaper articles and engaging in acts of philanthropy. It was to this side that Edith Maxwell's supporters in the National Woman's Party appealed in January 1937. McLean had responded with an ample contribution to the defense fund and apparently met Edith during the latter's brief stay in Washington.

The spring of 1938 found Edith in prison and McLean vacationing in Palm Beach, Florida. Still, McLean had not forgotten the convicted woman, whom she described as "simple and unaffected." In her *Washington Times* column of April 8, McLean pledged to do "anything in [her] power" to help win Edith's release and also managed to slander the entire Wise County population. "Just because Edith wouldn't be like all the other people around her in the hill-billy country—she had ambition and pride and got out and made the most of herself—is no earthly reason why the people in her county should condemn her for life, just through jealousy and spite," McLean wrote. "There's no use talking, you have to admire a woman like this. You never stand still in this world—you either go backward or forward, and Edith made up her mind to make the best of herself, which wasn't an easy thing to do, and I consider it an honor to have known her."

This was not the first time McLean had taken more than a passing interest in a criminal case. In 1932, at the height of national hysteria over the kidnapped Lindbergh baby, McLean hired Gaston Means, a former FBI agent and ex-convict, to recover the child. Unfortunately for McLean, Means had no real knowledge of the baby's whereabouts, nor did he have compunctions about conning the gullible heiress. Claiming to have contacts with a mysterious "gang" that had taken the child, Means succeeded in bilking McLean of more than $100,000 in "ransom money." He eventually was arrested and pleaded guilty to larceny and embezzlement.

McLean never recouped her financial loss—more than $1.3 million in today's dollars—but she had bought herself a real-life depression-era adventure. For years after the incident, she received mail from people interested in spinning out theories about the Lindbergh case and lauding her efforts to solve the crime. Now, with Edith Maxwell, she was ready to try her hand at intervention once more.

Sometime in April 1938, *Washington Herald* managing editor Frank C. Waldrop telephoned Governor Price at Newport News on McLean's behalf, trying to set up a meeting between her and Price. What the governor said on the telephone has not been recorded, but apparently he must have given Waldrop at least some slight encouragement. In any case, Waldrop followed up with a letter on April 19. "Mrs. McLean would like to call you at your convenience to bring exhibits and discuss this matter off the record and offer any further assistance possible," he wrote.[6]

This high-level lobbying apparently did get Price's attention. When he returned to Richmond, he took what might have been his first detailed look at the Maxwell case. The governor learned that Edith had served only a few months of a twenty-year sentence. He also was informed that she had two trials and that both verdicts had been reviewed by the Virginia Supreme Court of Appeals. Moreover, even her own lawyer, Charles Henry Smith, had not yet filed a petition for a pardon. Price then authorized his secretary of the commonwealth to answer Waldrop's letter with a firm no: "In view of these facts . . . and considering the further fact that Miss Maxwell is represented by able counsel, who may be relied upon to move at the proper time, Governor Price does not think it advisable to go into the case at this time."[7]

It is not known whether McLean had any further involvement with the Maxwell case, but the movement to gain clemency for Edith continued to steamroll. In May 1938 a two-thousand-signature petition from Loudoun County, Virginia—an affluent foxhunting and steeplechasing community near Washington, D.C.—was forwarded to Price's office. "The facts in this case are so well-known to the citizens of Virginia, and the injustice of this sentence [is] so manifest to nearly every law-abiding citizen," the petition read in part.[8] The *Coalfield Progress* editorialized against the wording of the petition, saying that the activists were "mistaking hysteria for the facts." The newspaper said it had no particular objection to Edith's obtaining a pardon, yet it did object to what it called "meddling" by northern Virginians. "This meddling, in every instance, has re-acted against Edith, rather than in her favor," the editorial warned.

Although the Loudoun County petition came and went, well-placed advocates kept reminding Governor Price of the state's famous prisoner. The Washington group that had backed Edith's appeals may have disbanded after she went to prison, but newspaper publisher Cissy Patterson still considered herself a staunch friend of Edith. Patterson had increased her influence in the nation's capital by purchasing the *Washington Herald* and *Washington Times* from William Randolph Hearst in January 1939 and then combining them into one newspaper, the *Times-Herald.*

Patterson wrote to the governor on April 20, 1939, to say that she would give Edith a job if Price would release her. "I understand that she is now keeping books, operating a typewriter, and is behaving herself very well," she wrote. "I like to believe that she would do as much if given her freedom."[9] Patterson also sought to clarify her motives for intervening in the case: "I have been informed that the Virginia Prison Board is under the impression that our interest in this girl is something in the nature of a newspaper stunt, and not a matter of sincere concern for a human being," Patterson said. "I simply wish to convey to you personally the information that if Edith Maxwell is permitted to leave prison while she is still reasonably sound both in mind and body, I guarantee to provide her with a job in our clerical force somewhere."[10]

No wonder Virginia authorities were wary of anyone who might be connected to publicity stunts. According to the *Washington Post,* in the first few months of her imprisonment Edith had been "nearly hounded to death" by people trying to exploit her story. One such scheme had even been hatched to take her to New York for an appearance at the World's Fair. Prison officials perhaps were beginning to see themselves not only as guardians of Edith's person but also of her peace of mind.

———

On February 5, 1940, the *Washington Post* revealed in a front-page, copyrighted story that James H. Price had decided to pardon Edith before leaving the governor's mansion at the end of 1941. Citing an unnamed source "of unquestioned reliability," the *Post* reported that the governor had "kept in close touch" with Edith through prison officials at Goochland and was eager to "do something" for Edith while in office.

"While the Governor has not yet made up his mind when to intervene in the celebrated case of the girl twice convicted of murder, it was also learned on reliable authority that Edith can expect pardon in the spring," the article predicted.

Somewhat surprisingly—in light of the effort that had been made—Edith was described as "not yet being ready for or wanting immediate freedom." Again using unnamed sources, the *Post* reported that she had adapted to prison life and was "happy, or at least contented." Perhaps for this reason, Charles Henry Smith chose to wait until May 29, 1940, to formally apply for the pardon:

> My dear Governor:
> As counsel for Miss Edith Maxwell, I hereby make formal application for a conditional pardon for her. . . .
> I understand that Miss Maxwell's prison record is of the best. She was incarcerated in the Wise County and Lee County jails for a period of something over 14 months. I understand that under the law she is entitled to credit for this period. She has now actually served about 2½ years of her sentence in prison. Considering her conduct, she would be entitled now to credit for having served more than 7 years.
> I feel that the verdict of the jury imposed on her was too much punishment for the offense committed, *granting that she was guilty as charged* [emphasis added].
> I understand that you have in your office many petitions requesting leniency. I am not bothering to forward any further petitions to you, but I understand that Judge Ezra T. Carter of Gate City, Virginia, who was the trial judge in this case, has certain recommendations

to make. He has suggested, however, that I file my application for pardon with you and when he hears from you, he will give you his recommendations promptly. I suppose you will, in the usual course, ask the recommendations of the Commonwealth's Attorney, Mr. Fred B. Greear, of Wise, Virginia. I do not expect him to make any favorable recommendation.

I may say that the brother of Miss Maxwell, who lives in New York City, has made arrangements whereby Miss Maxwell will be given steady, suitable and profitable employment, in the event she is granted a conditional pardon. Evidence of this fact will be furnished you within the course of the next week.

If your investigation of this case leads you to the conclusion that this is a proper case for executive clemency, I would like to suggest that any pardon that you may see fit to grant be conditioned upon Miss Maxwell's remaining certainly out of Wise County, and perhaps out of the state of Virginia.

Permit me to say in closing that I probably know as much about the details of this case as any other person, and that I honestly and conscientiously feel that this girl's case is one which merits and almost demands clemency at this time.

You will recall my conversation with you several weeks ago, in which I undertook to tell you honestly, frankly, and candidly all that I knew about the case—*the bad as well as the good* [emphasis added]. I hope you agree with me and that you will find yourself in a position where you feel that it is your duty to give this girl a chance to get back to a normal and useful life.

Thanking you and with my kind regards, I am

Sincerely yours,

Charles H. Smith[11]

If the particulars of Smith and Price's private conversation had been revealed to history, current understanding of the Maxwell case would have been enormously enhanced. Much could have been learned from Smith's recitation of what he called "the bad as well as the good." From the standpoint of a defense attorney, what does that mean? Did Smith have evidence showing that his client was all too human, a typical mixture of culpability and innocence? Or was he speaking of the actions of other players in the Maxwell case? Equally intriguing is Smith's remark that Edith received too harsh a sentence, "granting that she was guilty as charged." One can interpret this to mean that Smith was actually admitting that Edith *was* guilty of second-degree murder, or, one can argue, he *had to* admit guilt in order to get her released. It is unclear whether he could have maintained that she was wrongfully convicted and at the same time asked Governor Price to pardon her.

In any case, Price's office responded almost immediately to Smith's letter with a two-sentence reply.

> Dear Mr. Smith:
>
> As mentioned in your letter of May 29, 1940, petitions with numerous signatures have been filed in behalf of a pardon for Edith Maxwell, but thus far Governor Price has not felt that enough time has been served to justify an investigation. As soon as the evidence of suitable employment also mentioned in your letter is received, you will be advised as to Governor Price's feeling in the matter of completing the file.
>
> > Very truly yours,
> > Ex-officio Sec'y to the Governor[12]

Smith promptly documented the offer of employment for Edith by sending the governor a letter from the president of M. P. Kuczor Company Inc., a New York City firm that had employed Earl Maxwell for several years. The company, which imported Hungarian paprika, was offering to give Edith an office job upon her release. "Through our association with Mr. Maxwell, we are sure that she would have the proper home environment," added company president Roy R. Kinder.[13]

Along with the Kuczor document, Smith sent his own letter praising Earl Maxwell. "As I told you when I saw you," Smith wrote to Price, "her brother, Earl Maxwell, was the only member of her family who stuck by her in her trouble. He was very helpful to me and to her, and at all times cooperative. He holds a responsible position in New York . . . and is highly regarded by his employers."[14]

Smith's statement that Earl was the *only* member of her family who "stuck by her" is puzzling. Edith received legal assistance from her uncle, Gernade Dotson, and his son, A. T. Dotson; her sister and her mother were key defense witnesses; various relatives posted bond for her; and she often stayed at the home of her sister and brother-in-law, Gladys and Clay Robinson, while in Wise County. The remark is also hard to interpret in light of Edith's close and mutually supportive relationship with her mother. Perhaps Smith was just emphasizing to the governor that he thought Edith's living with Earl in New York would be the best possible placement.

A notation stamped on Smith's letter of June 3—presumably by someone on the governor's staff—indicates that Price ordered a copy of Edith's prison record on June 7, a clear indication that he was seriously considering the pardon request. Including 450 days spent in the Wise and Lee County jails, Edith had by now served three years, nine months, and three days of the twenty-year sentence. Her prison record, prepared on June 8, 1940, reveals that Prisoner Number 38599 had not violated a single prison rule since her commitment to the state penitentiary in 1937.

A separate questionnaire completed by Elizabeth M. Kates, superintendent at the Goochland facility, noted that "Work and conduct have been excellent and attitude towards the Institution has been excellent." Kates also described Edith's attitude toward society as "good," adding "[I] do not think she bears a grudge." Under "General Remarks," Kates completed the questionnaire with her most telling comment. "She [Edith] has shown marked improvement in self-control and [I] feel that she is determined to make good," she wrote. "However, I personally hope that some arrangement might be made which would not allow the brother to have a master hand during her readjustment. Further publicity would certainly ruin her future."[15]

On July 9 the governor advised Smith, through a spokesperson, that he had given the case "very careful consideration" and "[did] not feel justified in taking any action in this matter at this time."[16] It is unlikely that Smith was privy to Kates's warning. The machinery of a smoothly orchestrated pardon had slammed to a paralyzing—and perhaps inexplicable—halt.

26   The Two Eleanors

The *Washington Post*'s prediction that Edith Maxwell would be out of prison by the spring of 1940 had radically missed the mark. In October 1941, with Gov. James Hubert Price's term nearly over and Edith still behind bars, Cissy Patterson decided to play her trump card. She would seek help from a person even more influential than she and her moneyed circle—the First Lady, Eleanor Roosevelt.

The two Eleanors—Roosevelt and Patterson—had known each other socially since their debutante days. Many years later, in 1933, Patterson wrote a complimentary article about the then-new First Lady who was captivating Washington, telling *Herald* readers that "Mrs. Roosevelt has solved the problem of living better than any woman I have ever known."[1] Patterson believed that Price, reportedly a great admirer of the Roosevelts, would not ignore a sympathetic request from the White House.

Eleanor Roosevelt was not acquainted with the details of the Maxwell case, but she did possess at least a passing familiarity with southwest Virginia. Her beloved father Elliott, while estranged from her mother in 1892, had worked near the town of Abingdon, helping develop a vast tract of virgin forest owned by his brother-in-law. Eleanor, who was seven at the time, had corresponded with some of the daughters of Elliott's friends in Abingdon, on one occasion sending doll's jewelry as a present. More recently, in July 1934, she had driven through the Kentucky and Virginia coalfields on what, in that simpler time, was called an "off the record" vacation. The First Lady, traveling with two women friends, told the curious that she was "just running around," enjoying the mountain scenery and taking a look at relief efforts, particularly those aimed at providing hot lunches to mountain schoolchildren.

Eleanor Roosevelt had arrived in Wise County on July 3, 1934, after driving south on U.S. 23 from Pikeville, Kentucky. Sheriff Preston Adams, who escorted the First Lady's party, was surprised that they had no bodyguards and "were just driving like anybody else, afraid of nothing."[2] Outside Norton, the First Lady and her friends stopped for sandwiches at the Copper Kettle Inn. Word of her arrival spread quickly. By the time they finished lunch and continued on, an adoring crowd had jammed into the center of Norton, forcing them to make an unscheduled stop. As citizens pressed forward to shake Eleanor Roosevelt's hand, she had stood on the running board of her roadster and thanked the crowd for the thunderous welcome, appearing, as one observer put it, "plain, unaffected, genuine."[3]

Now, seven years later, she was about to be asked to help secure the early release of a Wise County woman convicted of murder—surely a controversial step even for a figure as popular as the First Lady. On October 6, 1941, Patterson sent Roosevelt an eight-page report summarizing the Maxwell case as she saw it. As Patterson had hoped, Roosevelt forwarded the report to Price, but not without some reservations, as her cover letter indicates:

> Dear Governor Price:
>   I am sending you the enclosed statement which has been sent to me. I do not feel that I know enough to make any personal decision in this case. I do feel, however, that the sentence has been unduly severe and there are certain extenuating circumstances. Whether the girl, if allowed to leave the prison, will be able to make good and become a useful citizen, is something for those who have been in contact with her to decide. I cannot refrain from sending this to you, because if an injustice is being done you will want to look into it carefully and rectify it before your term of office expires.
>   Very sincerely yours,
>   Eleanor Roosevelt[4]

Roosevelt wrote to Cissy Patterson the same day, telling her, as she had told the governor, that she did not know enough about the case to have an opinion. She asked the *Washington Times-Herald* owner not to publicize her involvement "because I do not feel that I have the slightest right to take any action."[5]

Patterson wrote back to reassure Roosevelt that her actions would be kept confidential and it was not necessary for her to form an opinion as to Edith's guilt or innocence. "Of course, I could not hope that you would *judge* the Maxwell case, dear Mrs. Roosevelt. I only wish that were possible, for your verdict would be fair and just. By calling the Governor's attention to the case, even without the slightest expression of any opinion on your part either way, you have done all I could possibly hope for."[6]

—

"I have talked at length with Edith Maxwell and believe her story, & this report to be *true*. C.P." Cissy Patterson had scrawled these words on the margin of her "Summary History of the Edith Maxwell Case," the document sent to Governor Price through the intermediary hands of Eleanor Roosevelt.[7] The report not only provides a fascinating insider's view of the Maxwell case but also a candid profile of Cissy Patterson as a journalist careless with facts, a condescending purveyor of upper-crust values, and a woman passionately determined to correct a perceived injustice.

Patterson starts her history by mentioning Pound, a hamlet she incorrectly places "in the heart of the Blue Ridge mountains of Virginia."

Introducing Trigg Maxwell, she says, "He was an average citizen of his community, ignorant and bigoted, but a popular character of the town, generous with his small money. He was somewhat rummy, inclined to drunken violence, and Edith frequently had to lead him home by the ear. He was also rough with his wife whom Edith habitually defended in family quarrels, and he was proud of being known as a strict parent."

Of the fatal fight between Edith and Trigg on the night of July 20–21, 1935, Patterson writes, "Exactly what transpired has never been developed." This was an amazing admission from a woman whose news organization had had nearly unlimited access to Edith over a period of several years—and whose writers had routinely reported the story of the high-heel shoe as fact. Here is Patterson's version of events:

> The sum of the story is that Trigg Maxwell attempted to whip his daughter for being out late, threatened to throw his wife out of the house, brandished a kitchen knife, was struck by Edith with (1) a shoe, or (2) an axe, or (3) a flat iron, or (4) a skillet. It was never established just what weapon Edith used to defend herself. She says (1) shoe and (2) skillet. The state suggested the other things. Edith's blouse was ripped off. There were definite overtones of *incestuous* tendencies, at least, in the whole business of Trigg Maxwell's opposition to Edith's "seeing boys" and "staying out late."
>
> Trigg spilled blood from a cut on the head. The battle ceased and all went to bed. Some hours later, Trigg was heard bustling about the kitchen. He fell to the floor, [and] died.

Patterson's statement that Edith had admitted hitting Trigg with a *skillet* is remarkable because nowhere in her court testimony was this ever mentioned. A half-century later, the rumor would still flourish in Wise County that Edith "did it in the kitchen with a skillet," but apparently the only recorded mention of a skillet as a weapon appears in Patterson's report. If one supposes that Trigg Maxwell was hit with the edge of a frying pan, the theory is consistent with the commonwealth's medical evidence about a "sharp-edged" instrument causing the head wound. That supposition, however, must be balanced against other testimony indicating Edith had told her best friend she accidentally hit her father with an iron. In Patterson's view, the type of weapon used was irrelevant because it was taken up in self-defense.

Likewise, her opinion that the fight had "incestuous" overtones is hard to evaluate. Did Patterson have inside information, or was she merely speculating? At any rate, her statement that "Edith's blouse was ripped off" contradicts Edith's own testimony at the first trial, in which she said she had already undressed and was wearing a princess slip at the time of the altercation. Did Edith purposely leave out this detail on the stand, or was Patterson again simply misstating the facts? Nowhere in any court testimony or newspaper article was the suggestion ever made that Trigg Maxwell sexually abused Edith or other family members. Although such a shameful secret might predictably have been suppressed, it is more likely that Patterson was expressing her personal opinion based on a shaky command of the facts.

Patterson goes on to characterize the prosecution of Edith Maxwell as a vendetta led by former sheriff Lee Skeen, whom she called "the prime mover for revenge." Calling up the myth that mountain people are not bound by the laws that govern civilized communities, she informs the governor that "in remote sections of the country as Wise County, murder of any sort is usually looked upon as demanding personal retribution, regardless of the course of official justice." Because of Lee Skeen's political influence and his being a cousin to Judge H. A. W. Skeen, Edith was "already doomed" before her first trial, according to Patterson. She incorrectly states in her report that Judge Skeen was an elected official and that he would lose office if Edith were found innocent. (He was, in fact, appointed.) This analysis also ignores the fact that Judge Skeen had ruled that a key piece of evidence against Edith—her alleged confession—would not be admissible at trial. This hardly seems to be the action of a judge in collusion with the prosecution.

Patterson deals with the fact that another of Judge Skeen's relatives, Alfred A. Skeen, was a defense attorney by saying that he eventually "was forced by family pressure to withdraw." It is difficult to prove or disprove this assertion, but a more likely explanation is that Alfred A. Skeen, who successfully argued Edith's first appeal in Richmond, was simply crowded out of the case by the arrival of three out-of-town lawyers.

Patterson also levels criticism at both the National Woman's Party and the Knoxville, Tennessee, Business and Professional Women's Club for their actions in the Maxwell case. The Woman's Party, she says, "sent a representative to Wise whose greatest talent was to offend the country people and make them all the more determined to uphold traditional parental authority regardless of the real issue of guilt or innocence of murder"—an apparent reference to attorney Gail Laughlin. Patterson lambastes the Knoxville women's group, which had withdrawn its offer of assistance after learning of Edith's deal with the Hearst organization, for worrying more about "customs and manners" than the real issue of guilt or innocence.

Patterson's criticisms of the heavy-handed tactics of the Woman's Party representative may be correct, but throughout the entire report she fails to acknowledge the role that her own newspaper had played in alienating a segment of the public in Wise County. After all, it was the *Herald* that had run the lurid five-part series in the summer of 1935, introducing the "mountain code" myth. She also ignores the fact that Hearst reporters had muzzled Edith at the Wise jail when the women from Knoxville tried to speak with her about starting a defense fund. Although she could see flaws in other well-meaning people, Patterson refuses to acknowledge in this report that actions taken by her own employees and Hearst colleagues probably were detrimental to Edith. If this is true, then her extraordinary effort to get Edith released from prison must be regarded not only as an act of compassion—but as atonement for reckless behavior.

What influence, if any, the report had on Governor Price is unknown, but on October 28 he responded to Eleanor Roosevelt's overture with a candid letter. Price acknowledged that he and the superintendent of the Women's Division (Elizabeth M. Kates) had "been working over this case for some time." He told the First Lady confidentially that it was his "full intention" to pardon Edith before leaving office.[8]

"The girl has been dreadfully exploited by newspapers and other agencies," the governor's letter continued. "What she really needs is an opportunity to get away from so much publicity and to have a free and fair opportunity to start life over again. I am devoting myself very earnestly to the accomplishment of this objective."

Clearly, the governor had come to regard Edith Maxwell as the victim of her own fame. Eleanor Roosevelt, proving herself the soul of discretion, did not share the contents of the governor's confidential letter with Cissy Patterson. She merely instructed her secretary to inform the newspaper publisher that Price was "giving the case of Edith Maxwell every consideration." Edith Maxwell would be a free woman within sixty days. In Eleanor Roosevelt's view, it was news best kept to herself.

As Charles Henry Smith had hinted in 1940, those seeking a pardon for Edith Maxwell had found an ally in Ezra T. Carter, the Scott County judge who had presided over the second trial. In late November 1941, while Edith's pardon application was being processed, Governor Price had written to Carter soliciting his opinion. Two days before Pearl Harbor, the judge responded with an unequivocal endorsement of the proposed clemency.

"I have given considerable thought to this case, more perhaps, than any other criminal case I have tried during my experience on the bench," Carter wrote. "I feel that the jury has convicted this defendant of the highest crime of which she could have been convicted properly under the evidence before them, and if the jury had come to the conclusion that the killing was merely manslaughter I do not feel that any one could have found any just fault with their finding." Carter upheld the jury verdict of second-degree murder in March 1937 with the observation that the jury was justified in concluding that Edith struck the fatal blow. Now he revealed to the governor how grave his own doubts about that verdict had been:

> I have always had serious doubts that this killing was a willful, deliberate and premeditated act upon the part of the daughter, but I have been impressed that what actually occurred was that the daughter returned home late that night and her father was angered on account of her being out late, and they got into an altercation, resulting, perhaps in a fight in which the wounds were inflicted, which resulted in the death of the deceased, either by the defendant or her mother, or perhaps someone else. We have no evidence from the defendant or her mother giving any explanation of this affray.[9]

After two jury trials and millions of printed words, the truth of what had happened that night was still locked within the memories of Ann, Mary Katherine, and Edith. Tales of the hatchet, the iron, and the skillet would flow through time indistinctly, like the murmurs of a babbling brook.

There is a scene, at the end of *Mountain Justice*, where the governor of New York denies Ruth Harkins's extradition back to "Durley County," where she has just escaped a lynching. A grateful Ruth looks at the kind-faced governor in amazement and asks, "You mean I may go now, I'm free?"

"Yes," replies the governor, "but I wouldn't go back to Durley County."

The two shake hands. "I don't know what to say, how to thank you," Ruth exclaims.

"Goodbye and good luck," he says gravely. The governor starts to leave his office, pauses cinematically to smile and nod at Ruth's good fortune, and makes his exit, firmly shutting the door on the past.

Edith Maxwell found herself walking through a scene that might have felt eerily similar as she entered the state capitol in Richmond on Friday, December 19, 1941. She had been working in the Goochland prison office earlier that day when news of her pardon came from the governor. With only thirteen days remaining in his term, Price had kept the promise printed in the *Washington Post* nearly two years before. "She left the farm with $10 worth of clothes, an undisclosed sum of money she had earned from the institutional work, and a very thankful look around," said the *Post*. A prison attendant had driven her the thirty miles to Richmond, where pardon documents had been prepared. It is not known whether she talked with the governor face to face, as the fictional Ruth Harkins had, but Edith attended a meeting in which she was formally released. In a twisted way, the ending written to *Mountain Justice* so many years before had finally come true. "I am very pleased," Charles Henry Smith told a reporter. "I knew, of course, that she would never serve the full sentence. I think she has served ample time and for her future I have the highest expectation."[10]

By evening Edith was on a westbound train, but she was no longer Edith Maxwell. With the help of prison officials she had already begun to reinvent herself. Edith had chosen "Ann" as her new Christian name, and her surname she had picked out of a telephone book at the Goochland farm.[11] Ahead of her beckoned a job in a midwestern city. It had been nearly six and a half years since it all began. Now she would start over at age twenty-seven in a quest to become that person so valued by Eleanor Roosevelt, "a useful citizen."

―――

Governor Price's office announced the next day that Goochland's celebrity prisoner—now gone from the state—had been pardoned. He kept her whereabouts a secret, saying only that "suitable employment" had been arranged. Edith's benefactors in Richmond had seen to it that she would have a day's head start on any reporter or curiosity seeker who tried to track her down.

Edith had served five years and three months in jail and prison, about one-fourth of her sentence. Governor Price gave Edith what was called a "conditional" pardon—one that could be revoked by a future governor—but in reality the only condition was that she not break the laws of Virginia in the future. Price told the press that she had been a "model prisoner" whose pardon had been recommended by both the superintendent of the State Industrial Farm for Women and Judge Ezra T. Carter.

How prosecutor Fred Greear, by then serving his third term as commonwealth attorney, regarded Edith's release is less certain.[12] Two weeks before granting clemency, Price had written to Greear asking his opinion. Greear later told the *Coalfield Progress* that he could not make up his mind, although he had given the matter "considerable thought." By the time Edith left prison, Greear still had not responded to the governor's letter and perhaps avoided taking a public stance.

As 1941 drew to a close, Edith's long and often overblown romance with the press was finally over. Newspapers that had kept her name before the public for years now seemed glad to relinquish her to anonymity. "Edith Maxwell Wins Pardon; Seeks Happiness in Seclusion," read the headline in the *Washington Post*. The *Washington Times-Herald* also lauded Edith's release but, predictably, insisted on playing up the hillbilly angle: "Edith Maxwell Victimized by Mountain Code; Condemned by Neighbors for 'Outland Ways.'"

One newspaper editor, however, had long believed that Edith—and Appalachian culture—had been victimized in a different way. "The nation was enflamed into believing that a barbaric persecution was in progress, in an isolated section in Southwest Virginia, where an entirely different family code existed," wrote Pres T. Atkins in the *Coalfield Progress*. "And then false hopes were planted in the mind of an unfortunate girl, whose greatest need was sane, wise, conservative advice, rather than the encouragement in the false belief of martyrdom, of a rainbow with a pot of gold awaiting her.[13]

Edith Maxwell would live for another thirty-seven years after her release, shadowed by what Charles Henry Smith had called "the tragedy [that] can never be entirely lifted." Once, while visiting a Richmond hotel with her husband, she unexpectedly encountered a Wise County historian who knew her story well. She quickly took the man aside and asked him to make no mention of her past.

Using the name she had gleaned from the tele-
phone book at the Goochland prison farm, Ann Grayson began working
as a secretary for an Indianapolis trucking company sometime in the early
to mid-1940s. Only a very few people besides her mother and younger
sisters, who had moved to the area, knew of her prior travails as Edith
Maxwell, and the skills she had learned in the prison office likely had
prepared her for the job. She was well on her way to building a new life.

Grayson and the owner of the trucking company soon fell deeply in
love. Nearly twenty years her senior, Otto Abshier was an Indiana native
who had served in the state legislature. By 1945 the pair had relocated to
Jacksonville, Florida, and were married there. They ran a mom-and-pop
grocery store for several years before developing a suburban shopping
center. In 1960 they sold their businesses and moved to a farm outside the
city, raising cattle and hogs. Four years later they returned to Jacksonville,
where Ann found a secretarial job with a local constable and occasionally
worked as a security guard for a department store.

A son was born to the marriage in 1946 and a daughter eighteen
months later. The family also included Ann Dotson Maxwell, affectionately
called "Mamaw Maxwell," who lived with the Abshiers until her death in
the 1950s. According to Ann and Otto's son, the Abshier family was tight-
knit and loving, going out for dinner every Sunday and often engaging in
a favorite pastime, putt-putt golf. Ann was a devoted mother who stressed
racial equality and the value of a college education. But she was something
of a mystery even to her own children, declining to reveal details of her
youth or even to tell her age. And though she did have occasional visitors
from the Wise County days, including Mary Katherine, they did not speak
openly of the past.

In the early 1970s Otto retired to his home state of Indiana. Ann,
Otto, and the couple's daughter and son-in-law bought motor homes and
intended to tour the United States, but their plans were sadly cut short by
Otto's death in 1974. Ann's son describes her as "a broken woman" after
the death of her beloved husband. She continued to live in Indiana until

her death in 1979 at age sixty-five. Although much younger than Otto, she lived only five years after his passing.

Ann Grayson Abshier apparently left no letters, diaries, or other documents in the family's possession that could connect her with her former life or explain events from her perspective. Even a trunk that Mamaw Maxwell had kept—lovingly stuffed with memorabilia of her idols, Franklin and Eleanor Roosevelt—was destroyed in a barn fire in the 1960s.

———

Just as the pioneer cabins were imploding in the 1930s, leaving only chimneys to signal their storied existence, Wise County today has already seen the passing of many depression-era landmarks. The little four-room house on Pound's main thoroughfare, where passions ran so high in 1935, is gone, the site now occupied by that all-American testament to progress—a gas station. The Pound River swept away the picturesque old mill in 1942, and a few years after that the river disgorged upon its banks a little hand axe. A small boy playing near the river found the axe and took it home to his mother, but its relation to the Maxwell case, if any, will never be known.

Over at Wise, just a ten-minute drive on the four-lane, the former Shorty's Restaurant was torn down in a street-widening project, and the old jailhouse was razed to make way for a modern brick structure in the 1970s. The high gallery in the Wise County courtroom from which spectators watched the Maxwell trials has since been boarded up, and circuit court proceedings have been moved to a windowless, carpeted room in the courthouse addition. When spectacular trials roll through every few years, they now attract out-of-town television crews rather than adventurers in fedoras and cloches. Coal trucks and SUVs, instead of cars with running boards and rumble seats, command the streets. Cows are officially banished from public traffic. And the voices that rang through the corridors of the former Colonial Hotel have fallen silent. The grand old building has been closed off and on for years, although talk of renovation yet hangs in the air.

And what of its former citizens? Although the Chant B. Kelly Memorial Bridge ushers travelers into Pound, and the Fred B. Greear Gymnasium sits on the University of Virginia's campus at Wise, the past has swallowed up many others. The jurors, judges, counselors, and courtroom spectators have begun to fade from memory. Trigg Maxwell sleeps in the Bolling Cemetery at Pound, while his wife is buried hundreds of miles to the south.

I would like to say that Edith Maxwell is different—that she has some-how escaped the passage of time, left an indelible mark upon a mountain community or even upon the world—but I cannot. Edith's case had the potential to change the legal status of thousands of women, yet it faltered. She was first a private person, and she ultimately returned to that private life. Would she wish to be remembered for her youthful celebrity or for her productive years as a mother and wife? Or would she prefer simply to be eclipsed by time? No matter. When our lives pass into story, they are no longer ours alone. It is up to those who hear the stories to decide what connections to the past may yet be made—and to give life to those stories through the march of years.

As literary critic Leslie Banner has observed, "Contrasts throughout the country between rural and urban cultures were still sharply defined in the 1920s and 30s, and the children of the Jazz Age were more distant from their parents' experience than any generation before or since."[1] This cultural divide played out vividly in the way some national newspaper editors treated the Maxwell case, promoting urban, "progressive" values while denigrating those of more traditional rural societies such as Appalachia. And it played out tragically in the conflict between Edith—herself a child of the Jazz Age—and her father, born in 1882. Although her approach was not at all ideological, it was Edith's desire to occupy the spaces previously reserved for men: the open road, the public square, and the street corners and cafes where female teachers seldom frequented.

Aggravating this generational conflict was her parents' troubled relationship, most likely rooted in Trigg's substance abuse and domestic violence and perhaps in Ann's disappointment with her husband's social standing. Even though Edith's flirting or staying out late likely sparked the fatal encounter on July 21, 1935, we can pinpoint an underlying cause in Trigg's threat earlier that evening to throw Ann Maxwell out of the house. A pattern long established over the years dictated that Edith would be her mother's defender, whether in word or in actual deed. She was caught up in a cycle of conflict from which she ultimately could not break free. It was mostly these factors, rather than a brooding, malignant rural culture, that evoked tragedy for this American family.

In puzzling over the Maxwell case, we might have some lingering questions: Who struck the first blow? What weapons were actually used? or even, Who exactly was involved? But these answers are hard to come by. It is as if we are watching a movie of Edith entering the house, only to find that the screen goes black as she shuts the door behind her. All we have to go on is the soundtrack that the next-door neighbors have provided: voices raised loud, feet shuffling across the floor, Mary Katherine saying that Trigg had blood all over his head, and his piteous moans. Finally, even that soundtrack is eclipsed by a loud radio. When Edith reemerges in the alley a few minutes later, disheveled and clad only in a princess slip, we cannot tell if she has been the victim or the aggressor. The answer probably lies in between.

So the question then becomes, Why did two Wise County juries deal so harshly with a defendant where the evidence pointed to accidental death or manslaughter? In the first trial, the wording of the jury instructions left jurors no option to seek a middle ground between a verdict of innocent and a murder conviction. And, of course, we may wonder if the prosecution's presentation of the evidence was more compelling. That is almost certainly true in the second trial, where the defense failed to put either Ann or Edith on the stand, relying instead on medical experts who tried to determine from afar that the victim died of natural causes. Other issues, however, must be addressed before we can conclude that Fred Greear simply outshone his legal opponents.

Was a prosecution conspiracy festering around Uncle Gernade Dotson's bucking of the Democratic Party and running as an independent, or was a conspiracy rooted in family revenge and orchestrated by Trigg's brother-in-law, Lee Skeen? Although Edith's supporters put forth both theories, there is little evidence to bolster such claims. Other issues are more pivotal to Edith's receiving a heavy prison sentence: the defendants' deception, the all-male jury, and the role of the press.

The Defendants' Deception

Ann and Edith Maxwell clearly had a moral obligation to seek prompt medical attention for Trigg and to give a truthful accounting of his final hours. In this they failed, probably because of panic and a desire to protect each other from the ramifications of the father's untimely death. Within minutes of Trigg's severe head injury, someone within the Maxwell home decided to execute a cover-up—a move that would have devastating consequences. The strategy to clean up any sign of a struggle and then call for help ultimately made the Maxwell women look guilty. They apparently compounded this error by moving Trigg's still-alive body to the porch from inside the house—and inventing the story of his falling on the meat block.

Writing in 1937, *Coalfield Progress* editor Pres Atkins believed that the dissembling of Edith and Ann Maxwell—through the "meat block" and "slipper" stories—backfired and resulted in Edith's murder conviction. Had she admitted to striking her father "during a hot-headed quarrel," she might have been acquitted outright or may have had to serve only two and half years for voluntary manslaughter, he wrote. "The mystery of the death room, rather than a straight forward story, is to blame, many believe, for the heavy punishment meted out [to] the former school teacher," Atkins concluded.[2]

The All-Male Jury

Although Edith was represented by competent counsel and was not forced to incriminate herself, she was not tried by a jury of her peers because of patriarchal state laws. The imbalance of power between men and women in the Wise County courtroom was illustrated quite dramatically by the appearance of Gail Laughlin, who was shunned by a fellow defense attorney and patronized by the prosecutor. Had women been allowed to serve on the jury, the trial outcome might have been different.

The Role of the Press

Media coverage outside southwest Virginia was overwhelmingly favorable to Edith between 1935 and 1937, yet her lawyers consistently tried to move her trials out of Wise County because of this very coverage. Especially in 1936, the defense tried to convince Judge Carter to move the second trial because of prejudicial pretrial publicity. The judge declined to do so, and his ruling eventually was upheld by a higher court, which stated that the Wise County citizenry was prejudiced against the yellow press rather than against Edith herself. Yet it would be at least two decades before jurists would more fully understand the effects of massive pretrial publicity; it would take a while for the law to catch up with the onslaught of the mass media and celebrity culture. Although, typically, a defendant's right to a fair trial can be compromised by negative pretrial publicity suggesting guilt, in Edith's case the excessively laudatory articles trumpeting her innocence had much the same effect in Wise County. The courts of the 1930s ruled otherwise, but I believe that for every compliment heaped upon Edith at the expense of her fellow citizens, resentment accrued against the yellow press and, by extension, against the defendant with whom "the scandalmongers" enjoyed such a cozy relationship. Had the second trial been moved to another county, the verdict perhaps would have been otherwise.

The role of Edith's own advisors in feeding the media frenzy is troubling. While her lawyers complained in court about the damaging effects of the articles, they were either benefiting financially or basking in the glow of publicity from Hearst, one of the most egregious offenders. We may also question whether the Hearst organization, and to some lesser degree the *Washington Post*, were ignoring the conflicts of interest inherent

in these arrangements—not to mention being disingenuous with readers. On the surface, the newspapers seemed to be crusading to correct
a perceived injustice, hiring some of the best legal talent in the East to
represent Edith. Yet it is unclear whether the decisions of Edith's handlers
were always made with her best interests in mind or with an eye toward
boosting circulation. What if Edith, at some point, had wanted to recant
her story, or perhaps to accept a plea bargain, but could not do so because
she already had been cast as the saintly "Joan d'Arc of the Mountains"?
Of course, one could argue, as the *Post* did, that Edith would have been
"just a number in prison" had the press not stepped in to help her. That
was true by late 1935, but we will never know to what extent the publicity
before her first trial contributed to her murder conviction. In the Edith
Maxwell case the demands of justice and the needs of the press ran parallel at times but ultimately diverged.

As we consider the thousands of articles written about Edith in newspapers and magazines, the Hollywood interest—and even a Johnny Dollar
mystery radio program as late as the 1950s—we may wonder, Why did
the world care so much about the fate of an obscure schoolteacher in a
remote mountain village? The short answer, of course, is that the press
made people care, setting the agenda through relentless, sensational, one-
sided coverage.

Beyond that, the Maxwell case was a story packed with human interest.
In a world where men commit the huge majority of crimes, the entrance
of two female murder suspects always generates interest, as evidenced by
the crime film *Chicago,* set in the 1920s and voted best picture of 2002.
Not only Ann and Edith's gender but also the fact that an eleven-year-old
girl was a crucial defense witness fanned the flames. The tale was further
enhanced by the Dotsons and Maxwells being "prominent" within their
community, holding numerous posts in politics and government.[3] That
the story was set in dark, mysterious Appalachia added to its allure.

Another element of intrigue revolved around the question of guilt or
innocence. As the Virginia Supreme Court noted, most of the testimony of
the three defense witnesses was uncontradicted.[4] Having no eyewitnesses
to the fatal struggle, the prosecution had to rely on circumstantial evidence
to try to disprove its story. The wide array of weapons suggested—high-heel
shoe, smoothing iron, and Coma Tiller's axe—made for copy so lively that
it fairly leapt out of the newspaper columns.

The reading public also may have been fascinated by the daring behavior of the defendant herself. On the night of her father's death she had gone with a young man to a roadhouse where liquor was served. Second, she had been seen earlier that day standing close to a man in the street, an encounter that drew a rebuke from Trigg Maxwell. According to the majority opinion of the Virginia Supreme Court, "The evidence does not disclose that she was guilty of any more reprehensible conduct than keeping late hours with young men."[5] Such atypical behavior for a woman in Edith's position, however, may have been as scandalous to readers as it undoubtedly was to her neighbors and kin. By testing the bounds of conventional behavior and parental authority, Edith represented the zeitgeist of flaming youth.

Looking at depression-era history through a twenty-first century rearview mirror by necessity warps the images displayed there, as did the funhouse mirrors that Ruth Harkins frolicked with in *Mountain Justice*. We must resist the perennial temptation to judge the Maxwell case by current standards. Less encumbered by our notions of multiculturalism, women's equality, and journalism ethics, the players in the Edith Maxwell drama moved by the only available light.

Yet from those early glimmerings we can trace an arc to present-day dilemmas. The impact of celebrity on the justice system has grown enormously since Edith's time, and checkbook journalism can scarcely be said to have faded away. Youth culture is more influential than ever, and women still die daily at the hands of male relatives and lovers. And in the eyes of much of the nation, Appalachia—although now wired to the Internet and thoroughly WalMart-ized—remains steadfastly the American other, a shadowland where youthful dreams are quickly extinguished.

NOTES

Chapter 1: "No Fire Here"

1. All direct quotations in this chapter were taken from the trial transcripts.

Chapter 2: The Purloined Peas

1. "Appalachia: The Economic Outlook through the Eighties," *Appalachia: Journal of the Appalachian Regional Commission* 17 (Nov.–Dec. 1983): 5.

2. "A Region of Contradictions," *Appalachia: Journal of the Appalachian Regional Commission* 18 (March 1985): 7.

3. Herbert Little, "Four U.S. Areas Held Blighted," *Knoxville News-Sentinel*, Aug. 4, 1935, B8.

4. Luther F. Addington, *The Story of Wise County, Virginia* (1956, repr. Johnson City, Tenn.: Overmountain Press, 1988), x.

5. I do not mean to imply that Wise County remained unchanged from the time of its settlement until the advent of coal mining; as Appalachian scholars point out, connections existed with other parts of the country through trading and travel. However, limited forms of mass communication and the absence of hard-surfaced roads and railroads made the county relatively isolated in comparison with urban areas in the nineteenth century.

6. James Taylor Adams, clipping from unidentified publication, Oct. 18, 1936, James Taylor Adams Collection, Special Collections, John Cook Wyllie Library, University of Virginia's College at Wise.

7. James Taylor Adams, clipping from unidentified publication, Wyllie Library.

8. Addington, *The Story of Wise County*, 196. Milling became a family tradition, and his son, James, built the last mill, this one water-driven, in 1875. The mill would remain a town landmark until floodwaters claimed it in 1942.

Chapter 3: "A Two-Hour Grilling"

1. Skeen's marriage to Trigg's sister, Clora, is recorded in volume 1 on page 67 of the Wise County Marriage License Book. Luther F. Addington, *The Story of Wise County, Virginia* (1956, repr. Johnson City, Tenn.: Overmountain Press, 1988), 292.

2. *Knoxville News-Sentinel*, July 24, 1935, 4.

3. James Cantrell, a deputy at the jail, testified about overhearing this conversation (transcript of second trial, 364).

4. Edith Maxwell as told to Walden B. Snell, "I Am Innocent," *Actual Detective Stories*, Nov. 1937, private collection of Evelyn Slemp.

Chapter 4: Becoming "Miss Edith"

1. Charles A. Johnson, *A Narrative History of Wise County, Virginia* (Norton, Va.: Pres T. Adkins, 1938), 215.

2. Her marriage license gives her age as sixteen, but if the birth date of April 30, 1860 is correct, she would have been only fifteen.

3. Edward T. Folliard, "Edith Maxwell Starts New Life under Death Trial's Shadow," *Washington Post*, Oct. 21, 1936, 3.

4. Trigg Maxwell's paternal grandparents were Audley and Zepporah Maxwell, who at one time lived in Mercer County, Virginia (now southern West Virginia). Marriage records indicate that Elbert Maxwell, Trigg's father, was born around 1851 in Mercer County. Apparently the family had moved to Wise County sometime before 1865, because one report places Audley Maxwell living in a two-room log house in a remote section of the county during the latter years of the Civil War. Emory L. Hamilton, "Legend of the Clark Camp," in *The Heritage of Wise County and the City of Norton* (n.p.: Wise County Historical Society, 1993), 7.

5. Johnson, *A Narrative History of Wise County*, 240.

6. The precise date of the Maxwells' departure to Kentucky is unclear. Edith notes in her *Washington Herald* autobiography that the family moved to Jenkins when she was six years old, which would have been between April 24, 1920, and April 23, 1921.

7. *Washington Herald*, Dec. 19, 1935, 6.

8. *Washington Herald*, Dec. 20, 1935, 13.

9. *Washington Herald*, Dec. 19, 1935, 6.

10. *Washington Herald*, Dec. 21, 1935, 8.

11. James Taylor Adams, clipping from unidentified publication, Dec. 30, 1928, Wise County Historical Society files.

12. James Robinson, "Christopher Gist High School," in *History of the Pound*, 272–75.

13. Edith apparently attended high school for five years (1927–28, 1928–29, 1929–30, 1930–31, and 1931–32), although only four years (grades 8–11) were then required. It is unclear if failing mathematics was the reason.

14. *Washington Herald*, Dec. 26, 1935, 12.

15. *Washington Herald*, Dec. 27, 1935, 6.

16. Ibid. According to court testimony, Trigg asked Lockie; in the *Herald*, Edith says she did.

17. *Washington Herald*, Dec. 26, 1935, 12.

18. *Washington Post*, Dec. 3, 1935, 7.

19. Goodridge Wilson, "The Southwest Corner," *Roanoke Times*, Nov. 14, 1937.

20. *Washington Herald*, Dec. 28, 1935, 4.

21. Joe Young West to His Excellency, Governor of Virginia, June 6, 1938, Office of the Governor, Letters Received and Sent, record group 3, the Library of Virginia.

22. *Washington Herald*, Dec. 28, 1935, 4.

23. *Washington Herald*, Dec. 30, 1935, 6.

24. The *Washington Post* would report in 1941 that Edith "never took much to school teaching, anyhow." This may have been a self-serving statement, however,

because by that time she did not intend to return to teaching. Yet the observations support its accuracy.

25. *Washington Herald,* Feb. 2, 1936, 1.

26. *Washington Herald,* Dec. 17, 1935, 6.

27. Arthur Mefford, "'Slipper Girl' Was 'Furriner,'" *Daily Mirror,* Dec. 15, 1935, 3.

28. *Maxwell v. Commonwealth of Virginia,* 187 S.E. Rep. 509 (1936).

Chapter 5: "A Man of Easy-Going Disposition"

1. It's assumed she arrived before the time of the Tuesday funeral service and was planning to attend.

2. Flora M. Branham to Editor, *Bristol Herald Courier,* undated clipping (likely, fall 1935), Wise County Historical Society files.

Chapter 6: The Mountain Code

1. The term *yellow* refers to "The Yellow Kid," a character in a popular comic of the same name that ran in Hearst's *Journal* and in Pulitzer's *World.*

2. H. L. Mencken, "Reflections on Journalism," *Journalism Bulletin,* new. ser., 2, no. 2 (June 1925): 3.

3. Mencken, "Reflections on Journalism."

4. Nelson Antrim Crawford, "Do Newspapers Thwart Criminal Justice?" *Journalism Bulletin,* new ser., 2, no. 2 (June 1925): 19.

Chapter 7: Buying Time

1. *Washington Post,* Dec. 2, 1935, 1.

2. Johnson, *Narrative History of Wise County,* 216.

3. *Variety,* Sept. 22, 1926, cited in John D. Stevens, "Social Utility of Sensational News: Murder and Divorce in the 1920s," *Journalism Quarterly* 62 (1985): 56.

4. One of the leading roles went to Henry Fonda, whose film character became the inspiration of Al Capp's *Li'l Abner* comic strip personality. "Trail of the Lonesome Pine," in *The Motion Picture Guide, 1927–83,* ed. Jay Robert Nash and Stanley Ralph Ross (Chicago: Cinebooks, 1987), 8: 3521.

5. Carl Knight, quoted in Virginius Dabney, "Edith and Her Pappy," *New Republic,* Feb. 26, 1936, 69.

6. So notable was the lonesome pine that two scientists from Washington, D.C., scaled the steep terrain of the Virginia-Kentucky border near Pound in 1936 to find the real tree that supposedly was Fox's inspiration. They found a great pine, fallen and decayed, but managed to collect a few chunks for study.

7. *Daily Mirror,* Dec. 22, 1935, 4.

8. Marguerite Mooers Marshall, "Hill-Billy Girl's Own Story," *New York Journal,* Nov. 26, 1935, 1.

9. "Man's Justice to Woman in the Hills," *Literary Digest,* Nov. 30, 1935, 26.

10. *Washington Post,* Nov. 18, 1935, 2.

11. All quotations in this account are from Luther F. Addington, "The Tabloid Journalists Visit the Town of Wise," unidentified clipping, probably from *Bristol Herald Courier,* filed Nov. 23 [1935], Wise County Historical Society files.

12. L. Sprague deCamp, *The Great Monkey Trial* (Garden City: Doubleday, 1968), 274.

13. *Knoxville News-Sentinel,* Nov. 17, 1935, A6. Perhaps Ferguson should have said that Christian fundamentalism, rather than the theory of evolution, was actually on trial in the Scopes case, but he is nonetheless on the right track.

Chapter 8: Witness for the Prosecution

1. *Roanoke Times,* Nov. 21, 1935.

2. For reasons unknown, Carson Hubbard did not testify.

3. Edward B. Lockett to Jack Warner, Oct. 15, 1936, USC Warner Bros. Archive, School of Cinema-Television, University of Southern California, Los Angeles.

4. Grear did recall Sowards later in the trial, but his story was again ruled inadmissible.

5. Fred Greear, "She Is Guilty," *Actual Detective Stories,* late 1937 or early 1938, private collection of Evelyn Slemp.

6. Greear, "She Is Guilty."

7. I have been able to locate only three sentences from her statement, an unverified excerpt appearing in the *Knoxville News-Sentinel* on July 24, 1935.

Chapter 9: The Men Decide

1. Transcript of first trial, 209.

2. None of the witnesses—prosecution or defense—could remember what had been playing.

3. *Roanoke Times,* Nov. 19, 1935.

4. *Washington Post,* Nov. 19, 1935, 1.

5. Edith Maxwell as told to Walden B. Snell, "I Am Innocent," *Actual Detective Stories,* Nov. 1937, 147, private collection of Evelyn Slemp.

6. Fred Greear, "She Is Guilty," *Actual Detective Stories,* late 1937 or early 1938, 114, private collection of Evelyn Slemp.

7. *Washington Post,* Nov. 20, 1935, 1.

8. *Richmond News Leader,* Nov. 20, 1935.

9. *Knoxville News-Sentinel,* Nov. 18, 1935, 1.

10. Greear prepared ten instructions for the jury, all of which the judge approved; Edith's attorney submitted seven instructions, five of which were approved. Of the fifteen instructions read to the jury, not one mentioned the possibility of a manslaughter verdict because neither side asked for it.

11. *Coalfield Progress,* Nov. 21, 1935, 1.

12. *Knoxville News-Sentinel,* Nov. 18, 28, 1935, 1, 3.

13. *Washington Post,* Nov. 19, 1935, 1.

14. *Knoxville News-Sentinel,* Nov. 26, 1935, 10.

15. *Coalfield Progress,* Nov. 21, 1935. 1. It is unclear whether the judge was directing his criticism at specific members of the press corps.

16. *Knoxville News-Sentinel,* Nov. 20, 1935, 1.

Chapter 10: A Mouse in a Trap?

1. *Roanoke Times,* Nov. 21, 1935.

2. Ishbel Ross, *Ladies of the Press: The Story of Women in Journalism by an Insider* (Manchester, N.H.: Ayer Company Publishers, 1974), 95.

3. The photograph ran in the *Chicago American* around November 26, 1935. A similar one appeared in the *Washington Herald.*

4. The same photograph appeared the next day in the *New York Daily Mirror* on page 1.

5. All quotations in Marshall's account are taken from Marguerite Mooers Marshall, "Hill-Billy Girl's Own Story," *New York Journal,* Nov. 26, 1935, 1.

6. Ross, *Ladies of the Press,* 94.

7. James Thurber, "A Reporter at Large: Crime in the Cumberlands," *The New Yorker,* Feb. 29, 1936, 30.

8. *Knoxville News-Sentinel,* Nov. 21, 1935, 1.

9. *Knoxville News-Sentinel,* Nov. 26, 1935, 9.

10. *Knoxville News-Sentinel,* Nov. 29, 1935, 1.

11. *Knoxville News-Sentinel,* Nov. 29, 1935, 14.

12. Stair letter in *Letters—A Magazine,* Dec. 23, 1935, compiled by Roy L. Sturgill in "The Maxwell Case: Pound, Wise County, Virginia," *Historical Sketches of Southwest Virginia,* no. 18 (1984): 15–24.

13. *Roanoke Times,* Dec. 29, 1935. In this slightly different version of the incident, Skeen was on hand as well as the Hearst employees, and it was he who told Edith not to speak because of the contract.

14. *Knoxville News-Sentinel,* Nov. 29, 1935, 1.

15. *Knoxville News-Sentinel,* Nov. 21, 1935, 1.

16. *Knoxville News-Sentinel,* Nov. 28, 1935, 2.

17. Edith Kane Stair to Hon. George C. Perry [*sic*], Dec. 2, 1935, Office of the Governor, Letters Received and Sent, record group 3, the Library of Virginia.

18. *Washington Daily News,* Nov. 30, 1935, 3; U.S. Department of Labor, Bureau of Labor Statistics, Consumer Price Index Home Page at http://www.bls.gov/cpi/. Accessed Jan. 17, 2004.

19. Virginia Lee Warren, "Gifts to Finance Maxwell Girl's Murder Appeal," *Washington Post,* Dec. 24, 1935.

Chapter 11: Trading Places

1. *Coalfield Progress,* Dec. 5, 1935, 7.

2. *Washington Post,* Dec. 2, 1935, 6.

3. *Coalfield Progress,* Jan. 2, 1936, 3.

4. Ibid.

5. *Washington Post,* Dec. 5, 1935, 4.

6. Esther Randolph Hawkes to Governor Peery, Nov. 22, 1935, Office of the Governor, Letters Received and Sent, record group 3, the Library of Virginia.

7. George C. Peery to J. H. Ruffin, Nov. 27, 1935, Office of the Governor, Letters Received and Sent, record group 3, the Library of Virginia.

8. George C. Peery to Judge Henry A. Skeen, Nov. 25, 1935, Office of the Governor, Letters Received and Sent, record group 3, the Library of Virginia.

9. *Washington Post,* Dec. 13, 1935, 1.

10. Ibid.

11. Ibid.

12. Ibid.

13. All quotations in this account are from Virginia Lee Warren, "Edith Maxwell Weeps as Retrial Is Refused," *Washington Post*, Dec. 13, 1935, 1.

14. *Washington Daily News*, Dec. 16, 1935, 5. It is unclear whether Edith actually received $500 for selling her photograph or whether this is a whimsical reference.

Chapter 12: "Country People without Much Money"

1. Emile Gauvreau, *My Last Million Readers* (New York: Arno Press, 1974), 225. Gauvreau is summarizing Stanley Walker's critique of the *Mirror* in Walker's best seller *City Editor.*

2. All quotations in this chapter that are from Mefford's series appeared in the *Daily Mirror* between December 11, 1935, and January 1, 1936.

3. In "The Parting," his column of June 29, 1936, Ernie Pyle bids goodbye to the Ford coupe he bought three years earlier. He traded for a Dodge convertible.

4. Ernie Pyle recounted his visit to Wise County in five columns in the *Washington Daily News:* "'Furriner' Finds Wise, Va., Is Just Like Other Small Towns" (Dec. 10, 1935); "Townsfolk in Wise No Different from Townsfolk Anywhere" (Dec. 11, 1935); "Ernie Finds Neither Curfew nor Child-Beating in Pound, Va." (Dec. 13, 1935); "Opinion Strongly against Edith Maxwell in Her Own County" (Dec. 14, 1935); and "Edith Victim of Circumstances; Should Be Freed, Says Ernie" (Dec. 16, 1935). Quotations from residents are taken from these columns.

Chapter 13: "The East" Steps In

1. Texas musician Dave McEnery, about to become famous as Red River Dave, penned a song, "Pleading of the Pine," about the Maxwell case and performed it over station WPHR in Petersburg.

2. *Washington Post*, Nov. 27, 1935, 1.

3. "Man's Justice to Woman in the Hills," *Literary Digest*, Nov. 30, 1935, 26.

4. Susan D. Becker, *The Origins of the Equal Rights Amendment: Feminism between the Wars* (Westport: Greenwood Press, 1981), 3.

5. Janet K. Boles, *The Politics of the Equal Rights Amendment* (New York: Longman, 1979), 41.

6. Becker, *The Origins of the Equal Rights Amendment*, 27.

7. *Equal Rights Independent Feminist Weekly*, Dec. 7, 1935, 317. It appears that funds were solicited for "the Edith Maxwell defense fund and the jury service campaign" as early as December 7, *before* Edith had granted her permission to Elsie Graff.

8. *Knoxville News-Sentinel*, Nov. 26, 1935, 9.

9. *Washington Post*, Dec. 2, 1935, 6.

10. Mrs. J. Templeton to Rebekah S. Greathouse, Dec. 7, 1935, National Woman's Party Papers, William Oxley Thompson Library, the Ohio State University, Columbus (hereafter NWP Papers).

11. Rebekah S. Greathouse to Jane Norman Smith, Nov. 25, 1935, NWP Papers.

12. Rebekah S. Greathouse to E. Hildegarde Swenson, Jan. 8, 1936, NWP Papers.

13. Rebekah S. Greathouse to Mrs. J. Templeton, Dec. 9, 1935, NWP Papers.

14. Rebekah S. Greathouse to Elsie M. Graff, Dec. 3, 1935, NWP Papers.

15. *Richmond News Leader,* Nov. 26, 1935, 1.

16. *Equal Rights Independent Feminist Weekly,* Jan. 4, 1936, 347.

17. Ibid.

Chapter 14: Big Shots in Town

1. "Observer" to Editor, *Washington Post,* Jan. 15, 1937, 8. This letter was not written until after the second trial and is anonymous, but it captures the reaction of some Appalachians in the 1930s and even today.

2. *Roanoke Times,* Dec. 17, 1935.

3. *Roanoke Times,* Dec. 18, 1935.

4. *Washington Herald,* Nov. 28, 1935, 1.

5. Ibid.

6. Editorial, *Coalfield Progress,* Nov. 28, 1935, 2.

7. *Roanoke Times,* Dec. 26, 1935.

8. *Equal Rights Independent Feminist Weekly,* Jan. 18, 1936, 363.

9. Ruth Sargent, "Laughlin, Gail," in *Notable American Women, the Modern Period: A Biographical Dictionary,* ed. Barbara Sicherman and Carol Hurd Green (Cambridge: Harvard University Press, 1980), 410.

10. Ruth Sargent, "Portland's Remarkable Gail Laughlin," *Maine Sunday Telegram,* June 10, 1979, 2D.

11. M. J. Fulton to Governor Peery, Jan. 6, 1936, Office of the Governor, Letters Received and Sent, record group 3, the Library of Virginia.

12. Governor Peery to M. J. Fulton, Jan. 9, 1936, Office of the Governor, Letters Received and Sent, record group 3, the Library of Virginia.

13. *Coalfield Progress,* Jan. 16, 1936, 3. The article states that both Fulton and Laughlin cited the Alabama case in their arguments before Skeen. According to a brief drafted by Laughlin, the defense also relied upon *Stauder v. West Virginia.*

14. *Richmond News Leader,* Jan. 15, 1936, 1.

15. *Washington Post,* Jan. 16, 1936, 1.

16. Ibid.

17. *Richmond News Leader,* Jan. 16, 1936, 1.

18. *Richmond News Leader,* Jan. 18, 1936, cited in *Equal Rights Independent Feminist Weekly,* Jan. 25, 1936, 375.

Chapter 15: Let's Have a Show

1. *The New Yorker* placed the attendance at eight hundred, while the *New York Times* estimated five hundred.

2. Except where noted, the account of the rally and related quotations are taken from James Thurber, "A Reporter at Large: Crime in the Cumberlands," *The New Yorker,* Feb. 29, 1936, 30–35.

3. *New York Times,* Feb. 15, 1936, 11; see also *New York Times,* Feb. 17, 1936, 3.

4. All quotations from Skeen's courtroom address are taken from the *Roanoke Times,* March 10, 1936.

5. Alfred Skeen maintained that blood had probably never been deposited on the shoe in the first place because the blows landed "in the hair" of Trigg Maxwell's scalp.

6. *Maxwell v. Commonwealth of Virginia,* case record 3886A, 1–13.

7. *Roanoke Times,* July 22, 1936.

8. It can be deduced from this statement that Edith did not attend the funeral of her paternal grandmother, Martha Gilliam Maxwell, who died in February 1936 at age seventy-five.

9. Author's conversation with Mildred Davis, Rose Hill, Virginia, April 17, 2001.

10. Edward T. Folliard, "Sympathizers in Thirteen Countries Send Letters to Edith Maxwell," *Washington Post,* Sept. 13, 1936, 17.

11. *Washington Post,* Sept. 12, 1936, 1.

12. Ibid.

13. All quotations from the opinion are found in *Maxwell v. Commonwealth of Virginia,* 187 S.E. Rep. 509–13 (1936).

Chapter 16: "A Change of Scenery"

1. Edith's conversation with her lawyer outside the Wise County Jail was recorded by the *Washington Post*'s Edward Folliard (Sept. 20, 1936, 1).

2. *Roanoke Times,* Sept. 18, 1936.

3. *Washington Post,* Sept. 20, 1936, 1.

4. Ibid.

5. *Roanoke Times,* Sept. 20, 1936.

6. *Washington Post,* Sept. 20, 1936, 1.

7. *Washington Post,* Sept. 21, 1936.

8. *Richmond News Leader,* Sept. 21, 1936, 1.

9. *Washington Post,* Sept. 21, 1936, 1.

10. A similar picture ran in the *Post,* which reported that Edith was "earning her keep" while staying with relatives.

11. A. T. Dotson was described as the owner in the *Richmond News Leader,* Sept. 21, 1936, 1. Yet his son, A. T. Dotson Jr., told me that his father did not own a farm in Chesterfield County. Perhaps the solution is that the farm was rented *by* Dotson on behalf of the Maxwells.

12. *Richmond News Leader,* Oct. 13, 1936, 1.

13. Earl Maxwell apparently had a wife during this period, but she took no public role in the case and it is unclear where she lived.

14. *Equal Rights Independent Feminist Weekly,* Nov. 14, 1936, 296.

15. *Coalfield Progress,* Nov. 12, 1936, 2.

16. Ibid.

17. *Roanoke Times,* Nov. 23, 1936.

18. *Kingsport Times-News,* Nov. 28, 1993.

19. The defense had previously submitted these affidavits to Judge Skeen at the November 7, 1936, hearing, but Skeen, like Carter, wanted to hear testimony from the affiants. No witnesses were presented, because Skeen disqualified himself (*Richmond News Leader,* Nov. 7, 1936, 1).

20. *Maxwell v. Commonwealth of Virginia,* 193 S.E. Rep. 508 (1937). The testimony that follows is taken from pages 39–150 of the record of the second trial.

21. Edward T. Folliard, "Edith Maxwell Plea for Venue Change Denied," *Washington Post,* Nov. 24, 1936, 1.

22. *Richmond News Leader,* Nov. 23, 1936.

23. *Roanoke Times,* Nov. 24, 1936.

24. Ibid.

25. *Coalfield Progress,* Nov. 26, 1936, 1.

26. *Washington Post,* Nov. 24, 1936, 1.

27. Edward T. Folliard, "Edith Maxwell Counsel to Ask Venue Change," *Washington Post,* Nov. 6, 1936, 32.

Chapter 17: "Roman Holiday"

1. *Equal Rights Independent Feminist Weekly,* Dec. 5, 1936, 314.

2. Unless otherwise noted the quotations and points of view in this chapter that are attributed to Gail Laughlin can be found in E. B. W. (E. B. White?), "Maxwell Trial Mockery Says Gail Laughlin," *Lewiston* (Maine) *Evening Journal,* Jan. 14, 1937.

3. *Washington Herald,* Dec. 9, 1936, 1.

4. *Coalfield Progress,* Dec. 3, 1936, 1.

5. Ernie Pyle, who wrote several columns for Scripps-Howard *after* the first trial, did not cover this one either.

6. Anne Suydam, "Edith's Sister Tearful, Grim in Testimony," *Washington Herald,* Dec. 15, 1936, 4; Anne Suydam, "Edith's Neighbors at Pound Hope She'll Be Convicted," *Washington Herald,* Dec. 14, 1936, 4.

7. W. A. S. Douglas, "Jury Picked to Try Maxwell Girl Again," *Washington Herald,* Dec. 10, 1936, 8.

8. Douglas, "Jury Picked."

9. *Washington Post,* Dec. 10, 1936, 1; Anne Suydam, "'Town for Edith, Hills Against,' as New Murder Trial Starts," *Washington Herald,* Dec. 10, 1936, 8.

10. I have been unable to determine whether the judge used tobacco.

11. *Richmond News Leader,* Dec. 9, 1936, 1.

12. *Washington Post,* Dec. 10, 1936, 1. W. A. S. Douglas's account in the *Herald* suggests that some of the defense attorneys, and Edith herself, laughed at Greear's joke. I have been unable to verify this through other sources.

13. *Washington Herald,* Dec. 10, 1936, 8.

14. Edward T. Folliard, "Maxwell Girl Again on Trial for Patricide," *Washington Post,* Dec. 10, 1936, 1.

15. *Roanoke Times,* Dec. 10, 1936. Another source says that thirty-two were questioned and twelve discharged (*Washington Herald,* Dec. 10, 1936).

16. Suydam, "'Town for Edith, Hills Against.'"

17. Edward T. Folliard, "Edith Maxwell Retrial to Open at Wise Today," *Washington Post,* Dec. 9, 1936, 1.

18. *Roanoke Times,* Dec. 10, 1936.

19. *Washington Herald,* Dec. 10, 1936, 8; *Washington Post,* Dec. 10, 1936, 1.

20. *Washington Herald,* Dec. 10, 1936, 8.

21. *Washington Post,* Dec. 10, 1936, 1.

22. Ibid.

23. Ibid.

24. *Washington Post,* Dec. 9, 1936, 1.

Chapter 18: Coma Tiller's Axe

1. The defense immediately asked the judge to strike the evidence because it related only to Ann and not to Edith. Special prosecutor Oscar M. Vicars countered that it was a joint indictment and that the commonwealth would show "a concert of actions and conspiracy" between the two women. Smith shot back that Edith had not been charged with conspiracy and had been granted a separate trial. Judge Carter allowed the testimony to remain in the record for the time-being. The quotations in this chapter are taken from the transcript of the second trial unless otherwise cited.

2. Branham evidently thought well of Trigg Maxwell and wrote a laudatory letter to a newspaper about him shortly after his death.

3. As Greear finished questioning Branham, the attorneys entered into a lengthy debate over whether her testimony should be admitted. Judge Carter eventually allowed it to stand but added, "It is quite apparent that if they [the prosecution] can't get any farther than that, there is not much to this evidence."

4. W. A. S. Douglas, "D.C. Coroner Called to Aid Maxwell Girl," *Washington Herald*, Dec. 11, 1936, 1.

5. Edward T. Folliard, "Defense Calls Coroner to Aid Edith Maxwell," *Washington Post*, Dec. 11, 1936, 11.

6. *Roanoke Times*, Dec. 11, 1936.

7. Folliard, "Defense Calls Coroner"; Carter Lowance, "Axe Presented as Evidence in Maxwell Case," *Roanoke Times*, Dec. 11, 1936. To justify this controversial tactic, Greear later said that the introduction of the facsimile axe was no more outrageous that the defense's introduction of the lady's slipper at the first trial. The shoe was not handed over as evidence until the trial and thus was not kept in a proper chain of evidence, but neither was it brand new.

Chapter 19: "The Least Said, the Least Mended"

1. The quotations in this chapter are taken from the transcript of the second trial unless otherwise cited.

2. Edward T. Folliard, "Ax Boomerang to Prosecution in Edith's Trial," *Washington Post*, Dec. 12, 1936, 1.

3. The reference is likely to Vernon Maxwell the elder, who was Trigg's brother, rather than to Trigg's nephew.

4. According to the court transcript (359), the witness was Walter H. Hubbard, but both the *Washington Post* and the *Washington Herald* identified the witness as R. S. Hubbard.

5. W. A. S. Douglas, "Counsel Open Fight to Bar Edith's Story," *Washington Herald*, Dec. 12, 1936, 1.

6. Smith objected to Fortner's testimony on the ground that being a trusty had made Fortner a "quasi-officer" with an incumbent duty to warn Edith not to confide in him. Judge Carter noted that a statement made to a police officer, if given without coercion, can be admissible.

7. Anne Suydam, "Hill Folk Enchanted by Greatest Romance," *Washington Herald*, Dec. 12, 1936, 8.

8. Pres T. Atkins, "What Nots," *Coalfield Progress*, Dec. 17, 1936, 1.

9. According to the *Washington Herald*, snowy roads had prevented the witness from getting to Wise from the town of Appalachia, some fifteen miles away.

10. *Roanoke Times*, Dec. 17, 1936. The report says the incident happened "during the week-end."

11. The defense did question Clay Robinson about his in-laws' medical history. Robinson said he did not know what caused the deaths of Trigg's parents, Elbert and Martha Gilliam Maxwell. He did recall that Fred Maxwell, Trigg's brother, had died suddenly. On cross-examination the prosecution revealed that Fred Maxwell reportedly died from a fall.

12. This is something of a puzzle because Henry Cantrell was listed in court records (and the newspaper) as the administrator.

13. "'Hill Girl' Loses Appeal," *Daily Mirror*, Dec. 13, 1935, 20. A photograph of Jessee accompanying the article shows an attractive woman with dark hair.

14. Hillman later moved into a building near the Maxwells but was not home when the family trouble broke out.

Chapter 20: "The Little Sister with the Golden Curls"

1. *Washington Post*, Dec. 15, 1936, 1.

2. *Washington Herald*, Dec. 16, 1936, 6.

3. *Roanoke Times*, Dec. 17, 1936.

4. Ibid.

5. "Hill Folk Heard Edith Branded 'Murderer,'" *Washington Herald*, Dec. 17, 1936, 2.

6. *Washington Post*, Dec. 17, 1936, 1.

7. *Washington Herald*, Dec. 17, 1936, 2.

8. *Washington Post*, Dec. 17, 1936, 1.

9. "Hill Folk Heard Edith Branded."

10. *Washington Post*, Dec. 17, 1936, 1.

11. *Washington Herald*, Dec. 17, 1936, 1.

12. *Washington Post*, Dec. 17, 1936, 1.

13. *Edith Maxwell v. Commonwealth of Virginia*, petition filed by the defense with the Supreme Court of Appeals of Virginia, June term, 1938 [*sic*], 29. The correct date is June term, 1937.

14. Quotations from Greear's summation and Fulton's objection are taken from the *Washington Herald*, Dec. 17, 1936, 1.

15. The *Roanoke Times* gave one hour and twenty minutes; the *Coalfield Progress* gave one hour and thirty-seven minutes.

16. *Roanoke Times*, Dec. 18, 1936.

17. *Coalfield Progress*, Dec. 17, 1936, 1.

18. *Washington Herald*, Dec. 18, 1936, 1.

19. *Roanoke Times*, Dec. 20, 1936.

20. Ibid.

21. Anne Suydam, "Edith Hears Jury Verdict with Chin Up," *Washington Herald*, Dec. 18, 1936, 3.

22. *Richmond News Leader*, Dec. 18, 1936, 1; *Equal Rights Independent Feminist Weekly*, Dec. 26, 1936, 34.

23. *Washington Herald*, Dec. 21, 1936, 20.

24. *Roanoke Times*, Dec. 20, 1936.

25. Ibid.

26. Katherine Warren, "Edith Gets Place Here as Restaurant Cashier," *Richmond News Leader,* Dec. 19, 1936, 1; "Edith Goes to Work," *Roanoke Times,* Dec. 21, 1936, n.p.

27. *Roanoke Times,* Jan. 2, 1937.

Chapter 21: Marry in Haste, Repent at Leisure

1. *Equal Rights Independent Feminist Weekly,* Dec. 26, 1936, 1. Passage of the amendment would open the floodgates of women's freedom in many areas of the law, but if that failed, the party could still be assured of a partial victory by winning its argument in the Edith Maxwell case.

2. Elsie M. Graff to Florence Bayard Hilles, Jan. 1, 1937, National Woman's Party Papers, William Oxley Thompson Library, the Ohio State University, Columbus (hereafter NWP Papers).

3. Helena Hill Weed to Evalyn Walsh McLean, Jan. 6, 1937, Evalyn Walsh McLean Papers, Library of Congress.

4. Ibid.

5. Corinne Mitchell Poole, "Where Is This House?" *Washington Star Magazine,* undated clipping, series 5, NWP Papers. In this article the address is given as 144 Constitution Avenue, N.E.

6. *New York Times,* Jan. 9, 1936; see also the letter from —— to Florence Bayard Hilles, Jan. 9, 1937, series 5, NWP Papers.

7. *Washington Herald,* Jan. 3, 1937, C2.

8. Letter from —— to Florence Bayard Hilles, Jan. 9, 1937, NWP Papers.

9. Anne Suydam, "Maxwell Girl Benefit Dance a Melting Pot," *Washington Herald,* Jan. 16, 1937, 3.

10. Helena Hill Weed to Evalyn Walsh McLean, Jan. 16, 1937, McLean Papers, Library of Congress.

11. *Richmond News Leader,* Feb. 24, 1937, 1. Graff's statement also can be found in the NWP Papers, in her letter to Helen Hunt West, Feb. 23, 1937.

12. *Washington Herald,* Feb. 24, 1937, 1.

13. New York City Committee to NWP National Council, Feb. 1937, NWP Papers.

14. *Washington Herald,* Feb. 24, 1937, 1. I have been unable to determine whether Laughlin and Fulton received any fees or whether they worked pro bono.

Chapter 22: Six Coonhounds from Kentucky

1. Charles Higham, *Warner Brothers: A History of the Studio: Its Pictures, Stars and Personalities* (New York: Scribner's, 1975), 93–94.

2. The transcript was prepared by a stenographer hired by the defense, and copies were provided to the prosecution and the court. Although it was a public record, it is uncertain when the transcript was actually filed in a public location where people could have accessed it.

3. I have chosen to focus on *Mountain Justice* rather than *Career Woman* because the latter seems to be much farther removed from the actual case. Fox's seventy-five-minute black and white comedy/drama "teeters between farce and stark realism," according to *Variety.* The *Career Woman* script, found at the Margaret Herrick

Library of the Academy of Motion Picture Arts and Sciences, suggests that the Edith Maxwell character, "Gracie Clay," is not the central character in the film.

4. Telegram to R. J. Obringer from Morris Ebenstein, Jan. 28, 1937, Warner Archive.

5. Unsigned telegram to Morris Ebenstein, Jan. 28, 1937, Warner Archive. The telegram also said "the picture won't be released until July or August" but the date later was changed.

6. Edith Maxwell to Warner Bros. Pictures Inc., Jan. 29, 1937, Warner Archive. Earl also signed a letter with almost identical wording, substituting "my sister" for "I" in one sentence.

7. Edward Amron to Morris Ebenstein, March 15, 1937, Warner Archive. Amron also wrote in the letter that "the Maxwells . . . have admitted their liability" but this cannot be verified. It is unknown whether Amron ever got his fee.

8. It is also likely that Edith received at least some of the money from the Women's Party benefit ball, but I have not located supporting documentation.

Chapter 23: Smith Redux

1. Paul F. Healy, *Cissy: The Biography of Eleanor M. "Cissy" Patterson* (New York: Doubleday, 1966), 137.

2. James Boylan, "No Sissy She," *Columbia Journalism Review* 19 (May–June 1980): 81–82, cited in Jean C. Chance, "Eleanor Medill Patterson," *Dictionary of Literary Biography,* vol. 29: *American Newspaper Journalists, 1926–1950,* ed. Perry J. Ashley (Detroit: Gale Research, 1984), 268.

3. Harold Brodkey, "The Last Word on Winchell," *The New Yorker,* Jan. 30, 1995, 74.

4. Eleanor Patterson to Eleanor Roosevelt, Oct. 14, 1941, Franklin D. Roosevelt Library, Hyde Park, New York.

5. *Roanoke Times,* Dec. 20, 1936.

6. On page 15 of his petition filed with the Virginia Supreme Court of Appeals in 1937, Smith argued that another guilty verdict was a "foregoing conclusion" unless the trial were moved. He alleged that pretrial publicity and "sinister and unwholesome political influences" made a fair trial impossible in Wise County.

7. This description of Pennington and Lambert, taken from the *Washington Post,* doesn't quite square with the *Herald*'s earlier report that there were "nine middle-aged and three young" men on the jury.

8. Except where noted, quotations from the March 1937 hearing in Wise County Circuit Court are taken from the record of Edith's second appeal (700–747).

9. *Coalfield Progress,* March 11, 1937, 1.

10. Ibid.

11. *Roanoke Times,* March 10, 1937.

12. *Coalfield Progress,* March 11, 1937, 1.

13. *Roanoke Times,* March 10, 1937.

Chapter 24: "The Wishing Book"

1. *Motion Picture Herald,* May 22, 1937.

2. When, if ever, she saw the film remains a mystery.

3. "News of the Screen," undated clipping, Warner Archive.

4. Frank S. Nugent, "Mountain Justice," *New York Times Film Review*, May 13, 1937, 31:2.

5. Review from *News*, cited in *Hollywood Reporter*, June 1, 1937.

6. *New York Times Film Review*, May 13, 1937, 2.

7. *Film Daily*, May 15, 1937, n.p.

8. Review from *Post*, cited in *Hollywood Reporter*, June 1, 1937.

9. Morris Ebenstein to R. J. Obringer, Sept. 30, 1936, Warner Archive.

10. See, for example, Morris Ebenstein to R. J. Obringer, Sept. 30, 1936, Warner Archive.

11. Morris Ebenstein to Hal Wallace, Feb. 25, 1937, Warner Archive.

12. A. Sachson to M. Ebenstein, March 22, 1937, Warner Archive.

13. Morris Ebenstein to Albert Howson, March 22, 1937, Warner Archive.

14. Frank Cunningham, "Blue Ridge Justice in Hollywood," undated clipping, Warner Archive. (The original script called for Ruth Harkins to strike her father with a shoe, but the instrument was later changed to the whip handle.)

15. "I Am Innocent," private collection of Evelyn Slemp.

16. *Maxwell v. Commonwealth of Virginia*, 193 S.E. Rep. 508 (1937).

17. For some reason that is unclear (probably an error), the opinion mentions allegations against four jurors, rather than three.

18. 193 S.E. Rep. 507.

19. The federal case, *Taylor v. Louisiana*, 419 US 522 (1975), is discussed in Elizabeth Frost-Knappman and Kathryn Cullen-DuPont, *Women's Rights on Trial: 101 Historic Trials from Anne Hutchinson to the Virginia Military Institute Cadets* (Detroit: Gale Research, 1997), 115–18.

Chapter 25: Goochland

1. Entire scene and quotations from the *Washington Post*, Nov. 12, 1937, 1.

2. All quotations in this scene are from the *Richmond News Leader*, Nov. 15, 1937, 1.

3. Joseph A. Fry, "George C. Peery, Byrd Regular and Depression Governor," in *Governors of Virginia, 1860–1978*, ed. James Tice Moore and Edward Younger (Charlottesville: University Press of Virginia, 1982), 261.

4. Alvin L. Hall, "James Hubert Price, New Dealer in the Old Dominion," in *Governors of Virginia*, ed. Moore and Younger, 276–89.

5. "A Friend" to Mr. Price, no date, Office of the Governor, Letters Received and Sent, record group 3, Library of Virginia.

6. Frank C. Waldrop to the Honorable James H. Price, April 19, 1938, Office of the Governor, Letters Received and Sent, record group 3, the Library of Virginia.

7. Secretary of the Commonwealth to Frank C. Waldrop, April 21, 1938, Office of the Governor, Letters Received and Sent, record group 3, the Library of Virginia.

8. *Coalfield Progress*, May 5, 1938, 2.

9. Eleanor M. Patterson to James H. Price, April 20, 1939, Office of the Governor, Letters Received and Sent, record group 3, the Library of Virginia.

10. Patterson to Price, April 20, 1939.

11. Charles Henry Smith to James H. Price, May 29, 1940, Office of the Governor, Letters Received and Sent, record group 3, the Library of Virginia.

12. Ex-officio Secretary to the Governor to Charles Henry Smith, June 1, 1940, Office of the Governor, Letters Received and Sent, record group 3, the Library of Virginia.

13. Roy R. Kinder to Charles Henry Smith, May 31, 1940, Office of the Governor, Letters Received and Sent, record group 3, the Library of Virginia. Perhaps this company also sold sweets as well as spices, for Earl was often identified in the press as a "candy salesman."

14. Charles Henry Smith to James H. Price, June 3, 1940, Office of the Governor, Letters Received and Sent, record group 3, the Library of Virginia.

15. Elizabeth M. Kates to R. M. Youell, June 12, 1940, Office of the Governor, Letters Received and Sent, record group 3, the Library of Virginia.

16. Secretary to the Governor to Charles Henry Smith, July 9, 1940, Office of the Governor, Letters Received and Sent, record group 3, the Library of Virginia.

Chapter 26: The Two Eleanors

1. *Washington Herald,* April 5, 1933, cited in Joseph P. Lash, *Eleanor and Franklin* (New York: Signet, 1973), 500–501.

2. *Crawford's Weekly,* July 4, 1934.

3. Ibid.

4. Eleanor Roosevelt to Governor Price, Oct. 8, 1941, Eleanor Roosevelt Collection, box 1616, Franklin D. Roosevelt Library, Hyde Park, New York.

5. Eleanor Roosevelt to Eleanor Patterson, Oct. 8, 1941, Eleanor Roosevelt Collection, box 1616, Franklin D. Roosevelt Library.

6. Eleanor Patterson to Eleanor Roosevelt, Oct. 14, 1941, Eleanor Roosevelt Collection, box 1615, Franklin D. Roosevelt Library.

7. Letters Received and Sent, Oct. 1941, Office of the Governor, record group 3, the Library of Virginia.

8. James Price to Mrs. Franklin D. Roosevelt, Oct. 28, 1941, Eleanor Roosevelt Collection, box 1615, Franklin D. Roosevelt Library.

9. E. T. Carter to James H. Price, Dec. 5, 1941, Office of the Governor, Letters Received and Sent, record group 3, the Library of Virginia.

10. *Washington Post,* Dec. 19, 1941, 1.

11. Author's telephone conversation with Burgess Cantrell, February 2000.

12. Greear left public office in 1944 and maintained a private law practice in Norton until his death in 1960.

13. *Coalfield Progress,* Nov. 25, 1937, 1.

Afterword

1. Leslie Banner, "John Ehle and Appalachian Fiction," *Iron Mountain Review* 3 (Spring 1987): 12–19.

2. *Coalfield Progress,* Nov. 25, 1937, 1.

3. This analysis owes much to Mitchell Stephens, *A History of News* (New York: Penguin, 1989), 108.

4. *Maxwell v. Commonwealth of Virginia,* 187 S.E. Rep. 508 (1936).

5. Ibid., 509.

BIBLIOGRAPHIC ESSAY

The full retelling of Edith Maxwell's story would have been impossible without the availability of voluminous court documents. Although the original file at the Wise County Courthouse regrettably has been lost, a complete record of *Edith Maxwell v. Commonwealth of Virginia* (case number 3886A) is preserved at the Virginia Supreme Court in Richmond. Petitions for Maxwell's appeals include transcripts of her trials held November 18–19, 1935, and December 9–17, 1936. Many of the direct quotations in this book are taken from the trial record.

Newspapers from 1935–37 and 1941 provided another rich source of information. I relied primarily on the *Washington Post, Washington Herald, Knoxville* (Tenn.) *News-Sentinel, Roanoke* (Va.) *Times,* and (Norton, Va.) *Coalfield Progress.* Additional reports came from the *Washington Daily News, Washington Times, Richmond News Leader, Richmond Times-Dispatch, New York Journal, New York Daily Mirror, New York Times,* and the *Bristol* (Va.-Tenn.) *Herald-Courier.* Popular magazines of the day added context and commentary, including *News Week, The New Yorker,* and *The New Republic.*

Chapter 1: "No Fire Here"

The account of the final hours of Trigg Maxwell's life was compiled primarily from the testimonies of Chant Branham Kelly, Verna Hubbard, and Lovell Sowards. A report of Orbin Baldwin's death appeared in the *Roanoke Times* on July 22, 1935. Guy Roberts, who was "on the lam" when the Maxwell story broke in newsreels, shared fascinating stories about past bootlegging practices in Pound. The story of Fred Greear's entering the jail with the Maxwells' electric iron was told to me by attorney Kenneth Asbury, who was a youngster delivering newspapers at the time.

Chapter 2: The Purloined Peas

The two standard reference books on Wise County history are Charles A. Johnson, *A Narrative History of Wise County, Virginia* (Norton, Va.: Pres T. Adkins, 1938; Johnson City, Tenn.: Overmountain Press, 1988) and Luther F. Addington, *The Story of Wise County, Virginia* (Wise, Va.: Luther F. Addington, 1956; Johnson City, Tenn.: Overmountain Press, 1988). Another valuable resource is *The History of The Pound,* edited by Rhonda Robertson and Nancy Clark Brown (n.p.: Historical Society of The Pound, 1993). Discussions of the Swift silver mine legend are found in *The History of The Pound* (25, 28–29) and in Johnson, *A Narrative History* (289). Delightful sketches of southwest Virginia in the 1930s and earlier were written by *Roanoke Times* columnist Goodridge Wilson, who retold the story of

Betty Ramsey's peas on May 1, 1938. Wilson credits Wise County historian James Taylor Adams as the source. Both Wilson's and Adams's writings are preserved in the archives of John Cook Wyllie Library at the University of Virginia at Wise. For theories about how Pound was named, see Addington (*The Story of Wise County*, 196) and *The History of The Pound*, edited by Robertson and Brown (9), as well as the *Coalfield Progress* (July 18, 1935, 1).

A now-classic work of regional economic history is Ronald D. Eller's *Miners, Millhands and Mountaineers: Industrialization of the Appalachian South, 1880–1930* (Knoxville: University of Tennessee Press, 1982). For more recent Appalachian scholarship regarding preindustrial Appalachia, see Wilma Dunaway, "Speculators and Settler Capitalists: Unthinking the Mythology about Appalachian Landholding, 1790–1860," in *Appalachia in the Making: The Mountain South in the Nineteenth Century*, edited by Mary Beth Pudup, Dwight B. Billings, and Altina L. Waller (Chapel Hill: University of North Carolina Press, 1995), 50–75, and Alyson Baker, "The Flanary and Co. Store: A Century of Connections between Southern Appalachia and the Wider World," *Journal of Appalachian Studies* 8 (Fall 2002): 421–30.

Chapter 3: "A Two-Hour Grilling"

Fred Greear's quotations and point of view are taken from his first-person account of his investigation into the Maxwell case; see "She Is Guilty," *Actual Detective Stories* 1, nos. 1–3 (late 1937, early 1938). A biographical sketch of Greear is found in Charles A. Johnson, *A Narrative History of Wise County, Virginia* (Norton, Va.: Pres T. Adkins, 1938; Johnson City, Tenn.: Overmountain Press, 1988), 243–52, and he figures in many stories in the *Coalfield Progress*.

Chapter 4: Becoming "Miss Edith"

Marriage licenses for Trigg and Ann Maxwell and for Martha and Elbert W. Maxwell are on file at the Wise County Courthouse. For the genealogy of the Dotson clan, see Fannie Steel, "Bold Camp," in *The History of The Pound*, edited by Rhonda Robertson and Nancy Clark Brown (n.p.: Historical Society of The Pound, 1993), 186–87. Information about the Gilliam family comes from Virgil Craft, "John Gilliam," in *The Heritage of Wise County and the City of Norton, 1956–1993* (n.p.: Wise County Historical Society, 1993), 1:234, and Luther F. Addington, *The Story of Wise County, Virginia* (Wise, Va.: Luther F. Addington, 1956; Johnson City, Tenn.: Overmountain Press, 1988), 109. Trigg Maxwell's family members are listed in the Records of the Thirteenth U.S. Census (1910). Trigg and Ann's purchase of a farm is documented in the Wise County Deed Book, Wise County Courthouse. For an illuminating discussion of feuding myths and stereotypes, see Altina L. Waller, *Feud: Hatfields, McCoys and Social Change in Appalachia, 1860–1900* (Chapel Hill: University of North Carolina Press, 1988).

The most detailed account of Edith Maxwell's early years comes from a newspaper "autobiography" serialized by King Features Syndicate in December 1935 and January 1936. Although it was an authorized biography based on information she gave to the Hearst newspapers, she almost certainly did not write it. A second "life story" was also published by the *Daily Mirror*, a Hearst tabloid, in 1935. Both versions must be viewed with caution because they were intended to create an idealized image of Edith, sometimes in disregard for the facts. Nonetheless, the King Features series contains credible information not available from other sources.

For the history of Jenkins, Kentucky, see Geoffrey L. Buckley and Timothy G. Anderson, "The Consolidation Coal Company Photograph Collection, 1910–1945," *Appalachian Journal* 27 (Fall 1999): 66, and Teresa Bevins, "Elkhorn Coal: A Way of Life," paper dated April 28, 1993, Vertical File, Mary Jo Wolfe Library, Jenkins, Kentucky. The grand opening of the Pound Gap road and the subsequent lynching of Leonard Woods were covered in *Crawford's Weekly* (Nov. 26, 1927, 1; Dec. 3, 1927, 6). Another account of the lynching is found in Roy L. Sturgill, "The Murder of Hershel Deaton," *Historical Sketches of Southwest Virginia*, no. 12 (1978): 28–29. For an overview of Radford State Teachers College, see Virginia Writers' Project, *Virginia: A Guide to the Old Dominion; Compiled by Workers of the Writers' Program of the Work Projects Administration in the State of Virginia. Sponsored by James H. Price* (New York: Oxford University Press, 1940), 434–35.

Chapter 5: "A Man of Easy-Going Disposition"

Details about Martha Maxwell's church work come from an interview with her great-granddaughter, Frances C. Roberson, in April 1994 in Wise, Virginia. The circumstances of Trigg Maxwell's funeral are related in the *Bristol Herald Courier*, July 23–25, 1935, and the *Coalfield Progress*, July 25, 1935, 1. Background on Earl Maxwell comes from Edith's autobiography published in the *Washington Herald*. For Edith's account of being whisked away from the funeral, see Edith Maxwell, "I Am Innocent," *Actual Detective Stories* (late 1937, early 1938). A similar but more dispassionate report was given by Sheriff J. P. Adams, who testified about the event on two occasions in 1936 (the hearing on a motion for change of venue and the second trial).

Chapter 6: The Mountain Code

For a biographical sketch of Fulton Lewis Jr., see *Journalist Biographies Master Index*, edited by Alan E. Abrams (Detroit: Gale Research, 1978), 414. A general discussion of the history of yellow journalism is contained in Frank Luther Mott, *American Journalism, a History, 1690–1960*, 3d ed. (New York: Macmillan, 1962), 519–45.

Chapter 7: Buying Time

For lists of Wise and Dickenson County attorneys, I consulted "Big Stone Gap," "Norton," "Wise," and "Clintwood" in the *Martindale-Hubbell Law Directory* (New York: Martindale-Hubbell Law Directory, Inc., 1936). Background on Alfred A. Skeen comes from an entry dated October 13, 1948, in *Pioneer Recollections of Southwest Virginia*, collected, compiled, and edited by Elihu J. Sutherland and supplemented by Hetty Swindall Sutherland (Clintwood, Va.: H. S. Sutherland, 1984), 338. Gernade Dotson's political career is outlined in Charles A. Johnson, *A Narrative History of Wise County, Virginia* (Norton, Va.: Pres T. Adkins, 1938; Johnson City, Tenn.: Overmountain Press, 1988), 216–17, 241. Information on Judge H. A. W. Skeen also comes from Johnson (363) and from an interview in the *Coalfield Progress*, Dec. 28, 1938. Ida Baldwin's trial was reported in "Maxwell Murder Trial Scheduled Today in Wise County Circuit Court," *Bristol Herald Courier*, undated clipping, story filed Aug. 19, [1935]. The postponement of the Maxwell trial was reported in the *Coalfield Progress* (Aug. 22, 1935, 1); *Roanoke Times* (Aug. 21, 1935); and "Defense of Mother and Daughter Not Prepared" (unidentifed clipping, datelined Aug. 20 and likely from *Bristol Herald Courier*). Sandra Lee Barney has written about the coming of modern medicine to the mountains in *Authorized to Heal: Gender, Class and the Transformation of Medicine in Appalachia, 1880–1930* (Chapel Hill: University of North Carolina Press, 2000). For an account of the Scopes trial, see Edward Larson, *Summer for the Gods: The Scopes Trial and America's Continuing Debate over Science and Religion* (New York: Basic Books, 1997).

Chapter 8: Witness for the Prosecution

The history of the Wise County Courthouse is recorded in Luther F. Addington, *The Story of Wise County, Virginia* (Wise, Va.: Luther F. Addington, 1956; Johnson City, Tenn.: Overmountain Press, 1988), 94–97. For a biographical sketch of the chief prosecution witness, see Nancy Clark Brown, "Chant Kelly—Pioneer of Pound," as well as Kelly's own article, "Grandfather Tanned Leather and Made His Shoes," both in *The History of The Pound*, edited by Rhonda Robertson and Nancy Clark Brown (n.p.: Historical Society of The Pound, 1993), 243–45, 376. The bulk of the narrative in this chapter, as well as all direct quotations except where noted, comes from the transcript of the first trial.

Chapter 9: The Men Decide

The testimony of Ann, Mary Katherine, and Edith Maxwell forms the basis of this chapter and is supplemented by newspaper accounts. All direct quotations are from the trial transcript except where noted.

Chapter 10: A Mouse in a Trap?

An account of Albers and Marshall's perilous trip, along with Marshall's exclusive interview with Edith, made a splash in the *New York Journal* on November 26, 1935. For a flattering sketch of Marshall, see Ishbel Ross, *Ladies of the Press: The Story of Women in Journalism by an Insider* (Manchester, N.H.: Ayer Company Publishers, 1974), 94–96. The activities of the Knoxville Business and Professional Women's Club were covered extensively by the *Knoxville News-Sentinel*.

Chapter 11: Trading Places

The story of Lelbourne Falin's death and his son's exoneration was covered by the *Coalfield Progress, Washington Post,* and *Richmond News Leader.* For a biographical sketch of Governor Peery, see Joseph A. Fry, "George C. Peery: Byrd Regular and Depression Governor," in *The Governors of Virginia, 1860–1978,* edited by James Tice Moore and Edward Younger (Charlottesville: University Press of Virginia, 1982), 261–75. For the history of the Colonial Hotel, see Rhonda Robertson, "The Inn," in *The Heritage of Wise County and the City of Norton, 1956–1993* (n.p.: Wise County Historical Society, 1993), 1:94. Edith's December 12, 1935, hearing before Judge Skeen was covered by the *Coalfield Progress, Washington Post,* and *Roanoke Times.*

Chapter 12: "Country People without Much Money"

For a general history of the tabloids, see Frank Luther Mott, *American Journalism, a History, 1690–1960,* 3d ed. (New York: Macmillan, 1962), 519–45. Background on Arthur Mefford is found in Emile Gauvreau, *My Last Million Readers* (New York: Arno Press, 1974), 225. The *Coalfield Progress* reported on the movements of the "foreign" press during December 1935. Mefford's "life story" of Edith Maxwell ran in the *New York Daily* and *Sunday Mirror* from December 1935 to early January 1936. For details of Ernie Pyle's life, see *Ernie's America: The Best of Ernie Pyle's 1930s Travel Dispatches,* edited by David Nichols (New York: Random House, 1989), and James Tobin, *Ernie Pyle's War* (New York: Free Press, 1997).

Chapter 13: "The East" Steps In

To read about the suffrage movement and the National Woman's Party, see Catherine Clinton, *The Other Civil War: American Women in the Nineteenth Century* (New York: Hill and Wang, 1984), 201; Susan D. Becker, *The Origins of the Equal Rights Amendment: Feminism between the Wars* (Westport: Greenwood Press, 1981) 3; Janet K. Boles, *The Politics of the Equal Rights Amendment* (New York: Longman, 1979) 41; and Christine A. Lunardini, *From Equal Suffrage to Equal Rights: Alice Paul and the National Woman's Party, 1910–1928* (New York: New York University Press, 1986) 170. I viewed the archives of the National Woman's Party at The Ohio State University's Thompson Library in Columbus. The archives contain microfilm copies of correspondence, reports, and the two NWP journals. Especially valuable was the *Equal Rights Independent Feminist Weekly.*

Chapter 14: Big Shots in Town

The kidnap-murder of the Lindbergh baby is discussed in Joyce Milton, *Loss of Eden: A Biography of Charles and Anne Morrow Lindbergh* (New York: HarperCollins, 1993), and Jim Fisher, *The Lindbergh Case* (New Brunswick: Rutgers University Press, 1978). The obituary of Minitree Jones Fulton appeared in the *Richmond Times-Dispatch* on July 4, 1954. Ruth Sargeant has written extensively about Gail Laughlin; see, for example, "Portland's Gail Laughlin Fought for Women's Rights," *Maine Life* (Jan. 1980): 35, "Portland's Remarkable Gail Laughlin," *Maine Sunday Telegram,* June 10, 1979, 2D; and *Notable American Women, The Modern Period: A Biographical Dictionary,* edited by Barbara Sicherman and Carol Hurd Green (Cambridge: Harvard University Press, Belknap Press, 1980). Charles Henry Smith is listed in the *Martindale-Hubble Law Directory* (New York: Martindale-Hubble Law Directory, Inc., 1936), 1361. The January 15, 1936, hearing on Edith's appeal was covered by the *Washington Post, Coalfield Progress, Richmond News Leader,* and *Roanoke Times.* For an enlightening analysis of the Scottsboro case, see James Goodman, *Stories of Scottsboro* (New York: Pantheon, 1994).

Chapter 15: Let's Have a Show

Information about Alfred A. Skeen's youth comes from *Pioneer Recollections of Southwest Virginia,* collected, compiled, and edited by Elihu J. Sutherland and supplemented by Hetty Swindall Sutherland (Clintwood, Va.: H. S. Sutherland, 1984), 338. The defense team's legal manuevers during March 1936 were covered consistently by the *Roanoke Times,* and for details about Edith's sojourn in the Lee County jail I consulted the *Washington Post.*

Chapter 16: "A Change of Scenery"

For Edward Folliard's obituary, see Jean R. Hailey, "Edward T. Folliard, Prize-Winning Journalist, Dies," *Washington Post,* Nov. 26, 1976, B13. The uproar at the Norton diner was reported in the *Coalfield Progress,* Sept. 24, 1936, 1. The *Richmond News-Leader* covered the Maxwells' move to the Richmond area in the fall of 1936. The description of Fred Greear's abilities is found in an April 1972 interview with Kenneth Asbury, cited in Joseph E. Wolfe, "The Legal Career of Fred B. Greear," in *The Heritage of Wise County and the City of Norton, 1956–1993* (n.p.: Wise County Historical Society, 1993), 469. Judge Skeen's exodus from the case and Judge Carter's entry were reported in the *Coalfield Progress* and *Roanoke Times.* A transcript of the November 23, 1936, hearing is located on pages 39–150 of the record of the second trial.

Chapter 17: "Roman Holiday"

The pretrial atmosphere and courtroom proceedings were covered extensively by the Washington, D.C., Virginia, and local newspapers. For background on Anne Suydam, see "Mrs. Henry Suydam; Wife of State Department Chief Dies at Fifty-four," *New York Times,* Oct. 16, 1955, 86.

Chapters 18–20: Coma Tiller's Axe; "The Least Said, the Least Mended"; "The Little Sister with the Golden Curls"

The information in these chapters was gleaned from the transcript of the second trial and newspaper accounts. Except where noted, quotations are from the transcript.

Chapter 21: Marry in Haste, Repent at Leisure

The National Woman's Party Washington headquarters was described in "It Happened Here," *Washington Post,* June 21, 1936, and in Corinne Mitchell Poole, "Where Is This House?" *Washington Star Magazine,* undated clipping, series 5, NWP Papers. Information about Sarah Thompson Pell is found in "These Fascinating Ladies," undated clipping, series 5, NWP Papers.

Chapter 22: Six Coonhounds from Kentucky

E. B. McElroy's correspondence, along with many revealing letters written by studio executives, is preserved at the USC Warner Brothers Archive, School of Cinema-Television, University of Southern California, Los Angeles. The files also contain the press book used to promote *Mountain Justice* as well as scrapbooks of newspaper clippings about the Edith Maxwell case. To read about movie-making in the 1930s, see Charles Higham, *Warner Brothers: A History of the Studio: Its Pictures, Stars and Personalities* (New York: Scribner's, 1975); Carlos Clarens, *Crime Movies from Griffith to the Godfather and Beyond* (New York: W. W. Norton, 1980); and John Baxter, *Hollywood in the Thirties* (New York: Paperback Library, 1968).

Chapter 23: *Smith Redux*

For information about Eleanor "Cissy" Patterson, see Jean C. Chance, "Eleanor Medill Patterson," in *Dictionary of Literary Biography* (Detroit: Gale Research, 1984), 29: 265–66, and Paul F. Healy, *Cissy: The Biography of Eleanor M. "Cissy" Patterson* (New York: Doubleday, 1966). Patterson's letters to Eleanor Roosevelt are housed at the Franklin D. Roosevelt Library, Hyde Park, New York. Except where noted, quotations from the March 1937 hearing in Wise County Circuit Court are taken from the record of Edith's second appeal (700–747).

Chapter 24: *"The Wishing Book"*

Miraculously, the film *Mountain Justice* has been preserved at the Library of Congress Division of Motion Picture, Broadcast and Recorded Sound in Washington, D.C. It was reviewed in various contemporary publications as indicated in the notes. Details about Edith's second appeal came from newspaper accounts.

Chapter 25: *Goochland*

For a description of Governor Price, see Alvin L. Hall, "James Hubert Price, New Dealer in the Old Dominion," in *The Governors of Virginia, 1860–1978*, edited by James Tice Moore and Edward Younger (Charlottesville: University Press of Virginia, 1982), 278. Evalyn Walsh McLean's papers are archived at the Library of Congress. Information about McLean's parties at Friendship comes from a letter from Archie Butt, cited in Chalmers M. Roberts, *In the Shadow of Power: The Story of the* Washington Post (Cabin John, Md.: Seven Locks Press, 1989), 115. To learn about McLean's role in the Lindbergh case, see Joyce Milton, *Loss of Eden: A Biography of Charles and Anne Morrow Lindbergh* (New York: HarperCollins, 1993), 232–33.

Chapter 26: *The Two Eleanors*

Eleanor Roosevelt's early years are recounted in Joseph P. Lash, *Eleanor and Franklin* (New York: Signet, 1973). Governor Price's and Fred Greear's statements about the pardon were carried in the *Coalfield Progress* on December 25, 1941. The account of Edith at the Richmond hotel was told to me by Rhonda Robertson, whose relative, the late historian Emory Hamilton, related the incident to her.

INDEX

SHARON HATFIELD grew up in the Cumberland Mountains of Lee County, Virginia. After college she became a newspaper reporter in Wise County, Virginia, covering the justice system in the same courtroom where Edith Maxwell was tried for murder. Hatfield now lives in Ohio, where she works as a freelance editor and college writing instructor. She is coeditor of *An American Vein: Critical Readings in Appalachian Literature.*

The University of Illinois Press
is a founding member of the
Association of American University Presses.

Composed in 10/13 ITC New Baskerville
with Ruach and Meta display
by Jim Proefrock
at the University of Illinois Press
Designed by Paula Newcomb
Manufactured by Sheridan Books, Inc.

University of Illinois Press
1325 South Oak Street
Champaign, IL 61820-6903
www.press.uillinois.edu